NEW MIND, NEW BODY

A 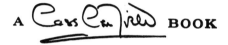 BOOK

Books by Barbara B. Brown

NEW MIND, NEW BODY
  Bio-Feedback: New Directions for the Mind

Edited by Barbara B. Brown

THE BIO-FEEDBACK SYLLABUS

THE ALPHA SYLLABUS (with J. Klug)

NEW MIND, NEW BODY

Bio-Feedback: New Directions for the Mind

BARBARA B. BROWN, PH. D.

HARPER & ROW, PUBLISHERS

New York, Evanston, San Francisco

London

1817

FIRST EDITION

Designed by Sidney Feinberg

Library of Congress Cataloging in Publication Data

Brown, Barbara B.
  New mind, new body; bio-feedback: new directions for the mind.
  (A Cass Canfield book)
  Bibliography: p. 423
  1. Biofeedback training. I. Title.
[DNLM: 1. Feedback. 2. Psychophysiology. WL102 B877n 1974]
BF319.5.B5B76   612'.022   73-14249
ISBN 0-06-010159-6

For the people whose Government has financed the journeys
of so many minds, including mine

Contents

Acknowledgments

There are moments when one is privileged to glimpse the threads of consciousness that span the minds of living things. There is such a moment in realizing the reality of bio-feedback. Its thread that leads within and beyond the mind is stouter by far than earth world ties. Journeys into mind space need mind support. For this I thank the friends who nourished me with friendship during my sojourn through an unfinished scientific maze. Whatever errors I made in its alleyways were, of course, my own. And for leading me to daylight by imaginative and understanding editing, my thanks to Dr. Jean Houston. A bouquet of thank-yous goes to my typist friends: Barbara Teets, Jeanne Hunter and Jean Quist.

Foreword *by Hugh Downs*

In this remarkable book on bio-feedback, Barbara Brown observes that people grasp the idea intuitively and with surprising ease.

It is not really a simple idea. The details of the actual training and experimenting are not only complicated but require some knowledge of the related fields of computer technology, electro-encephalography and other small-current detection devices, and some aspects of psychological theory. It is new and complex and uncharted, but still people latch on to the idea rapidly. People who wouldn't have the foggiest notion how an inertial guidance system works or how television pictures can be stored on "pictureless" magnetic tape (both of these things are intrinsically simpler than bio-feedback) can usually get a good grip on the principle of bio-feedback training (BFT) after one explanation of it. I have no idea why this is true, but I have noticed it.

Presently I want to offer one explanation, after which you will probably say "of course," but then when you charge on through the book you are going to find out things about yourself and hints of things about yourself you will long to know about in greater detail. Not that you will be "converted" to bio-feedback—it isn't a religion and, God help us, it shouldn't become a cult—but it is powerful and promising, and if you come to believe in its importance, you will sense the parallel importance of Dr. Brown's careful address to the subject, trying to keep it at once from the ditches on either side of the road of fad-panacea exploitation and traditional-hidebound stultification. She is a scientist, and her approach appears to retain all the worth of traditional scientific method, but it cuts away the shackles of doctrinaire body-only behavioral attitudes, much as early-twentieth-century physicists dismantled the rigid mechanical model of Newtonian reality, to replace it with the more versatile relativistic model of the universe complete with the Heisenberg indeterminacy principle and Planck's embarrassing constant. At the root of Barbara Brown's world of bio-feedback there is still the human will, clanking around like a loose nut, and she is brave enough to acknowledge it and open up a methodology for dealing with it as a factor, instead of attempting to banish it by seeking the safer refuge of operant-conditioning theory.

This is not a philosophical skirmish between determinism and free will. It is a scientific study of something new—a study broad enough to avoid the mistake of jamming the whole field into pigeon-holes and shearing off whatever hangs out.

Feedback is the return to input of some of the output of a system.

An indefinite mutual modification of input and output results from this, even when the fedback input is "damped" to converge and stabilize. The system has acted on information generated by itself and this influences further conditions and information about the conditions.

There are feedback systems in all living organisms. All muscular activity, for example, all learning of motor skills, involve feedback. Some information about a situation is fed back through the senses to the brain or nervous system directing action on the situation. (I reach for a light switch. My eyes inform me when my hand is close and because of this information I put the brakes on my arm muscles so as to arrive at the light switch without crashing into it. Or groping in the dark, my sense of touch will send back the signal of contact with the switch and appropriate instructions will be issued by the brain to the hand. This is kinesthetic feedback.)

Kinesthetic feedback interacts constantly with our conscious decision-making apparatus where muscular activity is concerned. But what about decisions to alter blood pressure or bile flow or pulse rate, decisions to digest food, or to sweat, or to set secretion rates for glands? These are not normally within the grasp of the conscious will. And while the body by and large runs itself quite efficiently without conscious interference, there are times when it would be desirable to seize the reins in given situations: to turn off useless pain, to tranquilize an alarmed heart, to instruct the body not to reject a transplanted organ, to recapture or to re-create an emotion or to banish an unwanted emotion—in other words, to bring a harmonized body-mind under full and rational control. This is not a George Orwell picture. Control would not rest with Big Brother but with the individual controlled. Medically this is government by consent of the governed.

By arranging for individuals to have access to meaningful information about their own insides, thus making the knowledge part of the "exterior" environment, bio-feedback researchers are making it possible for people to experience and for the first time control themselves, and to harmonize body and mind.

It may be that man has not heretofore had volitional control of his interior processes because most of his survival techniques were developed prior to the emergence of intellect. Although intellect has been recruited for survival purposes, it has not had intimate access to the dynamics of physical functioning.

Dr. Brown's far-reaching applications of this promising new discipline include a proposed technique for enabling subjects to strive for attitude change. This is really going to the roots of motivation. In a case where chronic unemployment is the result of job-related anxieties, the subject may really wish to change those attitudes which (unknown to him) cause anxiety, but the way to do this—even recognition of the need to do this—may not be in his grasp. Standard psychotherapy requires a doctor to help a patient understand the need and develop a way. The feedback technique in handing understandable data from the subject *to the subject* for re-evaluation and control represents a directness that promises at the least to eliminate some drudgery and frustration from the work of therapists. There is more than a hint here of a breakthrough in the understanding of emotional dynamics. The book is packed with enticing glimpses, experimental results, imaginative speculation, evidence of the compatibility of knowledge-seeking with the deepest roots of life, and an unabashed awe (which you will feel) at the emerging shape of the thing that is being studied.

NEW MIND, NEW BODY

Bio-Feedback Is Interacting with the Interior Self

In his physical dimensions man is a full foot taller than he was last century. In the confusion of a rapidly expanded material life it was to be expected that growth of the mind would be more difficult to recognize, perhaps more difficult to realize. Today the world is filled with signs of an approaching era of extended mental abilities. It may be that a first step toward realizing these is becoming aware that the failure of minds to achieve a world of harmony is because they have been diverted from an original purpose of knowing the harmony between mind and body.

The Forgotten Mind

As a literate civilization we are now more than five thousand years old. Through the rigors of these years we have become expert in giving comfort to the body, learning to protect it against the extremes of nature, and to heal it after assaults. These accomplishments that mark our evolution and civilized growth have been gained with the mind in the employ of the body. From mundane occupations with food, houses, and transportation to the most extended moon-walking venture, the struggle to live has continually milked the mind's resources of ingenuity. Physical needs have always kept the mind well occupied.

It is extraordinary that rarely has effort been made to nourish *mind* processes. No consistent scientific explorations have been made to explore the limits of the mind nor to expand the mind's capabilities. Our mental capabilities remain the same as they were in the days of Pythagoras. Only our tools and the environment have changed: perception, observation, and logical thought remain exactly the same.

1

Technical advances have extended our eyes and ears and modes of locomotion. We have invented new symbols to simplify verbal and conceptual expression, and they serve as techniques for expediting the transmission and ingestion of enormous worlds of information. But as yet scientific attention has not been directed toward developing new facilities for the mind nor toward making the mind itself more efficient. Mnemonic tricks are still used to assist memorizing; documents and pictures are still needed to recover memories; extended concentration has to be practiced assiduously, and creativity is still elusive. No one knows how insights occur; inspiration and motivation have been characterized but the secrets of their origin remain secret. Attention to the mind has been limited to filling it with information, allowing it to create fantasies, or permitting it to decay into confusion. By and large the education of mental faculties has been guided and controlled by technologic* advances, not by advances in philosophy or natural psychology. Until the very present, when experimental courses are just now beginning, there have been no academic courses directed toward exploring the abilities of the mind, to encouraging development of mind processes, nor to exploring the limits of the mind.

In this century the scientific study of behavior has concentrated almost exclusively on the physical aspects of biological organisms including, and most particularly of, man. The unique quality of his complex interior life and his subjective world of experience, feelings, moods, and thoughts are judged to derive from physical events. The behavioral scientist has studied only those external and internal events for which we have measuring devices and the existence of which we can agree upon by virtue of their physical reality. Nearly all bioscientific knowledge about behavior has been obtained by observation of the interaction of an individual with the *external* environment; neurophysiologic information about subjective activities, for example, is generally obtained in terms of properties of the physical stimuli inducing subjective changes. What the individual *feels* or *thinks* about his or another's behavior has until now defied accurate measurement in terms of physical change. There are too

* Where appropriate, the -ic suffix is used throughout. It implies a closer relationship to the substantive being qualified than does the -ical suffix. (Webster's Collegiate Dictionary)

many varieties of experience, too many shadings of meaning when it is communicated, and so our interior feelings that color all behavior have not been considered legitimate subjects for the scientific study of behavior.

What the individual feels or thinks about his or another's behavior remains secreted deep in the subjective domain, pulsing with power, dissipating without recognition and without constructive use. In the concern about pollution, for example, it is not a difficult task to measure the toxic effects of smog on animal tissues. But if you live in smog areas, you know that the average man agrees beyond question that on smoggy days there is also a mental irritation. The mind just isn't up to par. No doubt the frustration over the continued presence of the smog plays a part, yet it is these subtle discomforts of mind that are left unstudied and unexplored, uncorrected, and ignored, although experiential knowledge over time widely agrees that these fleeting mind effects can change personalities and even physical patterns of living.

Nearly all formal emphasis has been on emotion and behavior and how to control behavior by external means. It is somewhat terrifying to realize that the bulk of biological and psychological scientific effort has been devoted to learning how to control man's emotion and behavior, yet the reins of control are rarely, if ever, offered to the individual being controlled. The majority of academic, governmental, and industrial societies embrace varying types of behavior control and cybernetics, and delight in the prospect of automatized man.

Suddenly the technologic ingenuity of the scientist has brought the biomedical researcher face to face with the capabilities of the human psyche. Only now are we learning that if we provide man with accurate and recognizable information about the dynamics of his functioning being as part of his external environment, he can then experience himself. That is, he can verify certain relationships between himself and the internal, nonexternal world, and then interact with himself. The biological phenomenon which underlies this confrontation is the revelation by bio-feedback of the ability of individuals to regulate and control a wide variety of their own physiologic functioning once information of such functioning is presented in a form that can be perceived by that same individual.

Bio-Feedback, the World Inside

Bio-feedback is the newest, most exciting and potentially farthest-reaching discovery ever to emerge from the busy basements of biomedical research. It has been a virtual explosion of discovery, and it is currently causing a revolution in both scientific and public thinking. Sometimes called Bio-Feedback Training (BFT), the new phenomenon is a mind-machine communications technique which, for the first time, allows man to communicate with his inner self.

Bio-feedback is simply the feedback of biological information to the person whose biology it is. Feedback is a shorthand term for something being "fed back" to the same something. The expression developed in the field of engineering to define control systems that operate via feedback mechanisms; those systems which operate by their ability to detect changes in the environment of their operation, then to make internal adjustments so that their functions remain both optimal and continuously appropriate to the demands of the environment. The most common example is the thermostat. The terms "feedback" and "feedback control systems" were borrowed by physiologists when they began theorizing about how the functions of the body are performed.

Biological feedback systems have been known for some time as they operate *within* the body. There are perhaps millions of individual feedback systems in the human body. Information about the external environment is sensed by any of the five senses and relayed to a control center, usually the brain, where it is integrated with other relevant information, and when the sensed information is significant enough, central control generates commands for appropriate body changes. Responses of scratching an itch, hitting a baseball with a bat, pupil accommodation for near and far vision, perspiration, sneezing, sleeping, urinating, eating—all are examples of feedback control systems. The body responds to external and internal changes by its self-contained control systems.

The real biological feedback drama unfolded when it was discovered that we could tap the hidden secrets of the completely internal, life-governing functions of the body, that we could capture the internal signals and transform them into externalized information-bearing signals that could be sensed, perceived, recognized, and acted upon by our brain's control system.

The discovery allows man to sense signals of his own internal body activities and then to translate these signals into outward signs that he can observe to learn what is going on inside of himself. The consequence of this rather ordinary business of sampling a person's interior activity, with methods much like those used in every medical examination, is the new magic of the mind. For once a person tunes himself (rather than the doctor tuning in) to monitors of his internal being, be they a moving index of body temperature or the complexities of his brain waves, that person becomes acquainted with his internal behavior. And just as with his externally directed behavior, with practice he can learn to control it.

There are relatively few naturally occurring signals such as the pulse which give us information about the extraordinary universe which is inside us. Normally we are most acutely aware of respiration. We can become aware of muscle activity or heart action only by directing our attention to them and using some effort. Occasionally when temperature is elevated, we can "feel" our temperature. But for the most part, our functioning selves give very little external evidence of the inner activities. For example, you can't see, hear, feel, taste, or smell your own brain waves, or your own blood pressure, or the activity of muscle cells, yet each of these can be detected and displayed as signals which give you access to them. And with your body signals now in the external environment, the inner being can be experienced and can be interacted with. And eventually learned to be controlled.

Tuning in to the interior self is an ancient yet ever new concept . . . old in the sense that it is everyman's dream to know and understand his inner being, and new in the sense that current changes in social awareness are breaking down the taboos against explorations of the inner self. The new freedom to know the self is lucidly expressed in the thousands of new encounter groups, the new "awareness-raising" groups, in the new seeking for religious inspiration, in the changing curricula of universities. To many people, however, such self-analysis techniques border on the blasphemous, being either an insult to the word of God or an insult to the word of science. Bio-feedback cannot blaspheme either; it is merely a temporary technologic station along the path toward knowledge of the inner being. The technology pleases science, and understanding of the natural inner life cannot violate the wisdom of a knowing God.

In its present state bio-feedback employs simple devices to detect signs of inner physiologic activity, signs which have been used conventionally in medicine and in biologic research for many years. Many of these are familiar: the thermometer for reading temperature, the device for reading blood pressure, the stethoscope or EKG machine for reading heartbeat activity. There are a host of other devices that can detect deeply hidden or elusive body activities, those that we are normally never aware exist. For the greater part of our body's interior functioning, however, there is no convenient or objective way for the individual to learn what is going on inside of himself. There are, however, instruments capable of monitoring the function of nearly every internal system which are used routinely for medical and research purposes. These and other devices for tapping into the internal biology provide relatively simple information about the functioning of complicated physiologic body systems.

At one time or another we have all waited anxiously for the doctor to interpret for us the information he learned by tapping into our interiors. When *another* person reads your body signs, such as the doctor, the information is interpreted within a frame of decision about wellness or not-wellness. If, however, *you* are permitted to read that same information about yourself, you interpret the information in a frame of reference about how you feel inside. That is bio-feedback; you are being fed back biological information about your biological self. If you know little about your inner biological being, or little about how illness affects the signs of your inner biological self, then you store in memory information that relates the way you feel to what the sign read and what the doctor said the sign meant. The next time the sign reads similarly, you are already aware of its meaning. That too is bio-feedback.

Actually, there are two aspects to bio-feedback. First is the technology, the use of biomedical devices that are capable of taking a reading of your physiologic activity, such as temperature, heart rate, etc., and second is the aspect of training, i.e., what you do with the device. You may sit quietly in a chair or lie comfortably on a cot, linked to the device by delicate wires or tubes that carry the body information back to the device from bits of special sensing materials taped on your skin. In bio-feedback, the instruments that read the body signals are modified slightly so that they can display the body information in terms of visual or auditory information—lights or tones. It doesn't matter whether the body information is read in numbers or by lights or tones, the changes in body activity and their signs are all relative to a reference of normal readings.

Your biological information is there for you to perceive, but now, rather than a single reading, the device is continuously reading the body signals as they reflect the constantly changing activity of the body. Thus bio-feedback brings a new perspective to the understanding of internal states: not the single readings of the body's biologic state that medicine relies upon, but the almost *continuous* availability of information. In bio-feedback procedures body activities are monitored and can be perceived as they are performing in the dimension of time and in the spaces of the body.

In some forms of bio-feedback you simply watch or listen as the monitor sign of a selected body function fluctuates over its operating range. If you continue to work with the device, as, for example, fifteen or thirty minutes a day, then over time some association appears to develop between certain changes in the body sign and different subjective feelings, either consciously or subconsciously recognized. In essence the monitor gives you information about your successes. In time you develop control over fluctuations of the sign, and often may learn to exercise precise control, at will, over how the body sign changes. There are, of course, variations of the bio-feedback procedure, such as the one in which you are informed that the body signs can be seen or heard only when you change your body function in a certain way. When you are successful, the sign tells you so.

The new opportunity offered by bio-feedback to become aware of the biological functioning of the interior self, must, a priori, have both medical and psychological consequences. The tendency for experiential knowledge to suggest that not only medical and psycho-

logic causes, but also medical and psychologic cures, are inseparable is now in the process of being supported by scientific research.
The therapeutic potential of bio-feedback in physical illness is
apparently under psychologic, or at least mental, control. The most
obvious, immediate results of bio-feedback training techniques will
probably be in the prevention and relief of medical problems, but
the inherently associated or underlying psychologic changes cannot
be ignored.

Suppose, for example, that you suffer from regularly occurring
tension headaches. Along with other tension headache sufferers, you
have tried drugs, hypnosis, massage, and perhaps a dozen other
techniques with little relief of the headache pain. The headaches
have persisted for years, devouring whole days with their intense
discomfort. Your doctor has always noted that you would have fewer
and less severe headaches if you could only learn to relax. But how
far and how quickly can you relax with only the ordinary clues of
muscle tension to judge your progress? You are an adapting human
being, used to tolerating rather marked fluctuations of muscle tension and adjusting to the changes unconsciously. You have not been
taught to become consciously aware of the small increments of
tension which keep adding together to keep the body tense because
the muscles adapt to the increased tension without awareness of it.
It is an enormously difficult task to learn to become aware of the
real state of muscle tension without accurate indicators.

Bio-feedback can provide the accurate, continuous indicators
you need to know when and how your tension develops, and when
and how it diminishes. It can reveal small differences never before
within the realm of human perception, and perception is the basis of
experience. Now suddenly you can have the experience of breaking
the muscle barrier . . . you can experience small, localized changes
of muscle tension. You can get inside of the muscle, learn to perceive it directly, learn to experience its activity. It is a new world of
experiences and insights.

What can we expect from our new feedback techniques? It is
immediately apparent that they can provide major assistance in the
control of a wide variety of medical ills. One has only to look to
disorders of the cardiovascular system to see that learned control

over blood pressure, heart rate, and peripheral vasodilation and vasoconstriction will add immeasurably to a patient's comfort and life expectancy. Similarly with problems of the respiratory system, control over both respiration and the secretions of the respiratory mucosa will ameliorate the discomforts and serious sequelae of asthma, bronchitis, emphysema, sinusitis, and so on. Learned control over muscle systems, individual muscles, and even individual muscle cells will provide extraordinary help in all types of muscle problems, ranging from the simple muscle tension of anxiety to the rehabilitation of inactive or disordered muscles. So it is with each body system.

Although bio-feedback may find considerable usefulness in physical medical problems, a large percentage of medical problems, variously estimated to be from 60 to 75 percent, are either caused or aggravated by psychologic accompaniments of anxiety, fear, pain, and depression, which are equally well relieved by appropriate bio-feedback procedures. Because of the intimate interactions between the mind, emotion, and body function, and because the process by which bio-feedback is effective is largely a mental function, its uses are relevant to most medical, psychosomatic, psychologic and behavioral problems.

One bright horizon of the bio-feedback vista is the temporary quality of the need for the feedback device. Many research studies, including those dealing with clinical applications, have shown that once learned well, control of a physiologic function stays in memory for a long time.

A New Awareness

Bio-feedback is a curious mixture of startling simplicity and challenging complexity. It is deceptively straightforward: tap into the mysterious within directly from the surface of the body, use a simple device to convert the activity of the body system into a form which can be sensed, and *voilà*, the person can identify the feelings he has when the body is signaling the monitor device to say "blood pressure up," or "blood pressure down," or "heart rate up," or "temperature down," or "more alpha." It is very simple as a part-psychologic, part-medical compass on the road to satisfyingly better physical and mental health. Yet it is deceptively complex in the way it achieves its results.

Bio-feedback is simple in concept only. It is probably the most complex of all of the discoveries about man's being, for it points straight to the greatest mystery of all: the ability of the mind to control its own and the body's sickness and health. The mechanisms of the mind-body complex which are used to integrate the fedback information and lead to control of inner functions still elude understanding. Bio-feedback involves endless interactions among arrays of deep and surface emotions, interactions among the higher mental activities of reasoning and judgment, as well as the convoluted dynamics of highly complex body circular processes (such as those carrying messages through the brain–spinal cord–motor nerve–muscle–muscle sense–spinal cord–brain circuit). The mechanism of bio-feedback is deeply affected by the malleable, manipulable aspects of the psyche, those interacting emotion-thought complexes that are so susceptible to influences such as rapport, warmth and understanding, indifference or insensitivity. If you are, for example, in a therapist's office to learn how to relax your muscles via bio-feedback (perhaps to reduce anxiety and so to heal your ulcer), you can be just as readily turned off by a cold, impersonal attitude on the part of the therapist as you can be turned on and ready to learn by a warm, encouraging attitude. These flows of human beingness can be crucial to the ultimate success of bio-feedback techniques.

There is a popular misconception about bio-feedback by some traditionalist psychologists that in order for bio-feedback to be effective one must be strapped to a bio-feedback instrument for a lifetime. This is untrue. Many research studies have demonstrated surprisingly long-lasting effects of bio-feedback *once the concept has been realized.*

Bio-feedback merely helps the individual to become aware of his own internal world of psychologic functioning. The awareness need not be conscious awareness; it may spread only through subconsciousness, where it mobilizes the mind's intelligence to direct the body's responses according to the meaning of the fed-back information. Recently, for example, a group of researchers published a report on the remarkable success of their subjects who rapidly learned dramatic degrees of voluntary control over their heart rates via bio-feedback. The investigators suggest they were so successful because they "maximized" the efforts of their subjects' mental abilities by providing them with the full knowledge of their learning task and by asking them to change their heart rates "by purely mental means."

Precisely my point. Bio-feedback acts primarily as a temporary intermediary to give you information not ordinarily available to you about the deep within. As with any technique for self-improvement, gratifying results can be obtained only with adequate preparation, reasonable persistence in practicing the technique, and a modicum of patience. One should *not* expect results exactly similar to those of someone else. Bio-feedback is a very private process. It unquestionably will lead to genuinely individual explorations of the subjective and physiological self. It has the potential to offer one the security of one's own mind, the capacities of one's own body.

The "Black Box"

Despite the simplicity of its principle, and despite the apparent simplicity of its procedure, the actual use and success of bio-feedback depend upon an intricate complexity that defies even passable scientific definition and understanding. Both as scientists and laymen we are inexperienced in the phenomenon of internal self-control. Neither the uses nor the procedures and technology of bio-feedback have yet emerged from the research phase wherein new therapeutic developments are evaluated and tailored for specific therapeutic needs. At present bio-feedback is in its "clinical trial" phase, in which its effectiveness is being explored for a variety of medical and psychological problems.

Prolonged trials of new procedures are deemed necessary where drugs or devices with effects on the body are concerned. Bio-feedback is neither; moreover, its relevance to human problems is so striking that the customary procedures of evaluation seem to jar the logic of the bio-feedback phenomenon. And indeed, many physicians, psychiatrists, and psychologists believe so too, for many are hurriedly developing clinics where bio-feedback procedures are available. Although they are now relatively few in number, it is likely that the concept of bio-feedback therapy centers will spread rapidly.*

Under ordinary circumstances, new developments in medicine are subjected to long years of study under controls and guidelines specified by government agencies charged with protecting the nation's health. Where the *mind's* health and well-being are concerned, however, it is quite a different matter. Government supervision extends only to drugs and to what credentials are needed to use procedures that influence the mind, i.e., credentials from psychology, psychiatry, counseling, etc. It is, nonetheless, readily acknowledged that unwise or indiscriminate use of mind-emotion influencing procedures can be quite as dangerous as the use of drugs. Drugs and chemicals that influence mind and emotion, it seems, are one thing, but probing, persuasive, verbal and otherwise humanly communicated mind-emotion changing influences are quite a different thing.

This curious dichotomy between society's need to protect itself against assaults on the body and its failure to be concerned about assaults on the mind does indeed exist. It may be healed or at least brought into focus as bio-feedback continues to demonstrate the indivisibility of the human mind and body.

The critical and quite new element that bio-feedback brings to medical and psychologic therapeutics is the capacity to manipulate one's own body (and mind) by one's own mind. The implications of this newly discovered capacity are enormous. The uses are obvious, but the misuses are not obvious at all. Because we have been well educated to be cautious about doing things to the body, we hesitate when we see the harmless attachments of the bio-feedback devices. We have, however, had almost total freedom to explore and toy with the mind and emotions, and so are tempted to explore the mind with bio-feedback without proper precautions. We forget that now bio-feedback has made the mind and the body all one and the same thing.

In the following chapters I describe the biological bases of bio-

---

* At the present writing the best bet for information on bio-feedback is through your local college psychology department or medical school, or through the information service of the Bio-Feedback Research Society. The universities and medical schools also often can use volunteers for their bio-feedback research.

feedback for each of the body systems—first because we need to understand the body's physiology in order to understand bio-feedback, and second, because the historical evolution of the research leading to the psychobiologic concept of bio-feedback has not yet been brought into unifying focus.

The chapters begin with the skin, a body system almost without parallel for its ability to reflect the mental and emotional life of the body. The skin's bio-feedback use has been confined to studies of conditioned learning in the laboratory; its extraordinary communications ability is only now beginning to be recognized.

The study of biologic functions in everyday behavior has historically proceeded according to principles of conditioned learning, particularly those deriving from the work of Pavlov and of Skinner. The procedural details of bio-feedback and conditioned learning can often be strikingly similar if not occasionally identical. It is, however, the influence of mental processes and the interpretation of body activity in the light of mental activity which suggest that the two learning processes may be as different from each other as their procedures are similar. In the laboratory both conditioned learning and bio-feedback procedures have all the appearances of simple procedures. This may be true for conditioning, but bio-feedback, with its added dimension of mental influence, is far from being simple. The procedural oversimplifications stem from experimental psychologists who tend to view the body and its internal functioning as a "black box."*

It is not generally known or appreciated that, except for strictly physical measurements, study of how the body's physiology behaves during normal and normally stressful living is conducted chiefly by psychophysiologists who are concerned mainly with what happens on the *outside* of the black box of the body (i.e., behavior, psychol-

---

* A "black box" is an electronics term to describe some electrical system that puts out a signal when a signal is put into it. A popular black box is the one that automatically turns on a room lamp at dusk. The disappearance of outdoor light is a signal that activates a photoelectric cell and through circuitry then activates a switch which completes the electric circuit to the lamp that turns it on. There are a variety of electrical circuits that can be in the black box, but you who use this handy household black box are not concerned with what is inside. You are not concerned by the insides of black boxes unless, that is, the black box happens to be you. And in bio-feedback the black box *is* you.

ogy) and have relatively little background in the inner biological workings of the human or animal black box.

Now that the concept of bio-feedback is proving itself to be valuable in the regulation and self-regulation of the body's physiologic and subjective processes, it becomes important to understand the workings of the human black box during the normal ranges of human behavior.

In order to understand the biological information that is fed back in the bio-feedback process, we need to understand the biology the information is about, and what the biological information means in terms of the way in which the body functions. The need for background knowledge of biology is clearly shown in studies demonstrating that the more information an individual has about the bio-feedback procedure, about its mechanisms and objectives, the more successful the individual is in learning to control internal functions.

A further reason for giving exposure to both the biology and history of bio-feedback is equally or perhaps more important. For the most effective use of bio-feedback it is important *to know how the body expresses its emotional and mental activities through changes in its physiologic functioning.* It is, after all, the ability of the body to communicate that is the mechanism by which bio-feedback achieves its success.

It is surprising how ideally bio-feedback reflects the contemporary mood and technology. Aside from its therapeutic and self-analytic capabilities, bio-feedback is a new mode of communication. For the first time the mental self can communicate intelligently with the physical self. If desired, the interior self can be communicated directly to another human being such as counselor or therapist. The early course of bio-feedback communication will undoubtedly be as difficult to understand and to instrument as were other modes of communication when they were first new. In Chapters 12 and 13 I will offer some conjectures on the significance of this new means of communication for the future of bio-feedback.

The body's communication function and its potential for solving human social and emotional problems has been overshadowed by the more physiologic, medical usefulness of bio-feedback. Science has long been familiar with the ability of the body to communicate important information about itself, and uses this ability extensively in both medical diagnosis and in many varieties of biological research. Thus this book emphasizes the wealth of means of communication the body offers and the wealth of information the body can readily communicate about itself both to its owner and to others.

The Social Impact of Bio-Feedback

One of the most dramatic, yet curious, phenomena occurs when someone, either scientist or layman, first learns of bio-feedback: an almost immediate recognition of the validity of the process.

People *intuit* that bio-feedback is real. If it were simply a few people who have this reaction, it wouldn't merit comment. But it is significant, to the point of exposing a universal truth, that almost everyone reacts to an explanation of bio-feedback by a kind of whole-body acceptance.

The remarkable impact of bio-feedback on both scientists and the public is a phenomenon in itself. It has a startling revolutionary flavor, for even ten years ago we were chastised and taken to scientific task for exposing the thought that the mind did indeed control the body. The condemnation of such thinking dominated our intellectual and scientific speculations, despite a growing acceptance of the concept and success of psychosomatic medicine, and despite the experiential evidence of improved physical health with improved mental health. The experiences and observations of nonscientists on the feelings of health and illness have been, in the last fifty years, regularly in sharp conflict with the authoritarian conclusions and "hard data" of the medical establishment. But the current widespread social revolutionary activity is giving us room to test intuited truths as well as to voice them. We are, as at no previous time, questioning the decisions of authorities, including those decisions affecting our own behavior. We are becoming individuals rather than succumbing to the ancient tradition of permitting the cultural reality to shape our behaviors into a mass of almost identical behaviors. We are questioning and even acting upon the principles of behavior that have trapped us into someone else's categories. We are learning that what we call mind is unique and unexplored. Only now is our attention turning to the interior universes of our own minds.

Awareness of the Within

In Eastern cultures, achievement of self-awareness has long been intimately related to the art of physiological self-discipline. And people everywhere who have paused long enough from their socially imposed activities have discovered that attention to the inner self allows a fair amount of mastery over the inner physical being.

To yogis, Zen masters and mystics of other spiritual disciplines, awareness and fine control of the physical self are merely the worldly resources within the reach of every man that can be used to learn spiritual awareness. Long lifetimes are spent in controlled discipline of the mind, probing for spiritual awareness of communion and unity with the all and nothing of the universe. Accompanying this process of inner search there is almost invariably a profound and often beneficial change in human behavior. Not until bio-feedback has Western thought entertained the notion that the insights and awarenesses achieved by explorations of the self by the self may provide a far more solid base for ensuring mental health than can be achieved by all of the Westernized psychologic, psychiatric techniques combined.

The interior universe of man, his inner space, can be opened for new exploration. As man learns more about his internal functioning, he will learn how to communicate information about the new horizons of the mind. But perhaps the greatest consequence will be the possibility that bio-feedback will allow the individual to regain control of his own being and body.

We can become aware of new feelings and how they relate to the interior self, and perhaps can become aware of the unexplainable: the self teaching the self to control the inner self. Bio-feedback is an experience: at the same time it may be the mind watching itself evolving. The personal, social and even psychic implications are enormous.

There are many precious jewels in the storehouse of the subconscious which our consciousness rarely permits us to view, and then only fleetingly . . . the ecstasy of the daydream or the intriguing imagery just before sleep . . . or the mysterious logic of the dream. There are strong research hints that we may soon be able to recapture these moments of the other-mind, perhaps even learn to hold them in view and become well acquainted with the world within.

One of the most profound disturbances of our social well-being in recent years has been the burgeoning of the drug culture. Why has it had such remarkable, widespread appeal? We are only now beginning to understand that dangerous drugs offer a fleeting journey into the world of other-being, albeit a hazardous trip. We do not teach mind expansion; we only legislate against it. The seekers of new mind states—the mind-control devotees, encounter-group enthusiasts, the drug takers, the psychics, the meditators—all are on a journey into the interior universe trying to burst the limits of the socially conditioned mind. Whether acceptable or unacceptable, moral or immoral, wise or foolish, the mind of man is stirring toward a new evolution. Because of the undeniable general attraction for adventures of the mind, scientists are now beginning to study and to talk about altered states of consciousness.

Bio-feedback has the potential to make the journey into inner space one of controlled safety, as were the journeys of the astronauts into outer space.* The more we can provide feedback information about discrete mental and subjective activities, the more we can extend recognition of our mental and psychic universe. This brings us to the paradox that we may have to employ such techniques in order to understand the full implications of future mind explorations. Each new increment of knowledge about the inner self will be discovery and will immediately evolve a new permanent perspective of self and mind and being that we cannot even begin to conceptualize at the moment.

The pages that follow present the backdrop for the bio-feedback drama—the psychobiologic-philosophic foundation of the phenomenon. The antecedents and the framework of mind-body cooperation are described, beginning with the skin, where the least amount of bio-feedback potential has been realized, and moving on through the bio-feedback potential for muscles, heart, and blood vessels, and

* See Appendix A, page 409.

finally to brain waves, where some of the most remarkable and puzzling bio-feedback effort has been realized. Because of the vast potential of bio-feedback, this is more a book about possibilities and expectations than a book about conclusions. In a sense bio-feedback crystallizes the field of psychosomatic medicine, but it is also crystallizing the new work of the mind.

ONE

The Anatomy of a Phenomenon: Me and BFT

Laymen are rarely admitted into the intimate business of science. They are especially banned from the back streets of medical science where the vagaries of human nature are bared and the frailties of human emotion are mirrored in the frailties of science. Because I am an iconoclast in the world of science, and because I was *there*, a midwife attending the delivery of a hidden bit of mind, I have been impelled to share both the turmoil and the excitement of the birth trauma of bio-feedback.

Color, Imagery, and the Brain

As with all discoveries of great impact, the discovery of the bio-feedback phenomenon is also rooted in a particular gathering together of psychic, biologic, and social forces which, if we were all-seeing gods on a distant planet, could easily have been predicted as bursting forth upon the present scene. Historians have, in fact, often remarked that special sets of such circumstances seem to direct minds toward new developments particularly suited for the time. It could be said to have happened in the creative, burgeoning world of the eighteenth century that chafed with a vague yet anxious need for an omnipotent catalyst, for a new magic to lighten man's work and to assuage the agony of limited communication. The answer came unexpectedly from the accident of Luigi Galvani's discovery

19

in the leg nerves of headless frogs that the energy of electricity could flow in instant current and move its enormous power from here to anywhere.

Some years ago, like other researchers, I was salted away in the isolated confines of my highly specialized laboratory, laboring to define the physiologic underpinnings of a few selected bits of human behavior. There were few thoughts that I or my colleagues could ever uncover anything really new and dramatic about human behavior. It all seemed so well known and well theorized. We weren't thinking then in terms of new limits of the mind, only about trying to explain what we already knew. Then suddenly the work turned a corner, and there laid bare before us was a new, unexercised phenomenon of the mind: the happening of bio-feedback. No doubt my fellow researchers were as overwhelmed as I when the real import of the new directions of our work first crystallized in our minds. I can't speak for them, but I can perhaps recapture the flavor of how bio-feedback really began by recounting my own experience. Bear in mind, though, that many other researchers were doing work which led to the uncovering of the bio-feedback phenomenon, and that my efforts were only a part of the early research.

My work has rarely suffered the constraints of the traditional ways of science. I belong to the scientific elite only by the accidents in my work. Unable to profess true belief in much of current scientific theory, I prefer to make observations in the laboratory and let *them* dictate the theory rather than follow the custom of making research fit the theory.

The particular accident in my work which led me to the bio-feedback concept strangely enough probably began in childhood. When I was six years old, and on rung three or four of the neighborhood social hierarchical ladder, three very young girls sat under a mulberry tree one summer's day discussing the mystery of how one thinks. My best friend's head was flung back knowingly, her dark hair shining in the sun. Her black eyes flashed. "It's so easy. I just close my eyes and see everything I want to know. It's all bright and colored and beautiful. I just pick out what I want to. That's all. It's so easy." The other girl pumped her head in vigorous agreement.

I choked in disbelief. In one movement I brushed the dust free from my legs and began running, not stopping until I reached our house across the street and the safety of my mother's arms. I was sobbing with fear. "Mother," I cried, "they think in colors. They close their eyes and they think in colors. What's wrong with me? I close my eyes and all I see is gray. Just gray."

Fortunately some childhood traumas do not produce later mental and emotional disturbances simply because there are no echoes. The devices people employ in thinking are rarely, if ever, discussed. It was, in fact, nearly thirty-five years later that the occasion to discuss "colored thinking" arose again. I was in the laboratory with my technician and a bright fifteen-year-old who was spending the summer as a helper. The youngster began by wondering whether his vivid visual images could be recorded so that this memory and thinking device could be studied scientifically. To my everlasting relief, my technician promptly rejected the validity of this as an experimental approach since, as he said, "When I close my eyes, all I see is a gray field." Now there were at least two of us.

"Well," we conjectured, "if some of us think with visual images and others of us don't, why don't we study how our brains differ?" We could at least see whether the *colors* of mental visual images might be reflected by differences in brain electrical activity in the same way the actual perception of colors seems to be reflected in brain electrical activity.

None of our little research group had had any experience recording the brain waves of human beings. We were, however, deep into studies determining the brain electrical characteristics of cats, and how these related to a variety of behavioral characteristics. "Why not cats?" we thought. There was much against doing such work with cats. First of all, how could they report visual images to us? Worse yet, it was (then) an accepted physiological fact that cats did not have color vision.

Although older and supposedly wiser, I shared the enthusiasm of the two boys for the problem. It wouldn't hurt to explore whether colors did have any meaning to cats, despite cold scientific opinion. Certainly personal experiences with cats give one the *feeling* that colors do mean something to them. Yet the scientific literature told us that colors had no significance to cats because they couldn't be conditioned to color, i.e., they couldn't discriminate between any two colors to obtain a food reward. We were still not deterred.

There was the lingering thought that cats are pretty balky, perverse creatures anyway.

Our experiments were startlingly successful, but then we were looking for brain signals not behavioral reactions. The pampered cats who were our subjects had been regretfully but precisely implanted with electrodes deep into their brains; electrodes engineered into place to carry electrical messages of the brain to recording instruments. We flashed colored lights (softly, of course) to the cats, coaxing their brains to respond with brain cell impressions. (The cats had now recovered from surgery and gave us friendly cooperation.) Our job was to decode the messages and ferret out how, or even whether, a cat considered colors to be different. We found that the visual system of the cat was quite capable of responding in a discriminating manner to different colors. All of which makes the overt behavior of the cat even more puzzling. We never bothered to publish our results because the lure of learning something about man's thinking still beckoned us. (It has since been found that cats do indeed discriminate colors in their brains even if they don't let you know that they do. But then cats never let you know what they know about anything.)

The work with cats had given us a leg up, so to speak, on doing experimental work with visual imagery in human beings. The premise was simple enough: if cats' brains could discriminate color, human brains certainly should, and might not this brain judgment relate to the way in which people remembered and so have an influence on thinking? While this was our unspoken goal mainly because it seemed so unattainable, the scientific goal was to try to find whether any differences in brain electrical responses to color could be found between people capable of vivid visual imagery when their eyes are closed and those of us who are stuck in an eyes-shut world of gray. By that time we had interviewed hundreds of people and had confirmed the fact that some have intense visual imagery and others none at all. I hypothesized that if recall of imagery were dependent upon original input of visual information and all of us see the same objects and scenes, then there must be some central brain processes going on between storing the visual data and recalling it that differed in different types of people. And the different ways people recalled visual information had to have some relationship to their worlds of subjective associations and to their personalities.

The study was done, and the results were more dramatic than had been hoped for. It was as if there simply weren't any similarities between people who could visualize and people who couldn't. Not in their brain electrical responses to different colors, not in the structure of their inner worlds, nor in their outward personality characteristics. Although the imagery study was, in retrospect, more of a relay station on the way to finding the bio-feedback phenomenon, a brief summary of the study might interest some readers.

The experiments were actually duplicates of the experiments done with cats except, of course, that we did not surgically bury the electrodes into human brains. As in conventional brain wave recording, the electrodes were pasted to the scalp. But we did flash the same colors of lights, at a safe distance, to the eyes of the subjects and recorded the characteristic changes in brain electrical activity that always occur when new light suddenly appears in the visual scene. For one part of the study the flashes were slow, one every other second, to be sure that the message of the entire brain response to each flash of colored light was captured. Brain electrical responses to light all tend to show many general similarities in their shape and vigor and speed, but with close attention to these details, one can see special alterations that are specific for each different color.

In another part of the study the subjects watched flickering colored lights, presented at a much more rapid rate such as 5 or 8 or 10 flashes per second. Such rates of flicker somehow mobilize the visual cortex of the brain into "following" the rate and intensity of the flashes. When recorded, the brain responses look like rhythmic pen oscillations. The different patterns written out by the recording machines look like the different patterns possible by the new sewing machines and are extremely easy to catalogue by sight alone. The way these patterns gave us our results can be seen in Figures 1 and 2.

People who possessed vivid visual imagery showed a marked response to the color red, much as they would to an alarm signal. Their visual cortex suddenly failed to synchronize with the rhythm of the

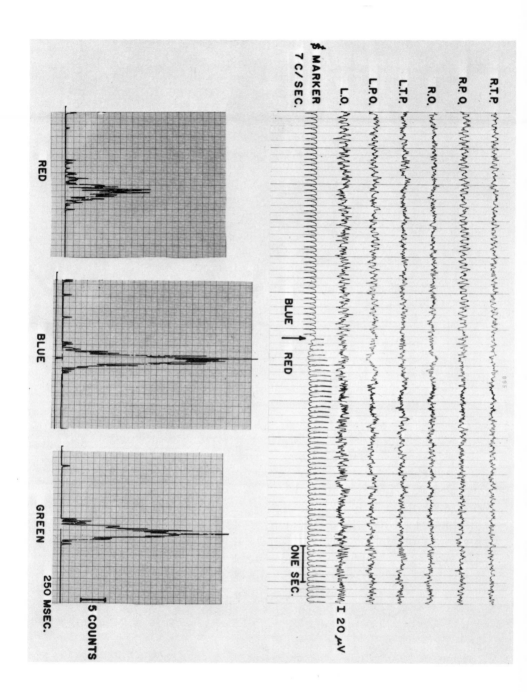

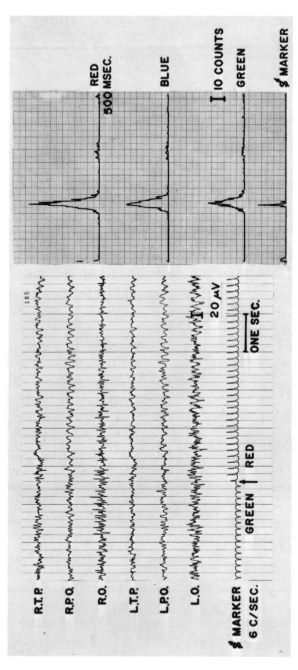

Figure 1. EEG records and frequency histograms demonstrating the difference in brain wave responses to flickering colored lights between an individual possessing vivid visual imagery (p. 24) and an individual incapable of visual imagery (p. 25).

The abbreviations to the left of the EEG records indicate placement of pairs of electrodes on the scalp (i.e., R—right, L—left, T—temporal, P—parietal, O—occipital). S—stimulus marker showing the rate of the flickering light. The frequency histograms were electronically constructed from counts of the rhythmic EEG waves in R.P.O. during the total time (15 seconds) each color was flashed.

In the first record, the typical visualizer subject showed EEG (R.P.O. and L.P.O. especially) brain wave "following" for most of the flashes indicated by the marker when the color was blue (or green) but showed very little "following" when the color was red.

In the record on p. 25, in contrast, the typical nonvisualizer showed very little brain wave (EEG) "following" when the color was green (or blue) but showed clear-cut "following" when the color flashed was red. The frequency histogram indicates the total amount of EEG following for each subject for each of the three colors. (From B. B. Brown, *Electroenceph. clin. Neurophysiol.*, 1968, 25, 372–379.)

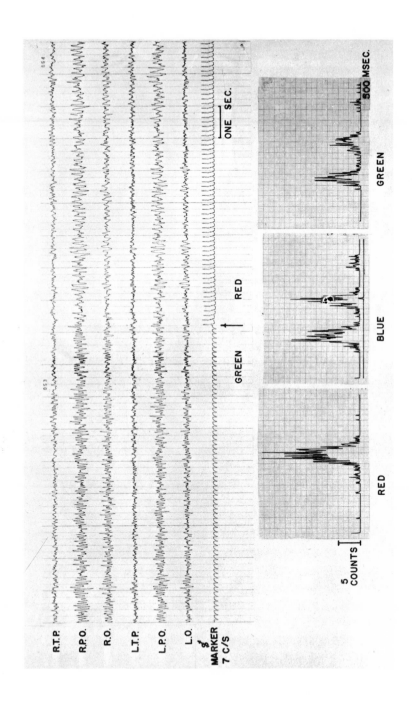

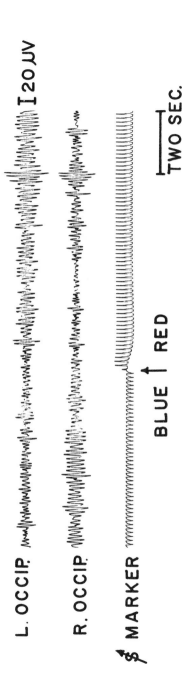

Figure 2. Some variations in the way in which the brain waves of different individuals respond to flashing colored lights.

In the record on p. 26, a subject whose brain waves followed the green flashing light at exactly twice the flashing frequency but when the color was changed to red immediately began following at the *same* rate as the flashing light.

The record on this page is that of a subject whose brain wave following of flashing colored light was better in the *right* cerebral hemisphere (right occipital electrode placement) with blue light and better in the *left* hemisphere with red light.

The EEG activity from both electrode placements has been electronically filtered.

(From B. B. Brown, *Electroenceph, clin. Neurophysiol.*, 1968, 25, 372–379; *Psychophysiol.*, 1966, 2, 197–207.)

flashes, while the brains of the nonvisualizers behaved quite differently, synchronizing their brain waves to the rhythm of the red
flashes with great vigor in a way that scientists interpret as indicating relaxation. The responses were much more complex than this,
but it was not difficult to distinguish the visualizers from the nonvisualizers by their brain electrical responses to color.

After the hard work of the experiment, we discovered a much
simpler way to distinguish people with such different abilities.
Although various standard tests have not been able to reveal differences in imagery ability, our study combined people-watching with
brain-color-response watching, and we found that we could predict
the ability of people to form visual images by their personality
characteristics alone. Vastly oversimplified, it was the energetic,
almost hyperactive, tense people who were often the nonvisualizers,
while their calm opposites generally were the visualizers.

From Brain Waves to Color to Bio-Feedback

I continued to speculate that if people using different kinds of
imagery in their thinking differed so in their brain responses and in
their personality characteristics, then certainly their subjective
worlds must differ also. The obvious next question was as old as
thoughts about the mind itself. How can the subjective worlds be
accurately and reliably characterized? This is really the heart of the
so-called communication problem. It matters not how sophisticated
and developed the ability to write or speak, the subjective world is
almost impossible to communicate with any degree of clarity. Until
now this has been the great divide. And until now neurophysiologic
researchers have failed even to find a clue of what brain matter
subserves the content of thought.

It then occurred to me that my studies indicated that the mind
processes between the act of putting perceived information into
memory and the act of recalling that information might be related
to how the brain appreciated differences in color. It seemed that the
associations between feeling, mood, emotion, and thoughts which
different people of different cultures had to different colors would
be a good starting point to explore this idea. Their different feelings

about color might begin to give us clues to mapping the almost unexplored inner life of man. At the same time it would also allow us to document actual differences in brain electrical activity. Part of this research was actually done, as is described in Chapter 11, but as soon as the experiments were started, I had my most impossible, foolish thought and stumbled onto bio-feedback. Why not let people use their own, personalized electrical brain energy to form colors? If I could perhaps offer them an array of colors their brains could choose, a palette of colors to be activated into vivid colored pictures by somehow internally, feelingly or mentally directing the energy of their brain waves; if I could offer this, then perhaps their inner selves could be expressed in colors of their own mind's choice, the epitome of nonverbal expression, alive, true and real. It never occurred to me at that moment that I, the investigator, would have to "program" a situation in which the different components of the brain waves could be directed to a number of different colors. And in doing so the brain wave component would be limited (by instrumentation) and so would be the color choices.

Yet I tried the experiment in highly simplified form. I devised an experiment in which a blue light was activated by alpha waves, thought to be the giant, rhythmic brain wave companion of relaxed feeling states. The objective generally was to let the subject of the experiment try to define his subjective feelings at times when the blue light glowed (actually signaling when his own alpha waves were present) and then, of course, report these feelings to us. By using different colors of lights, and possibly different brain wave components, I could then begin to log in information about the subjective worlds of different types of people.

I knew that part of the experimental plan had been foolish from the start, and I was soon aware that *whatever* the subject of the experiment might feel about the blue light at a specific time (when alpha waves were present), his feelings could be modified considerably by the information he was receiving about one of his own brain waves. I knew that this was bio-feedback.

It was an exciting time in the lab. The technicians and I rushed to work out all of the complicated electronics needed to transform the minute brain electrical current into a highly specific and accurate representation in the form of a light signal.* Finally everything was ready. The first subjects could watch their own alpha brain waves in the blue light as it came on and went off, as it waxed and waned in its brightness. The blue light was saying, here is alpha, now it's larger, now it's smaller, now it's gone, here it is again.

In the recording room we watched the EEG recordings. First the small diffuse brain wave (EEG, electroencephalogram) pattern typical of alertness or anxiety, an indefinable pattern of fast, non-specific waves of mixed frequencies. Then some bursts of alpha, then more and more. Over the intercom, we would check to make sure that the subject was alert and not drowsy, for we knew that more alpha waves would appear with growing relaxation. Time after time, with subject after subject, we watched the same surging forth of more and more alpha. And the subjects' reports were enthusiastic: "So restful but so interesting. I never get bored."

The conclusion seemed obvious. If a person could see something of himself that up to now had been unknown and involuntary, he could identify with it and in some way learn to exert control over it. If a person could learn this with an obscure brain wave, couldn't he then learn to identify with almost any functioning part of himself, and also learn to control that too?

New Wine . . . with Tom, Dick and Harry

Suddenly the long years of apprenticeship to the mind and body sciences had culminated in something infinitely greater than the scientist's "tentative hypothesis." My head swam with mixed thoughts of turmoil and peace. The hard, unbending facts of science had led directly to an explosion of knowledge of the very essence of inner being and the unifying thread of life.

What would medical science think? How would psychiatrists react? Could biology accept this new reality? Where were my scientific colleagues; did they know? Had they stumbled across the same bewilderingly unexpected ability of human beings? Where was everyone? The excitement cried to be shared. It was too great to be imprisoned by the ineffectual daily "My Gods"or "Gee whizes."

---

* Details are given in Chapter 10.

Then, like the eerie lull before the great typhoons, a gentle stranger visited the lab. Slightly bored with each other, we exchanged the usual kind of scientific information. Then without warning he observed, "An investigator up north is doing something similar." It was the psychologist Kamiya, an early pioneer in sleep and dream research. Moreover, he had been doing the "something similar" for some time. Why didn't I know? Oh, I reminded myself, he talked to psychologists while I talked with physiologists. It was always so, as if the branches of biological science were all sliced from the mother tree and transplanted in distant nurseries.

The first showers of the coming typhoon arrived. Another visitor to the lab said that *he* was "conditioning alpha." A letter told me of an investigator in the East who had studied alpha brain waves as an example of a control system in engineering. A researcher in the Midwest was also turning alpha waves into lights, much as I was doing.

It is rare in science, to the point of being exceptional if not unique, that researchers with different backgrounds and interests all simultaneously discover a new phenomenon. That scattering of a single event is a phenomenon in itself and speaks to the esoteric philosophy concerning the order of the universe, the intellectual and emotional recognition of which goes beyond awe and wonder to the drive to share with all mankind. The recognition of the biofeedback phenomenon and the almost supernatural order being imposed upon its development has continued to spur all of us to effective action. Even in the earliest days it was apparent that we were actually all heading in the same direction although we were all doing quite different types of research. It seemed that we should get together and share ideas.

Casting Bread upon the Waters

Dr. Joseph Hart, of the University of California at Irvine, started an information letter to be sent regularly to the six or seven researchers doing work such as ours. By the time the rest of us were ready to become active in writing information letters, Dr. Hart was off on a sabbatical. To rescue his effort, three of us held an informal conference in Washington. A few months later, with the stimulating enthusiasm of Dr. Gardner Murphy, one of the truly great fathers of modern psychology, and the sincere interest of psychiatrist-researcher Dr. Kenneth Gaarder, a letter and questionnaire were sent out to survey the number of scientists interested in the new discovery and learn whether they would like to join in forming a new scientific society.

The response was remarkable. Interest was obviously already high and widespread, and many were interested in a national meeting. With unbridled enthusiasm, and without consulting my colleagues, I planned a meeting and sent out reservation forms. What I had thought at first would be a rush to sign up for the meeting turned out to be an agonizing wait. Three dismal months passed with only driblets of replies. Then suddenly and quite unexpectedly in came 40 replies, then 50, and finally the meeting day arrived. There were 142 people registered for the three-day meeting.

From a slim six to the healthy figure of some 140 in less than six months to start a new scientific society and hold its first annual meeting in a field unheard of the year before was nothing less than sensational. And that is a phenomenon characteristic of bio-feedback. The meeting itself was a smashing success. The society was officially formed and named The Bio-Feedback Research Society. That was in 1969 and each succeeding year has seen another annual meeting.

The embryo BFRS looked ripe for an experiment—one to see whether scientists would or even could accept a sudden revolution in the way of doing scientific business. I instituted a new format for the meeting, one where each topic could be discussed in full by the audience along with a sort of self-selecting panel to lead them. No long, dry papers. Not only would there be a scientific meeting, but it would be a liberated, honest, and personal exchange of concepts. Everyone would have his scientific say. No one would be tightly scheduled for a locked-in appearance at the podium where he could drone on about the minutiae of his experiments. This time we could concentrate on ideas, and if people had gotten out of the habit of creating new scientific thoughts, then, by God, here was an opportunity to stimulate them to their best efforts.

Science on the Assembly Line

For those of you not familiar with the classical format of annual or semi-annual get-togethers of "scientific societies," here is a brief description.

The scientists travel, at considerable expense and in the face of yearly rising hotel costs, to a pre-selected location for the meeting, chosen for two reasons: first, that the facilities of meeting rooms are large enough and the number sufficient to cope with anywhere from several dozen to many thousands of presented research reports; and second, as token recognition to the "society's" member whose home university it is. There are always difficulties of transportation to the meeting places and difficulties in finding restaurants, and bathrooms, and girls, and various other appurtenances which scientists feel are important to the progress of their science.

Papers are strictly scheduled, and Important People (politically or scientifically) may or may not be found at the meetings of their specialties. The "scientific reports," which often sum up the research of a year's effort, are squeezed into a scant ten minutes. That's all that is allowed because there are many scientific papers to be read. And *read* is the right expression. It is the rare scientist who can extemporize about the details of his work, details without which apparently no one would trust his work. After the 10-minute reading, 5 minutes are allowed for discussion.

Confusion reigns. Scientists rush madly in and out of the meetings, for there is not only one schedule, but typical scientific meetings consist of many schedules of papers to be read and schedules of other presentations all running simultaneously. One must rush from place to place. There isn't time to discuss important aspects of the research in the time allowed so it is necessary to make appointments or try to catch other scientists in the halls. It is an old saying that most of the important business of "scientific meetings" takes place in the halls. Much of the "important discussion" is about "university politics or institution jobs," and if you hear the expression "happy" or "not happy," you know someone is probing about a job situation.

So the traditional "scientific meeting" is an unrealistic, ultra-programmed efficiency-directed, computerized construction for handling masses of scientific reports. The objective of exchange of research information has been lost long ago. Efficiency is the name of the game. The scientists play it because attending meetings is a convenient way of getting expenses paid for a trip. And presenting a paper at the meeting counts as a publication in the publish-or-perish society of scientists.

The formal rituals of intellectual snobbism have always struck me as an impediment to the real business of research—communication. In the old days when scientists were few in number and decorum was a gentle way of life, scientific gatherings compensated for the constraints of formality by allowing the earnest investigator an hour or more to detail his intimate involvement in his work. There were long and full discussions. Over the years, and particularly since World War II, membership in scientific societies has increased nearly a hundredfold. Time limits became a necessity, multiple session scheduling became needed, and more meeting rooms and hotels. The meat of the scientific gathering was nearly sliced out of existence. The new masses of new scientists became little more than pawns on a chessboard. Their seniors, department heads, issued work directives to be performed for the rewards of university degrees, for elevated positions, for raises. With students thronging into graduate schools, research facilities and advisors became stretched thin. The most expeditious solution to the masses was to limit research ventures to those with predictable results. Descriptive, exploratory research virtually disappeared because it was inefficient, because it could not bring in financial support since monies were for positive answers only, for products, for advertising data.

So it really hasn't mattered much that the discussions of most research efforts at scientific meetings are limited to ten minutes. The interested researcher, the imaginative, dedicated scientist had to play a new game too. If not, he was denied the tools he needed, the recognition from his peers, and the money for his research.

I was determined to hammer a wedge into the system. All I hoped for was that one or two people would realize that the contemporary scientific society of the forties through the sixties was criminally misdirecting research talent. I had seen too many brilliant research minds either become lost in the trappings of the status rituals or drop out in disgust. I had watched scientifically talented youngsters become frustrated by the lofty inaccessibility of scientific elitism and move to more psychologically honest if less scientific pursuits. There seemed to be no question but that our tradition had become a self-contained, self-limiting system taking new young minds bursting with the ability to create new worlds and derailing them into dull, unimaginative efficiency.

Meetings with a Conscience

The Bio-Feedback Research Society represents a novel, perhaps revolutionary, departure from the traditional "scientific society." The story of its organization needs telling if only to encourage less adventurous scientists to examine the usefulness of large, impersonal traditional scientific societies where political maneuvering for prestigious positions ranks with meaningful communication of scientific research.

Probably the first break with the formalized traditions of scientific meetings actually occurred two years before the BFRS meeting. In 1967 I attended the annual meeting of the Society for Psychophysiological Research being held in San Diego where the same Dr. Joe Hart presented a paper on his alpha conditioning studies. Hart really should be given the lion's share of credit for breaking with scientific tradition and the tiresome stupidities of the typical scientific meeting. His presentation at the 1967 San Diego meeting was the supreme satire on scientific meetings. Joe solemnly passed out mimeographed copies of his talk, took the podium, and announced that his allotted 10 minutes would be devoted to the *audience* reading the distributed copies. The audience could then ask questions with the data in their hands. It was a foolish, silent ten minutes. The tradition of the formal readings of scientific papers rose like a ghoulish specter in the silence. There was a lot of fidgeting, some muffled snickers, and a seeping restlessness to escape the specter.

One really couldn't fault Hart's departure from the accepted practice of reading a paper jammed with condensed data and thoughts *to* the audience. He had supplied his fellow scientists with all the data they needed to understand his research. It was, if anything, unusual thoughtfulness to provide fellow scientists with a text rather than continuing to permit the usual exasperating exercise of taking notes from rapid-fire talk and comments on twenty complicated slides of data all condensed into 10 minutes.

With bio-feedback research, however, most of the researchers were then actively conducting new experiments and only a handful of major studies had been completed. It was a time to share activities or interest, not simply to recount experiments already laid to rest.

Now came the next big test for the emerging chrysalis of bio-feedback. How would the drastic innovation of the meeting format be received? Would it work or fall flat? Would the participants cooperate?

Joy, Joy, Joy, Joy

The format for the first BFRS meeting was a considerable revolution in conducting scientific meetings. Instead of the formal research papers to be read, everyone working in a particular aspect of bio-feedback was assigned to a discussion panel. They all sat at tables in front of the audience, and were to report briefly on their interests, mentioning their most important results, then turn over the meeting to an exchange between the general audience and the panel. I had felt that the really important questions about research, such as *Why* did you do that experiment? or What do you *really* think your results mean?, were always omitted in formal presentations. With the major emphasis on exchange of research information between panel and audience, it seemed likely that researchers just beginning such work, or even those who were contemplating it, would benefit greatly from the ideas of those already having experience with new work.

It took a bit of time before the group was converted, but with the help of Drs. Kamiya, Green, Mulholland, Hart, Ax, Orne, and many others, the discussions opened up and both the panels and the audience began to feel their freedom. Ideas, information, and new concepts began flowing around the meeting room. Tensions relaxed. I noted another revolution taking place. Every participant began to assume responsibility for keeping the thing going. They were behaving like mature adults. The idea was working. All it needed was the time and the place and freedom from restraining rituals.

Even the business of the new society was arranged by open meeting. A very brief list of policies was developed. Membership would not be restricted. For the first year the new society would be governed by a group of members-at-large. I was elected chairman, presumably because I had performed a service. I was gratified that the service had been useful.

Buoyed by the success of the meeting, I arranged for the transcription of tapes of the discussions. The appetite of biomedical scientists throughout the country for the transcriptions was phenomenal. The thousands of requests were more than we could supply. Libraries from as far away as Sydney, Tasmania, Moscow, Prague, Madrid, São Paulo requested copies. The word of bio-feedback had spread more quickly than the proverbial wildfire.

Some Sticky Wickets

Bio-feedback attracted more scientists in different specialties, more students, and more professional people in a shorter time than any new development I can think of. Some VIPs of other biomedical, psychological scientific societies voiced considerable annoyance for the upstarts who insisted that bio-feedback was a new phenomenon and of such importance to warrant a special name and the formation of still another scientific organization to clutter up the fields and communication pathways of bioscience.

Within the professional scientific society there are also problems, for many are dependent upon continued exploitation of their own or their peers' theories to maintain personal security built up over years of work. And so some excellent researchers at first looked at bio-feedback as an intruder into the orderliness of their science which must be attacked and exposed as an illegitimate relative of their traditional, theoretical universe. The techniques used and the highly personalized, experiential events of the bio-feedback experience were foreign devils in the societal structure of formalized medicine and psychology. The new bio-feedback was escaping the stricture of classical thought; control was in the head, no longer in the hands of the experimenter. Experimental psychology had firm rules for laboratory conduct, and a syntax to discourage the intervention of feelings in the descriptions of human behavior.

This was sharply brought home during a Department of Defense conference where, as a bio-feedback pioneer, I was called as one of some twenty-five consultants. This is no Ellsberg revelation. We weren't even rated top secret or anything. Ostensibly the conference was to evolve recommendations about what kind of new research should be funded, particularly behavioral control research. There were certain "military needs," a tired but smartly turned out colonel told the gathering. He went on to explain that there was a particular need to have the troops psyched up for each "precision task" at hand. On an invasion, for example, how do you have the men calm and relaxed in the landing craft, then super-keen and alert for the fast action of the landing, single-minded and intense for the fighting, then shift their minds to instant relaxation for a good night's sleep? Even in theory, that kind of behavior control is nauseating. I promptly got a headache that lasted the entire two days of the conference. And it got worse as I listened to the procedures recommended by the gathered elite of the psychologists-straight-out-of-Pavlov. "Control their heart rates!" they cried. After all, emotion and states of mind are just the head reacting to the body. "Start with a heart rate conditioning procedure," they went on. And on. And I left.

Such researchers maintain the scientific establishment, without which there could be no revolution. For those bio-feedback researchers, such as myself, who exalt in standing at new horizons, the establishment is always there to keep us honest, to force us to explain our new ideas in familiar terms.

Behavior Is from the Inside

As it turned out, the scientifically established VIPs were only then discovering the true significance of their own research. They had, it is true, been the first generation to discover that the autonomic nervous system and its vital organs, the automatic functions of our body long believed beyond behavioral control, could in fact be subject to conditioned learning just as the muscle systems could be. And they were aware that their discoveries could be of critical

importance in the therapeutic management of psychosomatic illness. But they were looking at the control of inner man from the
outside, and bio-feedbackers were looking at it from the inner man
himself. As later chapters explain, the customary view was to
control behavior, including that of the inner self and body by
external control devices and procedures. The word is training, but
behaviorists train by exerting control on the outer side of man. Now
bio-feedback was talking about self-training and controlling man
from within.

The bio-feedback antagonists were entangled in a net of their
own theories. The entire modern history of psychobiology rested on
physical foundations, the subjective universe and its power being
viewed as too capricious and inconstant, too unstable to indulge
with scientific effort. Now, almost without warning that bogey of
psychology, the will, had returned to plague the researchers. It became their duty, as the medieval priests had warned about worldly
explorations, to warn us that it was all illusory. Behavior, they repeated, was controlled only by events in the external environment.
We have no argument with that, we replied; bio-feedback is simply
putting the inside on the outside, and so your inside events are now
outside events. Or, if you wish, those changes in the external
environment which you say are what shape our behavior are now our
inside events, except that they are outside. And incidentally, we
pursued the argument, in *your* work you controlled inside, internal
behavior by giving the reward of showing your learners how well
they were performing each time their inner selves performed correctly. If that reward was information about how well something
inside was learning, wasn't that bio-feedback? The silence that
followed has lasted several years.

My own experiences of being caught in the net of interest and
publicity mirror the public's excitement by bio-feedback.

It all began with scientists themselves. During the year that the
Bio-Feedback Research Society was forming and the word was out
that I operated a brain wave bio-feedback laboratory replete with
advanced electronic equipment, not a day passed without a visit
from professional researcher or therapist. They were full of questions, they wanted to experience brain wave feedback, they wanted
to dream about the future of feedback, and they wanted to initiate

collaborative research studies. My technicians patiently wired up every visitor and led him through an alpha bio-feedback session, and I sat for hours of explaining, conjecturing, planning and sharing, as best I could, the gold dust mined from the laboratory. The visitors were insatiable. It was as if they felt suddenly confronted by the impossible dream, a panacea for all time and for all things. It was a gut feeling, for bio-feedback was just being born, and there was none of the conventional, hard scientific evidence actually down on paper to warrant the wild dreams of the future. Yet the gut feeling persisted, an insight like the illumination of faith when all experiential knowledge fits together and reason must come later.

Cloud Nine

The drab, depressing Veterans Administration building where I work began to breathe with the air of high excitement. It was a time of open-eyed wonder for the visiting scientists and for the therapists. The magnitude of the future of bio-feedback was too great to allow anything else but wonder at first. Everyone was dreaming his own dream. A way to control the uncontrollable inner man, a way to know the self, a way to cure illnesses, a way to prevent illness, a way to make the mind more mindly, a way perhaps to genius. Everyone dreamed; it was no time to heave to and buttress the experimental shorings to conform to scientific architecture. The bio-feedback dream was too good, the intuition of its reality was too strong not to enjoy and revel in to the fullest. Nearly a year passed before the scientific feet began to walk the ordinary ground of scientific convention once more. We were all "high" on the drug of dreams, but they were dreams rooted in the realities of mind and body function. Suddenly, out of nowhere had come the lost thread between mind and body, the resurgence of a buried memory as ancient as man himself that there was indeed more to man than the physical self. The biomedical scientists had been born and had matured their intellects in a century of physical beingness shorn of its spiritual and mind dimensions. And now, like medieval priests, they were expounding the virtues of the human will.

In the second wave of spectators after the researchers and clinicians came the press and television, the magazine and movie people. It was science fiction come true, futurology in the research laboratory. We got used to microphones stuck under the nose, tape recorders humming, cameras clicking, technicians trooping through the halls with television cables, lighting banks being set up. It got to be a set routine, with all of us in the office and laboratory knowing our places and poses and lines. There were ABC, NBC, CBS, Canadian, Italian TV, BBC, and Public TV, and local stations, too. We began to rate the network crews for efficiency and artistry. We learned the different techniques for filming and taping, different interview techniques, where to put the lights and cameras.

It was interesting but tedious. Newspaper and magazine techniques were surprisingly different in their search for the most dramatic, and sometimes melodramatic, news delicacies for their readers. Television has a much more difficult time covering the scientist in his laboratory, always striving as it does for attention-getting devices and the edge of sensationalism. Laboratories are too often dusty bottles and cluttered work benches. But our laboratory was all visual, perfect for the media. We had the brain wave recording equipment, the banks of electronic devices then needed to isolate out the brain wave components we needed and convert them to feedback signals, and an assortment of fascinating colored light displays for the feedback signals.

And then we had the train, the delight of every reporter.

I had always been concerned by the relative abstractness of the bio-feedback signals; researchers mainly used dull, monotonous, unvarying tones, or unharmonious wavering noises, or simple on-off lights. And although my lab had always used colored lights in interesting combinations and settings, it seemed to me that if the feedback signal of internal body activity was to become meaningful to the individual, then perhaps it should at least have some symbolic meaning or interest other than ordinary shapes and colors. In thinking about how bio-feedback might appeal to children, the most obvious toy of childhood instantly popped into mind . . . the choo-choo train. Why not? Some toy trains were battery operated, and within a few hours, there was one in the lab, connected to the brain wave feedback apparatus.

It was typical for visitors to look glassy-eyed at the train, sure that they wouldn't be able to understand how their own alpha brain wave activity could possibly make the train run. Just like the feed-back light signals, we would explain. We extract the voltage of the alpha wave bursts in the EEG, and this is just like the voltage in your transistor radio, so when there are alpha waves in your EEG, the train starts, and the larger the waves become, the faster the train goes. Then when alpha waves disappear, the train stops. "Far out," they would usually mumble in amazement, then naturally ask whether they could try it. Adults loved the train much more than children did. Psychiatrists and psychologists agreed that the train idea was great for working with children, but what they didn't know and I was too embarrassed to reveal was that I had a whole racing car set which I had touched up to operate from brain waves. Two people could be wired up for brain wave recording and demonstrate their alpha wave control by racing their cars against each other, shooting the curves, plotting their track crossing tactics, all in their heads and with their heads. The racing cars are dusty now, their tracks corroded from lack of use, for science cannot be fun; it must be served by the inching tedium of measuring the symbols of science. In the laboratory science dictates that how fast a choo-choo train goes *must* be calibrated to the rate of change of the brain wave voltages.

Inevitably, though, the train triggered thoughts of practical uses for the electrical power of the brain. Almost everyone decided that in the future it would be possible to wake up in the morning, put on an electrode cap, think a certain brain wave and have the voltage start the coffee pot. Or come home at night, clap on the electrode cap, and have the voltage of a brain wave open the garage door. "Sure," I would agree. "It's possible." Scientists and TV crews alike began plotting brain wave electric companies.

Life, Look, Newsweek, Time . . . and Playboy, too

Scientists have a double standard about publicity. In their hearts they crave it, but in their public stance they eschew its leveling effect, offering the intellect of the elite to the uneducated common society. They argue that, in biomedical science, the public will appropriate the secrets of science, misuse them, and come to harm and be disappointed. Their emotional-intellectual double standard has been delightfully exposed during the unusually long period of publicity that bio-feedback has enjoyed. Several prominent bio-scientists guardedly asked me how I was able to get in touch with so many media people.* While the scientists were scheming to entice the media in their direction, they were publicly abhorring the rampant publicity about bio-feedback. It was, they argued, the scientist's responsibility to ensure that information revealed to the public was absolute and indisputable and of unequivocal benefit.

Like drugs that have a 70 percent success rate?

Like the dark night of the polio vaccines or heart transplants?

Like thalidomide?

The scientific research community has little concept of its own reality that nothing is ever 100 percent sure. Nor is any biomedical, psychologic procedure ever 100 percent safe. But our scientists argued further that even if bio-feedback were reasonably effective in illnesses, its safety had not yet been established. The public must be protected, even though protection creates a wall of ignorance; public education should await decisions from the scientific gods.

My own concepts about what the public is entitled to know about the activities of biological research are quite different from those of my colleagues. No longer must the public remain ignorant of the affairs of science. Education has been simplified by the media. Moreover, it is the public's money that supports the research. They're entitled. There are also the self-limiting aspects of scientific

---

* Aside from being amused, I was a bit shocked. It had never occurred to me to seek out publicity. How *did* the media get the word? Then I remembered that the large University of California system has its own press release service. For other scientists, however, the usual process was by having a scientific paper selected by a national scientific society as being of unusual interest or importance for release to the press. Over the years my research work had been selected a number of times for international press release. The press and television had covered so much of my research that I had gotten to be rather a veteran at scientific exposure. There had been the work showing that the way certain animals responded to ordinary drugs depended upon their social milieu (whether they were housed alone or in groups); there was the work showing that cats were like people in that the way they responded to two martinis depended upon their personality patterns; there was the experimental contact dermatitis developed for the first time in animals; there was the first of the modern psychic energizers and tranquilizers; there were the LSD studies, and the expedition to find the magic mushrooms in Mexico; and now, mixed in with the bio-feedback publicity were the studies on the brain waves of people who were addicted to cigarettes. My kind of science was obviously different; it was simply a wondering about what really happened in the behavior of living things, not the conventional science of trying to pin down reasons.

isolationism and scientific elitism. Thinking can get to be circular and encapsulated. The realities of public need should impinge upon scientific reasoning and its directions. New light is always helpful. It should be no chore for the intelligent scientist to separate the wheat from the chaff of public response. One has only to think of the public's influence in abbreviating the follies of modern war to understand that it might also be helpful in circumventing some of the research follies. It brings to mind the ninety million dollars spent on putting a trained lever-pressing monkey into space with only the smallest scientific justification. The monkey died within a few hours, and a public lawsuit followed. Good show, Mr. Public.

In general the media people expended good honest effort in their reporting. They too intuited the validity and the promise of bio-feedback. They were concerned about the misuse of alpha brain wave feedback by faddists, and they were careful to emphasize all of the potential hazards that I pointed out. There were a few good and bad exceptions. The unit manager of the "Chronolog" program was serious, kind, considerate, and careful. But when the program was aired, the long hours of considered taping of the interview and the efforts of the laboratory had been cut completely in favor of opinions of a brain wave expert who had scarcely heard of bio-feedback, to comment on the alpha fad. Although I had discovered that the careful and considerate unit manager was not at fault, nonetheless, with some pique and considerable justification, I fired off a letter to "Chronolog" citing their lack of honesty in production. We could not justify wasting the taxpayers' money to produce a selected, opinionated entertainment; we could afford such efforts only if the public was to be properly and adequately informed. I never had a reply.

Most of the TV shows were well done. The best experience was with Hugh Downs. Not only is he an ideal interviewer, his comprehension of the potential benefits of bio-feedback and its philosophic implications for the future left little to be desired. Six months later he returned for a week of detailed explanation and learning, to be prepared for the bio-feedback future. Understanding and interest such as his has made all of the research effort worthwhile.

The publicity created problems. Research offices and labs are poorly equipped to be information centers. We were already han-

dling the swelling demands of the Bio-Feedback Research Society;
the secretaries and technicians and researchers photocopying lists of
information, collating pages, sealing envelopes by the hundreds.
Most surprisingly the inquiries were largely from professional
people. There were letters from the education departments of universities, letters from lawyers and judges, letters from heads of penal
institutions, letters from ministers, social workers, neurologists, in-
ternists, surgeons, psychiatrists. Even high school teachers who
wanted to begin teaching students about bio-feedback. I recall
being stunned when, for the first time, I received a letter from a
large university with the letter heading Bio-Feedback Laboratory.
Bio-feedback had really arrived.

Then there were the volunteers for experiments, at times a
hundred a week. And the visits of groups from schools, scientific
societies meeting in Los Angeles, hospital staff groups, psychiatric
clinic groups, meditation groups, psychology classes from universities. One in particular was memorable. As I recall, it was a
psychology class from a well-known school of theology. The young
people were alert and excited, bright and thoughtful. They took
notes and asked questions for several hours. Then I discovered that
I was their class project for the semester. What a way to earn credit!

Bring on the Shamans

I've heard it said that there is a little bit of larceny in all of us. But
never did I hear the larcenous heart beat so loudly as in some of the
modern-day shamans who managed visits to the lab by some expert
verbal camouflage. Who knows where religion fits in science? There
was, unquestionably, a similarity between what bio-feedback could
accomplish and what practice of the Indian arts of yoga could
accomplish. In the early days of bio-feedback when the ability to
control one's own brain wave alpha activity was seized upon as
instant Zen or instant yoga, it was a new problem for the scientist.
Many bio-feedback researchers promptly became converts to the
Oriental mind-body control philosophies, partly because of their
own needs of the psyche, partly because it was mod and hip, and
partly because they had the magic machines right in their own
laboratories, mainly at government expense. I, on the other hand,

had been a student of the world's religions for some twenty-five years. When one has had the opportunity to study or to experience the many paths to a spiritual unity or the universal thread of consciousness, one is not likely to become profoundly attached to any single belief or practice for spiritual discovery. I was, in fact, highly skeptical of any promise for instant salvation, bio-feedback or otherwise.

Seekers of spiritual calm form as diverse a group as can be found in any population of human beings. Some of the ones who came to the lab actually did seem to radiate some kind of essence of other-knowing; some were simply young and eager, unspoiled and intense; but some were charlatans whose verbal raiments were stitched with the silk of the masters. Their eagerness was tempered with humility, their voices soft in an echo of practiced chanting. At first I could hear only faintly the overtones that rang a different bell, then gradually the notes became familiar. There is money here, and power, the words began to form beneath statements of compassion and all-lovingness. Where there is bio-feedback, there is money and power, disciples and customers. The tricksters mixed with the faithful and spurred them on to spiritual awareness with the bio-feedback Word. In the beginning was the Alpha. It was surprising how many electronics engineers emerged from the spiritual hut, how many myth makers were delivered fully statured into the camps of the seekers. And there too, in all of their transported glory, were my words and my bio-feedback instrument designs, cunningly purloined but little disguised. It was a new experience, and there was nothing I could do but name it: bio-feedback espionage.

Among the visitors there was one kind that deserves special mention. Although we researchers are accustomed to heartbreak and despair, there are times when the world touches us cruelly. Bio-feedback was, and is, a particular excitant to that kind of other-world visitor. I personally had five or six. These were the visitors who were wealthy and powerful. As the IRS knows well, each has a non-profit "foundation," that well-used tax-dodge, although no one can be quite sure which is and which isn't. They make appointments and come to the laboratory in an attitude of complete seriousness to learn more about the drama of bio-feedback. It is of great importance to society; it deserves financial support for extended research.

Would $300,000 do? Or would $100,000 a year help? (There were three of these.) All they ask is a few hundred pages of background, what researcher is doing what and where. Addresses, please. And please prepare a research plan for your future bio-feedback research. Then, armed with the nuggets of your labors, off they go to someone else's laboratory, and you never hear from them again. They have drained you dry, they have extracted every ounce of knowledge and planning they wanted, and they have departed. I like to coin names, and these were my "lab-hoppers."

The visits, the mail, the calls, the publicity; it began to consume all of our energy. I had been trapped between the desire to be of help to the seekers and the very practical need to do work for a living. It is an enormously sad decision to be faced with, having to decide to end the flow of information, to lend the little help I could, giving hope and sustenance to the earnest desires and needs of the searchers. There was no way we could continue despite my personal belief that the information about bio-feedback we supplied was truly owing to the public—who had paid for our research. It was perplexing to face the demands of the research administrators who refused to augment the staff to handle correspondence and visitors, insisting instead that we return to the machinery of the lab and plod our way to newer discoveries. I gathered that one discovered by rote, not by insight or by spirit. The office was forced into a defensive posture. No more appointments, no more visits, correspondence had to be left unanswered. It is an appalling sensation to be forced to refuse cries for help when one's whole life has been dedicated to be of service. I became ill listening to the secretaries explaining that I wasn't available for discussions or visits.

There was one thing that I could do to help answer the public desire for information about bio-feedback, and that was to lecture. As a laboratory recluse I was astounded to learn of the huge numbers of the public who take the time to learn, who make an effort to become involved with the new world. It was a humbling experience, one that doesn't become worn or oppressing or exhausting. Just yesterday I gave my four-hundredth or so talk on bio-feedback to the staff of a mental hospital and, rather than feeling stale, just watching the expressions of eager interest was more than enough to quicken my enthusiasm. Yesterday was typical in the response of the audience. I finished promptly at the designated time so that the staff could get back to work. But there was silence, no one moved, and as I began to wonder what I might have said wrong, someone spoke up. "Can't you go on, do you have to stop now?" That's the way it has been, talking about bio-feedback. It touches people, lay or professional, right in their gut needs and hopes.

TWO

Skin Talk: A Strange Mirror of the Mind

If the Tasadays, remnants of a stone age culture recently discovered in the Philippines, are an example of primitive communications, perhaps their constant use of warm, enfolding embraces and their loving touches should make us think more deeply about the communications power of the skin. The Tasadays have no words for weapons or war or hate. Has the natural love and wonder of man been disserviced by unnatural concepts of human behavior for so long that we have forgotten that skin communication once led to peace and understanding?

Voices in the Skin

One of the most feared, hidden, yet obvious properties of the human body is the ability of the skin to conduct an electric current. Everyone in the world feels apprehension about the potential disasters of electrocution or being hit by lightning. We are so used to the thought of accidents with electricity that for most of us merely approaching a broken electrical fixture is an anxious moment. Yet, in a very real sense we ourselves are charged electrical instruments, and few of us know that the body's electrical activity can be put to helpful psychotherapeutic use. Nor are many of us aware that when we take a lie-detector test it is the electrical capacities of the skin to communicate information about our personal thoughts and feelings that give us away. We have not been told that our skins readily provide a peep show into our most private emotions. In the follow-

49

ing pages is the story of some of the dynamics behind how the skin's emotional giveaway is accomplished and the great potential benefits that can derive from intelligent use of the skin's emotional speaker. I can only hope that such knowledge can suggest both a more direct route to the subconscious than conventional psychotherapy and a more enlightened use of the techniques and technology of lie detection.

Why do we know so little about this secret showcase of the inner self?

A very strange mixture of social, medical and scientific reasons has protected the public from both the benefits and the possible dangers of the powerful communications medium of the skin. And for apparently the same reasons science and man have appropriated this most personal body tool for use by the local police and the personnel departments of industry. One of the more fortunate bits of "fallout" from broad interpretation of the bio-feedback concept will, I believe, be a return to the individual of his most personal, but unsuspected, ability to talk with his skin.

Skin bio-feedback takes quite a different form than that of other body systems such as heart, muscles, or brain waves. The bio-feedback monitors of those organs or systems give information that appears to relate to changes directly within the systems themselves. Bio-feedback of heart rate information, for example, tends to emphasize primarily how the heartbeat is performing; brain wave bio-feedback tends to emphasize how brain electrical activity is performing. Because of their vital role, the fact that these body activities are expressing emotion and mind function as well as their life-supporting function tends to be a secondary consideration. But in the case of the skin, with its less well appreciated vital function, it is not the skin that skin talk is talking about primarily; the skin is talking about the *mind*.

With the skin, then, the priorities are reversed: the skin monitor is feeding back information *primarily* about the mind, and only secondarily, if at all, information about the skin itself. And what we can learn in skin bio-feedback is not control of the skin, but control of emotions and mental activity. This might seem to make heart muscle or any other kind of bio-feedback obscure indicators of emotion as compared to the skin's ability to communicate the inner being.

As with any communication made by human individuals, whether verbal, postural, facial, or behavioral over time and space, skin talk gives important clues about the personality and intelligence of the individual, his psychological state, his ability to learn; his motivation and memory; his awareness, perception, and how he thinks; his sex and age. As we have come to recognize in the twentieth century, communications are crucial to understanding the society of man. Yet for nearly a century the communications ability of human skin has been secreted largely in the cramped back laboratories of psychology departments, where it has been fondled, dissected, puzzled over and theorized on and lain fallow.

It can be estimated that probably more than 50,000 researchers have at one time or another focused their attention on the phenomenon. Probably, too, more than 5,000 scientific papers have been written on the subject. Surely out of all of this attention and effort something more useful to human life could have emerged than a way to detect lying. If lie detection is such a useful technique for police and personnel departments, why can't it be a useful adjunct to psychotherapy, where there is the need to explore the cryptic veil of emotions to relieve the medical ills that emerge from psychosocial difficulties? Basically it's a question of supply and demand. The stewards of social behavior know and demand the techniques, but society itself has been disadvantaged, knowing nothing of the skin's rhetoric, nor of its emotional sleuthing facility.

There has been at least one effort on the part of the public to claim its own; an effort, unluckily, lacking in expert guidance and sanction. To my knowledge the only nonprofessional, nonscientific use of skin talk adopted to any degree was in the nonestablishment, nonrecognized school of psychologic practice called Dianetics. They had their E-meter, a relatively crude device to monitor changes in the skin's electrical activity while flagellating the emotions. At the time of its greatest popularity the indiscriminate use of such devices made the psychoscientific community aghast. This upstart sect of pseudo-psychologists were untrained in approved techniques for dealing with human emotion. Medicine and psychology cried that the lack of authentic background of the practitioners could bring irreparable harm to the person whose emotions were so craftily being exposed. They suggested to medical authorities that the E-meter and its use were not to be permitted. Needless to say many legal suits ensued.

The attitude taken by the medical psychologists was probably correct; it was the reasons that were wrong. For in all truth, at that time the crude instruments of the psycho-sect and that of the psychoscientists were almost identical—both bad. Psychologists have had their problems with the physiology, biochemistry, and even the electronics that underlie most psychobiologic problems with which they deal. In turn, the physiologists, biochemists, and electronics engineers have problems understanding the theoretical frameworks within which the psychologists work. Even today, no really first-rate, accurate, versatile, and practical instruments for listening to skin conversation yet exist which can possibly be used effectively and efficiently in therapeutic applications.

If skin talk is or can reveal unconscious hidden inner emotional realities, why isn't it already in widespread use as a guide to better emotional health? There are many reasons.

First, as researchers entertained themselves with theories about the skin's choicest revelations, they deftly avoided the challenge of exploring useful applications. Yet even as they plied their conceptual trade in the laboratory, the cryptograms of the skin's communication gradually yielded signs of the profound influence of complex, higher brain processes on the conversation of the skin. Nearly one hundred years of research had failed to develop either adequate instruments or procedures useful for exploring the depths of emotional life with the precision and accuracy needed to reveal more about emotions than can be unveiled in conversations with a counselor or psychiatrist. Only in the past several years has the kind of knowledge about skin talk been developed that could convince a therapist of its usefulness. Indeed, these two chapters represent the first effort to bring together the considerable evidence that demonstrates the vast potential of skin talk to help solve the emotional problems of modern man.

Second, a universal language for skin talk has never been settled on. There are many dialects since skin conversation reflects cultural and environmental backgrounds. With so many dialects, skin language has been difficult to translate. With no universal language there could be no dialogue, and because communication about skin talk among the research psychologists was difficult, communications between researchers and therapist-clinicians were impossible. Then there has been the problem of recording instruments. Laboratory instruments are unwieldy and inconvenient, requiring constant adjustment because no one has cared to make them automatic. It may be convenient for the researcher to use instruments with innumerable knobs and dials and buttons, but for a practicing therapist facing a flood of patients, one knob to twist and one button to push is almost too much, especially if he also has to translate the dialect his patient's skin uses.

And finally, the psychiatric therapeutic community has been fooled before by the limitations of physiologic instrumentation which gave it information just as indirect and confusing as conversation. The clinical therapist needs an accurate instrument and an unabridged dictionary; he needs direct access to the problems of his patient. To him the jumble of skin talk is the same as the six hundred dialects of India—unintelligible.

The idea that bio-feedback has brought to the new frontiers of medicine and psychology is rapidly changing the directions of skin talk research and use. This is the concept that systems of the body are also communications media. This is strikingly true of the skin. Tomorrow the skin may take us to the threshold of nonverbal communication. Witness Ashley Montagu's new book, *Touching: The Human Significance of the Skin,* an enchanting account of the unsuspected power of the skin to receive communication. The importance of the skin as a sense organ takes the brilliant Montagu some three hundred pages to describe. He tells of the enormous variety of information which the skin is capable of sensing, and the importance of this information to the brain in making its judgments and its adjustments to the environment and to life. He notes that his book describes the neglected role of the skin: the meaning of the skin's information on the mind, in contrast to the descriptions of psychosomatic medicine which deal with the meaning of the mind's information on the skin.

These chapters stress the ability of the skin itself to transmit as well as to receive, to communicate intelligent information. Hopefully they will begin to bridge the two roles of the skin and give an explanation of how the skin monitors the mind's emotions, how the skin is one of the most sensitive and earliest warning systems of man's emotion.

The Voice Box of the Skin

It was nearly a century ago, in 1888, that a scientist named Féré discovered that the resistance of the skin to a small electric current changed in response to something that aroused the emotions. Behold, a looking glass into inner experience! Yet here we are in the 1970s, untouched and unserviced by a remarkable tool found in an earlier age. One must understand the superstitions of the times. In the nineteenth century scientists were fighting animal magnetism—the belief that a vital energy surrounds the body.* In the twentieth century scientists seek to reduce emotion to physical fact and primal body function; ergo, according to current scientific wisdom, the only way to explore the skin's electrical activity must be in terms of causes strictly related to physiology. But the skin and its mind have a greater wisdom little realized until the era of bio-feedback.

In the early history of the skin game there was great joy in the hearts of the researchers because the simple instruments that measured ordinary electricity were successful in detecting the conversation of the skin. They could apply a small current to the skin in a thousand different places of the body and measure the resistance the body offered to passage of the current. Or, they could simply measure the "voltage" of the skin.†

Over the years the body was mapped for its skin electrical activity, and in the doing it was discovered that the skin's electrical activity surged in intensity with emotion and excitement and fell to

---

* This nineteenth-century theory may have been the precognition of today's research into the bioelectric, magnetic fields that surround the body.

† In those days before the sophistication of electronics, the key to solving electrical mysteries was, and still remains, Ohm's law. This is a simple mathematical formulation, at a sixth-grade level of math, of how electrical current changes in an electrical circuit. It states that electrical current is directly proportional to the voltage and inversely proportional to the resistance in the circuit. It can be stated in a simpler way: current equals voltage divided by resistance. The researcher could measure any two of the three items and calculate the third.

quiescence with relaxation. The same thing happens with perspiration. The greater the excitement, the more the person sweats. It soon became apparent that the most dramatic electrical changes in the skin occurred in the areas with the most sweat glands. Then other researchers discovered skin activity where no sweat glands were. Electricity matured into electronics, and biochemistry uncovered the body's manipulations of atoms, and suddenly the simple electrical activity of the skin became very complex.

Where once it was thought that the electrical behavior of the skin was caused almost exclusively by changes in the underlying blood vessels, it has become apparent more recently that the sweat glands of the skin play by far the most important role. It has been found that every activity of sweat glands is important. The changes which occur as nervous excitation initiate sweating, the chemistry of the flowing sweat itself, and the chemical changes that occur during the resorption of sweat all contribute to the electrical behavior of the skin. With sweating and even in the absence of apparent sweating in some areas there is a change in the membrane permeability of the skin during its electrical activity and this change is the major cause of the electrical changes. Membrane permeability is simply the relative ease or difficulty with which chemical subparticles, ions, can pass through membranes, and all cells have membranes. It was certainly reasonable that the skin could produce an electrical current since there is movement of the ions of mineral elements in the body, and it is the movement of ions that is the basis of all electricity. One of these ions is potassium, one of the body's mineral elements concerned with maintaining the fluid balance that is critical to the electrical process.

Researchers are not yet content that these are the only physical mechanisms of the body which subserve the ability of the skin to reflect emotions, but it is likely they have already identified the main voice box of the skin. The principles of electricity are not easy to understand, and those of electronics are infinitely more complex. In many ways the electrical transformations in the skin through which it expresses fear, anxiety, worry or delight and passion may resemble much more the intricate electrical relationships encountered in electronics. This is true in the same way that the circuits of a color TV set are vastly more complex than those of doorbells.

Decoding the Inner Voice: Dermoglyphics

To listen to the skin's emotional talk all that is necessary is to tape several small unobtrusive electrodes onto the skin, connect these to a proper recording instrument and listen. The skin will tell you when there is emotion, how strong the emotion is, and even just how emotional a person you are. If the questioner is persistent, it also will very likely tell when you are lying.

How can one tune into the voice of the skin? Because it is an inner voice, there must be some intermediary mechanism to recognize and amplify the tiny voices. The electrical characteristics of the skin make it a ready match for a variety of electronic recording devices, like matching speakers to your stereo. In the laboratory the researcher amplifies the electrical changes and matches these to a device which produces a written record. At the same time he might use other devices to change the electrical activity into sounds.

Written records of electrical activity have been made almost since the discovery of electricity itself. The easiest form is by a writing pen whose metal shank is positioned midway between the jaws of a magnet. Because the magnet responds in a one-to-one fashion with changes in an electrical current, the changes in the magnet cause the pen to deflect back and forth between its jaws. If the pen is pulled by the magnetic force toward one side of the jaws this indicates a "negative" push of electrical force (voltage) and if the magnetic force pulls the pen to the other jaw, this indicates a "positive" push. These pulling effects cause the pen to write up and down (as illustrated in Figure 3, part A). Each of the three principal elements of electricity (voltage, current, and resistance) can be instrumented to be recorded by the movement of the pen. When the skin's electrical activity is recorded on paper, the resulting record is an irregular succession of hills and valleys, positives and negatives, and these on top of slower, less readily recognized waves of activity. In general, every small increase in emotion or tension or excitement is accompanied by bigger and better and more complicated wiggles of the pen while relaxation is accompanied by fewer and smaller electrical waves.

The jiggly pen movements drawn in Figure 3, part B are a

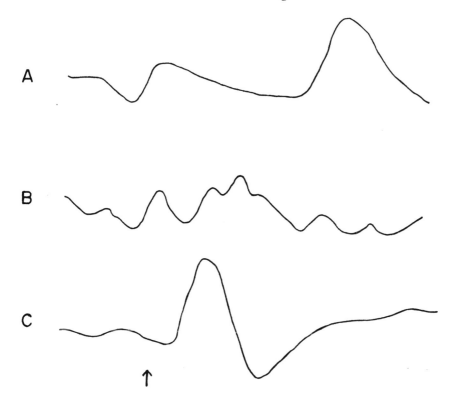

Figure 3. Records of skin electrical activity.

In A, the up-and-down writing of the pen reflects the changing electrical force, or changes in the resistance of the skin's electrical activity. This type of picture is very common in laboratory recordings.

In B, a rambling spontaneous conversation of the skin is recorded. Because the changes are generally much slower (as in A), the record was compressed.

In C, a specific question has been asked at the arrow, and the record shows the skin's response.

stylized set of recorded representations of the skin's electrical activity. Record B is from spontaneous skin activity, i.e., it is reflecting the normal changes in both underlying emotional level and responses to unknown or unidentified changes in the environment that are continually affecting the individual subconsciously or seeping into marginal consciousness. It is like a rambling conversation. In record C a specific change in the environment has occurred, say a question such as "Does love mean anything to you?," and the record shows an answer. If the recordings are continued over a period of time, there could be pages of written skin conversation. The records in Figure 3 had to be condensed into simple figures, but with a live person attached to the recording electrodes, the record will show endless variations on that stylized theme. Differences in heights of the humps are more or less directly indicative of the intensity of the emotion, as are differences in the quickness of the changes and how long they last. The relationships of these seemingly small differences will be explained further when we discuss factors of personality, intelligence, motivation and learning. It should be remembered that each of these discrete parts of the skin's electrical activity has its origin in the mental activity of the brain.

Each wiggle of the written record of the skin's electrical activity conveys information. One of the first decoding problems was that the recorded shapes of skin responses changed depending upon how the electrical circuit was arranged for recording. If the researcher measured either the ability of the skin to conduct or resist an electrical current, the record changed in one direction only (because electrical resistance and conductance are always measured from zero), one change being slow and the other change being composed of faster waves superimposed on the slow ones and lasting little longer than a second or two. The slow rolling waves registered the always changing underlying emotional state.

The faster changes were the spontaneous, unsolicited conversations of the skin, and these differed from each other in interesting ways. They might spurt forth or develop gradually, they might make a wide excursion of the recording pen or they might be small bips or anything in between. And finally, they might return to their starting point slowly or quickly. Each small change and every minor deviation from a typical wave form were found to be related to different expressions of emotion.

If, however, the investigator changed the electrical circuit and measured the voltage—which is the force of the skin's own electrical current—there were additional surprises. Now the recording pens deflected both up and down, making the wave forms still more complex (because voltage can be positive or negative from zero depending upon the way the investigator makes the current flow) and each of these two directions would be found to convey important information about interior emotion.*

Considerable argument has raged among scientific investigators as to the interrelationships among the skin's vocabulary and its meanings as written in recordings of the skin's electrical activity.† Some say it is a relatively simple process of one type of physiologic change following another, that first there is some neural excitation which initiates sweating followed by the flow of sweat. To most other researchers, however, the skin is a mirror of the mind's emotion. To one of the most imaginative researchers the hesitation of the skin in responding when spoken to suggested that rather involved cortical activity was at work, although it need not always occur. Dr. Chester Darrow in 1967 gave a beautiful description of the way the brain expresses itself by the skin. He wrote:

> The domain of GSR (skin talk) is thus a hierarchy wherein the "cortical most high" speaks only from the secrecy of the cerebral sanctum sanctorum through his ministers, and they through their emissaries, and they through their mouthpieces in the epidermis, including the orifices of the sweat glands. The "voice from on high" is never heard except by the whim and the disposition of his ministers, and of their emissaries, and of their mouthpieces, and they may sometimes be prompted to speak on their own. They may respond on

---

* For some of the underlying physiology, see Appendix B.

† Because the electrical aspects are complex, the non-electrician psychologist has floundered a long time over the best ways to measure the electrical changes. I have counted over twenty different names and abbreviations used, everything from EDR, meaning electro-dermal response; to PGR, meaning psychogalvanic reflex; to Sz, meaning skin impedance. In earlier times the most popular name for skin emotional activity was GSR, derived from the term "galvanic skin reflex." The term "galvanic" described the way the skin response was measured, referring to an early electronic technique using a magnetic needle or a coil in a magnetic field, the device being named for a pioneer in electricity, Luigi Galvani. When measurement was made of the resistance the skin made to passage of an electric current, the skin response was named SRR, skin resistance response. Other investigators concluded that this was not the most accurate measurement, and developed the rationale for a new measurement, SCR, the skin conductance response, indicating that the electrical conducting property of the skin was being measured rather than its resistance to passing electrical current. It had also been discovered in 1890 that the skin had its own source of electricity, but it was a long time before skin researchers simply measured the voltage produced by the skin. When they did, the new measure gave rise to a new set of names: skin potential level (SPL) and skin potential response (SPR) to indicate the electrical phenomenon which produces voltage, i.e., a potential force.

their own initiative to external stimulation without the word even getting through to the cortical most-high. And by the same token, silence of the emissaries or of their mouthpieces is no proof that the "most-high" has not spoken.

Thus those of us who watch the tapes for the write-out of the word from the cortical most-high must always interpret the leakings via the mouthpieces, in case what seems to come from above is only some more menial but independent agent speaking.

In a word, the mind of the skin is very complex.

Skin Language

The work of decoding the skin's emotional language has taken a very long time, and it is not yet complete. One must remember that the public has not been made aware that man's other, inner self is a stranger in a strange land, capable of complex communication. It could not petition science to explore what it did not know existed. Within medicine and psychology there have been too many pressing external problems to cope with, and no large-scale effort has been directed to the decoding. Yet despite the lack of attention to developing a sensitive mind-exploring tool, the language of the skin is known to reflect even the most subtle nuances of man's interior activity and may well prove to be one of the fastest, most direct routes toward the further exploration of inner space.

As people differ from each other in their verbal expression according to sex, race, creed, culture, and age, so do they in their skin language. Females and blacks have better skin electrical conductance than males and Caucasians. And it gets better with age in everyone. I have no comment on one research finding: that female skin talks more often than male skin. Ethnic differences too are reflected by different kinds of skin talk, perhaps a mirror of long cultural influence on the way one expresses emotion and attitudes. In skin electrical responses to shock, for example, Jews, Italians, and the Irish were found to adapt much less quickly than Yankees, suggesting perhaps that Jews, Italians, and Irish are readier to respond than Yankees. But then again, for everyone the skin talk of the right side of the body is louder and clearer than that of the left, regardless of whether one is right- or left-handed. The neurophysiologist who knows that man's speech center resides on the left side of the brain might have some interesting speculations about this curious fact.

The written record of the skin's conversation and its answers to questions does reveal a pattern and fabric that clothes the man in dress distinctive to his tribe. Not only can the skin expose your secret personality, but it can also reveal the way you solve problems, your level of motivation, the way you lie, every characteristic of your emotional life. For when you come to think about it, there is nothing which we communicate in whatever voice we use that goes unaccompanied by emotion. To the extent that we can identify people by hearing their voices, so we could identify them by the conversational records of their skins.

Not only can the skin talk profile personality and cultural backgrounds, it also reflects mood, that emotional tone of the individual around which his more immediate emotional reactions swing. Like the voice from the larynx, the voice of the skin rises and falls, becomes loud and soft, hesitates and delays, explodes with vigor. Every emotional nuance is reflected in transposing relationships of its electrical components, weaving them into ever more complex patterns to be puzzled over by psychophysiologists.

The reasons why skin talk profiles have not yet been attempted lie mainly in basic errors of procedure and critical evaluation by researchers. One has only to skim the vast field of skin electrical activity to be struck by the astounding number of different techniques which have been used to measure skin talk.*

It is an interesting commentary that no real compendium or dictionary of the meanings of the skin's electrical activity has been made while volumes of compendia have been written about the electrical activity of the heart. The components of the heart's activity are very few, five, as compared to those of the skin. If these few elements can reveal a host of details about the heart's health, it

---

* In a brief survey of twenty papers attempting to relate skin electrical activity to anxiety, for example, no two researchers used the same characteristic for reference. Some researchers count the number of electrical changes, some measure the height of the pen excursions, some measure the time before onset of a change while still others measure how long it takes for the subject to "forget" a conditioned response. Little wonder that there is so little agreement in the thousands of research papers on skin talk.

seems quite likely that an analysis of the skin's activity could reveal important aspects of the mind's conscious and subconscious activity. The heart's few electrical components carry relatively few bits of information, while the skin's activity ranges dramatically over many kinds of information and so there is a great deal more decoding to be done for the skin.*

Bio-Feedback Could Have Begun in 1904

To a large extent the ruling hierarchy of experimental psychology in the first half of the twentieth century has tended to support Adler's concept that the prime driving nature of man was his need for power. Whatever new tidbit of insight about the behavior of man, from stomach acid to mirror writing to the territorial imperative, the laboratory explorer has tried to bring it under his control. Sort out your valuables: your body belongs to the AMA, your mind to the psychotherapist, your spirit to the myth maker. Is there any way that we recover and protect our interior treasures? Do we want to? No one has ever discovered the source of the gold the conquistadores sought; have we human beings kept the secret of our own self-control?

It may be a delightful surprise to learn that some of the most dynamic, insightful studies of skin talk were done by the great psychiatrist Jung himself. Jung's approach to decoding the conversation of the skin was to engage his patients in a word-association test while wired to a skin talk recorder. Skin changes could then be observed as the patient verbalized his word associations and the skin would reveal the underlying emotion. One might assume that Jung had thoughts of using the skin's response of hidden emotion as a

---

* In recent efforts to standardize how and what to record of the skin's electrical activity and what terms should be applied to the various phenomena encountered, it was found that many researchers measure skin responses to emotional stimulation only and ignore the "resting" electrical level that indicates the normal emotional state of the individual. The skin's electrical state changes continuously and in different directions over minutes and hours in both cyclical and unpredictable fashion throughout the day because people normally are continuously responding to both internal and external changes. Thus, the kind of skin response elicited by stimuli depends upon the starting level of the slower shifting electrical state. These diverse, interacting voices complicate the reporting of skin talk, for what is being said in response to some event as emotion must be described in terms of what the tonic or ongoing emotional level was at the time.

therapeutic tool to explore subconscious emotion with his patient, the recorder documenting what associations were emotionally painful and disturbing. This would have been bio-feedback. Within months of Jung's initial studies experimental psychologists around the world were attracted to his laboratory and set off a flurry of new work. Then, at the very cresting of the wave of enthusiasm for skin talk to reveal the mysteries of mental life, the pioneers of modern-day psychology found a safer refuge for their thoughts. Pavlov had disclosed the principles of his conditioning theories of learning, and most of the experimental psychologic community was swept into the neater, simpler production-line experimentation of human behavior in animals. The whims of the scientifically elite are sometimes very difficult to understand, and the superseding of the dominant mode of human mind research by animal research is one of the most difficult to fathom. The consensus of the present and recent past in psychology regarding the Jungian research is despairingly commented on in a recent scientific paper. Paraphrased, the comment reads: "The notion that skin talk has a mind-reading ability has been responsible for much bad research. It has directed attention away from the important concept that skin electrical responses are primitive and automatic and are thus important only to the study of sleep and arousal. The connection of skin talk to the unconscious is incidental to its function as an automatic reflex."

Jung's early work from 1904 to 1907 had been the exciting demonstration that the skin's electrical activity changed remarkably when its ears heard words associated with emotion. It was obvious even then that mental activity, particularly that process of recall evoked by simple verbal stimuli, was consistently and continuously reflected by skin changes. In those days, however, electrical instrumentation was primitive and the subtle manipulations needed to sort out and decode the conversation of the skin were some fifty years in the future.

With few exceptions it is only in the 1970s that therapists have begun to use Jung's 1904 work with the skin as a communications medium to bring to light emotional and emotionally rooted physical illnesses. It was not the lack of refined instrumentation that slowed progress; skin language is complex and has required thousands of precise studies to grasp only a few of its relationships to the ever-varying activity of the mind. Yet it must be said that scientific politics have been a heavy deterrent to the evolution of practical uses of the skin's power to reveal mental life. The potential for use of skin language in diagnosis and treatment is strong; the efforts to explore the potential have been weak. At the moment the uses are understandably crude, but they augur well for future benefits.

Voice Lessons for the Skin

In the thirties and later in the sixties attention again turned to exploring the learning potential of the skin, largely in the framework of the simple reflexes of the autonomic nervous system. Both efforts were carried out in strict accord with conditioned learning theory. The efforts of the thirties flagged and have generally been ignored; the efforts of the sixties fortunately have synchronized with the development of bio-feedback concepts and the potential of skin talk has come alive again. Of the hundreds of scientific papers appearing on the subject since 1960, nearly every one of them has exposed some significant facet of the mind's activity as manifested in the conversation of the skin.

The few early experiments carried out with skin electrical responses in the 1930s were in the spirit of Pavlov, designed according to classical conditioning principles.* In the thirties, any activity or response of the autonomic nervous system (ANS) was viewed as a reflex action; there were no concepts of possible voluntary control— such as we have over our hundreds of muscles—and this "psychic," now scientifically proven power of the will moved unseen through the psychologic experiments like a many-fingered Beelzebub plaguing the researchers. The investigator "administered" a signal, a light, or tone, which he called the conditioning stimulus (CS), meaning that this was the neutral or inconsequential signal he hoped would, through conditioned learning, come to elicit the natural response always elicited by the "natural" stimulus (called UCS, the unconditioned stimulus). He knew that an electric shock to the arm or leg would cause an electrical skin response, just as it caused the accelerated heart rate, increased respiration and outpour-

* The dominant theories of conditioned learning are summarized in Appendix C, page 412.

ing of all autonomic activities. The electric shock naturally caused such responses (the body does defend itself!), and so it was designated as the "natural" stimulus. After a number of repetitions of the light or tone signal/electric shock pair, finally a form of the skin response would occur when the signal was given as well as after the shock. The skin could thus "learn."

In one sense it may have seemed rather foolish for researchers to waste time proving that skin electrical responses could be forced to surface to a supposedly meaningless signal such as a light or tone signal simply by constantly pairing it with a body shock that invariably caused the response. Foolish because bioscientists had already agreed that autonomic reflexes were involuntary surges of all of autonomic systems literally simultaneously in response to intense emotion, the primitive kind accompanying fear and uncertainty. It was, however, a portentous force that drove a few researchers to try to confirm that the skin's response repertoire was nothing more than a function of primitive, automatic reflex physiology, for no sooner had the first "learning" studies been attempted, than it was recognized that the skin's emotional vocabulary was sophisticated and complex and a result of the highest intellectual functions of the mind.

Research studies conducted to "teach" the skin to respond in a specific way desired by the researchers were, to say the least, perplexing to the scientists. They really weren't prepared for the variety of events happening in their experiments. For one thing, the skin was *always* talking electrically; their records showed humps and bumps and slow and fast wiggles at times, then at other times the skin would sink into an annoying silence. Then too, the skin of some people talked loudly and constantly, while that of others murmured or purred or even stuttered. The scientists were hard put to control the cacophony of the skin.

Looking back, it is a simple matter now to see where bio-feedback was an integral phenomenon even in most classical conditioned learning experiments. The formalizing of the bio-feedback concepts brought new sight to the experimental eyes by its focus on the fact that every stimulus, natural or associated, contains information meaningful to mind mechanisms, that every response of any organism or its parts feeds back information to the mind mechanisms, and that somewhere beneath or over this conceptually oversimplified notion of behavior are infinitely complex and interacting forces organized and directed by an agency unique in its ability to pinpoint its diverse recourses toward a specific learning task.

The Amazing Resistance of the Skin to Behavioral Control

The ogre of "scientific method" has always put a strain on psychologists because it requires the use of control measures to ensure that the experimental elements of interest are not contaminated by extraneous influences. This is a much easier task for the chemist or physicist who works in a setting where nearly everything can be identified physically. But for the psychologist the origins and influences on behavior are not so neatly documented. Because this science is still relatively in embryo, as compared to the physical sciences, the psychologist must make a judgment about the factors that he thinks may influence his experiment and then decide which of these are relevant and which he must consider. The judgment is based on his background knowledge, and this is where much of the difficulty lies. He may not, for example, be educated enough about the insides of the instruments he must use to recognize faulty performance of the instrument or he may not know enough electronics to recognize that it may not function the way it is claimed to function. The most persistent error lies in the fickle minds of the human beings he is trying to work with. They are a muddle of unknowns of attitude, motivation, ability to form concepts, different amounts of caffeine or nicotine they've imbibed, and lists of variations on the dimensions of human personality too numerous to mention. The experimenter must play God as best he (or she) can, but in all psychologic or psychophysical research it must be remembered that the researcher is human too.

Viewed from the standpoint of information content available to the human or even the animal mind, almost everything going on in the experiments could convey meaningful information to the consciousness of the subject being tested. Take the conditioning stimulus, the light or tone signal which is always paired with the reinforcement of behavior. It would seem natural for the subject's mind, human or animal, to become aware of its meaning, to attend anew to the experimental procedure, and to have a flood of thoughts about what was going on or to try to influence the experiment or to think the experiment foolish and become bored.

Then, too, throughout the conditioned learning era the researchers of human skin talk used control measures for their experiments exactly as had the conditioned learning researchers in animal experiments. One of the most interesting control measures was the interspersing of nonreinforced "trials." That is, for the proper Pavlovian experiment, the conditioning stimulus (the light or tone signal) was always followed in a short time by the stimulus eliciting the natural response. It had been found necessary, however, to throw in some trials where the conditioning signal was *not* followed by the shock so that the experimenter could be sure that no response occurred at about the time the "natural" stimulus was usually given. If responses did occur, their influence on learning could then be accounted for when the results were analyzed. Similarly, in Skinnerian conditioning, on occasion the behavioral response was not rewarded or reinforced. It was subsequently found that these negative situations where the signal was *not* followed by shock or reinforcement carried as much information to the brain, if not more, than did the situation when the shock was actually given.

It is hard to remember now that as late as the thirties bioscience believed the body's automatic nervous system was beyond control by the mind, even when they, the researchers, became flushed with success and their hearts raced with excitement exposing the powerful influence of their excited mind state. If they had been tuned to their skins, they would have heard shouting. But in those days skin talk was reflex, automatic, involuntary, primitive and inferior.

Nonetheless, the role of the mind was exerting steady influence during the skin learning experiments. It became aware of the meaning of the warning signal, it reacted, and even when the warning signal was not followed by the usual shock, the mind considered that to be very significant information and shifted its influence on how the skin electrical activity was responding. It was a long and tedious problem for the researchers to figure out.

Science has not been able to reduce the behavior of mind and body into simple elements over which full control can be gained. There are always surprises. All concepts, theories and models of human behavior are necessarily oversimplified, partly to make them feasible for testing, partly because man has developed a habit of thinking in only a few dimensions at a time. No matter that the data were often contradictory, or the influence of mind was ignored, or processes were more complex than conveniently recognized. Human behavior was nothing but a set of reflexes. Animals could suffice for human behavioral research. To the practicing behaviorist, animal intelligence was a simple matter of manipulating reflexes and deriving models for human behavior. Yet, despite the academic brouhaha for Pavlov and the partisan campaigns of Skinner there has been trouble all along the experimental way. For human beings have the advantage over animals; they can express their thoughts to other human beings; they have a wider range of mind action than animals, or perhaps they are simply more perverse. Whatever, the effect of the complex dynamics of the mind-body presents great complications for learning theory. Witness the present educational turmoil and inadequacy.

Skin-Minds with High IQs

A few researchers of the thirties were, however, intrigued with Jung's work and wove his concepts into learning experiments. One of the most exciting studies was the 1937 experiment by Cook and Harris, who wrote that it occurred to them that the electrical activity of the skin might be "taught" merely by verbal instructions, particularly if the skin itself first received some instruction as to what it was supposed to learn. First, they actually gave a shock to the subjects and paired that experience with the verbal explanation "receive a shock." Soon it was possible simply to say the words and the skin would respond. The next step was to transfer that response to another verbal stimulus, this time to the statement "green light" after first instructing the subjects that if they were in a *real* experiment the appearance of a green light would signal a forthcoming electric shock. The skin-mind learned so well that when the real experiment using lights and shock was subsequently carried out, no further learning occurred. It was somewhat anticlimactic that when the experiment was reversed and the subjects were told that the words "green light" no longer meant that a shock would follow in the make-believe experiment, the skin responses gradually diminished until they failed to occur at all. The responses to verbal suggestion even evoked the process of physiologic adaptation.

Now those kinds of results are enough to drive a dyed-in-the-wool conditioned learning experimental psychologist screaming out of his laboratory. Where is the simple reflex? I find it one of the more curious episodes of behavioral research that no one then asked the question: how can man remember a specific skin answer (that he was not consciously aware of, nor even knew occurred) to the word "shock" long enough or well enough that he can evoke *that same answer* when he is asked to make that skin answer to the words "green light"? Or that he performed this task better than when he actually saw the light and felt the shock? The light and the shock are the security tools of the experimenter, but if they are less effective than words, why are they still used? Is it a subconscious defense against the loss of control over another's behavior? The light of those experiments thirty-five years ago shining on man's ability to control the activity of his body has lain sleeping, imprisoned in behavioral control science. Today bio-feedback researchers have demonstrated unequivocally that the mind, the will, can and does control nearly all body activities. It is to be hoped that these efforts are not also swept away by the dogmatics of rigid behavioral methods.

In their 1937 study Cook and Harris had issued a warning that investigators should take all precautions to ensure that their learning experiments were not influenced or contaminated simply by the verbal instructions given to the subjects, and they even recommended that old work be checked for errors introduced by "verbal conditioning." It was not until the development of the bio-feedback concept that investigators began to realize the amount of information revealed in their instructions, the warning signals, the timing of the various manipulations, and that this information was used in a very active sense by the human mind, consciously or subconsciously, to direct the course of the experiments every bit as much as the researcher did. To my knowledge no one has yet re-evaluated the thousands of psychologic and psychophysiologic experiments now believed to be obviously and profoundly directed by the mind's consideration of the experiment itself. Even more inexplicable are the continuing practices which ignore these factors to this day. Myths usually die hard, but they are ensured of immortality in the minds of those who have won great rewards with them.

By the early 1960s behavioral scientists were again examining the possibility of bringing skin electrical activity under control, this time by the newer of the learning theories, Skinner's operant conditioning. As noted earlier, this technique (which incidentally had no real theory behind it) was exquisitely simple: any behavior of an organism when adequately rewarded could be made to recur as often as obtaining the reward was possible. Whatever behavior was instrumental to receiving a reward was reinforced by that reward. (Hence the second name for operant conditioning—instrumental conditioning.) It was not concerned with what went on to evolve or elaborate the behavior, only that an organism, man or animal, would continue to perform a particular behavior as long as the reward was in sight. It has long been argued that no real learning occurs in operant conditioning, simply repetition and sharpening of a performance.* Scientists have, since the inception of the technique some thirty-five years ago, played with changing schedules of reward, changing the type of reward, etc., but, amazingly enough, they have scarcely ever attempted to investigate *why* a bit of behavior is satisfied by a laboratory reward, or why some are not (we hear only about those that are satisfied), or why *no reward* is really adequate to keep any organism performing unless it has been severely deprived or has been rendered abnormal.

Operant conditioning may be a highly limited version of biofeedback. First, when a bit of behavior is rewarded, that event is feeding back information to the organism that something pleasant happens when he performs in a certain way. Depending upon the psychic or physical appeal of the reward, the organism himself shapes his behavior to receive more or less of the reward. He willfully manipulates his physical being to become appropriate to the demands of the reward. If the experimenter plays with the reward schedule, the organism responds in his old manner until he is fed back the information he needs to change his performance to gain the reward. Notice in the experiments described below all of the

---

* There are many kinds of learning—by instinct, by imitation, trial and error, etc., to satisfy certain drives, by observation, insights, imagination, by reasoning, etc.

kinds of information the researchers use in their experiments which can be used as feedback information.

The Independent Skin

One early modern-day skin learning experiment (1960) used pleasant and unpleasant odors as "reinforcers." That is, subjects were wired up with electrodes to record skin electrical responses, and the objective of the experiment was to determine whether a pleasant odor flooding the subject's nose at the same time that his skin was saying something quite definite could be used to train him (or his skin) to skin talk the same way every time that particular pleasant odor was in the air. Conversely, would the person be able to keep his skin from making that remark when an unpleasant odor was used? Since the skin was talking sporadically anyway, the measure of success was whether more or less skin talk occurred coincident with the odors. This, of course, was bio-feedback; that is, every time the skin spoke a pleasant odor was given, so both the individual and his skin knew the skin had spoken, and when an unpleasant odor blew in, they knew the skin had successfully refrained from speaking. From what we have discussed before about the sensitivity of the skin to its emotional mind, it might have been expected that the skin would have a mind of its own in experiments such as this. And it did. It responded all right, but quite at its own discretion. According to learning theory the skin should have answered the demand of the odor immediately once learning began. But the skin responded *after* the odor was taken away. This unexpected occurrence was only the beginning of a long series of discoveries that the behavior of the skin, that bright mirror of emotion, was startlingly independent of man's concepts of it.

Another early study used a different form of bio-feedback. Whenever a specific skin electrical event occurred, it was signaled by a dim white light. The light signal fed back to the subject the information that his skin was speaking. The dim white light is important to remember in view of later developments, for that faint signal was quite effective in reminding the skin to keep talking. There now seemed no doubt about it: in some way the body could recognize a signal which meant, please have your skin answer the way it did before. Still no one questioned the role of the mind. There were, instead, limitless controls to impose upon the skin's activity to ensure that skin learning was a real phenomenon, that it was accomplished by the skin itself and nothing else. Many experiments were devoted to determining whether the electrical changes of the skin were reflecting nothing more than indirect or secondary changes following muscle activity or from respiration. Nearly all results were negative, yet recently new research has reopened the question. At last count I found nine recent (since 1960) scientific papers all of which reported recording muscle activity and respiration along with skin activity. Six of these found no correlation between muscle and skin activity and three did. The consensus seemed to be that skin talk was special and independent. Moreover, in two additional studies subjects were questioned as to whether they were aware of any muscle activity during the skin learning experiments. You guessed it, one report said they did, the other said they didn't. The argument will no doubt continue for some time. There are many different muscles to measure, and bio-feedback is only now allowing explorations into relationships between subjective identification of otherwise imperceptible muscle activity and the actual levels of activity below the level of consciousness.

Among the various procedures deemed necessary to document skin learning as a reality were such things as learning whether skin talk would increase in volume or amount if the rewards were given when the skin was *not* talking, whether the reward itself would get an answer from the skin, whether good skin talkers were better learners than poor skin talkers, and whether age or sex influences the ability of the skin to learn. To sum up the findings from such questions is a prodigious exercise in dissecting the scientific literature, and although I have done this for years in various areas of bioscience, I have found nothing more confusing and perplexing than the literature on the electrical activity of the skin. While researchers were attempting to answer these questions, more fundamental characteristics of the skin's electrical activity were uncovered, and these were found to be of crucial importance to the skin learning process. And to make the matter more complicated, there were a multiplicity of the skin's own answers mixed in with the answers the researchers desired. The conversation of the skin, reflecting every nuance of human emotional response to the experimenter's situation, inserted itself in all unlikely moments of the experiments.

The Skin at Attention

One insightful deviation from classical methodology lengthened the time interval between "conditioning" (neutral) stimulus and shock and brought light to even more facets of the great conversational repertoire of the skin. For the skin was no mere respondent, it was a conversationalist, both responding and contributing. Although the discovery of these new voice tones played havoc with skin learning studies, each new skin vibration uncovered has been found to reveal much information about the inner emotional life of man. Skin talk was quickly becoming a dissonant Schoenberg symphony, and the new scale was hard to follow. Among other things there was a distinct, often booming voice whenever anything in the immediate environment of the subject changed. This voice was seized upon as the unfailing body signal of its orienting. In psychology talk the orienting response is the whole-body activity when something new and unexpected enters the environment, like a thunderbolt, or suddenly discovering that a diamond ring is missing. Like lightning you are all at attention, muscles move, eyes fix, ears prick up, and the skin screams. With all of these body signals so obvious, why on earth researchers felt they needed a hidden voice of the skin to herald such moments, one cannot guess. Yet, attending to the hidden "orienting" response of the skin has paid its debt of discovery, for it can reveal our hidden orienting, that kind of coming to attention of which we ourselves are usually not aware. In any event some researchers now believe that this skin voice of attention was actually what led them to believe they had brought the electrical activity of the skin under control. For it was present to any kind of signal in the experiment, and the larger it was, the more it decided to signal attention not only of the conscious mind, but also of the deepest recesses of the subconscious universe. So, regardless of what experimental learning procedure the researchers followed, the orienting response of the skin was an unexpected and troublesome intruder in their experiments, and when they believed that they had successfully trained the skin's electrical activity to respond on command what actually had happened in most cases was interference from the skin talking to itself. The orienting response essentially is the skin saying, "Pay attention to what's happening." If the researcher used a light or tone as the signal he wanted to get the skin to respond to, then naturally every time the signal occurred, the skin was recording the mind's noting to itself, in varying degrees of intensity, to pay attention. The concept of paying attention is very complex. If we see or hear the same signal all the time without any significant consequences occurring, then we quickly fail to bring ourselves to attention to that signal. But if the signal has interesting or important consequences to it, then we pay varying degrees of attention to it according to motivation, interest, satisfaction obtained, and so on.

The maze of influences that affect the way we pay attention is beautifully illustrated in a study where the effect of personal values was explored. The ability of the skin to learn was measured in some subjects who were asked to see how well they could accomplish a task for themselves and in other subjects who were asked to please do well to help the investigators make a good study. The skin of subjects who were trying to please themselves learned far better than the skins of the subjects who were trying to perform simply to help someone else. In a way as yet unknown to physiologists and psychologists, the mind decides upon the order of its body responses through a complex but nonconscious process of weighing the value of rewards. Learning is not simply working for rewards, it is the result of a collective mind judgment about all of the meaningful experiences we have had, good and bad.

Since the skin can signal rather small degrees of paying attention, the orienting response has been found to be very useful in detecting the effect of attention on the capacity for memory and ability to learn. While the average person is aware that he learns better and retains information better if he pays attention, it is comforting to know that his physiology attests to this fact. One researcher discovered that when subjects were verbally asked to "pay attention" they had larger orienting responses than when less cognitively meaningful attention-getting signals were used. Later, other researchers found that perception was improved when the skin was signaling that the mind was paying attention, and that memory improved also.

The Skin Is the Censor

Probably the most interesting use of the skin's orienting response has been in detecting subliminal perception. Naughty words or other emotion-arousing words were flashed on a screen so briefly that the subjects could not perceive them intelligently. Mixed in with the arousing words were some neutral words. Although it was impossible for the subjects to see the words and so consciously recognize them, something in their brains *did* recognize every word, and this recognition was voiced by the skin. For every naughty word there was an orienting response by the skin, but no responses to the neutral or bland words.* A number of brain electrical responses have also been found to occur at the same time, indicating that long before conscious recognition the body and its subconscious substructure both recognize and make judgments about what goes on in the environment. This enormously important finding has received little research attention, yet it offers a way to explore the universe of the subconscious. When the skin responds to such very mild emotional residues of trauma which are barred from consciousness, then the possibility arises that through the skin the whole world of the subconscious could be explored for its mode of operation and its organization and the way it communicates with consciousness. Yet a search of the biomedical scientific literature reveals that only two, perhaps three, researchers in the entire country are attempting to study the subconscious via physiologic indicators.

The delicate sensitivity the skin has to voice even the most deeply hidden emotions was also shown in a very clever study investigating whether the skin could discriminate the emotional tone of words describing attitudes or beliefs. Students with attitudes about the Church rated as strong pro-, strong anti-, and neutral

* It is a curious fact of the marriage between physiology and psychology that only one bit of physiology and one bit of psychology are studied at one time. In quite separate experiments it has been found that heart rate, blood pressure, brain waves, muscles (and probably much more) of the physiologic being all react to dirty words. In the above experiment, however, we are restrained to the electrical changes in the skin and are not informed about the possible influences from other body changes.

were asked questions about their feelings about the Church. The students who were strongly anti-Church literally exploded with skin talk whenever a pro-Church statement was made, and the pro-Church students made skin talk when anti-Church statements were made. The students who were neutral in attitude responded little, if at all. Moreover, the skin responses of the anti-Church students were consderably greater than those of the pro-Church students, suggesting that the body's emotional responses are much stronger when attitudes are challenged than when they are simply agreed with. Obviously our attitudes about social values are strongly supported by our emotions.

Anticipation and Expectancy

Still another part of the skin's vocabulary was discovered in the attempts to cause the skin to "learn" by the classical technique of pairing stimuli and examining the interval between. It was found that the skin could also signal its degree of expectancy or anticipation as well as its orienting or coming-to-attention action. After a few pairings of the two stimuli, there began to occur a distinctive skin response which followed the orienting response to the first stimulus signal, indicating pay attention. This new skin talk was found to be related to actively expecting the inevitable second signal, the shock when experimental subjects were asked to say whether or not they expected a shock which was given randomly throughout the experiment.

When the subjects verbalized their expectancy, their skin responses were very large, but when they decided that a shock was not forthcoming, the skin responses were very small. A sidelight was that subjects who were classified as quite anxious expected the shock more frequently and had larger skin responses and the skin forgot its experience with the shock more slowly than subjects who were classified as having little anxiety. In another instance subjects were given two different kinds of signals, one which asked for a behavioral response and one which did not. Again the expectancy wave appeared, but this time in closest association with the request to perform. In this case the expectancy wave was quite complex, suggesting to the researchers that there might be actual patterns of skin electrical responses which reflected the organization or mobilization of mind activity involved in initiating behavioral responses. Such expectancy waves are also found among brain waves when the individual is anticipating or preparing for muscle movement. The skin indicator is, however, much more sensitive. The skin is, in fact, such a sensitive herald of the mind's complex judgments (more complex than mere words can express) that it merits a new look at its unique ability to mirror reality as seen through the eyes of the subconscious.

This was shown by an experiment in which subjects were asked to rate the intensity of a noxious stimulus both verbally and by their skin responses. The subjects verbally rated the most noxious as the least noxious, but the skin's electrical response was largest and longest when the stimuli actually were the most noxious. This curious result was interpreted as indicating the effect of expectancy on subjective feeling; that is, subjectively the more noxious stimuli weren't as bad as expected, so the brain compared the expected bad with the real not-so-bad-as-expected. The skin, however, was with reality all the way.

Further evidence that the subconscious is not only more in touch with reality than consciousness but also has the facility to express its recognition of reality via the skin can be seen in an experiment where subjects were given shocks and told that these would vary in intensity when actually the shocks were all of the same intensity. The subjects reported that the intensity of shock became less and less, that is, they adapted subjectively to the shock, but their skin responded exactly the same to each and every shock. It seems faintly possible that the skin's mind was trying to tell the researchers something about their unrealistic use of electric shock as an experimental device for studying a sensible mind-body. The ability of skin to reflect judgments of the subconscious mind-body's ability to judge reality even more finely was revealed when noise was substituted for shock. The skin's mind seemed to discriminate the appropriateness of noise versus the inappropriateness of shock. Now it was the skin that adapted, judging each noise signal as of lower and lower intensity while the subjects verbally reported that the noise was becoming louder and louder. One might guess that expectancy also played a role here. The subjects expected louder and more disturbing noises and when they weren't, the skin, via subconscious judgment, noted the judgment by its response. That is, the noise signals weren't very threatening, in which case there was little use in wasting an answer or response, just as we tune out ordinary, everyday sounds that we have found to have no significance to us. On the other hand, the subjects' subjective evaluation continued to worry unnecessarily about the noise becoming more annoying, and as they paid more attention to it, the more distracting and louder it seemed to become although it hadn't changed at all.

THREE

Skin Talk: Conversations with the Subconscious

Emotional judgments expressed by the skin and those expressed by words are often at great odds. And more often than not the voicings of the skin cut through convoluted language and the pressures of consciousness with a remarkable accuracy about the nature of reality. Has man been so inordinately proud of his conscious mind that he has abnegated the beauties and extraordinary abilities of the subconscious? Is it possible that the genuine evolution of mind has taken place below the level of a consciousness busy with applying socially created brakes to the natural development of the psyche? Are we now ready to be Alice in Wonderland and look at the world of conscious constraints through the eyes and ears and skin of a wise and prudent subconscious?

The Skin and Subconscious Awareness

There are more good reasons for trying to teach skin talk to come under voluntary control than there are reasons to get out of bed in the morning. It is difficult to realize that not a few bioscientists have been privy to one of the most universal and basic abilities of man, the emotional mirror of the skin, for nearly one hundred years, and yet this extraordinary facility has been left to dissipate its energy into an insensitive vacuum of non-attention. For these one hundred years the revelations of the skin about inner man have been left unattended, to flow on like a babbling child whose language does not meet the consensus of what society deems language to be. If we think in terms of the electrical energy that flows in these skin conversations and liken it to the electromagnetic radiations that lay hidden in uranium ore until man needed to listen, we can have some idea of the potential force of the skin to guide expeditions to the furthermost horizons of man's mind.

As we have glimpsed in the preceding pages the electrical activity of the skin is a sensitive signal of a vast and complex mind-brain machine which performs our mental and emotional functions long before consciousness is set in motion. From many experiments there emerges a web of evidence indicating that nonconscious mental activity is often more realistic in its appraisals than is conscious mental activity. Popular notions of psychiatry have given us to understand that emotional problems arise from conflicts between conscious and subconscious feelings, and in general it is the subconscious which is held to be the offender, the immature self, the blind, unthinking demon within. Yet if we examine carefully the thousand bits of psychophysiologic evidence that reveal subconscious judgments to be sound and reasonable, it makes one wonder whether or not we have been fighting the emotional battle without knowing which side we're on. It makes one wonder whether or not consciousness might not be the real adversary, that part of us which is immature and incomplete. It could just as well be reasoned that the rightness of subconscious judgments and feelings, being so much more realistic and appropriate, are the real survival mechanisms of the self, and that the social group mind which shapes consciousness is, by comparison, naïve and juvenile. The social contract described by Robert Ardrey aids in survival of the group, but has it evolved to liberate the individual? Has it, on the other hand, been so occupied with protection of the purely physical survival of society that it has neglected to purify itself from within, or has it even deliberately stifled evolutionary tendencies of the mind because they might lessen the power of the group?

To most of us consciousness and subconsciousness are as different as day and night. We are embarrassed by intuition because the subconscious is unpredictable and a social maverick; security lies in conscious rational thought because it is only that which is socially acceptable in our particular culture. The intrusion of the subconscious into the domain of consciousness causes conflict and anxiety and we hie ourselves to the nearest psychiatrist or counselor to strengthen our defenses against the irrationalities of the consciously unacceptable considerations of the subconscious. The barrier between the conscious and the subconscious is well recognized, but our study of it has always been from the side of consciousness. Yet in a thousand springwells of laboratories the intelligence of the subconscious has been seen and documented and puzzled over, but consciousness has always capped the wells as if the subconscious were salt water instead of precious oil. Can a diligent physiology decipher the communications system of the skin, the heart, the muscles, the kidneys, the entire body, in such a way as to allow a flow of communications between the subconscious and the conscious? Can we begin to break the barrier from the other side?

Conflict, anxiety, tension and headaches are so prevalent in our society today that they are like a black shroud clothing the individual. Aspirin, Bufferin, Anacin, Compōz, Vanquish, Nytol, and a million other drugs, along with doctors, psychiatrists, therapists, counselors, and even ministers make up the largest conglomerate in the world, all attempting to relieve anxiety, tension, and headache. The emotional parasites thriving in the human body can be traced, in very large part, to a socially created barrier between the conscious and subconscious worlds. The entire body is reacting one way, crying out warning signals to a consciousness that is listening only to the consciousness of another socially evolved human product. If we are to relieve anxiety, tension and headache, we may do well to listen to the voices within. They are our survival signals. Later, in our discussion of bio-feedback and muscle systems, we will see the astounding braking effect that social consciousness has on the well-being of internal organs. From the muscle researchers has come the thesis that anxiety is incompatible with relaxation. Biofeedback is stirring a revolution in muscle relaxation techniques and therapy, but is muscle relaxation enough? If the skin and the heart seem to be able to respond to pure mentation, if they signal the conflict in our social ideas, if they detect down to the least significant event in our functional milieu, is it not reasonable to listen?

Who Needs Consciousness to Learn?

Although the controversy whether conscious awareness is integral or even necessary to learning still rages in the scientific pages of psychophysiology, one of the most intriguing studies conducted with skin talk would seem to give unequivocal evidence of the remarkably complex and organized learning ability of the non-conscious mind.

Patients anesthetized for relatively minor surgery were subjected to a routine conditioning experiment while still semi-comatose. To tell the skin what to do the investigators stroked the underside of the foot, rather a ticklish procedure normally causing a mild muscle contraction of the foot along with a good-sized skin response up at the hand level where skin responses were recorded.* They then preceded the stroking by sounding a buzzer, à la Pavlov, hoping to teach the skin to transfer its response during stroking of the foot to making a response when the buzzer was sounded. Absolutely nothing happened. There were no foot movements, no skin responses to either the stroking or to the buzzer. The anesthesia was blocking all of the normal responses, and certainly no "learning" could occur because even the thing to be learned could not break through the paralysis.

The next day, however, to the great delight of the researchers, the previously anesthetized, now-recovered and alert subjects were retested and all showed unmistakable signs of having learned while anesthetized. If both sensory function and the skin and muscle expression of responses to stimulation were blocked so severely that no evidence of either mind or body consciousness was present when the patients were under anesthesia, how then does one account for the learning? Is this another indication of the sensitivity and versatility of the subconscious to receive and judge and store sensory information? On evaluation the day after the anesthesia testing, the subjects learned better than nonanesthetized control partners.†

---

* The electrical skin responses, described in Chapter 2, as recorded on paper.

† For completeness the procedure was repeated twenty times in each of twenty anesthetized subjects, and for comparison, the entire experiment was done in twenty nonanesthetized subjects, all of whom showed normal reactions and skin learning.

Since none of the subjects could recall any conscious awareness of the experiment done under anesthesia, and the experiment itself was a simple buzzer/foot-stroking procedure done without informing the subjects of the purpose (which was to see if skin learning occurred during unconscious states, but the subjects were told that reflexes were being tested), the influence of conscious awareness would seem to be eliminated. That leaves subconscious awareness. One might conjecture that no prejudices were present in the conscious mind to prevent the subconscious mind from reminding itself that the procedure had been experienced before. If this were true, then one might deduce that subconscious memory of the experience made learning easier on the day after anesthesia.

Subconscious memories influence nearly every response we make to our environment. One simple study showed how the skin electrical activity of schoolboys was selective to the sound of their own names when read from a list of boys' names, and very ordinary skin responses were produced to all of the other names. This type of skin-mind recognition of one's self-image has been found repeatedly in all varieties of conditions of consciousness, from having the names pronounced backward to showing the names in scrambled letters, and each time there is recognition of one's own name as indicated by the skin responses at the very time when the "hidden" names could not jiggle consciousness into recognition.

The Skin Sees in Technicolor

Before we explore further the role of the skin as a wedded partner of the mind, there is yet another capacity of the skin to describe that is critical to an intelligent evaluation of most of the research done on skin learning. This is its ability to discriminate among colors. This subject is dear to my heart, and my research efforts in demonstrating the ability of the subconscious mind to react most specifically to different colors will be covered in the chapter on brain waves. The skin also is a good color detector and seems to reflect the way in which brain neurons process color information. Experiments demonstrating nonconscious body reactions to colors support the common belief that colors induce emotional states which are specific to different hues. We all know people who prefer the yellow-green part of the spectrum and others who like blues and still others who dote on reds and pinks. In general there are many more people who like the blue-green part of the visual spectrum. One author has postulated this is because it is the "safe" part of the spectrum, being in the middle, whereas colors at the opposite ends of the spectrum—infrared and ultraviolet—have dangerous connotations. First he compared skin responses to slides projected on a screen of the colors red and green, and found that skin responses were much larger to red. He then compared green to the color at the other end of the spectrum, violet, and again found that skin responses to violet were larger than those to green. When the experimental subjects were asked how they felt about the colors, they reported that the reds and violets were much more arousing, exciting, and lively.

While it is true that human beings have been educated to believe that red signals danger, my own concepts of the origin of body responses to different colors are quite different. Our learning that infrared and ultraviolet are dangerous is rather recent knowledge. In contrast, nearly all primates through thousands of years have had bad experiences with the color red. One has only to ask where we actually see red in the environment and we know that the most common, emotion-arousing place is where there is blood—so it is with animals and primitive man and warriors and advertising executives. Naturally red is arousing, alerting and exciting. For millennia red has signaled us to danger, injury, war, new life and death. Blue and green, however, are not only closer to the middle of the spectrum, but blue skies also signal calm days and green fields signal the coming of food. Perhaps nature plays a greater role in our body responses to color than bulletins warning about ultraviolet rays.

The information signals conveyed by different colors are picked up by the brain and are expressed by the skin, and experimental evidence suggests that the information value differs with the different colors. This is an extremely important consideration when it comes to the classical types of experimental learning studies. Colored light signals are used in a great share of such research, yet virtually no attention has been paid to the skin responses to color within the experimental design of learning experiments. We have talked about orienting responses and anticipatory responses, and now all of that is complicated by varying degrees of alerting responses to different colors of signals used by the researchers. One could suppose that similar effects occur with auditory signals. Some people love high notes, others favor low tones, and some prefer the middle ranges.

Many, perhaps far too many, research studies designed to study conditioned learning of the skin electrical responses used colored light signals. One very critical and illuminating study asked subjects to make a specific skin response to a red light signal and then later to suppress that same response when they saw a green light signal. This was a typical "operant conditioning" learning experiment in which the response desired by the researcher was "rewarded" (reinforced) whenever that desired response occurred. In actual fact, the subject (or his brain or his skin) was rewarded by being able to prevent a shock if he responded correctly to the different light signals. If, for example, the red light signal came on, this meant "please make a skin response," and if the subject did so he then avoided an electric shock. In the same experiment a light signal of a different color meant "don't make a skin response," and if the subject was successful in suppressing his skin talk, then he also avoided the shock.

Although none of the subjects was aware of what was actually going on during the experiments, they "learned" to discriminate the meaning of the two light signals and to respond appropriately. It seems obvious that some intelligent act had to have occurred, and moreover this intelligent act, this learning, was not consciously recognized. The authors of the study did not separate out results as to whether better or worse learning occurred with red or green lights as the signals, but they did note that all subjects learned to produce skin responses better than they learned to suppress them. This may have been a function of color of light or simply that a light signal, particularly a red one, existed which alerted them to a task. And because alerting is much more associated with positive action and also to the color red, it may be easier to learn to act than to learn to suppress an action. Even subconsciously.

Sometimes Science Has to Be in Quotes

Of course complexities of experiments of this type which attempt to isolate specifically elicited responses from a background of continuously fluctuating activity and endless responses to unknown events in the environment are somewhat like trying to extract a single color from a bucket of mixed paints. Or like trying to listen to a radio station that keeps fading in and out. Every vowel and consonant of the skin talk is integral to every other vowel and consonant if the talk is to make sense. So it is with experiments dealing with artificially elicited skin talk. The skin response discriminates alarming from tranquilizing environmental changes, i.e., whether the experimenter is using a strange shock or a familiar tone, or whether he is warning the skin to do something and then telling it to expect something quite different. One is forced to speculate that sometimes the intelligence behind the skin is correctly judging the experimental procedure to be a ludicrous waste of precious energy. For if the mind of the skin is as intelligent as the evidence indicates, then this indeed would be a reasonable judgment. Another example of the skin's intelligence is shown in experiments in which the effects of electric shock and noise as "natural" stimuli (i.e., stimuli which unfailingly produce body responses) were compared. Both heart rate and skin responses were diametrically opposed with the two kinds of stimuli. Common sense might have said that electric shock is *unnatural*—it has "bad vibes," unpleasant connotations—whereas noise is natural in the world of sound and is with us every day. Yet still today in a thousand psychology laboratories throughout the country, the favored stimulus is electric shock. Somehow common sense walks out the door when the eager scientist walks in.

Scientific judgment is often also sabotaged by the demands of the publish-or-perish principle in addition to an apparent lack of a guiding wisdom. I am hesitant to reveal the following series of studies on skin talk, mainly because the mythology of science is so thoroughly and universally believed that one doubts whether scientific Naderism can be successful. But the vestments of infallibility of biopsychology sustain its ineptitude in elegant isolation. Witness the following.

In 1963 a short study was published in the scientific literature detailing the effectiveness of a novel and daring shock to the skin-mind system which could elicit dramatic and reportedly controllable responses from the skin. This new stimulus was the projection of slides of female nudes on a screen for the exclusive enjoyment of male subjects. Such slides were presented each time the subjects showed a spontaneous skin response, and the results showed that skin activity became more and more active in the course of the experiment.

Some six years later the study was repeated with a few "design refinements" that revealed that skin activity zoomed to high levels and stayed there during the picture show of more and more provocative female nudes, provided that each picture was shown during an alerted moment. Pornographic magazines use the same technique. Suddenly seeing a taboo picture opens up the floodgates of the emotional reservoir, and the emotions flood the body fields until emotional pressure is exhausted. The entire being is involved. So much of the body is reacting that the skin's voice is nearly lost in the confusion. The skin is trying to signal that the mind has been caught in attention; it is expectant, anticipant. Its emotional voice is strident with confused motives: sexual arousal, moral attitudes, conflicts between enjoyment and self-criticism. The mind has also been stimulated to imagery, and imagery itself excites the skin to paint pictures of the pleasures of the mind.

If the hard bones of science are so aware of this maelstrom of activity, how can such a study be justified? The reported rationale was that the previously used rewards for skin talk were weak and ineffectual; stronger stimuli were needed. But, remember the dim white light in other skin learning experiments?*

Why Was that Weak Signal so Effective?

Another motive cited was that it was thought that either the jolting of emotions or a suppression of runaway emotions needed by various types of neurotics and psychotics and sufferers of psychosomatic illnesses could be implemented by such techniques. That is an interesting thought in view of the fact that psychologic patients are

* Chapter 2, p. 71.

already confused by the same problem. No matter, the investigators concluded that "affective stimuli can act as operant reinforcers of an autonomic response." Indeed they can.

While experiments such as these reflect a rather unfortunate scientific immaturity, nonetheless some of the incidental events during the experiments are interesting. For example, a second group of subjects who were used as "controls" were shown the nude slides only when they *weren't* alert and making skin responses. The idea here was to compare the skin responses for the two situations. Obviously the second group would have fewer total number of skin remarks about the nudes because they saw them only during significant lulls in skin conversations. On the other hand, the subjects who were said to respond by increased skin talk when the nude slides were shown *were already making skin comments,* and so if the number of comments are counted, the experimental group of subjects already has a significant figure going for it. What the experimenters should have done and didn't, was to equalize the changes in the two groups for the effect of an already talking skin. The fact neglected in their calculations (which incidentally were neither explained nor justified) was that the number of spontaneous skin responses normally changes markedly with basal state of rest or arousal of the skin. If the skin is already responding, it responds with more, rather than less, skin talk to a new stimulus. While some quite indirect indices of such states of rest and arousal were given, I took the pains to recalculate all experimental results in terms of changing numbers of spontaneous skin responses with changing basal levels of arousal. Unfortunately there were no differences from absolutely normal ways in which the skin responds during rest and arousal.

Research papers like this one are examples of the statistical games researchers play, especially in psychology. There are mathematical tricks galore to transform data into nearly any desired result, and nowadays it takes little time and trouble to ask a computer to fancy up results for a dramatic finding by burying it in inappropriate mathematical expressions. There is little scientific excuse for such shoddy treatment of the scientific readers who have little time to try to extract the actual results from a set of unwarranted expressions.

Keys to the Inner Physical Self

On the other hand, the scientific literature also contains some provocative studies concerned with a more realistic appraisal of mind-body emotional interactions. One study using skin talk to judge emotional involvement had the subjects make use of a remarkable method to avoid the inevitable shock of conditioned learning experiments. A regulation boxer's punching bag was mounted in front of the subjects. In typical research fashion, however, the subjects' attention was intentionally fully occupied by the many diversionary events of the experiment. They were shown a number of different types of slides on a screen, some simply different arrangements of lights, some a series of men's faces showing different emotions. They were told that sometime during the experiment they would receive an electric shock to the finger, but there was something they could do to avoid the shock. No mention was made of the punching bag. It was up to the communication between their subconscious and consciousness to figure out both which picture was followed by shock and then, that if they punched the bag they could avoid the shock.

The real purpose of the experiment was to uncover some of the subtleties of body activities which might develop into manifestations of anxiety and how people's bodies cope with developing anxiety. One always becomes a bit anxious knowing a shock is to come, and it is also natural to search around for ways to avoid it. The results of this study did much to expose the kinds of body changes that accompany the inching upward of anxiety and then the learning to cope with anxiety-causing problems.

One-third of the thirty-two subjects quickly learned to punch the bag to avoid shock and all of these subjects showed "physiologic discrimination," i.e., there was one very specific body response which signaled the mind's insight: large skin responses that preceded the bag punching while heart rate slowed during or slightly after the act. Another one-third of the subjects quickly learned to escape the shock after it had already started by punching the bag and these showed only modest and irregular skin responses before the punch. The remainder of the subjects failed to punch the bag at all, and none of these showed any related changes in either skin or heart responses. But the overt behavior, which includes both bag punching and skin responses, tells only a small part of the story. It seems to follow that the large skin response made just before the bag punch by the people who recognized (God knows how!) that a bag punch would let them avoid a shock is a reflection of the subconscious decision-making process that precedes conscious recognition of why one does something.

But how about the other people who either rather lazily decided to escape the shock after it had begun, or those who simply failed to punch the bag at all? Here is where differences in motivation and differences in appreciation of sensory information and personality characteristics exert their influence and bollix up attempts to do straightforward experiments. Some of the subjects who failed to respond just weren't that concerned about getting a shock. Others felt confused by the instructions of the researchers and decided they should "take" the shock as long as possible, while still others withdrew from the entire experimental situation to indulge in fantasies or ruminations about the curious situation they were in. Some just relaxed and said to hell with it, while others even failed to notice the punching bag in front of them, as many of us fail to see bulky barriers in our way when we are frightened or apprehensive in a new situation. Some subjects were hesitant to move although they recognized the problem almost immediately, because there was sensitive and delicate equipment around them that they felt the rough movement of punching might harm.

The "successful" subjects were those who viewed the experimental situation as a problem to be solved and then went about it methodically, step by step. In comparison to the other subjects, the successful ones were direct and aggressive, not dreamers or considerate or nervous or disinterested. And in general the skin responses of these different types of people tended to show what types they were and how they progressed with the problem.

The relevance of this study for psychosomatic medicine is at least twofold. First there is a very sensitive indicator of subconscious decisions to avoid unpleasantness: the skin responses, the revealing dialogue of the skin; and more, the signs that skin electrical activity give of subconscious-conscious equivocation and indecision and conflict. As we shall explore in the chapters on muscles, these skin indicators precede the muscle tensing that becomes so integral to psychosomatic illnesses.

There is, however, another side to the causes for emotional responses, and that is the worries we have about internal body changes. A tummy ache, a back pain, a thumping heart or even an unusual itch prompts immediate attention and usually a lot of worry, especially if it continues to prick consciousness. American investigators have been hesitant to manipulate people's innards, but the Russians have been doing it for years. Experimental work with people's interiors is much to be desired because our emotional responses to the unknowns of unusual things going on inside are just as serious and disruptive to emotional equilibrium as are emotional responses to changes in the external environment. Americans prefer to use animals for this type of work and take their chances with the accuracy of their extrapolations of animal responses to human behavior. The problem is that animals communicate very poorly about their anxieties and worries, frustrations and depressions. I don't mean to recommend experimentation in man that might harm has in- or outsides; perhaps someday we may learn that such work need not be done even in animals. But in many psychophysiologic studies where heart rate, respiration, blood pressure, muscle or skin responses are measured as they are in ordinary medical exams, and the psychologic stimuli are lights or sounds or even mild electric shock, one wonders why animals are used.

A study by Dr. T. Uno is, happily, a beautifully detailed examination of the skin's ability to reflect both conscious and subconscious detection of changes of the interior of one's self. To test for awareness of internal body changes, Dr. Uno used a balloon swallowed to lodge in the esophagus into which he introduced either warm or cool water. To compare this to awareness of an external event he used a tone which the experimental subject heard through earphones. Since this was an experiment in classical conditioning, the skin was "told" how it was to respond to both the internal and the external changes by giving an electric shock to the arm (to which the skin naturally reacts). That is, one objective was to pair the internal or external stimulus with the electric shock so that eventually the skin would "learn" to give the response it gave to shock to either the tone or a change in water temperature in the balloon in the esophagus. The more important objective was to determine whether the skin could learn to respond to *internal* changes without the individual being aware of the change, or whether awareness was necessary to learning.

The results of the study were extremely clear. There were no normally immediate skin responses to the warmness or coolness of the balloon in the esophagus *unless* the subject was consciously aware of the temperature changes, but there were plenty of delayed skin responses even when he was *not* consciously aware of the temperature changes. In fact the *amount* of learning required to detect the environmental change, whether it was the internal temperature change or the external tone, and then make a skin response like the response to the shock "reminder" was the same whether the subject was aware or not aware of the environmental change. Only the time of response was different in the case of nonawareness. The rather longish time taken for the skin to respond to a change of temperature in the esophagus when the subject was consciously unaware of the change suggests that perhaps internal changes are slower to be perceived or that we simply haven't been educated to become aware of nonbothersome changes in the interior. In any event, the study also brought out the fact that some conditioned learning parallels conscious awareness and some learning proceeds quite subconsciously.

Thoughts on Awareness

Just how much we are or can become aware of changes going on within our interior and within internal organs is and will be one of the greatest contributions of bio-feedback research. Nearly all of the "learning" experiments we have discussed concerning the skin were, in reality, basic bio-feedback techniques. In nearly every instance one of two bio-feedback conditions prevailed. Either the subject was rewarded for making a skin response, in which case the individual was receiving direct information about his body activity (that his skin responded well enough to get the reward); or, in other types of experiments, the mind, in its subconscious operational mode, was rewarded by avoiding the unpleasantness of shock when it produced the appropriate body response. The ten- or even forty-year detour taken by experimental psychologists in unraveling the marvels of the mind has been an insistence that the mind-brain serves little function in the way body activities learn how to behave. Yet we have seen in almost every research study that learning to control *any* body activity is dramatically enhanced when information about the body's performance is fed back to the "head" performer. Our culture, however, has taught us the animality of our beings; the sophistications of psychology and medicine have been built around the primitiveness and automaticity of our physical and behaving beings.*

No experiment yet has proved that our minds do not control our bodies. Quite the opposite: objective analysis of the mass of research evidence literally explodes with undeniable signs of direction by the mind. If the iron mask of behavioral control had not been sealed so tightly on the face of human intelligence by the feudal lords of academia, mastery of one's own physical and mental destiny could have begun long ago. It is difficult for me to imagine a schooled researcher watching any physiologic activity form itself into an intimate relationship with a signal of its performance, such as the rate of skin responses swinging into full stride when a light or tone continuously signals its success, and fail to recognize the significance of that event. Yet until the concept of bio-feedback became recently formalized this extraordinary phenomenon of the mind-body relationship was, like the midnight intruder, restrained behind a barricade of theoretical constraints and scientific hypocrisy.

Another problem rooted in scientific prejudice has been the consistent failure of experimental psychophysiologists to develop clear concepts about awareness. It is generally accepted in much scientific work that awareness means exclusively conscious awareness and, even more rigorously, it means the ability to verbalize concepts. To accept such a definition means that awareness is created *de novo* within consciousness and to limit the use of the elaborate associations that are made within the subconscious. In this chapter a fair number of experiments are described which have

---

* In contrast, so-called primitive cultures are based upon the sophistications of voluntarily controlled relationships between being and the ecology.

revealed the considerable influence of subconscious recognition and judgmental action on skin activity. When, however, researchers began testing the skin's activity according to learning theory, subconscious awareness was regularly excluded from consideration as an influence. Even so, it was a step forward when, in the late 1960s, a few research reports were published indicating that absolutely *no* skin learning could occur if the owner of the skin was unable to *verbalize* the fact that he had grasped the relationship between the lights and shocks and that if he did something, he would not get shocked. If the individual could not verbalize this relationship, there was no "learning" by the skin.

As in most experiments, there is a catch to this one too. In each case where the subject could verbalize the relationship, he had received helpful instructions from the experimenter *about what to look for*. Experiments of this type are usually done within thirty minutes, so these people had the jump on the subjects who weren't informed (the "controls" for the experiment). In addition they received a reward of no-shock if they performed successfully, and there was still more information being fed back to them when they failed to perform to command and thus received a shock. Other studies have shown that the more *relevant* the information provided for the subject is about his task, the better and faster he performs. Experimental results from different laboratories differ widely, and in another, similar study it was found that awareness of the task did indeed improve the ability of the skin to learn to respond to signals. That is, subjects who consciously figured out the task the skin must perform did best. Yet if the subject were so diverted in his attention that he was barely aware of what his skin was supposed to do, then he too could perform satisfactorily despite distraction of his conscious awareness, presumably because his subconscious was aware. And some subjects who were completely consciously unaware of the task also could perform well. One must conclude from this that some learning requires awareness and some does not, but awareness certainly helps, conscious or not.

On the other hand, other studies reported that exactly the same kind of skin learning occurred only when the subjects did *not* verbalize what was going on. Why is there such confusion, such disparity of results from such seemingly simple experiments? In view of the data on subconscious direction, one explanation might well be that, quite unintentionally, the laboratory environments of research investigations are loaded with information. In one case the bias of the investigator to prove the need for awareness in learning may easily be communicated in the way he treats his subjects—what he tells them about the experiment, perhaps a waver of the voice and shifting of the eyes when he is intentionally misleading the subject; the instruments lying about, where the electrodes are put, the *sotto voce* comments of the investigators filtering through the feeble soundproofing. Few of these effects have been systematically investigated, but one skin learning experiment illuminates the point quite nicely. Along with the other parts of the typical experiment, the investigator made ratings of the development of anxiety of the subjects. He found that those who were given misinformation about the objectives and events of the experiments became anxious and gave poor learning performances.

New Awareness or Just Overlooked?

The question of just how much the mind contributes to controlling the performance of so-called automatic body activities is, of course, of utmost importance to the cure and prevention of illness. More than 90 percent of medical science has culled its ideas about health and well-being from studies of illness, not from how the body behaves in *good* health. It is unfortunate that physicians rarely participate in psychophysiologic research dealing with body functions that fall within *normal* ranges of activity. It is in this research niche that the mechanisms of emotions causing body malfunctioning can be explored; it is here that the signs and symptoms of developing emotional and psychosomatic illness can be uncovered before the illness becomes disabling; and it is here where the mind or mind-body can be assisted in learning to control the potentially pernicious effects of undue emotion on body function as a convenient, inexpensive, and effective means to prevent and relieve illness.

It is paradoxical that experimental learning research has attended to body rather than to mind signals.* The mind-body bristles with receiver sets, like banks of radar and sonar sensors. Its antennae are not only the eyes and ears and skin-touching receivers; mind-body is affected by temperature, magnetic fields, love and kindness, being ignored or misled, by vibrations, physical and emotional. Mind-body is an omnivorous harvester of information, but it is only in this decade that the parallel evolutions of man's technology and his own mind have created the kind of interfacing, interlocking, friendly, understanding environment that can allow a readier understanding of the magnitude, the order, and the power of inner space.

One of the most difficult worlds to achieve awareness of is the autonomic nervous system, the regulator of automatic, life-supporting body activity. As with brain waves, we rarely have the opportunity or take the time to see or hear or touch or have any sensation at all of the normal operation of the ANS. Breathing continues without effort, the heart continues to beat, the gut digests food, the bladder fills and empties, all with little, if any, conscious awareness and direction. With bio-feedback techniques to transform the hidden signs of internal activity into the familiar space we live in, we are learning that the interior world can take direction from the mind, from what some call the will. Yet even the very real act of controlling this inner world need not require conscious awareness; indeed, in some cases conscious awareness may interfere with the ability of the mind-body complex to perform its controlling function effectively. This seemingly illogical action of the human mind may have its roots in the barrier between consciousness and subconsciousness, or it may be evidence of a mind evolution not yet achieved. If it is either, are there procedures to increase awareness of the inner being?

The Roots of Awareness

Sometimes the word perception is used interchangeably with awareness. To perceive is to define the dimensions of an event or an object in time or space with enough definition to make it retrievable from

---

* In the cold, impersonal laboratory of the biomedical scientist it has taken a long time for the mind to recognize the importance of the mind. When experiments are done with human beings, there is no way short of total anesthesia to prevent the unspoken but considerable influence of the minds of both experimenter and experimentee.

memory. Conscious awareness is not necessary to perception as we know from experiments with subliminal perception. We are so familiar with the dramas of the external environment that we scarcely need pay attention to many actual events or scenes—we reconstruct or "fill in" from similar events lodged in the subconscious. Do we do the same thing for perceptions from the interior environment, or is the internal universe such a completely new (or long-lost) experience that we must learn how to become aware of the interior physical self? Along with the fairly direct access afforded by bio-feedback techniques, are there ways to check one's progress in internal awareness?

Few scientists have studied internal awareness—we have no real idea of just how aware we are of internal sensations, nor how aware we could be. Medical science has assumed that man and animals perceive internal states and organs only when they are seriously disturbed, and so there seemed to be no reason to urge man to become sensitive to internal signals. Bio-feedback is changing all that. Better voluntary control of internal states may come with greater awareness of internal states.

The skin may be the key to learning how to "feel" the deep interior. While the skin needs electronic inventions that amplify and record to voice its awareness best, it is the skin that can serve as the spokesman for the body organs buried underneath. The concept proceeds logically, for both the skin and the internal organs are supplied in common by the nerves of the autonomic nervous system. The prevalent medical belief is that it is the ANS that arouses body organs to unnatural states of activity (as well as keeping them in balance) and it is these states that give the conscious mind its feeling of emotion. Many of the body organs are not accessible for us to measure their surreptitious ANS misbehavior (or if they are, they require analysis, such as heart rate and blood pressure), but the skin is an ideal source for such information. The skin is everywhere, it is a sensitive indicator of body emotion, and it can relay messages of consciously unrecognized turmoil below its protective cover.

A few years ago, in the late 1950s, some imaginative investigators devised an "Autonomic Perception Questionnaire," designed in part to be a somewhat more objective evaluation of anxiety than verbal descriptions, and in part as an initial step in quantifying people's awareness of their automatic functions. When the investigators related the results of the questionnaire study to traditional tests for anxiety, they found, surprisingly, only a relatively modest correlation between anxiety and the degree to which individuals were consciously aware of functioning of the autonomic nervous system. It was a surprising result since anxious people generally seem to be the ones who refer most frequently to internal distresses. Perhaps more surprising was the finding that individuals who are the keenest perceivers of interior perception do so whether the situation is pleasurable or anxiety-producing. These people who had a fair keenness of the interior ANS also showed a high degree of autonomic reactivity, i.e., a good bit of variability most of the time and were very responsive to mild stimulation. They tended to overestimate how much change their internal functioning was undergoing when stimulated. In contrast, those people who were relatively unaware (consciously) showed much less reactivity of the ANS and tended to underestimate what their ANS was doing. Of course the latter group was also less anxious.

The results of this study make one wonder about what favors more or less awareness of the internal milieu. Is it perhaps that some degree of anxiety sets in motion a more abundant skin talk, for example, or more frequent ups and downs of heart rate, or shifts from regular respiration, and that these slightly-more-than-normal changes constitute a form of internal bio-feedback? If so, there would be considerably greater opportunity to perceive an interior which is dancing in and out of the edges of comfortable normality, and sooner or later the accumulated subconsciously perceived information might burst through to consciousness. As noted in the chapter on heart rate, willfully increasing the heart rate to high levels results in feelings of anxiety, while conversely, as one becomes anxious, the heart rate increases. This is a good example of a closed bio-feedback loop within the body. Exactly the same thing occurs with skin talk and anxiety. Someday, perhaps, someone will begin to teach subjects to become aware of the many fluctuating parts of the autonomic system and use the Autonomic Perception Questionnaire to check the progress of awareness. One might then be able to determine whether the internal distress was real, in the organic sense, or due only to anxious moments or other types of emotion.

The authors of the study described above followed the inherent normal levels and the variation of a number of autonomic measures: heart rate, skin responses (talk), respiration, temperature and blood volume. They were interested in locating the best indicators of both the ability to perceive one's interior and of levels of anxiety. They found skin talk, heart rate and skin temperature all to be excellent indicators.

It was natural, then, for other researchers subsequently to use these well-defined indicators to observe whether individuals with high levels of awareness of internal states could be taught, via conditioning techniques, to produce more skin talk upon demand. Unfortunately, the next group of researchers gave no information to the mind of the skin.

A conventional "conditioning" experiment was conducted in which each spontaneous voicing of the skin was rewarded by continuously adding "ticks"* on a counter placed in front of the subjects (actually another form of bio-feedback). It had been theorized that "high perceivers" would "know" the state of their autonomic activity, and so would be able to discriminate when their skin was talking and when it was not. But the subjects were human beings, complicated and cerebral, and it was the "low perceivers" who learned better. In the face of unexpected results it is natural for investigators to rationalize why their experimental results refute theory. In this case the researchers suggested that being aware of the autonomic nervous system hindered learning partly because "high perceivers" could not follow the instructions to relax, partly because of the type of instructions given to them, and partly because they were trying too hard. The authors of the study also felt that the "rewards" of "ticks" failed to provide adequate incentive.† The investigators must have been impressed by the obvious

---

* Nonpsychologists generally tend to gasp in amazement at the assortment of "rewards" used by experimental psychologists to coax people into performing learning tasks. Whether or not people accomplish learning in a real sense when they are rewarded by toting up the sum of make-believe "ticks"—or getting to see slides of nudes—is something the reader can decide for himself.

† We thought so too. See previous footnote.

voluntary control and they suggested that further studies should be done in which helpful instructions, i.e., information relevant to the learning objective, were provided which could be considered and used by the mind to accomplish the objective.

A Skin Pill?

A related study may offer an attractive approach to the current perplexing problem of useful techniques for birth control, one which would not go against the moral and ethical suppositions of certain religious groups. A group of researchers studied the relationship between heightened autonomic activity and menstruation. Although they used a rating for ANS activity that averaged the activity for various organs innervated by the ANS, they found skin talk to be a dominant and powerful gauge. They found that during menstruation, in both the follicular (preparatory) and ovulatory phases, activity of the sympathetic division of the ANS was diminished and that sympathetic nervous activity rose during the intervening phase. Kindred studies have shown the relative ease with which important body hormones are altered by emotion. In one study, for example, a large number of subjects were "chastised verbally" while skin talk was being recorded. Both before and after the experiment two hormones, adrenaline and noradrenaline, the stress-anxiety related substances of the nervous system and ANS, were measured and were found to increase. The increase in urinary level of each hormone was directly related to changes in the skin electrical activity.

If there were a simple way for women to monitor one of the physiologic activities of the body that accompany the varying amounts of female hormones released during the estrous cycle (such as monitoring skin talk or even body temperature, and learning to control it), then there may be the possibility that learning to control these slow monthly rhythms might lead to a natural and simplified method for birth control. This possibility may not be such a long shot as it seems at first glance.

There are doubtless myriad therapeutic applications of heightened awareness of internal states obtained by patients being given information about how their interiors operate and interact.

Medicine and psychology have not actually tried to determine the extent to which awareness can substitute for drugs or psychotherapy. While I have stressed the remarkable positive capabilities of the subconscious, and before critics cite its inadequacies, one very important characteristic of living organisms, particularly of man, should be emphasized. Man learns best when he has information. He presumably could walk without being taught by knowing that unless he does food and shelter is unobtainable. The more information he has, however, the better he can optimize his living. His ANS may be the same; certainly it is part of him, and a dynamically performing, inseparable part of himself. Perhaps man has, to date, so little awareness and control of his interior self simply because his mind-body has had no information about its abilities and range of activity.

There is virtually nothing in our educational process that teaches us exactly how and what kind of excessive emotion pursues its treacherous attacks on the health of the vital systems beneath the skin. The anxieties of millions of human beings are imbedded in the not-knowing of their own insides. If the AMA and the ivory-towered scientists would spare just one leaf from their confidential books of body knowledge, how quickly the aspirin market would disappear. For some people a suddenly numbed arm trips the fear button and mobilizes the body's sweat and racing heart and gasping breath. Then if, for example, it is found that a tight overcoat armhole has pressed a nerve trunk under the armpit, the knowledge extinguishes the flames of fear like a blanket of soothing foam. It is knowledge and awareness that sustain life.

Skin Awareness and the Need for Intelligent Information

How much difference can knowledge make even to subconscious intentional control over internal events? This question has been tackled by a number of researchers. One particularly interesting approach was that of Shean, who, utilizing a classical conditioning format for the experiment, showed subjects slides taken of colored wooden blocks having nonsense syllables printed on them. Any one picture could show a wooden block which was either thick or thin, large or small, square, circle, etc., red or blue, etc., and a different nonsense syllable. The showing of the slides was the "conditioning" or warning signal. Of the many slides, only preselected slides with a certain quality of shape, size or color were followed in a few seconds by an electric shock to the calf of the leg. The psychologic objective was to determine whether skin responses could reveal when and if the subject realized the connection between the preselected slide and the shock. One group of subjects was given nearly complete instructions about the experiment, everything except the exact feature of the slides which would be followed by shock. That feature was the quality of *thinness*. Any wooden block, regardless of shape or color or nonsense syllable written on it, would be followed by the shock if it were *thin*. The informed group was informed specifically about the different characteristics (shape, color, etc.) and told that only one particular characteristic of the wooden block would be followed by shock. A second group of subjects went through the same experiment, but they were told only that they were to try to detect *which* characteristic of the wooden blocks was followed by shock. Actually this was a very subtle difference in the amount of information given to the subjects: the first group being alerted to what to look for while the second group was not. It was the informed group who learned best.

All the subjects were asked to try to formulate concepts about the relationship between the slides and the shock and to report their guesses about the relationship on demand. In view of what we have written about the ability of the skin to report the intelligent decisions of the mind, it would be expected, as actually happened, that the skin responses were equally as accurate as the verbal reports that any wooden block which was thin was followed by shock regardless of shape or color or nonsense syllable. It is unfortunate that it apparently was not possible for the author to analyze whether the reporting by the skin occurred earlier than the voice reporting. Nonetheless, there is still the striking conclusion that a little bit of information for the mind can speed up learning to control a body function even when that learning is proceeding subconsciously.

In a similar vein studies have demonstrated how the skin reflects the problem-solving activity of the mind. When new problems were given to subjects, skin talk was slow but loud, indicating, possibly, the time it takes to mobilize concepts from memory which are suitable for solving the problem at hand, along with indicating the tenseness and anxiety and concentration one has during the problem solving itself. Then, when the problem was mentally solved, the skin talk sank back to its resting state. A similar sequence occurred when multiple-choice answers were given along with the problems; the subject's skin also sighed with relief upon recognizing the correct answer. But if the subjects were told when their answers were correct (feedback), the activity of the skin subsided further still.

The skin really chatters during concept-formation tasks, when experimental subjects must identify a common element in a series of pictures in which many confusing shapes are introduced. Some researchers have speculated that this rapid chatter of the skin is reflecting a special internal state: that state when new information can be taken into the mind-body system most effectively and efficiently, sometimes called the "information receiving state." But this state, along with its skin indicator, can be dramatically altered by prior information. It becomes keener, more able to ingest new information, if there have been earlier successes, and it flags and seems inhibited if there have been previous failures. Some investigators have felt that such "inside information" about the experiment (feedback of successes) simply adds to the total sensory impact and is reflected by orienting responses of the skin. Orienting, however, is typically a response of alerting to the sudden intrusion of something unexpected and new. It is all over within a matter of seconds. The *use* of information during problem solving or during learning does not constitute novelty. Quite often researchers trap themselves by their own limiting definitions of phenomena. Certainly there are many examples of continuous digestion of new environmental bits of information, trying to fix one's self in a new situation, trying to relate to the newness. In problem solving there is internal orienting also, in the process of perceiving one's memory, digging for associations which can explain the novelty. These completely mind processes are reflected in the continuous chatter of the skin during concept formation. Someday, perhaps, sophisticated analysis of the chatter can be used to identify different phases of higher mental activity.

In an experiment where problems became more difficult but

followed a certain theme, it was found that skin talk did *not* herald increasing anxiety and uncertainty and attention when new problems to solve were given. Quite the reverse, there was more skin talk when the individual was confident that he could solve the problem because of the "theme" of the problems and his past successes. Thus the skin's activity does not merely signal orienting or the arousal of attention during problem solving, it also signals intellectual awareness.

Skin Signals of Disturbed Emotions

Direct, immediate bio-feedback information can be demonstrated to facilitate even further the effect of awareness and the skin's reflection of that awareness. Quite recently Glenn Shean, working with William Hughes, explored the problem of whether bio-feedback information actually could add to the combined effect of (a) the information given in explanations of the experiment, (b) knowledge of the objectives of the experiments and (c) information given in a quick course in the underlying physiology. The experiment itself was straight to the point. First the subjects were conditioned ("taught") to prevent a skin talk response when they saw a signal light, by the usual classical conditioning technique of following the light signal by shock. Then the researchers altered the experiment, not only by explaining the precise relationship between light and shock signals, but by actually helping the subjects to keep the skin from talking by explaining that relaxation and "thinking relaxing thoughts" would help them to be successful. These instructed subjects were then divided into groups, one of which additionally received bio-feedback, i.e., they were shown an external signal of their ongoing skin talk activity. The other group had no bio-feedback. The subjects who had received *all* of the information possible, i.e., explanations, instructions, assistance, *and* bio-feedback, were the best performers. They were considerably more successful in preventing skin talk than were the subjects who received all of the information except bio-feedback. Obviously the bio-feedback provided information and awareness about the skin response that was critical to success.

Shean and Hughes made one more comparison in their study

which is controversial but nonetheless intriguing. In essence they conducted two studies, one using subjects classified as "high neurotic introverted" and another with subjects classified as "low neurotic extroverted." Guess who did best in learning how voluntarily to control skin talk? The high neurotic introverts. There is a big to-do in medical literature about the biological characteristics of people with different kinds of personalities. It is not terribly difficult to demonstrate that people with the extremes of personality, such as those having severely depressed as compared to those having wildly excited, manic behavior, do differ in most of their physiology in a consistent and significant way from people whose behavior generally falls within the normal range. The problem is that personality disorders have to be fairly severe and have to have been developing over a rather long period of time before truly significant and reliable changes in body chemistry become evident. In some cases certain neurohormones indicate changes early in the course of emotional illness but require blood or urine samples and they are neither sensitive indicators nor convenient to use.

The skin, on the other hand, is a constant mirror of emotion. When decoded properly, it can detect even the *potential* for emotional and/or psychosomatic illness, as, for example, the most common neurotic tendency we all suffer: anxiety. In fact, it is doubtful practice to label anxiety as neurotic as so many psychologists and psychiatrists do, especially since psychophysiologists have been unable to make any sharp distinctions between "normal" feelings of anxiety and neurotic anxiety. Psychophysiologic research almost invariably relates anxiety to arousal level, alertness, attention, expectancy, anticipation and/or uncertainty. Not unexpectedly an exact correlation between arousal and anxiety is found. The laboratory man thinks more in terms of underlying physiologic states rather than day-to-day normal fluctuations of tension and rest, anxiety and accomplishment.

The most widely accepted theory today to account for heightened alertness and attention, for states of arousal, for vigilance and expectancy is the theory that the reticular activating system of the brain is excited by both external and internal stimuli. The core of this system is lodged deep within the brain, grossly designated as lower and midbrain areas, and in some ways the system resembles the telephone switchboard. It receives communications, via "collaterals," from nearly all of the sensory nerves ascending to higher brain structures, including the cortex, that modulate higher functions and in turn also it sends out communicating branches to modulate and buffer the brain messages which descend downward through the brain and spinal cord to the performing organs and parts of the body. Increased activity of the reticular activating system is believed to affect conscious awareness; with its decreased activity comes sleep. The essence of its action is to focus attention. The more stimulation it receives, the more alerted or aroused it becomes. When the RAS is aroused, it soaks up stimuli like a sponge, then wrings itself out to pour shaping impulses downstream to the body. All systems are not only GO, they are already in motion. The problem for the psychophysiologists is that some body systems respond more quickly and more violently than others when stress is added. One investigator, for example, attempted to demonstrate that cardiac and skin electrical responsivity differed according to where attention was directed, according to the type of stress encountered. It was postulated, and presumably demonstrated, that situations which involve perception, i.e., attention to the environment, were associated with a pattern of slowing of heart rate and an increased electrical conductivity of the skin while situations which involved cognition or problem solving were associated with an increase of both of these body activities. It was a nice little idea. Unfortunately few other researchers were able to confirm the original study, although there is considerable experimental evidence to support the concept.

The disparity of results in seemingly similar experimental studies emphasizes the complexity of the mind-body system. In some cases test situations are constructed to be stressful and anxiety-producing, while in other studies the faint hearts of the investigators may lead to use of quite mild experimental situations. The variation in the time each system needs to respond to the situation is also important; the heart responds quickly, the skin much more slowly, and it seems likely that many physiologic studies fail to consider sufficient time for recognition of complete responses. As the intensity of the stress increases, the responses of different body systems enter at different points in time. Each body system is unique, each individual is unique. But over and above all of the complications and complexities, for everyone, as stimulation increases the organism is stressed and becomes aroused, and arousal is the overture for anxiety.

The identity of skin electrical activity with anxiety and stress is so intimate that for every new increment of increase in anxiety, there is one also in the volume of skin talk. It is thus the ideal indicator of arousal level and the potential for anxiety. Its sensitivity in mirroring human emotion is so penetrating that it can actually empathize. In one experiment it was found that subjects not only naturally increased their skin electrical activity with the stress of putting the hand into cold water, but they did exactly the same when they watched other people putting their hands in cold water. There is little question that the skin can reflect the earliest, most subtle forebodings of apprehension and anxiety.

The Anxious Skin

There are a hundred ways in which anxiety can be defined. There is normal anxiety which keeps us alert, ready to take action; there is neurotic anxiety where fear and anxiety are not logical consequences of situations. And there are physiologic and psychologic anxieties, conscious and subconscious states of anxiety. For anxiety is an extension of normal alertness and uncertainty about outcomes. The many tuned senses of the body signal the mind to changing events and the body responds by arousal, alert to take action. Subconsciously, too, the brain alerts for action. It searches the memory: Is the situation new? Is it dangerous? Can I cope with it? Are there hidden meanings? Is it something to worry about? For the most part the brain searches its files and compares data and experiences, silently, automatically. In a matter of milliseconds the comparisons are made and decisions are reached. If pleasant associations or effective patterns for handling new situations are reached in this rapid-fire search of the memory banks, the comparisons are smooth; the body systems are not further aroused and usually the alertness subsides. But if unpleasant or worrisome memories are tapped in the search, then comes a new flood of comparisons between the new scene with its uncertainty and novelty and the old memories and associations. The sensing of the unexpected triggers the automatic system of nerves and muscles to increase in alertness, to become fully aroused and prepare its defenses. Consciousness itself may or may not be triggered and alerted to action; the subconscious alone may be triggered to action. If the change in external environment or the new situation has a pattern of unfamiliarity, the automatic self may respond with its usually effective survival defense mechanisms: the fight or flight reflexes, or culturally subdued modifications of these. In extreme instances anxiety is bypassed; the recognition of potential danger accelerates the mind-body to a numb panic.

In most circumstances new encounters are not a life-or-death matter, but are dramatic, swiftly moving serials of undulating demands for mental and emotional consideration. Here too the body is not divorced from the mind, and for every surge of newness and for every problem to be solved the automatic self becomes alerted. The skin talks and perspires, the heart speeds, the smallest arteries constrict and blood pools in muscles and near the surface of the skin and one feels the new warmth. When voiced in the lowest register, the awareness recognizes apprehension, the sensation of arousal. If the brain activity uncovers unpleasantness, the arousal may proceed to anxiety and worry. It is then that the mind begins to play strange tricks. Normally the body apprehension merely pricks consciousness from time to time, rather like the Secretary of the Interior reporting to the President for consultation. Interior may simply be informing or he may be seeking advice; no one yet knows such executive secrets. In these instances the Chief Executive may begin to worry consciously and perform the routine of rationalizing about the degree of seriousness of the new event, weighing different courses of action. At other times he may ignore the information, satisfied that the status quo is efficient and requires no special actions. All of these are essentially normal operating modes of interaction between consciousness and subconsciousness.

For all of us there are times of difficulty when our life's coping mechanisms falter. Apprehension builds swiftly into anxiety. If the experience is truly threatening to any of life's aspects: physical, mental, emotional or social, the anxiety is warranted and helpful because it alerts and mobilizes the resources of the mind-body. But if the experience is not threatening and yet mind-body still rushes headlong into action, enveloping itself with body answers to alarms of nonexistent danger, the balance between mind and body, between consciousness and the subconscious has been broken. No one is quite certain how the adverse balance occurs although most favor its origin in unresolved conflicts. Intense, pervading anxiety, the so-called "free-floating" anxiety which cannot be attributed to any single source of fear is now almost so common as to be, in its lesser forms, the norm of human behavior and the usual reaction to the constant stresses and pressures of today's life.

One of the reasons that bio-feedback may come to be of serious importance in the relief of anxiety is that many unresolved (and subconscious) conflicts are the result of social training. It is learning theory again, the simple kind of learning that says that repeated experiences shape behavior. Social traditions shape behavior, as do the smaller family traditions and the larger cultural customs. And misinformation and noninformation shape behavior just as effectively. I have previously spoken of the internal bio-feedback loops operating between mind and body. The conscious mind may be striving for social correctness: the lady arching her back in just-so elegance, while her subconscious intelligence is making a running commentary about the foolishness of bending her body to the cultural norms, or her physical self is groaning with fatigue. A simple conflict, yet unresolved. There is the logic from gleanings of the intellect of a subconscious, mind-body reality on the one side and the logic and intellect of a social reality on the other. Unless the compromise between realities is emotionally satisfactory, a base of body tension is laid, vulnerable to the assaults of further conflicts. More seriously, either realistic or unrealistic appraisals of one's own value or adequacy may be misconstrued or inappropriately fitted to difficult situations, and whether the inability to resolve the conflict is real or only apparent, anxiety heightens. The body excitement feeds on the emotional judgments of the mind and in feedback-fashion the emotions feed upon the taut alertness of the body.

The skin reflects each trivial detail of the anxiety process. Many movie and television companies use skin responses to estimate the impact of filmed emotional displays. If merely watching a disquieting or frightening scene sets the skin to chattering and whimpering, imagine what it does when the emotions are one's own. If one "listens" (via recordings), in anxious states the skin's voice is high-pitched, trembling in a fast vibrato, so on the *qui vive* that it responds explosively to just a touch to the body's senses. When people with high anxiety levels are studied in the laboratory and given simple repeated tone or light signals their skin accustoms itself to the intrusion much less slowly than people without such anxiety, and the skin extension of the mind forgets the experience much more slowly. These differences still remain even under sedation. This kind of readiness to respond by the skin of anxious people makes them good "learners" in the conditioned learning studies of experimental psychologists.

According to H. J. Eysenck, one of the leading authorities on personality and its biological underpinnings, anxiety patients are both introverted and neurotic, or at least have neurotic tendencies which can be evaluated by proper testing. He deduces that introverts are more readily conditioned in skin experiments than extroverts. Another investigator has confirmed Eysenck, but in studying the sexes separately discovered that males score more like anxiety patients during skin learning experiments. No doubt males can explain this by pointing out that they are more continuously under business and social stress than females. They could further bolster their position by referring to studies which show that persons with anxiety maintain higher levels of cerebral vigilance, constantly ready for mental activity. Moreover, sociopathic personalities have exactly the opposite skin learning abilities, their skin being sluggish to learn. Although experimental results claiming to document body activity as part and parcel of personality type are intriguing, difficulties in measuring the various dimensions of personality in *normal* people do not allow us to draw firm conclusions yet about whether the skin talk actually indicates neurotic tendencies or simply a happy, alive state.

Whether the bio-feedback of skin electrical activity is an effective tool in helping to relieve anxious states is yet to be determined, although all of the studies cited in this chapter would seem to be an extraordinary rationale for using skin BFT as a therapeutic technique. At least three major research studies are currently under way to prove the utility of skin BFT in psychologic and psychiatric counseling. The advantage which bio-feedback gives in learning to control one's skin activity by voluntary intention in subjects with high levels of anxiety suggests that the current studies will be successful. The new research uses recordings of skin responses during psychotherapy to pinpoint emotional difficulties. The simple process of recording the revealing skin talk promises to shorten the usual psychologic procedure that takes so long for emotional problems to be coaxed out from the battle in the mind between consciousness and subconsciousness. In my own projections for use of skin talk for psychotherapy, I envision both therapist and patient watching the recording indicators of skin responses so that they can agree about troubling emotions, and the patient himself can come to reconcile his emotional differences between mind and body. The technique offers a new and more accurate communication between therapist and patient.

Skin and Mental Illness

When anxiety cannot be contained and rushes inexplicably into panic, skin talk also explodes, and curiously dissociates itself from other body reactions to fear. The muscles do not become unduly tense, only the organs innervated by the autonomic nervous system and particularly the skin, which receives impulses chiefly from the sympathetic nervous system. Some clinical investigators have speculated that the explosion of the ANS during panic attacks serves a self-limiting function, that the organs are charged to full activity and can scarcely respond further. They have reasoned that this soaring activity is an emergency measure signaling that the breaking point has been reached and exciting the opposing, braking systems to action so that the panic is, by its own effects, ended. This self-limiting ability of the ANS is used as the reason for using desensitization therapy in anxiety—a series of "desensitizing" treatments in which the anxiety or panic patient is flooded with examples and images of his own personal stresses during therapy.

One would think that people with phobias are much like anxiety patients. Some are, but those with phobias about quite specific events or items possess skin responses more like those of normal people. With one exception: they respond to stimulation with a distinctive vigor which has led some clinicians to explore whether such marked skin responsivity would diminish during desensitization treatment. For example, in one study patients with spider phobia were constantly shown pictures of spiders while at the same time they were given therapeutic measures to produce muscle relaxation. As the patients began to report that their fear of spiders was lessening, so did their skin talk diminish to a whisper.

Skin responses are also used as indicators in the diagnosis and prognosis of schizophrenia. Confused patients generally have a markedly diminished skin electrical reactivity to external stimuli, and they adapt to repeated signals quite quickly, much as if a change in the external situation causes only the briefest kind of notice and is then ignored. The skin indicator has been interpreted as a sign of rapid but very diffuse assimilation of information by chronic schizophrenics. Those patients with acute schizophrenic episodes who have relatively more skin responsiveness have been found to have less emotional pathology and are more likely to show improvement with treatment. One especially interesting clue given by the skin response in young subjects evaluated as high risk schizophrenic subjects was that the "recovery" or return to normal ongoing levels of skin activity revealed the emotional significance of environmental signals to these young patients. Something in their minds was still functioning as it should; they were reacting to the reality of the environment and their skin responses showed it even if they refused to communicate that they grasped the changes by responding with the usual facial and verbal expressions.*

Can the Skin Lie?

The great emotional-giveaway, honest quality of the skin has been, of course, put to extensive nontherapeutic use. When the subject of lie detectors arises, there is, invariably, argument. The issue revolves around invasion of personal and constitutional rights. Few

---

* For many years my offices have been housed in the psychiatric buildings of the hospital. Nearly every day I fret about the stale and uninteresting world the patients face. Wherever they go and whatever they do, they are constantly fed back sad, despairing information about the way they are imprisoned and dispossessed. If any are like the young schizophrenics, the poverty of the feedback can serve only to increase frustration and divorcement from reality. If the dreary walls say "stay" and the body responds, then this is bio-feedback put to ill purpose.

people stop to question the validity of lie-detecting techniques or whether the instruments used as lie detectors do what they are claimed to do. Part of this is because we trust our law-enforcement officials to select the best tools necessary to assist in solving crimes against us, the society. But I feel strongly that there is a prior error: the misuse of lie detectors by overestimating their accuracy and reliability.

It has been variously reported that the lie-detecting ability of the skin is anywhere from 45 to 73 percent accurate. This is most probably why law enforcement has not insisted upon general use of the lie detector. But astounding as it seems, few if any have questioned the role of the instrument. The question of the morality of lie detection by an instrument may have impeded the development of more accurate instruments. There is also the attitude of the laboratory researchers. They are interested more in theory than in use, and moreover, they are not electronics experts. What is useful for laboratory experiments, where statistical analyses are so often used to compensate for inaccuracy, may be an impractical tool for use away from the laboratory. Now that the therapeutic use of the lie detector is on the near horizon, a moral justification for increasing the accuracy of lie-detection machines is at hand. Moreover, when therapists find that psychotherapy is more successful and can be accomplished in much less time by the use of such machines, there will be a demand for a better instrument.

Although I have not searched the biological literature for studies dealing with the efficiency or up-dating of lie detectors, I have rather thoroughly searched for research on the skin electrical activity part of lie detection. There appears to have been one study in which a new skin talk detector was designed, and it looks to be a rather efficient machine, but nowhere has there been evidence that it has been put to use.

Now that bio-feedback is upon us, the problems surrounding the practical and moral use of lie detectors will become increasingly important. The rush to manufacture bio-feedback instruments has already included in it the exploiter's version of a skin talk bio-feedback device for use by the general public. Even $10 kits are available for use by children. Fortunately these advance gimmicks are conspicuously inaccurate to the point of impossibility for use.

Nonetheless, the bio-feedback impetus is pushing forward the use of the skin talk machine for use in psychotherapy, and there will be sophisticated, accurate and reliable models coming on the market which do have real ability for lie detection.

Although law enforcement has not yet been authorized to use lie-detector evidence in courts of law, personnel departments of industries are using lie detectors as part of their employment criteria. As late as 1964 Congressional hearings were held on the use of polygraphs as "lie detectors" by the federal government. The conclusions drawn from the testimony of expert witnesses hinted at unrecognized and as yet unremedied cracks in the foundations for use of lie detectors.

In the 1964 hearings it developed that there was precious little concrete evidence for the effectiveness of lie detectors in actual criminal situations. The polygraph lie detector had been appropriated by law-enforcement agencies largely by drawing support for its efficiency from experimental work in research laboratories. It became obvious that experimental research studies are almost always conducted under "artificial" conditions. That is, the experimenter attempts to detect whether his experimental subjects are lying by tests which fail to consider the conditions for use "in the field." In the field the suspect is apprehensive and anxious, and, as described earlier in this chapter, skin talk is most revealing in the anxious condition. Yet in the researcher's laboratory, the conditions for testing lie detection are relatively benign. The difference should suggest that lie detectors may operate more effectively in the field than in the laboratory. This, however, has not been the case; in fact, the reverse is apparently true. The question is why?

One research team, following the 1964 hearings, inspected several factors that might account for the differences. They not only examined the effects of different levels of environmental or situational stress on their subjects, they also examined the different indices of body information recorded by the polygraph and used to detect lying. In government agencies the polygraph had been used as the lie detector. This is an instrument which records several indices of activity of the autonomic nervous system, usually blood pressure, heart rate, skin responses, respiration, and sometimes blood flow in the finger. The new, post-1964 study determined the lie-detecting value of each of these body activities rather than using them all together as in police work. The result was startling. It seems that the procedure of inflating the arm cuff in order to record blood pressure produced some extraneous effect which resulted in *decreased* efficiency of the other measures to detect lying. They found also that changes in heart rate as lie detectors were little better than chance, or simply guessing. It was, in the final analysis, the skin responses that were the best detectives. The skin detective was so good, in fact, that it picked up ethnic differences. People born in the Moslem countries of the Mediterranean area, for example, were less responsive than the European-born.

As for the rest of the newer studies, these have turned out to be more games that psychophysiologists play. One study developed a technique for detecting lies in groups of people. All of their skin talk was recorded through one instrument, meaning that if you looked at the record, you couldn't tell whose skin talk was whose. It was just one big record of all voices talking at once, but all using the same voice box. The particular game played was to have one group pretend to be guilty spies, and have in their possession a number of secret code words which they were sworn not to reveal under penalty of the total embarrassment of being disqualified from the experiment. A second group was not informed and was presumed to be completely innocent. Then the interrogators set to work with their little skin talk machines. They shot words at the subject one after another, interspersing the code words from time to time. Then came the delight of measuring the skin responses from the record, averaging all of the responses to the code words and comparing them to the responses from the rest of the words, which theoretically had no significance to any of the participants. That really was the purpose of the experiment (in all fairness): to design a situation to eliminate spurious significant responses which occasionally occur because all of us have emotional responses to seemingly innocent words that other people haven't. In any event, the experiment seemed to work and the researchers were able to weed out, by averaging responses to neutral words, these occasional emotional responses, and they were left with a spectacular demonstration that if a group of people are all lying about the same thing, the lie can be detected quite neatly. The problem, of course, is that it is rather rare that large groups of people are all privy to the same lie. Communists maybe, or kids pilfering apples from the corner store.

One other new study which seems a bit unimaginative at first glance was a lie-detection study using, in addition, conditioned learning techniques. In other words, most of the times when the subjects lied, in a simulated stealing scene, they also received a shock to the wrist. The effect of this was to make the skin responses during lying larger and larger, which of course became quite easy to detect. The real-life analogue is during repeated interrogation of a suspect. Perhaps the interrogator is only 50 percent right in his lie detection at first, but then so is the suspected criminal; i.e., the suspect has an uncertainty factor in that he doesn't know whether the interrogator has guessed correctly or not. However, if the questioning continues, it appears that his lying responses will probably get larger and larger and the lies easier to detect.

Bio-Feedback versus the Lie Detector

Even before bio-feedback, experimental psychologists knew for many years about the ability of the skin to reveal emotions that individuals may prefer to keep to themselves. This knowledge, without mature consideration, was shared only with law-enforcement agencies to extract information from often reluctant witnesses or with industries as part of the psychologic profile probing carried on by personnel departments. In some industries today it is mandatory to submit to a lie-detector test (that in large part is the skin voice) before employment.

Why are such uses of our most intimate mode of emotional communication allowed when we have not even been told that we reveal our inner selves by our skins, nor advised of our personal, constitutional right not to talk, even with our skins?

In the future it may not be a questionable inaccuracy of lie detectors that would preclude use of the evidence they obtain in the courts; it may be that with increasing knowledge of the bio-feedback process, the use of lie detectors may be found to infringe upon constitutional rights.

We have learned, in these chapters, that the skin voice can learn—it can learn to speak more loudly or more softly, to speak only when spoken to and not to speak when spoken to. Obviously the skin can learn to exert the same kind of control over its voice as the vocal cords have over their voice. After all, it's the same mind for both.

The whole point of course is that the average individual is not aware that a lie detector may tap his unconscious thoughts; that, unlike his verbal expressions, he has no choice but to answer. However, now that we know that the skin's voice can learn—just as does the voice itself can—to speak or not to speak, then it does have a choice which the individual has not been advised of.

With these facts in mind, perhaps every witness to crime, every suspect, every prospective employee should be taught control of his skin voice. Then they would be fair game for personal questions. Their skin voices would have the same option as their voice-voices; to refuse to answer or to answer as their consciences and circumstances dictate—but if the skin voice were given the same options there would be no need for lie-detector tests.

Recapping the Skin

The story of the hieroglyphic physiology of the skin has, to this point, revealed an array of clues to the health of the inner being that has a distinct potential for psychotherapy. What better way for therapist and patient to agree upon emotional problems than for them both to hear the same voice? One of the most devilish tricks man finds necessary to accomplish in today's sophisticated, stressing, hyperactive society is the sorting out and keeping straight his emotions that are forever bouncing between the self within and the cultural patterns without. If the skin's voice can help us to listen to the deep within, we can expand our perimeters of self-knowledge and keep our emotional health. Now that bio-feedback is bringing us to the possibility of widespread use of skin talk to delve the depths of inner reality, bioscience should be equally obligated to foresee misuse of skin voices. While the bio-feedback era of skin psychobiology has unprecedented potential for human and humanistic good, we should also become aware that the capacity of the skin to reveal our inner realities may be misused.

Is it possible that one day the skin will talk to the computer and have its innermost self coded on IBM cards for sale to psychologists or doctors or car salesmen? This, indeed, is what some people may believe mind control to be all about. The best antidote is education and understanding, but over and above understanding how the skin talks, the obvious antidote is training oneself to control what one's skin is saying. It can be done with bio-feedback training procedures. As we grow to maturity we learn to control our gestures, to modulate our voices, to shade meanings verbally. We come to control, voluntarily, what and how we communicate to others. If the skin is a communication medium, which it is, then shouldn't we have the option to learn how to control its communication? Should there be available skin talk machines not only for therapeutic use and the privilege of discovering one's inner self, but to be able to learn to control when to speak with the skin and when not to? This question opens up a myriad of moral, ethical, and social considerations. Who should talk to whose skin? Should we be taught early in life that the skin can be our emotional giveaway?

If we do learn to control our skin's emotional conversation, is there a chance that we are subverting or converting emotion to some other route of expression which may be harmful to the self? If emotion weren't expressed, would we become as zombies? Or is it possible that by learning to control our skin talk we are, in effect, reducing the *causes* of uncomfortable or inappropriate emotion and its expression? Would that be dangerous, or would it make for greater brain efficiency since there would be little effort wasted on unproductive emotion? Would the self-control lead us to more peaceful states, and then to new, higher states of consciousness, rarely experienced because learned and uncontrolled emotions block the way? That is a beautiful array of coconuts to knock open for a new nutrition, a new pantry full of succulents for mind growth.

FOUR

Muscles: Teaching Muscles to Work for the Mind

We have been so schooled in relating to the external world that we look upon muscles only as they benefit the body in our daily occupation with physical and social survival. Technology is now enabling us to make experiential voyages to the inner world of muscles. There is every reason to believe that muscle trips may take the mind to unexplored horizons where mind and body can join to find a better understanding of the self.

Updating Relaxation

There is an interesting bias of Americans in the way they view the muscles of their bodies. It is all exercise and no rest. Even embryo athletes are urged to fine specialization of muscle activity. In every social activity the goal of excellence of muscle performance seems to haunt each performance of the body. But it is in the world of sports that muscle specialization is carried to the extreme. Golfers often refuse to play tennis for fear of despecializing the refined muscle activity needed for the golf swing. Even the powerful strength and superb balance of the gymnast is subdivided into seemingly endless marginal differences in order to accomplish perfection of highly specific feats of muscular organization. To compete today the athlete

119

is called upon to hone his muscles into a precise, efficient machine, and his successes are exciting and appealing to watch.*

While the public is peaking its muscular self in sports, back in the research laboratories biomedical scientists are probing the benefits of the exact opposite of muscle activity: relaxation. Scientific relaxation. There has long been an underlying medical interest in the therapeutic effects of relaxation, but until bio-feedback techniques evolved, relaxation therapies required years of consistent practice and were usually so dull and boring that the patient could scarcely tolerate the doctor's prescription for relaxation. Medical doctors, psychiatrists, psychologists, sociologists and the man in the street all recognize the need to try to stay relaxed just to stay even with the tensions of social pressures. The new generation (the hang-loose generation) has coined a new word, "uptight," which, when you think about it, is a frightening acknowledgment of how prevalent tension is even in the very young. Some medical opinion interprets their use of marijuana as a means of relieving tensions as perhaps their parents do in their use of alcohol.

New research is showing that with bio-feedback deep relaxation can be learned fairly rapidly. The discovery promises much in the way of keeping us healthy and relieving hundreds of annoying physical problems. The great scope of uses for muscle bio-feedback therapy in medicine is because muscles are the vehicles of expression of nearly every aspect of our physical and mental life. They are the implementers of our existence. To live without tension (and tension is expressed in muscle tension) is the strongest protection known against the large family of psychosomatic illness, as well as being the greatest insurance against emotional illness.

It is a fair comment on our educational system that virtually no attention is paid to teaching the art of relaxation. From infancy we are taught to set our bodies to pleasing postures, to cramp our fingers to produce good penmanship, to form our bodies into a myriad of socially acceptable positions. To "relax" has meant simply not to use the muscles. Sleeping or simply lying down to rest is

---

* We might do well to recall Plato's observation in *The Republic* that the athletes' "habits of body" led to sleeping their lives away and becoming susceptible to dangerous illness if they deviated even slightly from their athletic regimen. Plato believed that the body should be entrusted to the mind.

essentially nothing more than not working the muscles in the performing mode. With few exceptions neither biological nor medical expertise has been directed toward either active or profound relaxation. Part of the excitement of bio-feedback as applied to muscle relaxation is learning about the consequences of real relaxation. To date we have learned that deep relaxation can vastly improve health, but perhaps more challenging is the finding that profound muscle relaxation can lead to startling changes in states of consciousness and awareness. We are now beginning to learn that in some way muscles can be not only *actively* relaxed but can give us new experiences and feelings different from the feelings, or non-feelings, present during simple resting or soothing our muscles. Not by devices like whirlpool baths, nor by the intervention of another person as with massage, but by the action of central control—the brain. The new discoveries that human muscle tension can potentially be reduced to zero by volitional control . . . by willing . . . may even revolutionize scientific concepts of muscle control.

Even at rest the cells of the muscles we use for all voluntary movements (even the muscles of eye movement) are working. If they weren't we would collapse like dishrags. Some part of the cell population of every muscle is always active—some part has to be, if only to bear up under the push of gravity. Nor can it be a one-muscle job. For nearly every potential movement we can make, at least two muscles or sets of muscles are required, and these work together essentially by opposing each other. The result is balance, just the right amount of push or pull. Some of the cells of each muscle type, push-pull or flex-extend, maintain their activity during rest, keeping the muscle masses in a constant state of preparedness for action. This complex system, which allows us to move and to respond, functions entirely by means of feedback systems. The muscle "sense" of one type of muscle signals its tension levels to the central nervous system, which sends signals to other and opposite muscles about how much to respond, and vice versa, and on and on, ad infinitum. This constantly monitoring control system continues to operate at rest; it is always poised for action.

The *amount* of muscle activity that takes place at rest, or during relaxation, can vary enormously from person to person. We may think that we are resting and relaxed simply because we aren't moving. The power of this deception lies in the automatic act of balancing muscle tension in opposing muscles. Somehow, as long as the body is in a position of rest, we have learned to believe that we are resting. We have no awareness of the real magnitude of the effort being made by the muscle cells just to keep us in a certain position. Bodies readily adapt to continuous stimuli, modifying and accommodating their activities to adjust to new situations. States of anxiety and nervousness, or such slight body responses as bracing for something unexpected, all stiffen the muscles, causing an outbreak of muscle signals that are sent back to the brain, causing feelings of tension. The muscle systems respond by their balancing act, and then adapt to the new condition of heightened tension. The problem is that the conscious awareness adapts also to the point that we soon forget that we are tense.

That's where bio-feedback comes in. Because the body adapts so beautifully, the mind accepts the different adaptations as appropriate. The mind either has not learned to explore the situation to determine whether its adapting is for short-term or long-term use, or the mind forgets along with the body's mechanisms for forgetting-adaptation. Bio-feedback acts as a reminder. It lets us look at our own muscle tensions, stirs our memories to make us aware that increased muscle tension is actually uncomfortable and inappropriate over the long run. Soon we become aware that less and less muscle tension is comfortable and restful and recharging, and is real relaxation.

From Muscle Sense to Mind Sense

Most people are aware that the mind directs muscle activity, but most people aren't aware of the enormous amount of planning, judging, reflecting, and repatterning of muscle activity that goes on when we learn new muscle movements. Take learning to dance, for example. We watch a pattern of activity, mentally sort out the required movements, then later subject images of our movements to trial and error by actual performance. But likely as not we may simply read about a new movement and plot out body patterns solely in our minds. And we are generally successful with the mental planning alone. We scarcely need more evidence that the mind leads and the body follows. It is feedback mechanisms which implement all of these processes.

Within the great muscle systems the sensing of relevant information, feeding it back to central control, and the directing adjustments are all assisted by a number of specialized feedback systems. The most important feedback system of the muscles themselves is the one called proprioception. This is the "muscle sense," meaning not the intelligence of muscles, but the resident sensing elements within muscles which detect what activities are going on deep inside the muscle cells themselves. As the tension of muscle cells increases or decreases,* the microscopic sensors read not only the degree of change but the rate of change as well. These sensitive detectors then send the information into special groups of cell bodies within the spinal cord where it can be modified by simple muscle reflexes and from where the information is relayed upward to a variety of specialized areas of the brain to be integrated with information coming from other feedback-sensing control systems. The muscle sensors rarely operate alone; the performance of directed, coordinated, refined movements requires the cooperative operation of the systems which perceive position, balance, direction and touch, and visual or hearing information.

The importance of muscle relaxation to the maintenance of health and to the relief of illness has not received the recognition it merits. The major reason may be that until bio-feedback techniques came along there was no way to measure the degree of relaxation that is more than simple rest, and so there was no way to relate the effects of such relaxation to the origin, progress, or relief of physical problems. The technology of bio-feedback revealed an unknown ability of the mind—to reduce muscle tension far beyond that ever before believed possible.

Bio-Feedback, 1901 Style

The mechanics of voluntary control over muscles have long intrigued physiologists. How does the organism learn to direct its

---

* Through bio-feedback techniques it has been discovered that the mind, in some as yet unknown way, can isolate and manipulate the muscle control system at an infinitesimal level. The voluntary control of the muscle cells themselves is described in the following chapter.

muscles to answer a mental purpose and command? Most studies concentrate on the influence of physical factors in the environment, such as how long it takes a muscle group to react to varying degrees of pressure. But such studies do not answer the question, why voluntary? In 1901 J. H. Bair reported a novel approach to the study of voluntary control of muscles. He selected muscles over which, through evolution, most people have lost control, the muscles that wiggle the ear. He undertook this study "because of the light its solution would throw upon the nature of the will." It may have been the first bio-feedback experiment ever. There were no fancy electronics in those days; instead Bair ingeniously rigged a small lever with a notch in it to fit the ear, resting the other end of the lever on a small air-filled drum. A rubber tube from this drum carried pressure changes to a second drum which had a second lever scratching its movement on a kymograph. The kymograph was the old-time recording instrument of the physiologist: a paper blackened by soot fitted over a metal tube which was turned by a motor. As the ear twitched faintly, the first lever pushed the enclosed air from the first drum into the second and the lever of the second drum transmitted the pressure change to a steel pen that scratched on the sooted paper. Presumably the subjects made all sorts of efforts to try to wiggle their unwilling ears. Probably quite by accident some unrelated movement, a concentrated thought or whatever, resulted in an ear twitch. The subject saw the scratch on the kymograph, and somehow used this bit of intelligence to bring his long-forgotten ear muscles under voluntary control. Soon everyone was learning how to twitch ears. Although Bair's comments are scarce, and he is no longer around to question, he did note in his report that he kept accurate records of the learning to control the process "and careful introspections of the accompanying mental states." He also noted, "As soon as the movement is effected, however feebly, the sensorimotor circuit is beginning to be made. The sensation at the same time is cognized and effort is made to increase the sensation." He was aware of the importance of the meaning of the experience in the learning process.

Sensing Tension: Progressive Relaxation

There apparently was no general interest in 1901, or even up until 1961, in learning to control unimportant, phylogenetically left-over muscles. There have been no research reports in the scientific literature describing further efforts. Perhaps Bair is groaning "I told you so's" from the grave. The difference between vogues in biological research and other fads is that fashions in research last a long time and Bair's work did not found a new fashion. He apparently found no followers of his thoughts and was left, perhaps, to dream lonely dreams of bio-feedback in 1901. It wasn't until the early twenties that another lonely researcher attempted to teach how to gain voluntary control of muscle tension. It was Edmund Jacobson who, at Harvard in 1908, began long years of persistent devotion to the single theme of relaxation. When he began, people thought of relaxation as pleasure from diverting amusements or recreation. But Jacobson was convinced even then that many illnesses were social diseases of tension and that release from muscle tension could be therapeutic. Over the years he sharpened his focus and understanding of the relationship between mind and muscles, emotion and muscles, and muscles and muscles. He was concerned primarily with translating his concepts into effective treatments for disturbed people. He evolved a detailed retraining program for muscles, and there seems to be no muscle he overlooked.

As a physiologist Jacobson inspected the internal signs of muscle tension, that tension a person is unaware of even at apparent complete rest. The difference between felt tension and unfelt tension he called residual tension. If an individual is lying down and seemingly at complete rest, he still may show a lot of resistance to having a muscle moved. If he is truly relaxed there is no resistance. As Jacobson pointed out long ago, residual tension can be measured by measuring the amount of muscle electrical activity. He detected even then that absolute zero muscle activity can be achieved by learning how to relax. Although Jacobson's techniques were never incorporated into everyday medical practice, partly because of the length of time and assiduousness of practice required, he did come to command a significant following among many physicians who also believed in his concept of tension as a prime cause of psycho-somatic illness.

Jacobson was probably the first to realize that even at apparent complete rest muscles still contain residual tension. He was able to prove this by the simple technique showing the resistance to muscle movement when someone else tried to move the muscle, and also by proving it in the laboratory by measuring the residual muscle firing going on during apparent rest. Perhaps because he was a physician, or simply because of his own deep understanding and compassion for his patients, he brought a new dimension to the therapeutics of medicine. When the field of psychosomatic medicine finally evolved, his work would later be a fundamental of its treatment programs.

The key to Jacobson's relaxation theory is teaching the patient to become aware of even the most elusive elements of muscle tension. The technique is so simple as to be scarcely believed. As originally described, it generally began by asking the patient to lie flat on his back in the most comfortable position possible and with the eyes closed. Then, with the arms resting at the sides, the patient was asked to bend the hand backward at the wrist, a hyperextended position. His mental task was to become aware of the feeling of tension developing in the muscles of the upper forearm, about halfway between the wrist and the elbow. The wrist bend was main-tained under a steady pressure for enough minutes to ensure tense-ness. Most people have described the tenseness in terms of mild soreness or tenderness. Then the wrist was allowed to relax, and the patient was to try to feel the difference between the tension of the wrist pressure and relaxation. He was to try to become aware of the feeling of "no-tension." The exercise was practiced extremely slowly; no more than three times in 10 or 15 minutes, then the patient simply rested for the rest of the treatment hour. It sounds a bit like the psychiatrist's 50-minute hour. Then after several repeated prac-tice sessions with this isolated muscle tension alone, the patient began work with another important muscle group. After weeks or months conquering the tension in large muscle systems, he began to isolate muscle tension more and more finely.

The technique for sequentially learning to control tension of muscles was named Progressive Relaxation (P.R.) and was de-scribed in a book by that name published by Jacobson in 1929.

Written for physicians and scientists, the techniques have been widely used professionally. The procedures were so clear cut and easy to follow that if one were persistent it is a good guess that his methods are the source of nearly all books written on relaxation in the last half century.

Jacobson was convinced that true muscle relaxation would also indirectly allow relaxation of certain internal organ systems having "smooth" muscles, those types of muscles not ordinarily under voluntary control. To demonstrate this in one study he first trained subjects to relax completely all of the major skeletal muscles. Then he inserted a balloon in the throat and monitored the rate of swallowing the balloon. When the subject went into voluntary profound relaxation, the balloon proceeded smoothly down the esophagus. When body tension existed, the balloon was held up by muscle spasms.

One of the more interesting aspects of Jacobson's work throughout the years was his exploration of techniques which might influence the awareness of internal states. He became interested in the power of imagination and, being a scientist, he undertook to provide conclusive proof of the effect of imagination on body functions. He was, no doubt, the first to make such investigations scientific, and his studies on the physiologic consequences of imagination have fathered many existing uses for psychology in medicine. In one experiment, for example, he asked his subjects to imagine trying to lift a heavy weight off the ground. The subject was to *imagine* only, not to move a muscle. To record the effect of imagination Jacobson had the subject wired to record the electrical activity of resting muscles. When the subject imagined lifting the weight, the resting muscle burst forth in electrical firing although it didn't noticeably move at all. In another experiment subjects were asked to recall mentally some motion, say a tennis game. Recordings of eye movements showed back-and-forth eye movements just as if the subject were actually watching the tennis game. Or Jacobson would ask subjects to read silently, while he recorded the muscle activity around the jaws. There was the "silent" muscle activity of reading that today we call subvocalization. Jacobson's point in these experiments was not so much to demonstrate that imagination arouses undetectable, hidden body activity as it was to provide a basis by which a person could become aware that muscles were being used actively even when seemingly at rest. The patient could learn to become aware of even the *energy* of imagining. Then there are even more marvelous discoveries the patient can make about himself, once he learns to become aware of the nuances of his muscles' activities. He can begin to analyze for himself the significance of his imagery. Perhaps the process could be named somato-analysis in contrast to psychoanalysis, even though the insights obtained might be much the same.*

Passive Relaxation: Autogenic Training

An equally productive technique for producing profound muscle relaxation, viewed particularly as a forerunner of bio-feedback relaxation techniques, was developed in Germany in the 1920s. It was developed as a medical therapeutic measure and given the name Autogenic Training because control of the muscles was developed almost entirely by self-generating means. The method stemmed from observations by Oskar Vogt around the turn of the century during a type of psychotherapy using hypnosis. Vogt found that intelligent patients were able to induce hypnotic states within

* I refer particularly to the imagery of relaxation and the sudden relief from muscle tension (a bit like that which we experience on the way to sleep) that many psychotherapists claim to be an important part of various kinds of psychotherapy. For reasons that are explained later, the self-stimulation of muscle cells that muscle tension itself produces appears to bombard the mind with messages which distract the attention of the mind from its other activities. The distraction however is usually subconscious because we have gotten used to it. In this view relaxation lessens the flow of stimuli from tense muscles and so lets the mind attend to its own mind business. In most desensitization procedures, images of traumatic or disturbing experiences are repeatedly recalled intentionally until they are no longer accompanied by emotion. In other types of psychotherapy a spontaneous flow of images is urged, and these have often been found to be more revealing than dreams. Something similar happens during deep muscle relaxation therapy when a reverie state occurs, distinguished by a spontaneous flow of images that can be used for insight into or the thinking through of emotional problems. Images of course actually generate emotion, from mild pleasant feelings to the explosive letting-go surge that releases body energy and exorcises emotional devils. Or, as is now practiced in varieties of humanistic psychology, the energy generated by the images can be directed into specific channels for use, such as re-experiencing and intensifying meaningful emotional states. Some of the newer therapies assume that whole patterns and hierarchies of emotional experience are locked into muscle tension patterns to the point that upon release and awareness the individual may even become aware of the once hobbled, now realized energy of his muscles, as well as being freed from a psychological bind.

themselves by autosuggestion because the auto-procedure reproduced the essential elements of the hypnotic procedure. With the help of clues from the patients, Vogt found that even a little time spent each day on such "autohypnotic" exercises gave considerable relief from the effects of fatigue and tension. A wide variety of the symptoms of psychosomatic illness, as we define these today, could be relieved by practice of the exercises. The neurologist and psychiatrist J. H. Schultz was greatly attracted by the benefits claimed for the exercises and decided to reformulate the procedure because of the then growing distaste for the use of hypnosis in medicine and the general worry about dependence of the patient on the therapist which hypnosis entails.

Schultz soon found that two different types of body sensations occurred almost invariably in his hypnotized subjects: a feeling of heaviness in the extremities often extending to include a heavy feeling throughout the body, and an associated feeling of warmth reported as quite pleasant. He isolated these two factors as being essential to the production of the hypnotic state. Because of the importance of the well-known physiologic changes which can be produced in the hypnotized individual, it became important to determine whether similar changes in body functioning could be produced by autosuggestion, beginning with formulas to develop feelings of heaviness and warmth.

Schultz was eminently successful. Over the years he perfected various series of mental exercises which proved to have profound effects on body functioning, particularly on the abnormal functioning which results from excess tension and stress. Exercises for the beginner are called standard exercises and are directed specifically toward physiologic activity. These consist of verbal formulas such as "my right arm is heavy"; then after some hours of practice applying the formula to various parts of the body muscle masses, the patient follows with exercises to induce warmth. This phase of the therapy requires some four to ten months.

After mastery of body relaxation exercises the patient progresses to meditation exercises which concentrate on visual imagery. From the imagery of simple elements such as color, it continues with the imagination of objects and finally to abstract concepts. Still later the meditation explores one's own feelings until the deepest level of meditation is achieved in which one communes with the unconscious.

"Let it happen" was the real key to Schultz's success. It is a surprisingly modern, almost faddish philosophy of behavior. During the exercises the patients were instructed to use passive concentration, never active fixing of the attention.

Schultz arrived at the concept of passive concentration through years of keen observation. Later neurophysiologic studies were to demonstrate a very real functional basis. The reticular activating system (RAS) of the brain is something like a brain guide which sorts out both incoming and outgoing nervous impulses between the body and the rest of the brain. With both conscious and subconscious alertness this system relays information about situations causing concern—whether a pin prick from the outside or the internal pain of an acid stomach—to the cortex, where the information enhances attention. As the arousing information is appraised within the cortex, the extracted information is fed back to the reticular activating system, which then assists in modulating the more primitive responses of fear and tension to situations of potential danger. The body, or the critical part involved, becomes tensed, ready to respond. It is, in terms of older concepts of psychophysiology, an attenuated form of the "flight-or-fight" response to danger signals. In man with the increased sophistication of his brain, the response occurs chiefly as a mental state of preparedness for action. Obviously such a state would not be helpful in learning how to relax. Thus active concentration is not desirable during the relaxation practice.

Autogenic Training (A.T.) techniques have been studied intensively in Europe and are used extensively in clinical practice. It might be guessed that one reason A.T. failed to gain popularity in the United States is the very long time involved in the treatment. Even with good success the results are more ones of the gradual subsiding of disturbing physical problems and aren't so dramatic as the sudden relief one gets after the proper pill. The New World society demands faster action, and drama along with it. That's another reason why bio-feedback is growing in popularity so rapidly. Bio-feedback is a good fit for Americans. It is technical with its instruments, and we are used to learning with technical aids.

Mind-Muscle Interaction

The real advantage and surprise of bio-feedback is the new dimension it adds. And the way in which it operates in the mind-body complex may be as different from that of A.T. as aspirin effects are from penicillin. Yet together they are both good combinations. Although we as scientists can't provide absolute proof, some of us feel that current evidence points to an unused ability of man to direct his internal body activities with pinpoint accuracy. The researchers of A.T. feel that their experimental evidence points to a decrease in the amount and type of information which the sensors within the muscle cells relay to central control (naturally if there is little information for the mind to "sense," the mind is less bothered by its distractions), and this in turn results in less brain "attention" being paid to the muscle tension. Neurophysiologically it is believed that the net result of the low-level occupation of the cortex with muscle information leads to a lessening of cortical, "higher" control exerted by the cortex on the lower brain areas which represent more primitive functions. In the case of A.T., at one point in the therapy this lessened control liberates the more primitive control centers and there is a flood of downward, helter-skelter, ungoverned motor impulses. The patient may experience a variety of "letting loose" feelings, from whole body shaking to muscle twitching with or without feelings of shifting body image, floating, warmth, heaviness, or even detachment.*

Many people have had the experience of sudden release of "pent-up" energy, and this is precisely what the A.T. practitioners believe is happening. Some people can live through a terrifying experience with great calmness and effectiveness, only to break out in violent shakes after the need for survival action has passed. Others tremble inside, only barely able to control the shakes (such as when one has to get up and talk before a group), and then this is followed by calmness and a regaining of normal control. Perhaps less dramatic,

---

* This too (see preceding footnote) stimulates imagery frequently described as dancing lights or formless visions. These altered states of consciousness also often release energy that somehow revitalizes the body and brings a feeling of euphoria. This is a common reaction in certain anxiety or panic states.

but even more relevant to everyday living, is the physical release given by sobbing after one has put on a brave face during a great sadness or deep disappointment. Nearly everyone realizes that these types of discharges of pent-up nervous energy give great relief and signal the real recovery from the experience which caused the tension. A.T. researchers, however, feel that the nervous discharge is actually of much more importance to the process of anxiety than a simple relief mechanism. They view the discharge as evidence of a safety device of the higher nervous system. We should indeed be able to recognize what consequences might follow a continuing state of mind-body tension—we've all had the experience of feeling "any more of this and I'll explode." And in psychosomatic medicine it is well documented that continuing aggravations become more and more manifest as bodily malfunctions such as recurring headaches, peptic ulcer, asthma, ulcerative colitis or the most common experience of profound fatigue. In everyday experience this is perhaps why businessmen are often devotees of massage—the relief from muscle tension helps to keep their emotions in check. When release doesn't occur, the disease may progress to such serious condition that treatment becomes ineffective or only temporarily palliative.

Of course the stored, misdirected energy can also be simmered away rather than boiled out in an uncontrolled discharge. Psychoanalysts might help us on this point, but so far they haven't come forward. It might be reasoned, though, that practice with A.T. techniques as with yogic techniques would lead to some awareness of the relative state of tension or relaxation of one's own muscles. Whether this awareness actually comes to consciousness or not, memories of different states of muscle tension are nonetheless stored in the subconscious (and even in muscles) and are subject to recall. Just how such awareness is concerned with the mind and body's safety regulation mechanisms to prevent psychosomatic and emotional illness is unknown. Bio-feedback methods may allow, as never possible before, exploration of the effect of awareness of the interior self on body performance because their ability to induce controlled relaxation is based upon awareness and experiential knowledge about the most concealed and masked features of muscle activity.

It is of some curiosity to me that the "safety mechanism" of the nervous discharge phenomenon has not yet been reported when deep muscle relaxation has been achieved by means of bio-feedback. Perhaps it is too early in the studies, or perhaps patients responding in this manner have not been included in the studies. Yet the very nature of bio-feedback would suggest that cognition and understanding, and vastly increased access to one's muscle activity down to a few cells that attend the bio-feedback process are prime elements in the success of the therapy. Not only is the knowledge of the muscle state more accurate and intimate, it can be perceived almost simultaneously in time with the actual muscle activity. The bio-feedback signal is providing a wealth of information, all previously inaccessible. The real question is: how does the body use the information to change the condition of the muscles? The neurophysiologist and the behaviorist of psychology may theorize that the changing type of information conducted by the sensory neurons and internal feedback systems is relayed directly to the proper set of effector nerves and organs, which respond quite appropriately to the changed input. While such a theory may be demonstrated successfully in animals or with isolated bits of human behavior, it is quite a different matter to explain how mechanical neural activity can formulate patterns, hold these in memory, and respond to selected parts of a pattern in a directed, appropriate, and useful manner. For example, the student busy learning in the classroom not only can follow the lesson, take in the mood of the teacher and gauge his own behavior of attending, but simultaneously he can also split off a bit of attention and put into memory the quizzical look of a fellow student and formulate an answer for later conversation.

While the majority of psychophysiologists tend to view body-mind mechanisms no differently from a mechanical model, some of us feel that the many complexities of body processes cannot be explained on the basis of present-day knowledge of the anatomy, chemistry and physics of the body. One rather neglected but functionally important piece of evidence for such thinking is the ability of the mental apparatus to understand, even on a non-conscious level, how to control and direct muscle relaxation to those lower levels previously unavailable for direct or apparently even indirect perception. Then too, there are the altered states of consciousness which often accompany profound relaxation induced with bio-feedback. The curious feeling of having an arm feel as if it were floating in space, or the feeling of levitation echoes reports of out-of-the-body experiences. Is this the experiential of the third reality, an experiencing of a state of consciousness where there is separation from feeling and from the impact of the sensory world, and where one can watch the entirety of being from the perspective of being itself? Is this the stuff supranormal experiences are made of, wherein the essence of the autonomous mind divorces itself from its normal operating mode and directs the experience into activities inexplicable in the known reality? Is it possible that whatever the mechanism of bio-feedback is, it is accompanied by an energy as yet undescribed?*

Bio-Feedback Shortcut

Until the advent of bio-feedback, practitioners of muscle relaxation techniques had no way to measure just how much relaxation was taking place, nor in what muscles. And because exaggerated muscle tension becomes a habit, so it is that the greater the tension, the more difficult it is to get the muscles to relax. Often in the course of therapy the patient will, in his desperation, consciously or subconsciously feign relaxation. Without some outside impartial indicator of just how uptight the muscles are, it can become a long, slow road to learning real relaxation. It is rather like having a faulty gasoline gauge. The needle keeps signaling you that there is gas in the tank, and you let it deceive you until suddenly you are out of gas. Only then do you know that your estimate was wrong. The only other way is to get a stick and physically measure the tank. At other times you think the tank is empty and hustle to a gas station only to find there is still plenty of gas. With muscles, it is easy to deceive yourself into thinking relaxation, but if the muscle tension is actually measured, the gauge would show a good bit of tension left. Part of

* It should not be unexpected that new and different forms of body energy will be discovered. As physics, chemistry, astronomy and biology probe more deeply into energy systems, our notions of energy are being vastly expanded. We are discovering lasers and the energy of light, the energy bonds of crystals that continue to revolutionize electronics, the black holes of stars that radiate gravitational waves, chemicals that direct and chemicals that repress genes, and there are thoughts that even time may be energy. As we explore further into the psyche it seems likely that other forms of psychodynamic and mental energy will be discovered.

the deception is the physiologic action of adaptation. We simply get used to different levels of tension, forgetting that the apparent state of relaxation is not the same as genuine relaxation.

Using bio-feedback to have a constant gauge of muscle tension does a good bit more than tell the therapist what the tension is or give the patient an objective way of relating accurately to his tension. It can also be thought of as a means of communication between patient and therapist. Physical data, the actual voltage of the muscle activity, is "hard" physical data that can be agreed upon and can be discussed in relationship to what emotional problems might be causing the increased muscle tension.

At least one group of bio-feedback researchers was quick to see the usefulness of Schultz's methods. Presumably proceeding from the objective of training people to learn deep relaxation by perceiving their own muscle activity via bio-feedback, these investigators were early concerned with obtaining results in the most efficient manner. One assumes they argued that if their subjects could become aware of the most subtle changes in muscle tension with bio-feedback, then helping them along with techniques such as Schultz's or Jacobson's couldn't really hurt. The chief difficulty with Autogenic Training and Progressive Relaxation was their very long course, taking something like two years to go to completion. But A.T. and P.R. had been proved over and over to correct disturbances of body function: Why not combine this certainty with the new muscle feedback procedure? At least the combination treatment could help to determine whether muscle feedback improved or shortened A.T. or P.R. therapy. Autogenic Training was chosen to use with bio-feedback training because of its greater emphasis on and use of mental activity.

Fortunately for thousands of muscle-tight people, combined BFT and A.T. proved even more worthwhile than had been anticipated. There have been a sufficient number of experimental and developmental studies conducted to date to lead us to say with some conviction that combined BFT and A.T. can produce therapeutic relaxation to a degree not before possible to experience. The explorations of Budzynski and Stoyva into the combined question of whether profound muscle relaxation, if realized without too much frustration, was in fact a basic therapeutic tool of wide applications and whether the bio-feedback of levels of muscle tension could bring relaxation techniques into a broader realm of usefulness were explorations which should, in my mind, be considered classics of well-directed, logical, common-sense, scientific studies in their own time. The research team was successful in putting relaxation on a standardized base, making all degrees of tension and relaxation specifically identifiable for both the patient and therapist to perceive and to use.

The Stoyva and Budzynski team is an ideal one, capable of bridging the gap between the interest of basic science and of applied therapeutics. Stoyva, a psychophysiologist trained in relaxation techniques and a sleep researcher, joined with Budzynski, an electronics engineer who completed a Ph.D. in psychology during the bio-feedback studies. These neatly complementing backgrounds allowed the researchers to define their instrumentation requirements precisely. They designed their experiments for measuring changes important to understanding the mechanisms of the changes, but at the same time to keep the study oriented toward maximizing therapeutic benefits.

The beginnings of these discoveries might seem very ordinary. It began by the two young men discussing the contributions of their special scientific talents to therapeutically useful relaxation, and ended with an ad in the newspaper. The ad solicited people suffering from tension headaches to participate in a laboratory experiment. The overwhelming response to the ad was a crowd crying for help. Unhappily the requests to participate, trustingly, in an untested therapy had to be screened in order to achieve useful, reliable results. Headaches which couldn't be classified as due to tension couldn't be considered for treatment, nor could people who couldn't be counted upon to keep accurate records of their feelings and headaches, nor people who had too many other types of physiologic disturbances—the hypochondriacs and the real neurotics. The exclusion of patients desperate for treatment is a traumatic experience for the clinical researcher. Yet he must keep to his objective, otherwise the true effectiveness of the new treatment could not be evaluated properly, and widespread use would have equivocal results.

The tension headache was chosen because the malefactor was

muscle tension and represented a clinical condition caused almost beyond doubt by anxiety and stress. Classically the tension headache is a dull ache across the frontal areas of the head, usually accompanied by the pain of tension in the neck muscles. It tends to begin in the mornings and may last all day. Although executives feel that the tension headache belongs to them exclusively because they can point out so easily the tensions they live under, tension headaches can affect anyone who has more tense and anxious situations than he can handle.

Over the years most people who have tension headaches become aware of the "knots" that gather in the muscles of the neck where they attach to the back of the skull. These may become excruciatingly tender and are usually fairly slow to relax even with the best of massage. It might have seemed that Budzynski and Stoyva should have chosen these vulnerable neck muscles as the muscles most crucial to demonstrating whether muscle bio-feedback could produce more effective and more accurate relaxation than other relaxation techniques could. But for scientific reasons they chose the frontalis muscle of the forehead. It is a muscle rather difficult to relax, one reason being, I suppose, that most people aren't aware of muscles in their foreheads.

First it was necessary to demonstrate that muscle tension of the frontalis muscle was high in tension headache. True enough, the tension levels were found to be considerably higher in people who chronically suffered from tension headaches, and true, too, that the tension of this muscle was harder to relax than the tension of other muscles. But one great, perhaps unexpected, benefit was that when relaxation of the forehead muscles was learned with bio-feedback, the relaxation effect spread to most of the other muscles of the upper body—to the neck, chest, and shoulder muscles.

Therapy Can Be Pleasant

In the general procedure for muscle bio-feedback you are put into a dimly lit room in a comfortable chair and then small electrodes are pasted on the forehead. You are told that a tone will tell you how relaxed or how tense you are. The higher the tone becomes, the more tension there is in the muscle. It is your job to relax and try to keep the pitch of the tone low. The tone is your guide. There may be an assistant guide as well: the box housing the bio-feedback instrument may have a counter which keeps supplying you with a numerical sum of muscle activity added up over successive short periods of time. It may seem to you a straightforward step between the small electrodes on your forehead to the soft tone in your ear and the subdued flashing numbers on the box, but the muscle bio-feedback instrument is actually a new technical development of startling complexity (see Figure 4). Its job is to sense the electrical firing activity of a relatively small number of muscle cells. Although the voltage developed when a single cell fires (during contraction) is quite large considering the microscopic nature of this muscle universe, the voltages occurring during recovery from firing are opposite to those of firing, and because the cells fire rapidly but at different times, when the voltages add, the total is often less than that of a single cell. The average voltage recorded from the frontalis muscle at moderate tension is about 50 microvolts, i.e., 50 millionths of a volt, and at rest it may go as low as 5 microvolts. It requires some electronic magic to capture such small electrical signals with any degree of fidelity. Then there is another problem. If the muscle signal were used directly to activate the tone, the extremely rapid cell firing would cause the bio-feedback tone to warble, with annoying auditory flicker between high and low tones. This problem is solved by adding the electrical signals in a way that eliminates the rapid fluctuations, and this in turn is used to drive an oscillator which emits (to the speaker) steady streams of auditory vibrations that reflect the level of accumulated electrical energy. You might hear a pleasant tone that changed in pitch as muscle tension changed. The accumulated muscle signals can also be used to operate a visual signal of how much muscle tension occurs over the preset time periods. This can be the counter, which would show a number to indicate the total amount of muscle tension that had occurred during the past few moments.

As efficient as the muscle feedback instrument is, there remains the problem of matching the person to the machine. In the case of initiating muscle bio-feedback the problem is, as with the faulty gas gauge, no one knows how much low tension relates to a low tone until it becomes zero. In other words, the lowness of the tone

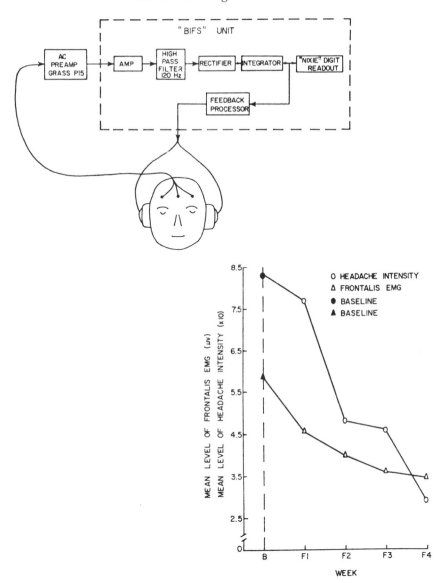

Figure 4. The diagram in the upper left shows the EMG bio-feedback system used with the temporalis muscle of the forehead.

The graph represents headache intensity and muscle tension for five patients over a five-week period of a tension headache study using EMG bio-feedback as therapy.

(From T. Budzynski, J. Stoyva, and C. Adler, *Journal of Behavioral Therapeutics and Experimental Psychiatry, 1*, 205–211, 1970.)

depends upon how the machine is set. What may be low for one person may be high for the next. If you begin a muscle bio-feedback relaxation session and you are tense but are not aware of how tense, how can you get a clue about the muscle relaxing if the tone stays high? Currently, bio-feedback researchers cope with this problem by regulating the feedback given to the subject. The therapist "cheats" a little in the beginning so that you can distinguish not-so-high muscle tension from just slightly higher tension. Otherwise the relaxation treatment techniques would simply be just another frustrating, anxiety-producing experience. For this reason, in beginning treatment the therapist "helps" you to discriminate between levels of tension by adjusting the gain on the bio-feedback instrument; that is, what pitch of the tone you will hear for the muscle tension you have. At first he makes it a little easy for you to lower the tone, just enough so that when the muscle relaxes even slightly, you can get the "feel" or the sensation of slight relaxation. After you learn that, the therapist makes it a little more difficult for you to lower the tone. You have to relax more in order to make the tone lower. By degrees, and over several treatment sessions, you pick up more and more clues which enable you to distinguish different levels of muscle tension. And finally, there is no need for the signal.

Before giving discouraged tension headache patients hope of a new treatment, Stoyva and Budzynski established the validity of their new approach in subjects *not* suffering from unusual increased muscle tension. The objective, of course, was to determine whether bio-feedback of muscle tension information of itself would assist in achieving a significant degree of relaxation. In such demonstrations it is necessary to provide evidence that every condition of the treatment *except* the single most important element does not produce the same effect. Some subjects, therefore, were placed in the same situation as those receiving the muscle feedback information, but they received either misinformation or were simply told to relax. In the Budzynski and Stoyva experiments some subjects heard a tone which varied such as the average person's might during muscle bio-feedback, but was merely a random sound and not the muscle activity of the subject. Other experimental subjects heard a consistently low tone which they were told would be conducive to learning to relax. But no feedback.

Almost anyone left alone in a dimly lit room with nothing more distracting than a low tone or a softly changing tone will relax some over time, and the subjects without bio-feedback did relax. But *with* bio-feedback, subjects relaxed at least twice as deeply as those subjects without bio-feedback. In other experiments the same persons were subjected to all three different conditions, and all showed only modest muscle relaxation when there was no muscle feedback but excellent relaxation when they had the opportunity to monitor the actual tension in their frontalis muscles.

Now that Budzynski and Stoyva had provided convincing evidence that bio-feedback possessed a unique and powerful effect in and of itself, research could move into the next phase, where its usefulness as a therapeutic tool could be evaluated. This is where the tension headache study actually began.

Tension Headache

When a researcher is first exploring a new technique in human beings, it is always a difficult decision to reserve some of the sufferers for what are called "control" groups. Such control patients may have to continue to suffer so that the superiority of the new treatment over no treatment at all can be proved beyond question. Other sufferers may be given a treatment known to be effective so that the effects of the new treatment can be compared precisely, including comparison of any undesirable effects that might occur. For the tension headache patients, one group received no treatment, while another heard a continuous low tone during the "treatment" sessions which mimicked the sound the patients heard who actually did receive muscle feedback. All subjects were, however, encouraged to relax as best they could. All of these subjects were controls. The muscle bio-feedback group had the benefit of the new muscle bio-feedback treatment as described above.

Again the studies revealed a most satisfactory effect for bio-feedback. The tension headache patients responded to muscle bio-feedback with a dramatic drop in both the frequency and intensity of their headaches. All of the subjects of the study kept hourly charts to document the occurrence and intensity of their headaches, and this was done for at least four weeks. By the second week of their training the average "headache index" had fallen off by 50 percent, and was down nearly 75 percent by the fourth week (as in Figure 4). All this was achieved by providing the patients with accurate and continuous information about the tension in a relatively obscure muscle in the forehead. (And, of course, giving the subjects the atmosphere and encouragement to concentrate on their muscle abilities; this will be discussed more fully later, for it may be a crucial factor in the way in which bio-feedback produces its effects.)

Learning to Be Tense

One school of bio-feedback researchers is committed to the EMG (electromyograph) machine and its promise for guiding the patient to effective, therapeutic relaxation. The EMG machine started out as an instrument whose function was to record on paper, or via an oscilloscope, the electrical activity of muscles. Early bio-feedback researchers simply made the record of muscle activity available, in modified form, to the person whose muscle activity was being recorded. One of the earliest researchers to report on studies using external indicators of internal muscle states was Ralph Hefferline of Gestalt therapy fame. As with most dedicated researchers, Hefferline arrived at new concepts by way of ingenious means for testing his theories. One concept, however, that then remained unrecognized even by Hefferline himself was bio-feedback. His underlying thesis at the time of his muscle studies was to develop both the theory and a technique for conscious body control. The specific concept of one part of his work was built around experimental evidence and clinical observations that chronic muscle tension (including mildly abnormal patterns of behavior) stems from learned *blocking* of signals from the muscle and tendon sensors. Such a blocking would mean that central control would be deprived of information it needed to make adjustments for the muscle system to be appropriate to the situation inducing the tension.

In the old days when children were to be seen and not heard, it can be speculated that the children, being social creatures, learned to respond to social situations by imitating what they saw as appropriate and acceptable behavior for the adults. Their elders had, however, quite a different notion: children must first learn to contain their spontaneous behavior until the rules were learned. In the absence of an effective outlet for the natural behavior, Hefferline suggested, the body activities accompanying or even implementing natural behavioral responses were held back. While it is not difficult for most of us to conceptualize the mental learning and conscious understanding which develops under the tutelage of authority, we are scarcely ever given the opportunity to examine the insides of our muscle cells to learn what the behaviorally blocked learning means to our only implements of behavior.

We can perhaps now imagine the but-not-to-be-heard-only-seen child holding back his emotional expressions by choking up at the throat, or by clenching the jaw, or perhaps by tensing the whole body so as not to be tempted to open the mouth. Psychology theorists argue this as a conditioned avoidance response, and the argument certainly seems to have merit from the experiential standpoint. As the child is continually reminded to repress his emotional expression, so he reminds his body to repress his emotion.* The implementing muscles are held back, and over time the conscious awareness of the holding back passes into unconscious nonawareness. But the muscles remain at the ready. Their tension becomes set, and the potential for truly appropriate responses is diminished. The adult evolved from such training might be your noncommittal friend or the shy, retiring acquaintance. He may be, too, the neighbor who is doctor-shopping.

Hefferline's concept of the learned inhibition of natural muscle responses led him to believe that the average human being could become aware of the exact amount of tension in his muscles. Aside from the implications for learning awareness of private muscle activity, he also showed genius by devising an experiment in which the learning ability of the muscle sensor systems could be demonstrated and then what the import of such learning was for un-

---

* More than daily experience, the total life experience may be affected by social and cultural influences which day by day repress natural muscle activity until every muscle tenses and bends with repression, fails to push forward the blood to nourish the body, the body becomes susceptible to infection and disease, the mind fails to cope, and finally comes a premature end to life. Today especially the social demands of machismo, radical new life-styles and the ambience of a drug culture seem to lead to even more violent consequences as large numbers of youthful suicides testify.

pleasant (or pleasant) living. His studies, reported in 1958, in retrospect now seem alive with the principles of bio-feedback. His work to support the contention that people could learn the precise amount of muscle tension they had did not result in the technique becoming the forerunner of bio-feedback technology because his objective at that time was only to provide subjects with the means for devising a "yardstick" by which to estimate the intensity of their muscle tension as they became aware of it. The yardstick was a meter which showed his subjects the relative amount of tension in the jaw muscles. For a portion of the experiments the subjects tried to match a preselected muscular tension of the jaw. In other parts the subject was asked to reproduce the selected tension simply by becoming aware of the proper tension and remembering it when the meter was not present.

The experiments were all successful although it was stated that "performance with visual feedback shows no improvement" (over simple recall alone). The subjects certainly did have the bio-feedback tool—but they were not asked to attempt to shift the amount of muscle tension intentionally, only to recognize how much tension there was.

Individuals in the study who were made curious by the challenge of becoming aware of the lost feelings in their muscles, and who persisted in exploring the messages of the previously ignored muscle sensors, reported the emergence of lost memories. These were usually associated directly with the experiences that had initiated the blocking of the muscle-sensing machinery. If the reader wonders why research such as this was not more vigorously pursued and why scientific curiosity failed to be stimulated, he is not alone in his wonder. As we will detail a little later, the discovery of man's ability to exert voluntary control over even as few as four single muscle cells came about by quite a different approach to man's interior functioning. Although the great bio-feedback revolution did not take shape following Hefferline's experiments, several very important directions that were ultimately important for useful, therapeutic bio-feedback did emerge from these studies.*

In real fact, Hefferline's studies fell under the broad theoretical

---

* See footnote page 145.

cover of the conditioning theory of behavior. His attention and that of those who read his reports was focused upon the shaping of behavior by stimuli in the external environment. Although the study provided an ingenious method for detecting previously inaccessible internal mechanisms responding to external events, it was considered unrealistic to entertain notions of voluntary control over internal, automatic, apparently self-contained physical processes. The community of psychophysiologic researchers was fairly well dominated by proponents of conditioning theory, the principle that argues that all behavior is simply a response to and is dominated by stimuli occurring in the external environment. Quite out of favor at the time were the advocates of the experiential influence on behavior, that school of thought which believes that reorganization of thought patterns, such as insights, developing new concepts, mental orientations, and other subjective phenomena are equally powerful determinants of behavior.* The dominant behaviorist school has successfully ignored such possibilities, and its task of proving theories is greatly simplified because evidence for its theories can be presented in purely physical terms. The withdrawal of a hand to painful stimulation can be documented in terms of physical change; the mental processes affecting the degree of resistance to such movement are infinitely more difficult to quantify.

The flurry of critical comments aroused by B. F. Skinner's recent book *Beyond Freedom and Dignity* illustrates a vigorous change in attitude in conditioning theory as being the ultimate answer to the origin and mechanisms of behavior. Aside from errors in the basic

---

* The Hefferline type of study actually provided more of a base for Gestalt therapy than it ever could for conditioned learning theory or behavioral therapy in whose mold it was designed. While it is not within the province of this book to discuss psychologic theory and its clinical practice, we should draw attention to all of the earlier experimental work that had unwittingly utilized bio-feedback principles, and to the fact that all bio-feedback work itself appears to fortify Gestalt concepts. In bio-feedback the mind and body use information about internal and external events in a remarkably efficient and effective way to change both internal processes and the relationship between the perceived world and the self. This information is *not* discrete, nor is it isolated; it is, rather, information about fluid relationships and dynamic function that is understood and utilized as an organized, meaningful, holistic pattern. Both the psyche and the body are in a state of continual flux—to change one element of it means that its entire sphere of interactions and relationships must also be changed in relative and suitable proportion. It is most parsimonious (as body processes are) to conceptualize the process of such complex changes in terms of patterns.

assumptions of conditioned learning theory, part of the current revolution brewing about what makes people tick is probably an intuitive revulsion to the idea of being controlled behaviorally by someone else.

Release from Anxiety

As Hefferline's concepts had suggested and Budzynski and Stoyva recognized early in their work on the muscle bio-feedback, high levels of muscle tension are a common denominator in many psychosomatic illnesses. The common sense of this statement is so well known by the average man that it is nearly always the first comment made when someone's new illness is discussed. The possibility, in fact the probability, that an illness is psychic in origin is so well known that it often hovers in mind even in established physical illness. Yet the psychic origin is almost assiduously ignored in medical treatment. The reverse is generally true of the psychiatrist or psychologist who rarely follows *physiologic* characteristics in his treatments. Perhaps bio-feedback is the medium which can unite the mind-body interactions and may give rise to a new school of therapists who can consider both aspects of human beings in their treatments. The presence of muscle tension overload in all varieties of physical and mental illness is widely acknowledged, but until the arrival of bio-feedback neither medical nor psychologic treatment approaches had any reliable way to measure either the seriousness or the extent of tenseness, and no way to measure effectiveness of therapy on the ubiquitousness of the involvement.

I am reminded of the work of Friedman and Rosenman in San Francisco and the work of many others who have demonstrated the uptight constitution of coronary patients. This is only one of countless distortions of healthy muscle balance which may be amenable to muscle bio-feedback treatment. If certain types of chronically uptight people are likely candidates for coronary attacks, then learning to keep relaxed under the constant stresses of life may add immeasurably to their lives. There is even the logical hope that such learning can be extended to the heart muscle itself, providing a learned, built-in life-saving device. There would be less total stress to require the heart to exert itself excessively and less total muscle tension on the arteries that acts to intensify vascular pathology.

In the realm of emotional and mental problems one of the most dramatic aberrations which human beings may suffer but still live with is the phobia, an acute fear about certain objects or circumstances, such as excessive panic about snakes or about leaving the house, or sometimes panic about nothing that can be consciously identified. These isolated bits of psychologic malfunction lend themselves to ready identification and the success of psychologic treatment is clear cut when it occurs. The development of panic or phobias is much like developing a chemical sensitivity. Over time one becomes more and more sensitive to the specific chemical—for example, certain detergents—until just a pinch of it can cause an excruciating response of the skin or nose. So it is with anxiety-producing situations: under special conditions the more often or the more intense a situation appears, the more emotional response it evokes. Along with Schultz and Jacobson and their respective relaxation therapies, behavioral therapists also have felt that such acute episodes of anxiety could not exist in a condition of relaxation, the antithesis of uptightness. Many therapists believe that relaxation and anxiety are almost mutually exclusive conditions of the body's response states.

Behavior therapy treats certain illnesses as learned phenomena. The conditioning theory of learning which has dominated in the United States for the past thirty-some years attributes learning of biological responses to changes in the environment. While I and many other biological scientists are convinced of the serious limitations and contrived oversimplified artificiality of conditioning theory, as is frequently pointed out in this book, nonetheless the definitive exploration of most any theory yields new insights. If we apply the conditioning theory of learning to the development of an illness, we discover that the individual, in some way through the continued impact of elements in the environment, learns to continue an undesirable response. A youngster may have gotten spanked at the end of an argument between his parents. His confused understanding and emotions are associated with his struggle to control the sobbing in his chest. Even without the spanking at the end of the next argument, his chest remembers. It grows into a spastically performing function, checking off the emotions at the chest, and depending upon the significance of the situation, the youngster may develop asthma. His mind-body responses gave him the only defense he knew, and the defense generalized to other traumatic situations. His mind and body have learned: asthma.

Behavior therapy is essentially the unlearning of a bad emotional habit by subjecting the individual to exactly the same kind of learning procedure that is postulated as causing the erroneous response. Except that now the consequence of the same learning is changed to a desirable one.

One interesting new application of therapeutic relaxation has been its incorporation into new behavioral treatment programs typified by Wolpe's desensitization technique. In such treatment procedures the anxious or phobic patient is faced with his own visual images of the events or problems causing his anxiety or phobia, and is trained to keep relaxed while reliving the situations through the images.* The patient is said to become "desensitized," that is, he becomes less and less sensitive to the events that cause him emotional distress. The anxiety-inciting problem is visualized as intensely as possible, beginning with the least anxious symbol. The patient is encouraged to stay relaxed, not to respond to the thought and the image of the problem. Since the patient has made a habit of tension even with the faintest thought of his problem area, he must be taught how to relax and stay relaxed. The initial procedure is thus learning how to relax and this aspect of treatment appears to underlie the majority of such behavior therapy techniques. Only after relaxation is learned does the desensitization procedure appear to become effective. The patient's task is to learn to *stay* relaxed while he visualizes the memories of his anxious moments. As he proceeds through the hierarchies of tension scenes from least to most traumatic, he becomes more and more keenly aware of degrees of tension and relaxation, and as this happens the procedure shifts to the real-life situation, gradually, as he has learned to do with the images. Finally the patient learns to stay relaxed in the real world of problems and anxieties.

* One of the most famous examples is the spider phobia.

The Many Faces of Bio-Feedback

The role of muscle bio-feedback in this type of treatment program is readily apparent. The patient uses the monitor of his muscle tension to identify particular states of tension. The bio-feedback indicator may be a meter that monitors the muscle tension, as illustrated in Figure 5. As with the experiments with the frontalis muscle, he uses the information to become more and more intimately aware of how his muscles are responding to difficult situations and even images of them. The therapist now has an accurate and reliable gauge of how the patient is responding. This benefit is also of considerable importance with respect to the continuing motivation of the patient. Without the bio-feedback there were no indicators of small changes in tension. Sensations of change previously occurred only with spurious episodes of relaxation. The long delay until the patient could become truly aware of body tension was frustrating and taxed the patience more than many patients felt able to bear. With bio-feedback the auditory and visual signals of even small changes are encouraging, and the morale boost that this gives is no doubt one of the many reasons why bio-feedback possesses inherent therapeutic value. And when low, low levels of muscle tension are attained, bio-feedback signals assure the patient that the reward of the goal is in sight.

The most profound and revolutionary feature of the bio-feedback technique lies in its involvement of man's conscious intelligence. This is in sharp contrast with characteristics of all other medical therapeutic techniques. As for psychiatric therapy, the long course required to cajole patients into discovering problems hidden in their subconscious has lost considerable ground to new techniques involving the body responses of emotion. This gap between the nonpsyche treatment by medicine and the nonbody treatment by traditional psychiatry is bridged by bio-feedback.*

The muscle feedback signal also contributes to success of the therapy because of its remarkable sensitivity. During the patient's

* Older forms of psychiatry, and particularly psychoanalysis, have also been losing ground to variations of treatments that consider the essential unity of mind and body: group therapy, sensitivity training, body awareness therapy, etc. Many are now combining these new psychotherapeutic forms with bio-feedback.

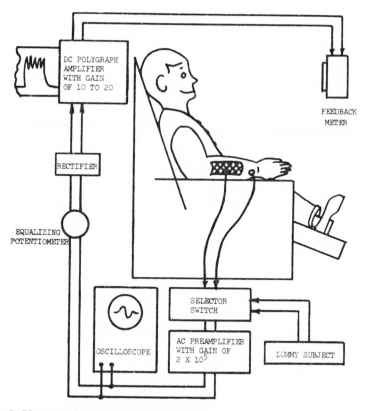

Figure 5. Diagram of another type of arrangement for muscle bio-feedback. (From E. E. Green, A. M. Green and E. D. Walters, in *Progress of Cybernetics: Proceedings of the International Congress of Cybernetics,* London, 1969 [ed. J. Rose]. Gordon & Breach, London, 1970.)

visualization task the muscle indicator can "read" anxiety expressed in tension long before the patient becomes consciously aware of it. If the image is one causing considerable anxiety, the therapist can watch the muscle monitor and "see" the build-up of anxiety, and can terminate the visual exercise before the anxiety becomes too intense and detrimental to therapeutic progress. The patient is not only spared undue anxiety, but can recover his relaxed state more quickly. By properly adjusting the amount of tension allowed during the therapy, the patient has the chance to gain longer and longer periods of anti-anxiety, the relaxed state. The effect carries over for longer and longer periods until eventually the tendency for relaxation is carried directly into the real-life situations causing the problem.

Changes in states of consciousness which accompany the release from muscle tension no doubt also contribute to the beneficial effects of muscle bio-feedback to help alleviate anxiety states. Although phobic and high-anxiety patients are likely to be much too preoccupied with the immediacy of their own problems to concern themselves with new sensations, such new subjective changes have been documented for the tension headache subjects receiving feed-back therapy. Some of the sensations are those that naturally follow achieving true relaxation, such as feelings of heaviness and tingling in the limbs, or feelings of warmth, and even increased salivation. These are the results of changes going on in the autonomic nervous system, occurring when the muscle tension is relieved and allowing better general circulation of blood. There are, in addition, sensations that are new in the sense that we have them so fleetingly that there is no opportunity to identify them. The bio-feedback relaxation subjects reported sensations such as lightness, floating, even turning. Many reported a flow of imagery. And at the end of the training sessions they described the experience as pleasant and restful.

Bio-feedback adds so much to both the underlying relaxation process and to the desensitization treatment program that the question arises as to the cogency of the popular behavioral therapeutic techniques. The very term desensitization means to reverse the process of becoming sensitive to particular irritations and to learn *not* to respond to them either emotionally or physically. Without the internal, intimate knowledge that bio-feedback gives, there would seem to be little chance to affect the mechanisms that underlie the subtle complexities and nuances of unsuitable, inappropriate, or destructive emotional behavior. The human mind is distinguished by its ability to diversify its perceptual associations. Each part of a scene is associated and interpreted differently depending upon the arrangement of the other parts of the scene. But every variation of every part can be remembered, associated, and reassociated. It is curious that repeated experiences, either actual or visualized, can first continue to intensify fears and anxieties, and then subsequently the same experiences effectively continue to diminish the same fears and anxieties. The only difference between the causative experience and the therapeutic experience is that during treatment the patient learns not to let his body respond, not to tense. The thrust of the therapy is to manipulate the external environment and to encourage diminished response to stress. Based on conditioned learning theory, this type of behavioral therapy is a human replica of laboratory animal learning experiments. Neither subconscious motivation nor subjective experience is considered. Although in wide use, the technique has been criticized on the basis that the "conditioning" process alone is weak therapy, becoming successful only when more personal aspects of the patient's mental and emotional needs receive attention.

Bio-feedback forces the participation of the patient's consciousness. Streams of information pour into the brain through the eyes and ears watching and listening to the dancing of the muscle cells. Where does the information go? Certainly not directly or solely to the muscles again. As with any information the individual perceives, the new data are distributed, filed, associated, stored, redistributed, refiled, reassociated and restored. Those researchers and theorists who believe that learning is the reorganization of perceptual information offer a concept of the way man learns that has greater appeal to those of us who feel that evidence points toward the mind's possessing activities as a whole that are different from the sum of its activities. If the concept has merit, then one would expect that the bio-feedback information could eventually be incorporated into the structure of other memories, and that its subsequent reorganization could account for the ability of human beings to use the fedback data for a positive action of changing its seemingly autonomic functions. Perhaps as the new information is circulated about, awaiting to be deposited in the appropriate file, it makes contact with memories of body sensation. This might lead it to an association with memories of profound relaxation.*

* One of my subjects for a study on the possible effects on anxiety of learning to control theta brain waves is a good example (although possibly exceptional in the rapidity of the therapeutic effect). She quickly became proficient in controlling her theta waves, which were "fed back" to her by a soft, diffuse green light. She later reported that she attributed her improved mental state and relief from anxiety to the fact that when faced with a frustrating or anxiety-producing situation, the "feeling" of the green light intervened. She would feel suddenly relaxed, as if the relaxing and insightful experience of the theta wave–green light was a timely and natural—and now automatic—response.

A Note on the Nature of Muscle Mind Power

I was gathering my notes on muscle bio-feedback together, thinking about the remarkable cases I'd heard about of the use of voluntary control to reduce muscle tension to absolute zero or to control a single motor-neuron and noted that I still felt wonderstruck because it all seemed so miraculous. In my school days all muscles of movement were labeled voluntary and that meant that men of medicine regarded them as under voluntary control. Definition 1. in Webster's dictionary defines voluntary as "proceeding from the will, or from one's own choice or full consent," and definition 4. reads "of or pertaining to the will; subject to, or regulated by, the will; as, the voluntary muscles." Somewhere in the history of psychology someone had forgotten to empty all of the old wastebaskets. They had thrown out the will, but kept the voluntary, possibly because they could define *their* voluntary simply as overt muscle action and that could be measured. But voluntariness still connoted intention, purpose, determination, premeditation. In experimental psychology and psychophysiology the idea of voluntary action was acceptable provided the action expressed a response to the presentation of external physical information which the body sensed and which could be appropriately shaped with respect to the physical dimensions of direction, time, pressure, force, etc. Now through bio-feedback *representations* of internal sensing muscle activity were literally being sensed.

What does it mean to the intentional brain to watch a *representation* of just a fraction of the electrical energy used to produce a movement? The monitor of muscle activity is a symbol, whether it represents accumulated residues of tension at rest or minute electrical surges of the activity of a muscle cell family. It is a translation of subatomic electron flows which organize electricity into a picture or ideograph which becomes significant only after it is explained. The explanation may be as simple as "the dimmer that light becomes, the less muscle tension there is," or even, "something in your body affects that light." There is explanation even in the very acts of attaching electrodes and placing the bio-feedback display in front of the subject. Human beings have the capacity for deductive thought, they put two and two together; they can make associations between abstractions.

I do not think that it can be successfully argued that bio-feedback merely extends the senses. In the early days of my work, I constantly fretted over the nature of the information the human being was being fed back about his physiology via the feedback monitor. I concentrated on the accuracy and fidelity of the information and synchronizing it with its actual occurrence in time and only recently have begun to realize that the information being fed back by monitors is not simple sensory information to be perceived by the sensing organs. It is complex, ideational, abstract, symbolic, associational information requiring cognitive effort before it can be appreciated. In the bio-feedback phenomenon the mind seems to be capable of responding directly and specifically to an abstract symbol. The process may take us into a new area of psycho-philosophy because responses to abstract representations require a mobilization of thought exploratory effort, judgments, decisions, intentions and the will.

FIVE

Nerve-Muscle Cells: Voluntary Control of a Single Cell

Once there was a man so wee
He stood on tippy-toe to see
The inside of himself.

The Quintessence of Voluntary Control

As we went into that first meeting of the BFRS in 1969, most of us were totally unaware that bio-feedback was an almost universal phenomenon. Working in our isolated laboratories, sharing thoughts only within cliquish scientific specialties, and insulated from the real world of battered bodies and emotions, each of us brought to the meeting only tiny, hopeful bits of knowledge none of us dreamed would affect world consciousness when they were all put together. We were confident of interesting and probably important consequences of individual research efforts. We seemed to sense that medicine and psychology were about to hurdle forward together in a great new adventure although no one quite realized the impact of a clearly changing research consciousness beginning with that moment. It was as if we had started on a journey to Mars, possessing workable but untested tools, and we were riding on the tensions of facing a faintly known but unpredictable world.

We had heard Stoyva and Budzynski, been reminded of Jacobson's Progressive Relaxation and of Schultz's and Luthe's Autogenic Training, reviewed neuromuscular physiology, and refreshed our memories about muscle sensors. Now we were listening to John Basmajian give a sparkling discussion of a new field of muscle research. Suddenly the ubiquitousness of man's muscles, the mediators of his mental and emotional intentions, was stretched out before us in panoramic dimensions. Like most people, we were used to thinking about muscles as generators of movement and locomotion. We were listening to what for many of us was our first glimpse of an unknown capability of muscles and the mind they served. As the exciting new research was skillfully interwoven with more familiar knowledge about muscles, we were struck by the universal role of muscles in health and illness, by the mysterious and powerful mind force of muscles, and we struggled to understand a new and different world of muscles. We were being reminded of the powerful influence of mind over muscles, its ready perversion to inexhaustible varieties of psychosomatic problems and its relieving therapeutic benefits of learning to control the subtle tensions of all the body, of learning to "tell" the muscles about new emotional insights.

Then came the climax. The revelation, in all the true meaning of the word, that in some way the human mind, without even telling itself, could learn to control the electrical activity of a single cell.

I was, perhaps, more startled and more stunned than any layman ignorant of biological science. After a lifetime of studying the intricacies of man's body in both good functioning and bad, my memory banks of physiological, pathological and biochemical information suddenly stalled. There was simply no scientifically explainable way in which man could learn to control a single cell of his body. How could he even identify a particular cell? And there were the matters of chemical systems involved in regulating the electrical activity of muscle cells. How could the mind control this complicated microcosm?

Basmajian first briefed us on the neuroanatomy of muscle cells, on how nerves coming from the spinal cord reached and made contact with muscle cells, and how nerve fibrils carried information from muscles back up to the spinal cord. Even experienced bioresearchers need refresher courses from time to time to keep straight the many varieties of physiologic processes. During all of Basmajian's talk the only reference to brain processes was a casual comment that the nerve pathway from the cerebral cortex to the cell connections in the spinal cord was the classical pathway. No one seemed to notice that there was no attempt to account for the new phenomenon by classical neurology. Nerve-muscle business began somewhere in the circular pathway endlessly carrying information between muscles and spinal cord. Deep in the spinal cord, grouped together in a colony with distinctive characteristics, lie the nerve cells whose conducting fibers stretch in remarkable elongation out of the encased spinal cord and course with other motor fibers down long lengths to the body muscles. Here they separate to innervate different areas of the muscles. Any one fiber from a single nerve-muscle cell in the spinal cord may carry electrical messages to anywhere from only three to many hundreds of individual muscle cells by dividing its fiber into terminal fibrils near the cells. It is much like the old-time telephone trunk line servicing a dozen or more home telephones. When a message comes through, the more connections there are, the more signals are sounded. In the case of muscle cells, if one fiber from one nerve cell in the cord services several hundred muscle cells, then the response to the message is one of considerable force. But one nerve cell may service only three or four muscle cells; then the response is weak, even though all three or four cells respond together. One might view the case of a few cells innervated by the same nerve fibril as a fine-tuning mechanism. Regardless of the number of cells innervated by a single nerve cell in the spinal cord, they are called, when taken together with their nerve cell, a motor unit. Like an army platoon, they have but one commander.

It is a great convenience for physiologists that nerve and muscle cells give off an electrical discharge when they are in action, and, subserved by much complex biochemistry, the energy dissipated in the active contraction is renewed almost as quickly as it is used. So there is a second change in the electrical activity of the cells which signals its build-up of electrical energy back to "resting" levels. This discharge and recovery of electrical energy is relatively large for any one cell and can readily be detected by suitable electronic instruments. When a researcher wants to study the action of a single cell, he can do so by "impaling" the cell with a minute electrode which senses the electrical changes in that cell alone. But for practical purposes it is not at all necessary to impale cells. Each motor unit, or family of muscle cells, whether three or three hundred muscle cells, receives its nerve supply from the same nerve fiber. These families of motor units with their motor nerve cell in the spinal cord discharge and recover their electrical energy in quite characteristic ways. Each motor unit has its own electrical signature, easily seen when the changes in electrical energy are allowed to flow across an oscilloscope screen or move a recording pen across paper (as in Figure 6).

It still seems a major miracle that ordinary people can so quickly learn to control such faint whispers of muscle cells so small that it takes many hundreds to be visible, cells buried deep within other muscle cells covered by layer after layer of other kinds of body tissues, muscle cells under the control of microscopic-sized cells deep in the spinal cord and responding to the infinite shading of brain directions. This is what Basmajian explored, and what before him Harrison and Mortenson had discovered.

Scientific history didn't record just how Harrison and Mortenson came to ask their subjects to watch their secret muscle potentials dance across an oscilloscope screen, but there can be no doubt of their surprise and wonder when they found the human mind to be capable of controlling these muscle whispers of infinitesimally small dimensions.

The diagrams in Figure 7 show the way the human subject is attached to the recording device, the oscilloscope, and the records in Figure 7 are enlarged simulations of pictures photographed from the oscilloscope screen while the subject is watching his muscle cell activity. Each pip marked A, B or C etc., represents the combined electrical response of those particular cells innervated by a single motor cell in the spinal cord. Each is the characteristic signature of those cells. These records show the way a subject can mentally and unconsciously select out a specific motor unit and control its appearance on the screen. Figure 8 shows records of a subject who learned conscious control over eleven different motor units, being able to isolate and fire each upon command. In real fact this means that he performed many complex mental-brain functions simultaneously. First, he must be able to distinguish response A

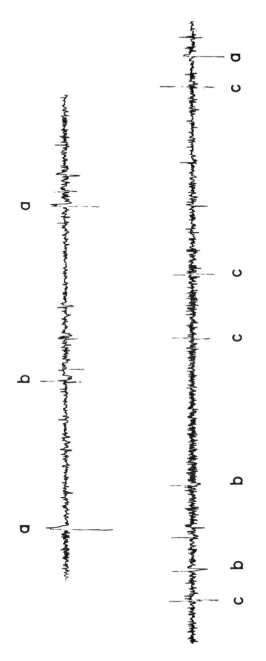

Figure 6. Polygraph recording of a forearm muscle at rest. The large amplitude "spikes" are muscle responses from different families of muscle cells and can be voluntarily controlled as to rate and rhythm of appearance.

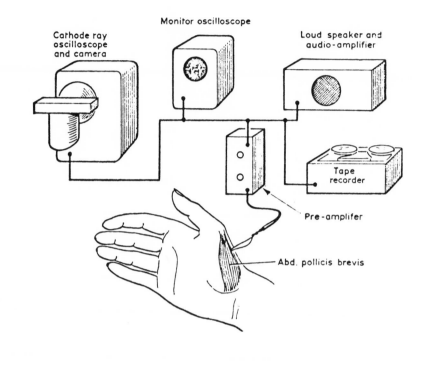

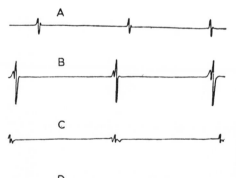

Figure 7. Above is a diagram of the general arrangement of monitoring and recording apparatus used in studies of muscle cell activity.

To the left are tracings of nerve impulses ("spikes") recorded from cathode-ray oscilloscope. A, B, and C spikes were recorded through the same electrodes from different motor units under conscious control. Tracing D is the result of a weak-to-moderate sustained contraction with many motor units "firing."

(From J. V. Basmajian, *American Journal of Physical Medicine*, 1967, *46*, 480–486.)

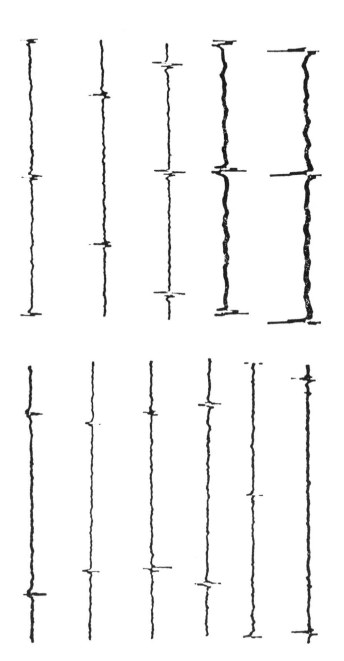

Figure 8. Eleven different motor units isolated by one subject by conscious control. (From J. V. Basmajian, *American Journal of Physical Medicine*, 1967, 46, 480–486.)

from B, and A from C, and so on, and then he must be able, in some
as yet mysterious way, to exert a discriminating and highly selective
influence upon the motor cells in the spinal cord so that all but one
are suppressed or prevented from activity while at the same time
the selected cell is allowed not only to continue its electrical activity,
but is forced to become active upon command.

The first researchers made a puppet show of the motor-unit
muscle cells. The puppets were the different groups of muscle cells
normally dancing in the anonymity of the muscle mass. Their electrical dancing is caught by the electrode, acting like a television
camera, and fed by cables into the television receiver, the oscilloscope version used in laboratories. Each small cell group dances
across the screen in distinctive shapes. Sometimes a sharp, tall
figure, sometimes a figure with a small top and a large curved
bottom, sometimes twins or triplets appearing together. The subjects watching their own interior, minute, unconscious body activity
would begin to say, "Oh, there's Charlie, and there's Sam, and here
come the twins." Then a very curious event occurred. Soon the
subjects began to announce, "Did you know that I can make Charlie
come by whenever I want," or, "Watch me make Sam disappear."

It seems to be a universal human trait to insist upon control over
one's very own possessions or property. And this may be a fundamental characteristic shared in the bio-feedback phenomenon. It
may be irresistible to try to control one's own being. It is almost
automatic for us to take control of those parts of us which we can
see. We look at a finger and move it just so. Or we look in the mirror
and try on different expressions by simple mental command. Perhaps it is so even with the most hidden recesses of our physical
selves. Once we become aware of a new bit or segment of our being,
we seem to be compelled to try to manipulate it. Like pimples, or
warts. Or noticing suddenly long hair or fingernails. Or a blister. Or
extra weight. Whenever we become aware of something new about
ourselves, there follows a drive to incorporate it into or disgorge it
from our body image. We must somehow maintain our body's
natural order.

This basic human drive may someday be found to be of fundamental importance in the bio-feedback phenomenon. The drive to
manipulate our being and existence extends far beyond the bound-

aries of the body; it reaches as far as our being and thoughts can extend. Our manner of dress, our living areas, work areas, we manipulate to adjust snugly around us as part of our being. So it is perhaps natural that once we are aware of their existence we try to bend the innermost, finest physical fibers of our being to our mental commands. This is such a fundamental aspect of animate life that we may never know the precise nature of this phenomenon. Some may call it a God-given ability, some may say it is part of the will. Whatever the source, it is a human capacity of near-infinite power.

Cell Rhythms

From the standpoint of basic medical research, the experimental designs and laboratory execution carried out by Basmajian and his co-workers are superb examples of clarity of purpose and parsimonious operation. Research scientists laud systematic investigations, but they are rarely achieved. Basmajian's work sparkles with precision and steadiness of purpose. It is the basic research counterpart of the clinically oriented research of Stoyva and Budzynski.

As a neuroanatomist, skilled in the sophisticated techniques of tracking the activity patterns of complex relationships between nerve and muscle cells, Basmajian knew better than others the code used by neurons to pass information along among themselves and to the organs they innervated. He knew that the most important variable of the code was the number of nerve impulses conducted down the long lengths of the nerve fibers, and so the information received by muscle cells of a motor unit family could be "read" by noting the rhythm of the electrical impulses. A bip-bip could mean, "Your cell is relaxing," while a bip-bip-bip-bip could mean, "Your cell is too tense." Messages such as this are constantly streaming down the neuronal fibers, and the conversation going on the large nerves enclosing hundreds of nerve fibers may be every bit as great as that being processed in our largest computers. Of course the bip-bips are our translations into sounds or symbols of the electrical changes constantly taking place in the nerves and the nerve-muscle systems.

It may have seemed to Basmajian that if such rhythms in nerve conduction are the sole source of information about how the muscle cells are to be active in different situations, then perhaps such rhythms might have a comparable significance to the human brain if they could be put into the brain via another sensory route, such as ears and eyes. He knew also that the messages flowing through each nerve fiber were different, that is, the rhythm of the impulses was different for each motor unit family. And rhythms are fundamental to living processes. The heart beats in a spontaneous rhythm; each body cell has its own inherent rhythm. Our whole functioning mode as human beings is keyed to rhythm: conversation, music, walking, waving, whatever.

The delicate sensing organs of the ear are exquisitely tuned to distinguishing even the most minor variations in rhythm, and so it may have been natural for Basmajian to choose to convert the rhythmic electrical charges carrying the messages of the motor nerve to the muscle cells into auditory rhythms to be heard by his experimental subjects. Although his sensing electrodes were unbelievably small (25 micromillimeters in diameter), they would sense many different cell families belonging to many different single motor nerve cells in the spinal cord. And in each of these a different rhythm would be heard. With so many different rhythms available, the listening ear at first might hear a mixture of dominant rhythms, much as one can distinguish two or more melodic lines in counterpoint in music, then become aware of the separateness later. So Basmajian's subjects listened, and when he heard an easily identifiable rhythm he would say, "Make that drum roll, rat-a-tat-tat, tat-tat come by again," and in a few minutes his subjects would be rat-a-tat-tatting like the British Imperial Drummer. And how did the subject say he accomplished this neural tattoo? "I don't know" was the consistent answer.

Here is a new puzzle. The human brain can, at a moment's notice, learn to control a few cells encased in his spinal cord. For the most part he doesn't even know what cells look like. He can't feel them, he doesn't even know where they are. But they have spoken to him, and he has answered with a mental command. Here is man in communication with individual cells of his own body.

Listen to Basmajian at the 1969 BFRS meeting:

Remember then, that normal human beings can quickly, in a matter of fifteen or twenty minutes, isolate only one motor unit from the population of perhaps a hundred or two hundred which are within an area of pick up of an electrode pair. They can suppress all of the units, fire single units, manipulate those units, turn them on and off easily, suppress the one they started with, pick up another one, train it, suppress it, turn to a third and then, on command, they can respond with signals from the unit that you chose from them to respond with.

Yet there is no sensation. There is no clue except the rhythm which, in a very real sense, is artificial to the person. It is an electronic conversion to sound, yet the primitive part of the brain is an old friend of rhythms. Is it that our complex brain machinery is so accustomed to the task of discriminating rhythms that no conscious mental effort is required? If so, then doesn't muscle bio-feedback offer us whole new vistas for exploring unconscious, *productive* mental effort? Shortly we will describe the experimental work of Dr. David Kahn, who has used the Basmajian technique to dissect subconscious motivations. But here we must still pursue the problem of how the mind controls a single cell. The scientific answer is a classic of evasiveness. Every neuroscientist knows that the control is a matter of cortical integration; that is, the interface between information coming to the brain from the sensory receptors of the body and the information which is sent out from the brain via the neural effector systems. An interface is a junction where two systems meet and are conjoined, chemically or physically, to communicate with each other; an integration is the combined coordination of all of the input information. These are abbreviated, cryptic definitions for the most complex processes known to man—and for giving a name to a complex process whose mechanism is poorly understood. So it doesn't tell us much that the ability to control a single cell resides in cortical integrations.

Basmajian himself made no real guesses as to the ultimate seat of control. Much to his credit, he may be the first of the modern hard-line bioscientists to use the word "will" in a biological research publication.

Why does this research seem so exciting? Why does it seem to be so important? Or is it really significant and important to the future of man's existence? Is the demonstration that man can exert voluntary control over a single cell simply another research gimmick, a new technique for exhibiting the already known capacities of the mind, or will these new data be a launching pad to send man into the unexplored realms of his interior world?

Skeptics in the frigid, body-only school of human behavioral research can put down experimental work showing voluntary control of single cells by pointing out that even primitive man was endowed with this capability. Fine-tuning control of muscles had to exist to make pottery, to use a spear, to stalk prey, to feed the baby. It should come as no surprise that man's muscles could respond appropriately and selectively as his tasks become more complex. The quickness and precision and shadings of pressure demanded of the pianist must require an extraordinary degree of voluntary control over an enormous array and variety of muscle cells. And these in turn are regulated by the single motor cells in the spinal cord. The heart of the question is, How does such refinement of muscle activity come about, and how is that kind of voluntary control different from the control learned by watching monitors of muscle cell action?

The learning of motor (muscle) tasks has classically been considered by physiologists to depend upon the external guides of position, relationship to objects, and other environmental clues such as perceived hardness (which tempers hitting an object), perceived distance, and so on, along with the internal mechanical factor of proprioception described in Chapter 4. Proprioception is perception of muscle cell activity obtained from the muscle cells themselves, as they undergo changes in length and strength of contraction. During activity the sensors within the muscle cells themselves "sense" the changes going on and relay this information to nerve cells in other muscle areas, to the spinal cord and to the brain. But the data about muscle activity which the sensors in muscle cells relay to the spinal cord and brain is all *post facto* data. It tells what *has* happened. If we read neurophysiology carefully, we find no such mechanical functions to account for the *mental* learning of new muscle tasks. As in dancing. Here is where Harrison and Mortenson's and Basmajian's bio-feedback work brought a new world of light to how muscles learn.

For the first time the importance of vision and hearing in muscle learning had been demonstrated. For all practical purposes the usual guides of tension and position were no longer factors in the muscle bio-feedback experiments. The only remaining clues to the affairs of the muscle cells were the peculiar shapes made by the dancing oscilloscope beam. Or in the case of Basmajian, the bips or clicks the muscle cell poppings triggered to signal their presence. Obviously the information taken in by the eyes and ears could be potentially as important as could the feel of the muscle itself, touching, and being aware of levels of muscle tension.

The Scientific Will

For more than fifty years behavioral science has tabooed the merest hint of willpower as a real product of the human mind and has admitted to study only the elemental forces of physical nature shared by animals. In all of their detailed analyses they have never made studies of love, or heart's desires, or fantasies or longing; and certainly no study of an intelligence higher than or different from that deriving from a vision of computer-programmed nerve cells. Yet here is the strict, scientifically conservative Basmajian talking about the will as the substance behind man's ability to control a single cell. Then again, why not? He was dealing with voluntary muscles, and since the beginning of time the whole world has agreed that the will of man directs the major muscle masses of the body. His brain recognizes and sorts the floods of incoming sensory information, it searches its memory, and somewhere in that interface between sensory and motor systems the strange process of "cortical integration" conceives and fashions a parade of decisions and judgments and conjures up a personal will. It expresses individual purpose, group purpose. But to the materialistic, behavioristic neurophysiologist the will is dismissed as a moral football, a toy created to entertain the mind. It has no substance, no chemicals to measure, no electrical currents to signal its whims. How curious that this mental-spiritual-moral-experiential entity has not been found a fit subject for scientific exploration. Now Basmajian admits it into the cautious neurophysiological literature. And after him, Dr. Elmer Green of Menninger's tags the different aspects of the will by the way in which his bio-feedback results are obtained, as active volition and passive volition. As we have seen, the will was expunged as a mind product early in this century with the revelations of Pavlov that selected bits of the physical environment (tones and lights and shocks) could substitute for certain causes of primitive behavior.

In the late 1890s and early 1900s the laboratory researcher of physiology and psychology still retained the passionate questing of the Renaissance man. Every experiment was an experience for and with the researcher; he was a part of his work, he identified with the subjects of his work, became so much a part of it that every detail was used in his own cortical integrations and he produced rare insights about the workings of man. Then came the upsurge of the physical sciences and Pavlov, whose disciples converted psychology into a simulated physical science, and the school of behaviorism was off and running. Off and running without the mind, outside of the universe of mind-brain, away from the subtleties of human behavior where cognition and reasoning and wishes and aesthetics play their nonphysical games.

The rediscovery of the will may well be a major landmark along the evolutionary path of man. Bio-feedback must be credited with having, at last, discovered new important links in the mysterious chain between mind and body. Not only has it uncovered a real, physical-science acceptable, measurable effect of the will, but it has further produced physically identifiable higher intellectual processes of the unconscious. The effect of these discoveries may soon assist in the evolution of man from a state of behavior control by others to a state of true self-control, a state more in harmony with the order of the universe.

The bridges between the physical world of matter and the wispy, elusive, impressionistic inner cosmos of man are now undergoing ordered construction by use of bio-feedback techniques. The physical manifestations of mind control over all its physical structure and operations bring us closer to understanding the future of man. Decade after decade more of the ultrastructure of man's being has been exposed, yet we have the barest glimmer of how our ordered selves perform the way they do. Science agrees about the ordered universe, including our beings, yet there is not one iota of information, other than that from faith, which even faintly suggests how nature is so ordered. Energies from the future, known but not acknowledged, may play a role. Why, for example, does the number of lemmings born determine the number of eggs the white northern owl will lay? Is it God—or ecologic necessity—or a biologic or mind energy that can be transmitted like radio waves? At this time we do not know. Cells may have their reasons that reason doesn't know. In the processes of our body there may be answers to events not just about our bodies, but about the environment at large. Through bio-feedback we may be able to cue in to the actual knowledge and structure of our body wisdom and learn about ourselves, about our environment, and why the number of lemmings born affects the most intimate biology of the white northern owl. It may be possible for the bio-feedback process to build firm bridges to lead to areas of mind known only in visions.

There has been one "scientific" approach to study of the will put forth by a neuro-psychophysiologist, and it typifies the overwhelming bias of biological science to deal exclusively with physically expressible nature of man. Hans Teuber of M.I.T. postulated a "corollary discharge" system which alerts the brain to compensate for certain physical activities of the body so that apparent stability of the external universe is ensured. He suggests that such an early-warning system is the brain mediator of voluntary or willed behavior, largely, one supposes, because it allows for anticipated behavior and gives the brain mechanisms a chance to plan and control actions. It has been further theorized that this alerting system, which puts a controlling brake on actions, resides in the frontal lobes of the brain. Yet, curiously, neuroanatomists fail to find concrete evidence of such pathways.

Despite the unknown mechanism of the will, the behaviorist psychologists can still take comfort in many of the observations Basmajian and others have made during the muscle bio-feedback voluntary control. For example, with bio-feedback in operation it is much easier to learn to control muscles and muscle cells we are familiar with using, and it is more difficult to learn to control muscles we've had little direct experience with such as back or chest muscles. We deduce then that muscles which have had a good bit of education, like those of the hands, feet and face, have acquired some special way of learning or are smarter than other muscles which haven't made much impression on our awareness. The behavioral scientist calls this generalization "learning to learn," or transfer of learning. That is, all learning, even that of single cells, lays down a "how I learned" memory trace, particularly if the learning was in some way useful to survival, and the cell remembers. The phenomenon of learning how to learn is still largely unknown but essentially it says that there are common denominators among the elements which cause responses, and among the varieties of responses themselves. So the cell or system always has some background information, and the more it has, the more quickly it learns something new. The motor nerve cells in the spinal cord which have had more "training," particularly those in most frequent "willed" or aware operations (fingers, arms, noses, etc.), are brought under voluntary control much more quickly than those supplying nerve messages to the large supporting muscles that are used in rather simple movements. At any rate, this finding seems to fit psychologic theory, except that the psychologists have not yet made it clear whether the principles of "generalization" and "transfer of learning" relate to the amount of physical training a muscle (and its innervation) has had or whether it is the increased mental awareness of the boundaries and capacities which develops when we refine muscle activity.

Another finding with muscle bio-feedback that fits with neurophysiologic theory concerns the sequence in which various muscle units become active, i.e., come under voluntary control, and the location of the different muscle cells innervated by a single neural axonal fiber. Anatomically it is known that the family of cells innervated by that single fiber are not necessarily all clumped together; some cells may be at some little distance from others. But the visual signal used in bio-feedback can sketch characteristic electrical changes such that the trained scientist can locate the scattered cells. And with the bio-feedback training, the conscious control encompasses the entire cell family, regardless of how widely the individual cells are scattered through the muscle. Moreover, the neurophysiologist knows that when a standard stimulus is given to the nerve, small muscle cell families become active first, then the larger families. And so it is with feedback training: the small units learn first, then the larger ones. So consciousness doesn't violate the known physical order of the nerve-muscle system. Also for the physiologist, it is known that functionally there are links among families of motor units, relatives so to speak. And here again the voluntariness of bio-feedback confirms hard medical data, for with bio-feedback training related units are easier to control than unrelated units.

The Will May Know Something Neurology Doesn't

But while some bio-feedback results comfort the physiologist, bio-feedback presents him with disturbing puzzles that are challenges which must be answered. And these puzzles are the strange nonconformities of bio-feedback influence on nerve-muscle events. An observation of Whitney Powers is most curious. He was particularly attracted by the 20 percent of the normal population who couldn't seem to learn to control a single muscle unit. In casting about for ways of improving his bio-feedback technique, he was startled to find that if the same muscle on the opposite side of the body was voluntarily contracted, the original motor unit on the other side began to learn. The muscle unit activity that filtered over to the untrainable side was almost invariably used as clues which the subject incorporated into his associations and eventually used to learn to control the muscle cells he couldn't learn to control before. This curiosity appears to relate to the phenomenon of mirror movement in which the mirror image (such as the other half of the body) is moved instead of the real part. There are medical reports which further suggest that there is cortical representation of the cross-talk between the mirror halves of the body.* Here again, bio-feedback was able to elicit information that previously was available only when damage had occurred in the nervous system.

Another puzzle was revealed from the investigation conducted by Basmajian in which he forced a gross contraction of the whole muscle under study and found that the entire muscle mass could thump loudly with its massive activity, yet all the while trained motor units, their cells scattered within that muscle, could still voluntarily be controlled to continue their tick-tick-ticking. Somewhere, somehow, the normal, "learned" but almost involuntary

---

* Contrary to popular belief, the two halves of the body are not symmetrical. They do have, however, neural communication with each other via the spinal cord at every level of body activity. One purpose of this is to maintain balance and efficiency of movement and purposeful activity. There are special cells in the cortex which monitor the cross-talk and apparently can assemble higher nervous influence to exert effects on the two body halves proportionately.

muscle contraction had been conjoined by a new mind-controlled ability to influence single cells. Dr. Basmajian calls this result "provocative," which is about as close as he ever comes to immodesty about his fascinating work. Basmajian cites an interesting illustration which occurred when his work was being filmed for a television program. The news commentator insisted upon being the volunteer to learn to control muscle units. Rank inexperience in a critical demonstration is always a hazardous business, but the situation was complicated further by the many duties requiring attention of the commentator, and the need for him to be physically active during the demonstration and interview. Again, listen to Basmajian speaking at the 1969 BFRS meeting:

> Now he happened to be what we called a motor unit genius and he, indeed, in the half hour he had available, learned to drive motor units, demonstrated the turning of a little wheel faster and faster, slow it down, turn it off, speed it up and so on, and conduct the interview at the same time. Conducting of the interview for him, although a complex phenomenon, was easy enough so that he could do this other very easy thing.

There are many other intriguing facets of the phenomenon. We have said that the subjects have no recognizable sensations, either about the activity of the muscle units they are controlling or about the feeling they have when they are in active voluntary control. But after a 20-minute period of exerting voluntary control over as little as a single motor unit, the subject is extremely fatigued. And his arm is stiff and perhaps a little sore. The minute energy consumed in controlling a single motor unit can scarcely account for the intense fatigue. One can only deduce that it is the result of the psychologic effort of trying, of the learning process. And while it is easy to ascribe the stiffness and soreness to simple muscle inactivity, we rarely experience such unpleasant after-effects following a period of rest and relaxation. No one has yet suggested the possibility that the stiffness could result from the mental effort expended in suppressing the activity of the many neighboring motor units whose electronic voices would otherwise interfere with the activating control of a single selected unit.

Then there is the subtle yet integral role of the subject's understanding of what the bio-feedback task is all about. Researchers seem to agree unanimously that cognition or understanding or awareness, or some kind of intelligent understanding, is a necessary element in achieving success in voluntary control of muscle units. In one study a high degree of success was achieved by telling the subjects of the importance of the study for future use in the muscle rehabilitation of disabled patients. Moreover it was found the instructions themselves had to be made completely clear for genuine understanding by the subject. This observation fits the theories of the "minority" behavioral psychologists, those who favor the field theory of learning in which the most important component for learning is recognition of the event, that is, it is the *meaningfulness* of a task that determines the nature of the response. This is quite different from the dominant theory that mere repetition underlies learning. Yet the bio-feedback phenomenon can give support to both theories. For if appropriate responses are rewarded or suitably reinforced, bio-feedback is more rapid and efficient, as is predicted in conditioned learning theory.

The voluntary control of a single cell is all the more incredible when one considers the complexity and extensiveness of the neural connections each cell can make with various parts of the cerebral cortex and other parts of the central nervous system. It is estimated that some 600 or more nerve fibers make connection with and influence each motor nerve cell. These in turn may connect with the interconnections of nearly 10 billion brain cells in one hemisphere. The complexity is not only structural, it is the challenge in understanding the functioning of related but separate motor units, each carrying a different message but all receiving the synthesis of information from the 10 billion brain cells. For few if any of the motor units fire together. They are not synchronous. If all individual muscle fibers became active at the same time (contracted synchronously), a large muscle mass such as the biceps could only contract and shorten. But each family of muscle cells fires asynchronously, just enough out of step with each other to allow for a smooth, coordinated muscle movement. It is an inherent and complex property of the nerve-muscle system. The mechanism is even more difficult to understand when anatomy tells us that there is marked asynchrony even among families of muscle cells receiving their nerve supply from motor cells in the same neuronal "pool." This means that the motor nerve cells that lie close together in the spinal cord are subject to quite the same influences coming down from the brain. Yet even with the aid of bio-feedback it seems almost impossible for an individual to select two motor units from the same muscle mass and drive them or control them at exactly the same rate. If the subject does manage to synchronize the rhythm, it is for only a few seconds at a time. It is as if there were a real battle between mind and matter in this instance, for the whole nature of man's physical being argues against the possibility of synchrony, yet there is a striking mobilization of directed neural energy. Even if muscle units from opposite sides of the body are selected, it is only with great difficulty that the two can be controlled to fire synchronously, and then also only for a few seconds. The relative inability to achieve control over synchrony emphasizes the strong natural defenses of the body against inefficiency. For when many muscle cells fire synchronously, the muscle tremors with rapid mass contraction-relaxation cycles and becomes incapable of performing its normal functions.

Reclaiming Muscle Power

There are, unfortunately, a myriad of disabling disorders which involve muscles and muscle systems, almost all of these resulting from a disease process or some damage to parts of the nervous system. Rehabilitation of the neuromuscularly handicapped is an enormous problem area in medicine, usually in the province of the two specialties of neurology and of physical medicine. To date bio-feedback techniques have been investigated as a therapeutic tool in everything from annoying jerking eye movements to incapacitating spastic muscle activity to learning control of artificial limbs, all with an encouraging degree of success. The most dramatic, and the most difficult, application of bio-feedback has been with assisting in the manipulation of prosthetic devices. Long before single motor unit control was investigated, clinical researchers had explored the use of graded whole muscle contractions as sources of different levels of electrical power to operate different directions of mechanical movements. This procedure became known as myoelectric control. Myoelectric assistive devices have been in use for some time in the U.S.S.R., England and Canada. Essentially they require the patient to learn only to tense a selected muscle to three different levels of tension. This is not a difficult task for normal people, but the more extensive the paralysis or nerve-motor damage, the more learning and engineering is required. Since muscle contraction is accompanied by a surge of electrical pressure, there is an abundant supply of electrical power which, after suitable amplification, can actually drive electrical motors. In one such system different degrees of muscle contraction could turn the motor on and off and reverse the direction. With the motor off, a desired movement was held, such as grasping. Other biologically operated devices have been found useful, such as using controlled eye movements to operate wheelchairs. One of the major complaints of this technique is that the muscle under learned control must *not* be one in habitual use. Otherwise normal muscle activity would have to be diverted for the special task of controlling a motor by the same muscle action. Some researchers have found success with vestigial muscles such as the no longer used muscles of the ear.

In terms of present bio-feedback techniques, a fairly primitive form was used in training patients to use biologically operated mechanical devices. While early in the research the patients simply watched their own muscle movements and learned to sort out the most important sensory information needed to accomplish mental control, a number of investigators incorporated elements of conditioned learning techniques by which the patients were rewarded for successful efforts. This meant supplying the patient with something meaningful, since the usual rewards for such human learning experiments, candy or coins, might have too many meanings other than "you made a correct move." The researchers chose, in some cases, a light of different color for each of three different movements to be mastered. According to the principle of operant conditioning, any behavior desired by the investigator (the behavior controller) is rewarded and any undesired behavior is either ignored or punished. With sufficient repetitions of the reward or punishment, the organism eventually selects for specific responding that behavior which is rewarded or suppresses that behavior which is punished. All of this works very nicely in animals, particularly since they give us virtually no evidence that they may be considering other behavioral expressions, but in human beings the conditioning procedure suddenly becomes endowed with a new dimension. That is, the reward or punishment is of itself a source of information. The importance of information-bearing signals is clearly demonstrated in the muscle rehabilitation efforts. Here the patient learns more quickly, more efficiently, and with less effort the more information he has and the more clearly he understands what is going on. This appears to be a universal characteristic and the value of the bio-feedback phenomenon; it takes advantage of human ability to make mental judgments and decisions to speed learning.

When the discovery of voluntary control over single motor units became known, investigators of muscle rehabilitation techniques immediately began to explore the feasibility of controlling artificial muscle devices by conscious control over individual muscle cell families. There was the hope that bio-feedback would obviate the need to use obscure muscles and could allow for more versatility in motor movement. But the same stumbling block that Basmajian encountered proved to be a major obstacle. Patients could learn to control as many as five different motor units, but when trying to operate five different directions of motion (implemented by motors) they could succeed with only three. The question remains: Is this limit a matter of how many different constantly shifting elements the mind can deal with simultaneously, or is each direction of motion a complex sum of several different functions as yet not understood? In Basmajian's opinion many difficult problems must be solved before muscle unit electrical activity can be used successfully and practically for the control of artificial devices to mimic muscle action.

At the same time that myoelectric control with bio-feedback was being studied, Dr. Therese Simard, a former student and co-worker of Basmajian's, was investigating the possibilities of motor unit control and its uses in children. She found that children under six could learn to control muscle units with considerable ease. Many youngsters found it an interesting game at first, but most quickly became bored. She also found that fine motor control was excellent in children between seven and nine years of age but that there was a decrease in skill level in nine- to ten-year-olds. The decrease in skill may be due to the rapidity with which patterns of muscle activity develop and become established in the young.

Next were thalidomide children, those unfortunates deformed at birth from the mother's use of the experimental sedative thalidomide. In general youngsters suffering such deformities had more difficulty in learning to control their muscles via bio-feedback, although most were able to achieve it. These young subjects were seen only once by Dr. Simard, and it is reasonable to assume that further training would have improved their performance. The outstanding difference in the thalidomide children from normal children appeared to be in their lesser abilities for understanding and for paying attention to the task. One explanation for this problem is that they have so little sensory information coming from the areas of the deformities that they receive less feedback than do normal children. Such work, nonetheless, holds considerable promise. Children learn motor unit training easily, even when they have serious muscle problems, particularly before muscle activity becomes set in its patterns. It seems possible that further study of training techniques tailored to children's needs can further improve the extent of motor learning capacity in deformed children.

Critical to the success of such training programs are the supportive measures used to assist people to control muscle units. Nearly every researcher has pointed out the importance of maintaining a relaxed atmosphere, giving clear instructions, and of persuading the subject to commit himself to the learning, and then giving confirmation of success as well as general encouragement.

In studies to determine the fineness and range of voluntary control over single units of facial muscles, Petajan discovered that an *awareness* of the level of effort was critical for achieving control. If attention strayed or the effort was neglected, the firing of the muscle unit slowed dramatically. The learning process, although it can be accomplished in an amazingly short time, is more difficult than it would seem on the surface. In order to maintain any muscle position, even that of apparent rest, opposing muscles must be in balance with each other. This means that many muscle units are active unless consciously directed to become completely inactive. It is not known, of course, whether *all* muscle cells of a normally working muscle can become completely inactive unless some external monitor is available. But we do know in bio-feedback experiments, such as those of Dr. Elmer Green, that large groups of muscle units can intentionally be made totally inactive. It is thus generally assumed that in order to control the rate of activity of a single motor unit, the activity of all other muscle units in the vicinity of the monitoring must first be suppressed. It may have surprised neurophysiologists to find that some kind of awareness was of such critical importance in learning to control single muscle units, yet clinicians attempting muscular rehabilitation have always known that successful rehabilitation depends upon a great complex of mental influences: attention, motivation, desire, and intimate awareness of the "feel" of the deep inside of muscles. Everyone, in fact, who needs manual dexterity for his job or profession understands the intimate relationship between mind and muscles.

The sad memory of hospitals filled with the disabled is never very far from the clinical neurophysiologist's consciousness, and he too dreams of miraculous devices to relieve the suffering. The undeniable evidence of brain control over the smallest portion of the body's systems encourages the dream that someday a mere thought will be sufficient to bring the muscles back to near-normal functioning. Mind activity may someday be read by the EEG machines, and if this is true, then the electrical energy recording the mind activity can be used to help the failing muscles. With this dream in mind researchers are already searching the vast complexities of the brain electrical code for the bits and pieces which can be used to carry out thought commands by salvaged tissue or substitute arms and legs.

Worden Waring, the dedicated bio-engineer who has devoted years to devising motor systems as body part substitutes, has listed a seemingly impossible set of conditions which brain electrical changes must meet in order to operate prosthetic devices and take over for disabled muscles. Whatever brain electrical activity is used to send out commands to the muscles, it must first be related to the desired movement; it must be clearly recognizable, that is, electronically isolatable from all of the other continuous jumble of brain electrical changes; it can't lag too much or precede the desired movement too much; it must be specific to the movement, and moreover, it must be incidental in the sense that it cannot require much, if any, attention; it must occur in most people; it must be accessible (not deep in the brain substance and requiring operation to implant an electrode); and it must be relatively simple to instrument. These are severe requirements indeed to attempt to extract from the ongoing business of the brain. Yet nowadays there are computers to assist, and they promise to save tens of years in the identification of all the minute interrelationships the brain electrical code describes. Thus, the hope for brain-assisted mechanical devices for the disabled is not a too unrealistic hope.

Brain Antecedents (the Muscles Are the Media)

With such a large involvement of brain activity in coordinated muscle movements, some researchers began to search for and found brain electrical activity that correlated precisely with voluntary muscle activity. Not too long ago in the early stages of this research, a large, easily identifiable brain electrical wave was found in the cerebral cortical area associated with muscle movement. It was found to precede the actual coordinated, willed movement of muscles by some half second and was thus labeled the "expectancy wave." No scientific studies have yet been reported in which attempts to use voluntary control of the "expectancy wave" or other muscle-related brain waves in the operation of mechanical devices to help replace or to assist weakened or paralyzed muscles, yet the kind of research described in the next few pages strongly indicates a promising future for both mind-brain assisted mechanical devices and mind-brain rehabilitation of neuromuscular problems.

Two Japanese investigators, Tanji and Kato, subsequently used the bio-feedback technique to pinpoint the relationship between "unicellular" voluntary control (control over single motor units) and brain cortical activity. They found electrical changes occurring in the cortex with each voluntary discharge of a motor unit and which mimicked, in their electrical shapes, almost precisely the sequence of electrical changes which accompanied voluntary movement of the entire muscle. Although some of the brain electrical changes preceded the voluntarily controlled single motor unit activity by half a second, some cortical changes were almost simultaneous, however, and still others appeared nearly a tenth of a second *after* the motor unit discharge. The "late" brain electrical changes might be more apparent than real because of the great difficulty in placing electrodes on the scalp in desired locations and because of problems of electrical interference that occur between the area of cortical change and the external location of the electrodes. "Outsized" cortical responses that were found to relate to the voluntary control of a single muscle unit were nearly the same in size as those related to contraction of the entire muscle. This encouraged the thought that the cortical electrical wave expresses the cortical effort required to select out and control a single unit. The energy used to suppress a number of other motor units in order to isolate and control a single motor unit may also be represented in the cortical electrical change that immediately precedes voluntary movement. The refinement and use of a procedure such as this may only await the cooperation of biomedical electronic engineers.

One very exciting bit of neurophysiologic data has recently been reported in the scientific literature by E. E. Fetz, and D. V. Finocchio, who have demonstrated that a *single* brain cell can be involved in directing a *number* of muscles used to produce a coordinated movement. They studied the relationship between single "motor" cortical cells in awake monkeys to the various muscles effecting a patterned coordinated arm movement. The design of these experiments was extremely ingenious, and by using conditioned learning techniques, the inability of the monkey to understand man's verbal instructions and to give a verbal report was circumvented. The originality of the study is worth reporting.

Monkeys were trained to perform several different tasks, first to simply sit quietly and especially not to resist the investigators when they moved their arms to different positions. Next they were trained to flex and extend the elbow, and finally the investigators "locked" the arm in place and conditioned the monkeys to contract the muscles isometrically when the arm couldn't move. (Try to contract your muscles in your arm for a movement, but don't move it.) In the beginning the monkeys were rewarded by fruit juice for learning the various muscle positions. Later on the investigators isolated and recorded both the electrical energy of the muscles and the electrical activity of the cortical cells. They then used the cortical electrical signal instead of fruit juice to "reward" or signal the monkeys that their muscle responses were correct. Finally, in order to find out what cortical brain cells were related to what muscles, they recorded the electrical activity of each and all of the muscles involved in the coordinated movement along with the electrical activity of a number of single cortical cells.

The results were startling and impressive. A single cortical cell was found to become active in a specific relationship to *all* of the muscles involved in any one coordinated movement. Then, when the monkey's task was to contract a single specific muscle of the group required for the coordinated effort without contracting the rest of the muscles in the group, they found that not only could the monkey isolate the activity of that specific muscle alone and suppress activity of the other muscles normally used in the coordinated movement, but the activity of the cortical cell also continued to accompany the activity of the single selected muscle out of the group normally performing the coordinated movement.

Later on the task became more difficult still when the monkey was rewarded for continuing the activity of that same cortical cell while suppressing *all* muscle activity. This meant that, with training, the monkey could produce a dissociation between the cortical cells used to command his muscles to action and the muscle activity that normally would respond to these commands. The study demonstrated a remarkable flexibility in the brain-muscle system to respond to a variety of different conditions.

While neurophysiologists class such studies as "operant conditioning," it is interesting to note the unusually large amount of bio-feedback information provided for the monkeys during the experiment. One form of the "reward" was a meter whose needle deflections indicated the time and amount of the fruit juice reward and the meter was placed in front of the monkey. Not only did the fruit juice tell him that his performance was successful but he apparently also used the meter as a source of information about what was going on between his brain and his muscles. The experimenters provided the monkey with even more information when they asked him to separate out the activity related to the several different muscles used in the desired movement. Here the activity of each of the muscles involved was represented by a set of colored lights on a panel placed in front of the monkey. Not to miss any bio-feedback bets, the muscle activity was made audible so the monkey could also hear his own muscle activity.

These added bundles of information available to the monkey are identical to those used in the experiments with human beings, and it makes one wonder how the monkey uses such information, and for that matter what his mental processes are when he is given the classical conditioning "rewards" of fruit juice, water, or milk. Behaviorists seem to be content simply to shape or control behavior by constantly reinforcing the animal behavior they desire to elicit, and to be terribly proud of shifting time schedules to have animals perform on schedule so that they can measure the "strength of drive" animals show by shifting their behavior (lever-pressing) schedules to get their rewards. I know if I were a monkey I would think it expedient to answer the desires of the researcher and have an end to the foolishness, and there still remains the possibility that animals think the same. When the scientist reduces behavior to defining the characteristics of the environment and the response to the environment they don't answer the question of *how* or why some information is attended and responded to and some is not. It reminds one of the dog personally trained by Pavlov's own technician. The dog was claimed to be trained to be afraid of the outside steps down from the second floor of the laboratory. On the day of an important demonstration of this conditioned behavior the technician was ill and was replaced by another. The pair, technician and dog, exited from the door, faced the downstairs, and the dog merrily trotted all the way down the steps. Why? Because only the original technician had been conditioned.*

Again it is the interface between the incoming information and the outgoing information that is decisive, the interface between the data coming into the central nervous system from all of its receptors and sensors and the commands transmitted back down the nervous pathways to the effector organs. We are all aware of the limitations

---

* With instances like this, one can't avoid a recurring thought about conditioned learning theory. Who is being conditioned: the rat, the dog, or the man to his own expectations? *What* is being conditioned, what is being learned may be the expectations of the operant conditioner (the instructor). Is it a Skinner in his own Skinner box? Does it have anything to do with what is really going on that is important to behavior and learning—or is it all a matter of expectations?

of the analogy of the computer to the human brain, not only for reasons of efficiency as compared to size, but also because of the versatility of a single functional unit of brain cell–muscle cells as demonstrated so exquisitely in the monkey study. Bio-feedback has rediscovered the importance of the other senses, the eyes and ears and mind, to learning of even the most minute portion of muscle control. Despite years of intensive effort and the development of remarkable electronic tools to identify the ultrastructure of cells, the way in which nerve cells receive and disperse discrete, *meaningful* bits of information is still poorly understood. The receivers, or sensors, that send information into the nervous system are chiefly the muscle spindle receptors located within the skeletal muscle fibers themselves and the Golgi tendon organs located in the tendons of muscles, which sense stretch or contraction. There are other receptors as well, deep in the tissues' surrounding muscles, in joints and joint capsules and around bones. But more than just muscle information is needed to effect coordinated movements. There must be sensors which detect changes in the external environment, such as eyes, ears, and the vibratory senses. Then there are sensors of the internal environment which can, at least indirectly, influence the muscle systems, such as sensors of internal pressures, of heat and of chemical changes. What puts it all together is the brain. There are also widely scattered areas in the brain which exert various types of influence. Some of these sort out incoming information and put order into it, others modulate near-ready commands by integrating anticipatory or novel or contingent information. It is an extremely complex operation. Yet by "mere" intention, this extraordinary, versatile, complex machinery can be precisely directed and controlled. What else can one call it but an act of will? And regardless of the number or intensity of distractions, the intent of the will is carried out.

An interesting digression from the muscles studies of Basmajian and others and a study which must have tickled a lot is that of Gray, who trained people to learn control over single motor units in the external anal sphincter muscle. His reason for studying this muscle was, as everyone is quite aware, that it operationally is in a constant state of tension, and for the most part is under reflex control. To the investigator this meant that under normal conditions there is a constant volley of tonic activity, and to learn to control a single motor unit of the anal sphincter would mean that relatively great numbers of active units must be suppressed. Using small electrodes in the anal sphincter, small bits of the electrical activity of its muscle were recorded on an oscilloscope screen which the subjects could watch. This was the feedback of the activity of the "automatic" muscles they were to learn to control. For additional feedback the muscle activity was also converted into auditory signals. Suffice it to say that the experiments were most successful. There were, however, some curiosities about events ancillary to the learning. First, the subjects found it necessary to rely on auditory feedback. They would identify the activity of the units to be trained by watching the electrical changes on the oscilloscope screen, then turn away their eyes from it to concentrate on the sound of the muscle activity provided by the amplified auditory signals. A second difference was that all of the experimental subjects attributed some of their success to the mental process of "thinking" motor units. This may be another way of saying that they were concentrating, eliminating distraction, and trying to "feel" the process that was evolving between watching the monitor of activity and the influence of their concentration.

Aside from its theoretical physiological significance, the clinical use of a more refined control over the activity of anal sphincters might not only reduce the need for laxatives, but might also be useful on vacations in Mexico.

Relief for Ailing Muscles

Some of the most common physical discomforts that plague people are muscle spasms, painful muscle tension, and the irritation to muscles during recovery from injury. Scientific reports now appearing indicate a future major role for muscle bio-feedback in relieving these relatively minor but most annoying muscle problems. An excellent study by Jacobs and Felton provides exciting proof of the possibility. These two psychologists were aware of the very real clinical problem of inability to relax a tense muscle, particularly one that sustains muscle spasms after an injury. Somehow messages from the muscle sensors become confused under such conditions, and if instructed to try to relax, the patient's muscles become more tense. It was theorized that under these conditions the muscles' sensors were not providing enough information for the cortical integration necessary to produce effective commands for relaxation. Muscle bio-feedback techniques were thus used to augment the amount of information about muscle activity.

The investigators compared a group of patients with recent neck injury with a group of noninjured normal subjects. Both groups were first given "treatment" periods where they tried to relax the shoulder-neck muscles purely by feel, i.e., by relying on the sensors within the muscles, joints and tendons. Then they were given treatment periods in which they could watch their muscle activity on an oscilloscope screen. There was considerable information on the screen; one line marker that indicated how much muscle tension was accumulating over time for various time periods, and a second line that indicated the amount of tension present at any instant. It was somewhat more difficult for the injury patients to get started learning how to relax with bio-feedback than for the normal subjects, but they very quickly caught up, and the total amount of relaxation achieved was the same for both groups. How simple it all seems now. A little machine, a little attention, and the plague of muscle tension disappears.

A case report of a single patient whose injury severed the major facial nerve and left the side paralyzed also merits reporting. The patient's case, reported by Dr. Booker and colleagues, revealed no voluntary function of the muscles on the left side of the face and the patient was unable to close or blink that eye. A surgical procedure was performed in which a nerve going to the big shoulder-neck muscle was sutured to the remaining portion of the facial nerve. Of course activation of the shoulder nerve would now cause movement of the face, but there was first the matter of learning; now it had to be retrained so that it could serve the face. In the treatment the patient watched an oscilloscope screen on which were two separate "tracks" of electrical activity. One track was an artificially produced electrical activity which simulated nerve-muscle action, while the second was a track of the patient's real facial muscle activity. The patient's task was to coax his facial nerve-muscle activity to coincide with the simulated signal in order to restore the normal activity of the facial muscles. In her case, a twitch of the shoulder would also cause, in the beginning, a twitch of the face. With bio-feedback information and practice, the patient soon learned to strengthen the facial muscles and eventually to isolate these for action while at the same time suppressing the shoulder twitch. Later her task was to track the activity of the opposite side of the face in an attempt to achieve normal symmetry of movement. The doctors reported excellent results: apparent complete recovery of both facial function and appearance.

Aside from direct muscle problems, there are a host of disabling muscle ailments that are due to seemingly relatively minor malfunctioning of neural elements as well as a number of serious nerve-damage disorders such as those following cerebral strokes, cerebral palsy, and in types of mental retardation. Dr. James Block, working at the Neuropsychological Center at New York Medical College, has been exploring bio-feedback techniques in patients representing most of these various disorders. He has had good success, for example, in brain-damaged patients who also suffered severe abnormalities of eye movements. After feedback of either auditory or visual information about the activity of their eye movements, the patients were able to bring these disabling, aberrant eye movements back to within normal range. As is usual in such patients, motivation was found to be of critical importance. In younger children, where it is difficult to convey adult logic for encouraging continuing practice (as practicing the piano), improvement in eye muscle activity was consistently less than in older patients. Neither the adults' reasoning insistence nor the "do it for Mother, dear" approach appears to be an appealing reward for children sufficient for them to endure the boredom of practicing the control of an unfelt muscle. It can only be hoped that some of the newer methods of working with children can be applied to improving the training of young disabled children. One questions the assumption that lack of motivation is the chief reason why children between three and six have greater difficulties learning to control hidden parts of their bodies, particularly since most researchers have agreed that the critical element in bio-feedback learning is the development of an awareness of a feeling between subjective reality and the external indicators of the muscle activity.

Dr. Block also reports initial success with bio-feedback conditioning methods in cerebral-palsied children. For these young patients he developed simple devices especially designed for their particular difficulty of managing fine muscle movements. A string is tied around a problem spastic finger, that then is led around pulleys to a system of weights which can control the amount of tension created by the finger when it contracts and straightens. The string is also led to a meter which records the tension in the finger by the fluctuations of the meter needle. The meter is ever so much more sensitive an indicator of tension than is the sensation one gets by trying to change muscle tension by very small degrees. In cerebral palsy, the meter needle would jump out of control the very moment the patient began to move the finger, reflecting the jerking muscle problem of the illness. In Block's laboratory the patient's task was simply to watch the meter reading of the smallest muscle efforts of the finger and to attempt to bring these under control, then to go on to control of more and more small movements.

There is a surprising amount of information in the movement of a meter needle, especially when it is in some way related to the body of the watcher. The rate at which the needle moves, whether it is a smooth or jerky movement, how far it goes, and whether it stops and goes back or goes forward—all of these changes convey different kinds of information. The watcher records these changes through the eyes, the brain sorts out the messages, and in some unknown way begins to make sense out of the total picture which the individual comes to understand on some conscious level.

The problem of spastic fingers and limbs occurs in older people as well as in spastic, cerebral-palsied children, and Block's simple technique seems to be as useful in the older patient as it is in children. It may be that Dr. Block's different kind of neurologic thinking was the key factor in his success. Rather than thinking in terms of joined nervous pathways to convey parcels of information, Block recounts his view that perhaps a thought is a *pattern* of neuronal activation.* In some way, generally because of brain damage, the spastic patient's motor-nerve system is dominated by thought patterns of continuous muscle contraction. But somewhere in the brain

---

* The research of E. E. Fetz and D. V. Finocchio and that of J. Ranji and M. Kato described earlier gives rather specific neurophysiologic support to this concept.

there might still be residual thought patterns of relaxation. If a simple task presented the opportunity to express one of these relaxing patterns during one of its rare appearances, then the patient might be able to apprehend the pattern, at least parts of it, and gradually bring it forward into a more dominant position in his nerve-motor hierarchy of thought patterns. This is essentially what the muscle-string-meter experiment allowed to happen. Gradually the patient learned to replace spasticity with relaxation. It is of course a long, slow, tedious job. The next problem is to make this task more attractive.

Muscle Routes to the Subconscious

The work of Dr. David Kahn, an unusual and brilliant combination of psychoanalyst and psychophysiologist, is striking in its imagination and ingenuity. Dr. Kahn used the voluntary (but subconscious) control of single motor units to track the activity of the subconscious. For the scientist, this is a very ticklish area. If he is a neurophysiologist or neuroanatomist, he doesn't deal with vague subconscious meandering; he may not, in fact, recognize that productive, rational thinking can occur on a subconscious level. There is simply that black hole of the unconscious, where the electromechanical events of the nervous system carry on their patterned functions. But if he is an experiential psychologist or psychiatrist, he tends to be too familiar with the very real influence of subconscious processes and he intuitively assumes that the subconscious is capable of some very high-level mental activity. But his source of information is mainly through anecdotes, not through measurement of physical changes in a body part accompanying subconscious operations. One way to capture and perhaps identify the subconscious is to shape a bridge between the loose, flowing structure of the subconscious and the stolid objectivity of external reality. The bridge must join the subconscious world with the external physical world and be subject to physical measurement. This is the gap Dr. Kahn is briding in his work, and which my own work confirms from quite a different standpoint.

Kahn, of course, is boldly attempting to bridge the abyss of understanding the link between mind and body: a neurophilosophic link to define the complicated, obscure integrative function of the cortex that philosophers call the will. And it is the act of will which can govern the electrical discharge of a single motor nerve cell. Clearly, then, in cortical integration a conglomerate of mental and emotional details are sorted out and evaluated, and thus there is the possibility that changes in the activity of the motor unit while under voluntary control might reflect various aspects of the subconscious. Part of this thinking does, in fact, fit with what we know about the influence of our memories on our behavior. For the most deeply imprinted memories, whether by having them repeated often or because a single experience was so profound, are the most likely to exert a dominant effect. The probabilities are high.

The immediate problem for Kahn was how to control the flow of memories within the subconscious. The storm of activity deep below consciousness has kept itself well hidden; until now we could only reconstruct it long after the storm has blown off in surprising changes of behavior. Sometimes in the laboratories researchers have tried to arouse the subconscious by controlling the input to memory. To accomplish this the psychiatrist may ask what the dream meant, or demand a stream of consciousness to account for an incident of unbecoming behavior. In this process consciousness must first be requested to perform in the hope that it will stir the memory banks of the subconscious and up will come a wish, an emotion, a thought that had been blocked from consciousness. Kahn conceived the idea of arousing the subconscious by means of a subconscious but voluntary act of the individual, believing that this might trigger a direct route to subconscious memories as well as an expression of subconscious activity without any apparent intrusion of consciousness. This would be a bypassing of consciousness, as it were.

To accomplish this, he designed a system in which a meaningful picture could be seen on a screen by means of a light flashing on the screen. The amount of light on the screen was controlled by the action of a single motor unit. The subject first underwent training as in Basmajian's experiments, learning how to select out a single motor unit and then how to exert voluntary control so that the rate of muscle electrical firing would fire right on the dot, precisely at, say, one every second. When the muscle unit was fully trained, the electrical power of that single motor unit was amplified and made to operate the strobe light flashing on the picture projected on the screen. The flashing of the light could be externally controlled as to the duration and intensity of each flash so that at whatever rate the subject's motor unit was firing, the total amount of light flashing would be too weak and dim for the picture to be seen. After that the amount of light on the screen was strictly dependent upon the subject's voluntary but subconscious direction of his motor units which in turn controlled the strobe light. Then the experimenters sat back to see what would happen. The subject might complain that the flashes were too fast or too dim to see a picture he thought was on the screen. Then after a short time some subjects would increase the rate of the electrical muscle firing and be delighted that they could see the picture on the screen. Yet others who subconsciously fired their muscle units faster and saw the pictures voiced a contrary emotion, exclaiming, "Ugh, I don't want to see a picture like that." Then there were subjects who would slow down the muscle firing, diminishing the light still further, and then contrarily remark, "Why don't you put on more light so I can see the picture?"

Why these changes? The subject had already learned to fire the muscle unit at a steady rate; why did he change? And why did he express emotion about seeing or not seeing the pictures? How did the cortex seem to know that the picture might be pleasant or unpleasant to see and do its integration thing so that the light was increased and the picture could be seen, or why did cortical instructions cause the light to decrease so the picture couldn't be seen? Meaningful information had to have been transferred long before a conscious impression occurred. Did this mean that the visual system could transmit a perception which could exert strong influence without ever arousing consciousness? Then again, are people quite different, some individuals having only a narrow line between the conscious and subconscious, and still others having obvious blocks between their two conscious selves?

There are no simple answers, only a host of conjectures. Are there perhaps sets of personality factors, gained by inheritance or by experience, which govern the expression of physical activity even at the cellular level just as they seem to govern our social behavior? Accumulated effects of personality and experience might exert their influences during the "cortical integration" process. Certainly dominant characteristics would have a more powerful effect than fleeting impressions, whims, or indecision. Then again, how was an impression gained through the senses able to "tell" the cortex what the picture might be, whether its contents might stimulate memories of anxiety and so the picture should be suppressed before it is seen?

The research scientist does not know. All the data allowed him to say is that the picture on the screen can't be seen until the person changes the voluntary (yet subconscious) control of his single muscle units to put more light on the picture. The data also indicate that some subjects go so far as to turn the light and picture off subconsciously.

There are other experiments, however, which nourish the subconscious influence theory. Other work has shown that a percept, a sensory impression, can be put into memory completely without conscious recognition. Nearly everyone can remember instances where you have watched an exciting scene with your total attention focused on the drama, only to recall much later parts of the scene that you had not attended to consciously. Or the times when you suddenly remember "peripheral" events which occurred when you were asleep. Or failing to remember what happened under hypnosis when the hypnotist instructed you to forget, then being able to remember when he said "remember." There is a great deal of evidence to indicate that we tuck away volumes of sensory impressions by bypassing consciousness.

The next question is, then, How much does this subconsciously stored information influence our actions? The psychoanalyst describes the process as the suppression of emotional information, preventing it from being in the conscious domain although it remains a powerful force subconsciously. So perhaps that is what also happens with peripheral subconscious impressions. They may churn around, making associations just as consciously manipulated information is handled, only to produce an effect on our behavior that we can't seem to account for. In other words, the subconscious peripheral information is incorporated into the cortical integration and a judgment is made partly with its influence. That is what I believe happens in Kahn's experiments. The subject perceives the picture at a lower level of illumination than is required to make a strong conscious impression, and this perception is routed through brain pathways where it is able to make an impression in that large gray area of cortical integration. The impression then changes the commands flowing down the spinal cord to the single nerve motor that in turn commanded the muscle cell firings to slow down or speed up and so controls the light on the pictures. The picture might be one of horror such as of the Kennedy assassination, or one of sexual excitement, or one of fat dollar bills, or children quarreling. Not very specific, but then how does one take a direct route to subconsciousness when so little is known about that hidden, secret life of the mind? But the pictures do stir memories when seen; we associate the scenes with interests, desires, needs, pleasures or unhappiness, sadness, terror. The results of Kahn's experiments suggest that we do the same long before we are consciously aware of the visual picture that jogs the memory.

Dr. Kahn's psychoanalytic training impelled his thinking ahead to another basic formulation of analysts: the subconscious conflict. In the extreme form the individual feels one thing but expresses his behavior as if he felt quite a different thing. He might desire sex, but live as a prude. He might want to be loved, but behave with a forbidding reserve. If people expressed some emotional reactions to pictures perceived only subconsciously by changing the rate of muscle unit firing, then could a subconscious conflict be inspected by observing how a person's muscle cell responded to conflicting subconscious impressions? This experimental work is only now beginning, but its potential for critical use in psychiatry warrants considerable investigation. The actual electronics and psychologic considerations necessary to bring this investigation to a reality are enormously complex. Briefly, the experimental subject first learns how to bring under voluntary control the firing of two different motor units. He learns both so precisely that whether each motor unit is active or suppressed is entirely at his control, albeit subconsciously. Then each motor unit firing is "tagged" to different pictures capable of inducing opposite emotions, so that increased firing of one unit causes one picture to be seen and increased firing of the other causes a different picture to be seen. For example, most of us have some sensitivity about the racial problem. One picture would be the figure of a black person, the other of a white person. Or the general ambivalence about sex could be used, with one picture of a sex scene and the other of a bride in white. Both pictures can be seen on a split-image screen. Will the subject consistently subconsciously and willfully increase the muscle firing of the one motor unit to flash more light and see the white person's picture while his conscious mind says, "But some of my best friends are blacks," or will, perhaps, his subconscious consistently direct his muscle unit firing to decrease so that he can't possibly see the sex scene while his consciousness says, "Wow, I really had a sexy experience last night"? Gross reactions, perhaps, even a gross experiment perhaps in some respects, but it is a wedge into the secret self.

Many more tricks can be played on the puzzling communications system between the subconscious and the conscious mind. One might "condition" the individual so that he becomes trained to see the picture of the white figure every time, then begin him on training to see the black figure. What then? Would his social tradition or his social consciousness interfere or facilitate learning to see the second figure? And would his verbal comments agree with the subconscious directions he gave to the muscle cells?

The psychologist and psychiatrist have a vast store of picture tests, and it seems that any of these could be used with the trained motor unit to delve into the further reaches of the subconscious. One other experiment of the type Kahn has tried is with the ambiguous picture. These are ill-defined drawings that can be interpreted differently according to how one's experience and feelings emphasize different parts of the picture or how one completes certain lines of the drawing. A picture of a face may be quite neutral, yet personal emotion may make it seem to be crying, while another emotional feeling may make it seem to be laughing. The apparatus showing the picture is set so that the learned rate of muscle firing is not quite enough to illuminate the picture to be consciously seen. The subject is urged to increase the firing rate of his muscle units to see the picture. The objective of this experiment is to find out if the increased muscle firing necessary to *see* the picture differs from the rate needed to *interpret* the picture. The subject is instructed to "hold" the picture, once it can be seen, for twenty seconds, which means sustaining the increased rate of firing.

The results of the preliminary experiment were not, unfortunately, immediately apparent. There seemed to be no differences in the rate of muscle firing when the subject was able to see the picture and during the period when firing was sustained so that the picture might be interpreted. But when the regularity of muscle firing was examined, meaningful differences were found. The rates during simple seeing were of one pattern, but the rates during interpretation followed a different pattern. Although the work is in too preliminary a phase to allow conclusions, this unique experiment gives psychology still another new way to inspect the subconscious, one which can be measured accurately and offers a measure for comparison among different kinds of people. The patterns of the rates of motor unit firing might be examined under various other conditions. In addition to interpreting scenes, patterns of firing might be different when the individual is describing them or imagining them or using them for free word association tests.

The psychiatrist pursues mental causes of emotional problems. That is perhaps where Dr. Kahn's work ends and Dr. Whatmore's begins. George Whatmore is a practicing physician and neurologist whose chief concern is the physical well-being of his patients. One specialist must mend the social life of the patient, the other mends the physical life. Beginning at either end, careful treatment can mend both. As we have kept repeating in this chapter, the muscle systems of the body are prime expressors of emotion. We all know that, unless deeply anesthetized, the body's muscle systems expend great amounts of energy. Every moment of living requires effort, nearly 90 percent of it through the muscles. Some of the effort is easily recognized, as in walking, eating, driving, talking and writing, but many muscle efforts are difficult to recognize. There are the small movements of the eyes in focusing, the muscles around the ears which tense when trying to be very alert and sharpen seeing and hearing. Yet there are other muscle efforts we are rarely aware of that involve nearly all of the muscle masses of our bodies. These are the efforts accompanying the mental processes of paying attention, of preparing to perform, of responding emotionally to words or visual scenes, of boredom, or of waiting. It is this group of efforts, working without the benefit of awareness, that can cause body problems difficult to unravel. Problems in walking or writing or talking are obvious; problems of wrong eye movements or aberrant muscle twitches are easy to diagnose. But problems of minor errors of posture or resting or waiting are too much a part of society's normal behavior. Dr. Whatmore seems to have spent a very long time thinking about these annoying misuses of muscle energy and has done a great deal to correct them. Obviously aware of the significance of Jacobson's relaxation techniques as a certain path to improved physical health, Dr. Whatmore began inspecting the correctness and efficiency of muscle activity as an underlying mechanism in the proper functioning of the body.

He reasoned that a functional disorder must arise from misuse of a system since no physical disease could be detected. And if it were misused, this meant that a great deal of effort was being wasted. Further, since muscle systems are the prime expressors of effort, then perhaps misuse of muscles was at fault. He simplified the concept of this process by defining a condition of misdirected effort. Suddenly the whole process became clear. Suppose you are anticipating a decision affecting your future. You don't wait in healthy relaxation, you become uptight, tense. Every muscle becomes expectant; you brace yourself for the news. You do this while waiting for the appraiser for your car accident, or waiting for guests at the biggest party you ever gave, or even during the minor expectancy of waiting to catch a ball just thrown to you. Under these circumstances it can be a normal, useful body response, and you become accustomed to it. But if you wait expectantly for a longer time, you forget that the muscles stay expectant. It is only long afterward, when relaxing, that you become aware of the fatigue and soreness in the muscles. Too often it becomes an entire life-style. There is no relaxation; tenseness is habitual and unconscious. It is only when you become aware of frequent extreme fatigue or have a headache that you become aware that something is wrong. Whatmore labeled the root cause as "misdirected or wrong effort." Actually he coined the word dysponesis to describe this state—from the Greek *dys*, meaning faulty or wrong, and *ponos*, meaning strenuous effort. I suspect that there are many who feel that the term dysponesis is a good example of dysponesis. Nevertheless, the dysponetic concept and definition finally pin down to a real entity an entire family of functional disorders.

Whatmore's techniques are an interesting combination of those used by Budzynski and by Basmajian but are quite different from both. To make his diagnosis, he puts muscle electrodes in as many places as possible and convenient. Then he records the muscle activity for a time to detect whether the patterns are normal or not. After cataloguing patterns of muscle activity of hundreds of normal people, Whatmore can quickly determine, with his equipment and knowledge, whether the patient is expending excessive amounts of muscle energy when he should be at rest. If so, the patient is likely to be what he calls "bracing." The patient is expectant, anticipating some event affecting his emotions. He is wasting and misdirecting energy. The treatment is to teach the patient to become aware of the difference between misdirected and efficiently useful muscle energy. How? The patient *watches* his own muscle records. His muscle errors are pointed out to him; he trains himself to reduce the number of errors. Then he must memorize the awareness of bracing and the awareness of corrected, directed energy and learn to discriminate these in his normal daily activities. It is a long training and requires much practice. He must continuously monitor his awareness of his muscle energy expenditure. If he becomes successful, he frees himself from his functional disorder, his headaches, his fatigue; if he fails, he lapses back into headaches or his other disturbing problems.

Some patients are found to misuse only one muscle system such as the diaphragm or neck muscles, while others may show bracing in almost all muscle systems. So each must learn to become aware of his special problems and where correction is needed. And he must learn to become aware of those special situations which cause bracing. Are they only with the boss, or when he gets the pay check? The patient must expand his awareness to catch the beginnings of his bracing movements, remember his practice, and suppress the bracing. With practice, the effort to suppress wrong muscle action becomes less and less. One might wonder about the energy source used to suppress wrong movements, and how it differs from the energy expenditure in misdirected efforts. Apparently the latter is in the muscles themselves, the "good" energy is in the will. And we come back again to the will, and the disparity in energy use, and the nature of the will.

SIX

Heartbeats: The Heart That Nobody Knows

> Bio-feedback has an intimate appropriateness for the human heart. Only with the heart does man view his body with such violent opposites of emotion. His hunger for love brings the heart to life; his fears of life converge upon the frailness of his heart. He is now to learn that the heart is not alone. It is the gracious servant of a still evolving mind.

An AP release to the Los Angeles *Times,* March 5, 1972, headed "Six Patients Learn to Alter Heart Rate. . . .without drugs," described a scientific report to the American College of Cardiology. Six patients suffering from atrial fibrillation (a condition where the upper chambers of the heart flutter wildly instead of beating regularly) had received bio-feedback heart rate training as their medical treatment, apparently with great success. The article reported that no medical explanations were offered, but, "it apparently involves an exercise of willpower."

One can imagine a crusty, pompous, medical Dr. Scrooge snapping out, "Willpower, bah! Humbug!" Anyone schooled in our traditions of physical exams, X-rays, drugs and physical therapy would be brought up short by this turn-around in medical attitude. How can an act of will be as good or perhaps better than a drug to treat organic malfunctions of the body, especially of the heart? How did medical opinion come to change its mind? Did it suddenly give up medicine and turn to philosophy? No, but the story behind the news report is a fascinating one of changing medical research attitudes and of the re-entry of the human mind into the concerns of the heart.

Did the patients learn, or did their hearts learn? If some medical researchers are now teaching hearts, or the minds of hearts, to reverse a pathological condition, then medicine must be learning that relationships between mind and body are more powerful than they thought. The concept of "psychosomatic" is generally accepted as indicating the emotional origin of disease processes; research into bio-feedback is the first medically testable indication that *emotion and mind can relieve illnesses as well as create them*. Mind power and willpower, however, are not always with us; they are elusive attributes of human beings. But the overlay and underlay of emotion surrounding the activities of our beings *is* accessible for study. Openly expressed or hidden in the recesses of our being, emotion is always with us.

The Emotion of the Heart

The heart is so inextricably tied to emotion that all a mystery drama needs to do to ensure attention of the audience is to have the heart's lub-dup beating in the background. We are normally unaware of continuous rhythmic sounds in the chest except for those quiet moments just before sleep. But at rest, shifting positions and with the pillow as a sounding board, we can hear the heart beat. The sound can be distressing, for sudden awareness of heart sounds is almost always associated with moments of fear and anxiety. Long before the Greek natural philosophers, the ancients believed that passion and all emotion resided in the chest. But in the first century A.D. the brilliant physician Galen took the romance out of the heart myth and decreed, on an anatomical basis, that the heart was simply a natural pump, a mechanical organ to circulate the nourishment of the blood to nerves and muscles. Yet, despite these 1,800 years of acknowledging its mechanical function, personal experience daily witnesses the reality of the heart as an organ of emotion.

The experience of every man has told him that his heart expresses his emotion. In love it is an early-warning system. Suddenly the new lover feels his heart race or skip or seem to stand still. If he had any questions about his feelings before, his heart confirms his emotions. It is expressing his experience. But if the new lover happens to be a psychologist or physiologist (or worse, a combination of the two), he takes his experiential knowledge into the research laboratory and dissects it down into bits of physics or chemistry or animal instinct, and somewhere in the translation between feeling-man and laboratory-man the power and knowledge of his interior self becomes screened off from his operational, reasoning mind. In the laboratories of science he has learned that behavior is what can be observed happening between man and his environment, not, it seems, what happens within man, within his bubbling cauldron of experience that finds a million devious, buffered, modified, modulated routes for expression. So lab-man has pursued the nature of the mechanics of the heart, and for some 1,800 years it has been acknowledged as a mechanical fixture. Yet when he, the scientist, deduces new information about the heart's physical action and then finds his own heart racing with the excitement of his mind's discoveries, he fails to heed its signs.

This paradox, I think, would be the fascination of a Martian looking at Earthman's understanding of mind-body relationships. He would see us feeling and experiencing body changes with every mind activity; yet formal knowledge neither admits of nor recognizes virtually any connection between mind and body not explainable by old Newtonian cause-and-effect laws of physics. To a Martian, seeing through and around us with an all-knowing vision, the scientific community may appear to have been suffering from hysterical blindness, a refusal to "see" parts of the mysterious unknowns of our own mind world that could lift us out of the security of the empirical womb we believe we live in. But the world is changing rapidly now, and with it some scientists are beginning to admit that the elusive psyche is a thing unto itself which has its own peculiar way of behaving.

It was the poets who first observed that the heart was a faithful executor of emotions. As in most spheres of life, literature antecedes "official discovery." Poetry discovered psychosomatic medicine, biological drives, the power of sex, and it has excelled in matters of the heart. Long before the invention of writing, poet chroniclers of history endowed the heart with the ability to express nearly every human emotion. The ways of the heart give life to legends. The earliest recorded legend-history, the epic of Gilgamesh, set down on clay tablets in the third millennium B.C., attests to the words of the heart:

". . . he longed for a comrade, for one who would understand his heart"; "Because of this do not be sad at Heart"; "The eyes of Enkidu were full of tears and his heart was sick"; "Here in the city man dies oppressed at heart, man perishes with despair in his heart"; "Why did you give this restless heart to Gilgamesh"; "If your heart is fearful throw away fear; if there is terror in it throw away terror"; ". . . let him lose the desire of this heart"; ". . . why does your heart speak strangely?"; "Despair is in my heart"; ". . . but the heart is oppressed with darkness"; ". . . is it for this I have wrung out my heart's blood?"

The heart was the center of all emotion—sadness, fear, desire, despair, oppression, sickness, understanding. It was even the conveyor of messages. Today we feel the same emotions with our hearts. Modern literature and songs are still filled with cardiac similes, and we seem not to tire of the most worn heart cliché, for it is the most powerful body symbol of our own experiences and feelings.

Death by Heartbreak

One of the stories about the heart that never fails to fascinate is the story of a parent or lover or dear friend dying of a broken heart. Those who "know better" have traditionally ridiculed such reports as romantic fantasies. But it is not a fantasy, it really happens. One of the better and more extensive studies documenting death by heartbreak was done in England in which the fate of people close to a person who had recently died was followed. In this survey the medical records of nearly all residents of a small market town in Wales were investigated for deaths occurring within a one-year period of bereavement caused by the death of a loved family member. Over a six-year period 371 of the residents died, and these had a total of 903 close relatives living in the area who had survived.

This group was compared with a control group of another 371 living residents and their 878 close relatives. These were matched with the survey group with the people who had originally died as to age, sex and marital status. Nearly 5 percent of the bereaved close relatives died within one year as compared to only .07 percent of the matched control group where no deaths occurred. Deaths continued to be more frequent in the survey group for the next three years. Although the average age of the bereaved relative who died was seventy years, this was still an earlier age than usual for deaths in the community. It was also earlier than the age of the relatives who predeceased them. While the average age of the bereaved relatives who died was seventy, the younger relatives were not excluded from the risk. Many of the deaths of the bereaved occurred at age fifty or sixty, much earlier than usual for the community. Females were more resistant; death by bereavement was much more frequent in males.

There were other rather startling facts that emerged from the study. If the primary death occurred in the hospital rather than at home, deaths among the bereaved relatives were twice as frequent. But if the deaths occurred in some inappropriate site such as on the road, in a shop, or when out on a walk, deaths among the bereaved jumped to five times the number when the relatives died at home.

Perhaps even more astounding are the implications of a study that investigated a group of young U. S. soldiers whose deaths were so sudden and unexpected that there had been no opportunity to discover the cause. Most of the young men believed themselves to be in good health, and certainly they had received complete medical examinations when they were inducted into the Army. At autopsy some of the deaths looked to be from meningitis, others from cerebral hemorrhage, but most were found to have types of heart disease. Nearly all of the disease pathology found at autopsy was concentrated on organs most intimately involved with the effects of stress. Could death be from sublimated emotion? Despair of the military? Broken hearts? Sad, despairing hearts? Perhaps it was voluntary. The extraordinary prevalence of sudden body failure is a phenomenon that ordinary medicine cannot account for. Recent studies of voodoo deaths abundantly verify the lethal effects of deeply felt beliefs. The victim of the voodoo priest's curse believes in the power of the portend; his mind carries out the prophecy of evil.

The Biologic Basis of the Heart's Emotion

The heart is, by all odds, the most confounding organ of the body. It is mechanically simple, a pump, nothing more. It receives circulating blood, gently pushes it into the lungs to collect the body's nutrient, oxygen, brings it back again, and with a powerful contraction sends the re-oxygenated blood out to nourish the body. It is a simple four-chambered pump with a detour circuit to harvest the work of the lungs. Yet, what tells it when to beat and how often? The genesis of the heartbeat is as unknown as the genesis of man, and equally a miracle. A squib of tissue so small and so well camouflaged as to be unseen by the naked eye is the progenitor of beats. By some unknown ultrachemistry, this squib of tissue generates a flow of electric impulses, bip-bip-bip, one after the other with bewildering unmatched regularity. Each bip swarms across the thin-walled auricle, the upper chamber, which responds in a gentle swelling contraction, and the electrical bip swims directly into the muscular band between upper and lower chambers where it becomes channeled into special heart-impulse-conducting cells, then to spread out in guided fashion and in one concerted move makes the ventricles contract. For an entire lifetime that squib of tissue, the sinus node, spews out electrical impulses in an unbroken rhythm. The generator is inborn, inherent. It is programmed by genetic chemicals to perform regularly and efficiently and for a long generation. No one knows how the program is decided upon. The best evidence suggests that the rate of the heart is related to the metabolic requirements of the organisms. And that means another program to relate metabolism to the heart.

As man goes through life, he learns that his heart rate accelerates with exercise, races in a fever, and slows with periods of rest and relaxation. Other than that, he is scarcely aware of its changes. Physiologists long ago found that it wasn't the sinus node that changed the heart's *rate* of beating; it was special nerves finding their way to the heart. Tracing these nerves, they found two completely different pairs which connected to two quite different parts of the central nervous system. The very large pair traveled straight down the neck area, one on each side, almost from the brain itself. Their origin was buried in the highest portion of the spinal cord. Once stimulated or disturbed these nerves caused a profound slowing of the heart and could stop the beat completely. The second pair of nerves were fine fibrils, traced to small nerve swellings lying alongside the spinal cord but at a much lower level than where the large nerves connected to the nerve conduit to the brain. Once stimulated these finer nerves caused the heart to accelerate rapidly. Ultimately both sets of nerves were traced into the brain itself to areas labeled control centers.

These two quite different sets of nerves belong to what is called the autonomic nervous system, the ANS, a relatively simple nerve network anatomically, but a most puzzling intricate system in its action. Its name came from the belief that it functions autonomously, apart from the massive nervous system that provides nerves to and from muscles. Anatomically and physiologically it has been far easier to trace the neural systems concerned with motor functions, and detailed maps of the human cortex have been made which indicate just where sensory clues interface with brain neurons and give rise to commands for muscles to perform. But the nerves of the ANS are scattered widely, and they can be fine and delicate and cannot be traced with any specificity above the primitive lower brain.

The discovery that all of the nerves controlling the heart's rhythm of beating seemed to derive from a brain area so primitive and so ancient in its development that it shared its name and functions with that in fishes and insects has, until recently, reinforced the idea that nervous control of the heart rate was indeed automatic. The autonomic nerves were simply tied here to the primitive stem of the nervous system. Through the accidents of evolution this vital area had risen to become encased in the skull. It was the ancient brain, superseded in man by the complex brain structure that had grown above it. The "higher" brain took care of man's more recent business of the thinking brain.

It is true, however, that from this life-essential, ancient brain the relationship between the nerves controlling the rate of the heart and the rest of the brain becomes lost in the endless interconnections of brain neurons. It was always thought that it was the concerted force from the more primitive emotions funneled by the lower brain that had the greatest influence. Yet nearly every part of the brain examined has, in some way, an influence on heart rate. Higher brain areas and functions are now being found to have an even greater influence, and although the higher brain modulates and influences the lower, more primitive brain, the "inferior" part carries out the basic needs for survival. It is only by vague, indirect associations that we have become aware of the great sensitivity of the heartbeat to the most subtle and submerged secrets of our sophisticated emotional life.

The two sets of nerves, the large and the small, of the ANS, performing their speeding and slowing effects on heart rate, are also called by more general terms which tell the physiologist something about their role and function with respect to the control of internal function in general. The ANS is composed of two separate divisions. Just as the heart is supplied with two sets of nerves, each with the ability to oppose and balance the effect of the other, so are all organs vital to the physical survival of the body supplied with two sets of nerves. Long ago these sets of nerves were grouped into larger sets of divisions of the ANS. One was called Sympathetic (presumably because its actions for all organs were sympathetic to protecting life), while the other group was labeled Parasympathetic ("para" simply meaning parallel to the sympathetic division). Unlike the nerve arrangement for the motor system with its sensory nerves for receiving information and its motor nerves for producing effects or responses to the information, both divisions of the ANS excite internal organs to activity.* The two divisions do, however, generally more or less oppose each other in the functions they control, such as constricting and dilating blood vessels, contracting or relaxing the intestine, or slowing and speeding the heart. Overactivity of one division of the autonomic system generally tends to call its opposite into action, and by such cooperative activity the two divisions tend to maintain internal life-support organs and

---

* There are some "sensory" nerves coming from the visceral organs which continually input information about the internal state of affairs into the central nervous system. Until very recently it has been believed that these were merely part of a neural reflex arc, a way of directly communicating with the ANS nerves going to visceral organs as part of the balancing act. Now, with voluntary heart rate control demonstrated, these concepts may all be changed.

systems in a state of balance optimal to the survival of the organism.

Over and above its balancing function the ANS is a chief mechanism by which emotion is expressed, and this also is a survival mechanism. Whatever emotion is displayed, whatever action is to be taken depends upon the brain's appraisal of the specific situation at hand. If the situation is threatening, the emotion is alarm and fear. Here the sympathetic division of the ANS generally dominates and implements the body's responses: breathing becomes rapid, the heart speeds, eyes widen, palms sweat, the gut stops moving. In some situations the parasympathetic division becomes dominant, as for example in deep meditation where the body becomes calm and tranquil, and heart and respiration slow.

There are three frequent major influences on heart rate: muscle activity, as in exercise and work; infections; and emotions. Under abnormal situations there are the pathologies of the heart itself, or disease processes in some way related to the nerves supplying the heart. Whatever the cause, there are a variety of organic problems which can directly affect the heart rate. When, by any of these influences, the heart rate is accelerated, the sinus node is forced to spew out impulses faster and the heart muscle responds. The faster the heart contracts, the less time it has to rest, and after a time it becomes fatigued. With high heart rates there is also the problem of one contraction coming almost before a preceding one is finished, fostering the tendency for not quite complete and less effective contractions. Or when, for as yet unknown reasons (although fatigue is suspected), the heart slows excessively, some impulses from the sinus node seem to get lost and the heart skips a beat. Of course, the same events may occur when the heart rate is disturbed by emotion or exercise or infections. All these factors suggest that the ability to control the heart rate by willpower, by voluntary action, could be most useful in conserving the energies of the heart and protecting it from undue stress.

One of the easier things a medical student learns in his studies is the pharmacology of the heart rate. It is a simple task because heart rate can go only up or down and there are only two major areas of fault: the auricle and the ventricle. Or to put it more medically, problems of the sinus node and problems of the auriculo-ventricular (A-V) junction, that special heart-impulse-conducting band lying between auricles and ventricles. Then there are only the two sets of nerves influencing the rate, each having an opposing action: the ones that accelerate and those that slow the heart. So the drugs to be prescribed are chosen for one of the two actions and one of the two sites to be affected. Clearly there are relatively few drugs to choose from. When I was in medical school, we were chiefly concerned about slowing abnormally high heart rates or breaking through blockage of impulses at the A-V junction. Later, working for a Ph.D. in cardiovascular physiology and pharmacology, I was mainly concerned about the mechanisms producing abnormal heart rhythms and how to develop more efficient drugs for their treatment. Never once were my colleagues and I concerned about the psychologic origins of abnormal heart rates. Medicine is medicine, and you work with physical realities, not with unknowns of a tangled subconscious.

I recall vividly a case of suspected thyroid tumor which medical consensus sent to surgery. Months later I saw the patient quite by accident in the clinic. Her chief symptom, an annoying and frighteningly erratic and rapid heart rate, persisted. As a result of surgery there was no excessive thyroid hormone to keep the heart so excited. This time my supervisor was a different doctor, one interested in psychosomatic medicine. We probed the patient's emotional life and found enough trauma there to trip the hearts of ten people. Over the weeks as the social workers helped her with her problems, her heart responded. Then she understood. Her heart expressed her fears, her thousand worries. It was a different, an excessive, but quite normal mechanism to express boiling emotion, and understanding settled it down under her knowing, feeling, conscious control. (But, alas, her thyroid was gone forever.)

Studies of the Heart's Other Function

Scientific study of the heart as an organ of emotion has been rather a higgledy-piggledy, disorganized effort, never taken too seriously. Physiologists are familiar with the multitude of brain centers and influences on heart rate but it is not within their scientific province to study the effect of emotional reactions or mental activity on these central control systems of the heart. That is for the psychologists to do. But the psychologists are not, on the whole, well educated in the physiologic mechanisms which they encounter in studies of behavior and emotion. And neither type of scientist has been willing to spend time trying to correlate the eccentricities of heart rate performance with loosely defined, poorly verbalized subjective reports of mental and emotional impressions of how the heart "feels" when it beats in different rhythms. Until the principle of bio-feedback gradually became conceptualized, nearly all information about the behavior of the heart during emotion was derived from the emergency theory of adrenaline secretion expounded by Professor Cannon many years ago: the fight-or-flight reaction. When confronted with a threat to life or when suddenly startled, animals and man react with an emergency explosion of adrenaline secretion, and the adrenaline fires up the sympathetic nervous system, which is already aroused by the threat. One of the first effects of this emergency reaction is the racing of the heart. Later in psychobiology it was observed that anger or fear or even anxiety was accompanied by rapid heart rate.

Only within the last decade has refined instrumentation allowed a more precise evaluation of the heart's response to emotion. At the same time some of the more courageous psychophysiologists began to explore the behavior of the heart during ordinary emotion and mental activity. Heart rates *were* higher in states of anxiety; to be sure anxiety rightly or wrongly heralded danger. But why did some hearts seem to slow in the face of danger, and was the change in heart rate due to the thought alone or was it part and parcel of the whole body response to impending danger?

As research became more sophisticated and less parochial, the reactions of the heart were found to be even more challenging. In one experiment, for example, anxiety and anticipation were separated as emotional overtones by manipulation of anxiety-producing stimuli and instructions about preparedness for the stimuli. It was not a very exciting experiment, as experiments go, bearing the stamp of acutely objective, simplistic approaches to the complex human emotion of anxiety. But it is a first-rate example of how laboriously and unempathetically many an experimental psychologist approaches the vast, intricate inner world of man, and how utterly superficial is the knowledge that is acquired. (Not to mention the high cost of research.) In the experiment some of the test subjects were shown a series of simple digits given one at a time every few seconds and exactly in the right order (1, 2, 3, etc.). They were told that when number 10 appeared they would occasionally receive an electric shock to their fingers.

Actually the rascally experimenters shocked them at least 50 percent of the time anyway, and to be scientifically sharp about it, they gave some subjects stiff shocks and others quite weak ones. It really didn't matter anyway because as soon as the numbers started appearing everyone's heart rate started accelerating, a clear case of anxiety the researchers tell us, especially since the hearts beat faster in the people who were getting the strong shocks. But then, just when number 10 appeared, the hearts slowed dramatically. And this, they tell us, is a clear case of anticipation, since it occurred at the actual point in time when the shock was expected. As a check on the accuracy of their interpretation that the speeding heart was a result of anxiety, the experimenters repeated the experiment using a tone instead of a shock, assuming the tone would not cause anxiety as the shock did. Amazingly, hearts did not accelerate, they actually slowed all during the time the numbers shown were inching up to number 10. Then, as in the shock experiment, they slowed still more.

It is a matter of great convenience to biological scientists to have complex phenomena all tied up into neat little packages, as in this experiment that concludes that heart rate acceleration is a component of an anxiety response whereas heart rate deceleration appears to be related to anticipation. But good old realistic you and I have good reason to query the inferences of such experiments on an experiential basis alone. If I am anxious, isn't it because I am anticipating something? Why does my anxiety grow through seeing numbers 1 through 9 and suddenly give way to anticipation on number 10?

The Anticipatory Heart

What the heart does during different emotional experiences is both very complex and very individual. How could it be viewed otherwise, knowing about the vast neural mantle of the brain's network that holds together every part of the body with every thought that forms? Yet the experimental psychologist has plowed his way through dozens of expensive research projects to confirm what you and I observe every day. They found that the heart rate decreases gradually during a night's sleep, except for dream periods, when the heart becomes erratic. How many mothers have felt their sleeping child's pulse, noting contentedly the slow, regular beat, or owners watched their dreaming cats or dogs show a storm of body activity, including a dancing chest of heartbeats? Some researchers even made scientific headlines when they reported that the way the heart rate changed depended on where the attention was: it decreased its rate when the mind attended to external events, but it increased its rate when the mind ignored the outside environment and was assumed to be thinking or problem solving. These different changes were attributed to different types of central nervous system arousal.

Another report has verified the tendency for people to perform poorly when their hearts were running fast—for example, they failed to hear high tones, suggesting a deficiency in mental function. Of course one can ask the question that if the person's attention isn't on the high tones when his heart is beating rapidly, then where *is* his attention? Does attention just fade away? Perhaps his attention is on experiencing his heartbeat, or wondering why he was sitting there involved in some nonsensical situation with high tones pounding in the ears, or devoutly wishing he were home with the TV on.

Sensory perception, such as the perception of visual, auditory or tactile information, reaches the interpretive cortex of the brain most accurately and effectively at the time when the electrical impulse that makes the heart beat is flowing across the auricle. But at the time when the impulses are actually initiating the beat of the ventricle, the sensory information is much less effectively transmitted to the brain. We all have experienced our inability to sustain attention over long periods of time, and such experiments suggest that we attend to events in the environment much more closely when the upper chamber of the heart is contracting than when the large lower ventricle begins its contraction. So, as the powerful ventricle beats and then relaxes, our attention to the outer world fluctuates through mini-cycles. If the heart is beating rapidly, there are more ventricular beats with an accompanying waning of attention and less sensory information arriving at the brain (the "deficit of sensory input to the central nervous system"). This would account for the poor performance of tasks during fast heart rate activity.

Some researchers have interpreted this lesser ability of the brain to handle sensory information when the heartbeat deviates from its accustomed rate to be an effect produced by information about the heart's activity being fed back to the brain via the ANS. They postulate that the fedback information activates the ANS to produce a condition which actually prevents sensory information from arriving at the cortex. They believe that the condition preventing the awareness of outside information exists because the brain receivers are busy paying attention to the internal data, the information coming from the heart. Other researchers have interpreted the effect as a result of actual feedback of information from the heart via the ANS which actively and directly inhibits the brain receivers from properly receiving sensory information, being occupied by receiving internal data.

The emotional responses of the heart are also modulated by the internal milieu, by experiences the mind and body have had and how they have found it most expeditious to behave. In one cogent study the effect of anticipating an electric shock (which never came) was compared to the effect of *imagining* that a shock would be given. The study is of particular interest because the investigators exerted considerable effort to document the anxiety potential of normal people, rather than following the usual procedure of comparing obviously anxious people with obviously calm people. The degree of anxiety proneness was found to be the most crucial determinant of how the heart rate changed. In general, as the time approached for the shock to be given, the faster the heartbeat. It became fastest in subjects most anxiety prone. At the moment the shock was expected, those with the most tendencies for anxiety jumped higher in rate, while those with the least tendency for anxiety sharply dropped in rate. The heart rates of people with average tendencies toward anxiety fell slightly if at all at this point, and all subjects' heart rates, regardless of anxiety potential, behaved rather similarly during the imagined anticipation of shock except for the medium-anxious people. The researchers felt that these reactions indicated that people with only an average amount of anxiety were the most adaptive; that they could modulate their autonomic nervous systems and hearts to meet the changing demands of the environment, for they were also the only group to distinguish the real and imagined shock threats by changes in their heart rates. The sudden slowing of their heart rates at the moment of anticipated shock brings to mind research showing that such cardiac deceleration actually facilitates performance in a work task.

The basis for this concept was extended by an experiment in which heart rate changes during mental tasks were measured. Heart rates continued to increase during attention to and work of the task, and decreased back to normal as the subject reported his mental work. The faster rate is believed by some to be associated, as noted above, with inward attention, and "resting" or slowing the heart with facilitating outward attention. In a performance task in which subjects pressed a button every time they saw a light (activated on different time schedules), it was found that good learners of this simple task had higher heart rates during rest periods while poor learners showed faster heart rates during the work periods. It makes one wonder whether bio-feedback might not be put to good use for the ordinary problem solving we are continuously faced with in everyday life. If we trained our hearts (as we will see later that we can easily do) to stay slow while thinking about problems, or at least teach them to stay steady, perhaps our daily efficiency would take a great leap forward.

The consensus of one school of researchers interprets heart rate changes occurring during the anticipation of an event and preparing for a response solely as part of an emotional response of the organism produced by central nervous system activity preparing for a motor (muscle) response. To them the changes in heart rate are strictly secondary to getting ready to move. It would indeed seem reasonable to consider that if the sensory information about demands of the environment sent to the brain is undergoing extensive cortical integration in order to excite the appropriate nerve messages to the muscle system, then it certainly would be possible that somewhere in the process connections are made with other nerve cells which relay information to the brain areas which influence the autonomic nervous system. Current knowledge of the interacting functions of the CNS make this a logical hypothesis. If some psychologists, however, prefer an experiential explanation involving a reasoning subconscious rather than a simple result of muscle reflexes as a major influence in some emotion (as I do), then the burden of proof is on them.

The Cardiac Communications Gap

Although the information the heart sends out about its activity does go directly to the brain, there is little if any communication between brain and mind about the normal activity of the heart. In the section on the heart and bio-feedback we will explore this apparent communications barrier. At this point we can note that several experiments have revealed a startling dichotomy between what the heart was really doing and what its conscious mind thought it was doing. When, for example, people see a *series* of pictures, the more interesting the pictures are to them, the more the heart actually slows. *But,* they report that they feel their hearts are accelerating. Moreover, they also believed their hearts speeded up with the most interesting pictures, when their hearts actually slowed. This is surprising in view of the common belief of most people who habitually attest to acute awareness of their heart rate (I was so frightened, my heart stood still!). The foul-up in communications between heart and mind is probably a function of inexperience. Perhaps, as we may learn with bio-feedback, our attention has not been drawn to the subtle changes of a normally beating heart since we've come to trust the heart to serve us well without paying attention to it.

The matter of variability of heart rate has also occupied researchers. Some have related a high degree of variability to the degree of "arousal" (increased readiness to respond) of the central nervous system. Curiously, it was not until 1971 that one research group suggested that *how* a particular heart responded to emotion, to attention or to stimuli was dependent upon what kind of heart rate it normally had. The investigators did not bother to review their data in this light, but at least they suggested that future experiments on heart rate, attention, etc., might be clarified *if* experimental subjects were separated into heart rate accelerators and heart rate decelerators. This suggestion had been indicated in earlier scientific papers, yet has remained unexplored. It is likely that a great many experimental results will be changed when evaluated according to this distinction.

As we begin to pay attention to such distinguishing characteristics of human beings, we may develop entirely new ways for mapping our physical distinctiveness. We need not be simply black or white, short or tall, stout or thin. Our inner differences would not only strengthen our identities, but our qualities of being and reacting could shortcut communicating our qualities to others. We might be heart rate accelerators, or high alpha producers, or regular breathers, or variable blood pressure people. Shorthand notes of our interior selves might also convey our spiritual essence or our psychologic attitudes.

Where does the following fascinating facet of the heart's behavior fit? Heart rate synchronizes with the rhythms of music—especially rock music. To the weary parent, however, it may be helpful to know that your child is not always in synchronization with the music. A few extra calls will eventually get his attention as the heart rate fades in and out of synchrony with the beat of the music. In neurophysiology it is well known that rhythmic auditory signals can "drive" the cortex to discharge the electricity of its nerve cells in rhythm with the signals. It is much like the driving of the visual cortex with flashes of light that we discussed in Chapter 1. In both auditory and visual "driving," the responding brain cells lose some ability for their usual functions, such as forming thoughts and making thought associations. Rock music is an outstanding way to drive the cortex; the beat and the loudness overwhelm the brain and mind. Another lab-man might argue that musical rhythms are stimuli which set in motion our muscles at a less than noticeable level, that it is the imperceptible muscle movements that make the heart synchronize with the beat of the music, and that may be true.

But perhaps the scientists don't have the whole story. Clearly the heart is telling us something . . . something to the effect that there is more to man than stimulus and response, that man is infinitely more complex than lab-man's ideal of a layer-cake collection of simple one-to-one behavioral reactions. Perhaps we do have sensory and response body systems which receive and respond to totalities of patterns and that it is these patterns of our sensory information input which can selectively remind our body system of ancient, community forms of expression. It might well be that this discovery of the physiologic basis of mental patterns would reinforce Jung's notion of the archetypal unconscious. And if you can't buy that, then just remember that cows and chickens produce better when they are allowed to hear music.

The Yogi in the Laboratory

The heart as the indicator of emotion has a mystique and significance and complexity that make Western researchers shy away from making guesses about its meaning. Those who have seriously searched for the wellspring of the heart's emotion have found one enigma after another in the tie between emotion and the heart. This enigma is compounded further when we consider the education of the heart. Long before bio-feedback crystallized as a fundamental phenomenon in the mind-body relationship, experimental psychologists were challenged by the curious "learning" characteristics of the heart. Learning theorists experienced a real biological rebuff when they tried to apply their theories to determine whether the heart could "learn" and the heart performed in exactly the opposite way from what they had expected.*

Nonetheless, if we can teach our muscles not to betray our inner emotions, why not the heart? Every day we hold back a frown, a

---

* For example, the earliest efforts to educate the heart were made according to the classical learning theories of Pavlov, theories usually interpreted as involving chiefly the more primitive, lower-level, involuntary functions of man. Trying to apply these principles to the behavior of the heart proved to be a vexing problem. As the script went, to show the heart what it was being trained for the researchers gave a shock to the body which caused the heart to accelerate. They then preceded the shock by the sounding of a buzzer. According to theory, a dog would learn to associate the two and thus learn to accelerate the heart when he heard the buzzer in order to avoid the ensuing shock. But the heart decelerated, it slowed. The heart was independent, it misbehaved. (Today's young new scientists might have said, "Wow, that's great, it's doing its own thing." But laboratory-man relentlessly pursued shaping experiments to fit the theory.) One intriguing aspect, however, was that the heart kept misbehaving in a regular and quite characteristic way. This was interpreted to mean that there must be some specific or regularly occurring influence operating during the act of associating the shock with the buzzer or between the association of buzzer and the heart's response. The persistent perverseness of the heart became an elaborate puzzle, and hundreds of experiments have been conducted to discover the nature of the heart's peculiar learning habits.

smile, a motion, a shrug, a tear. The muscles mind the mind. Why not the heart? Would we lose the ability to express emotion if we taught the heart to stay steady? Would we learn new ways to express emotion? Would there be any emotion at all? Or if we teach the heart to stay calm, will we become so aware that we become more enlightened (because new ways of looking at things bring new ideas)? What harm might follow learning to control the rate of the beating heart? Could we become so proficient that we could mask the signs of real cardiac problems when they arose? Could certain emotionally disturbed people use their power to control the heart to use it as a "clean," "efficient" way of suicide? Or is that physiologically possible? These are some of the questions to be answered before medicine and psychology plunge into recommendations about learning to control heart rate. Yet the benefits may outweigh possible hazards. If patients with problems of heart rate control can learn to maintain a healthy heart, won't this also be controlling the emotional life of the heart? Just how much does biomedical science know about control of one's own heart rate?

The question of whether the heart can "learn" has been clouded by the prejudices of Eastern versus Western philosophies and of physiologists versus mystics. Of all the differences between the Eastern contemplative tradition and the outer-directed activist Western tradition, the views on the relationship between the heart and the mind are an exceptionally striking example of the contrasting philosophies and attitudes toward physical science. The cultural elite of the East developed the practice of subjective voluntary control of internal functions; the cultural elite of the West harnessed the physical world with tools and machines, and where the heart was concerned attempted to control it by surgery, drugs, exercise and electronics. For this reason it was no wonder that Western physiologic opinion tended to deny the ability of yogis to control hearts exclusively by voluntary subjective means. Although always excited by the possibility of its occurrence, official opinion has concluded that such control of the heart rate must be a trick, a fraud, a vaudeville stunt. As late as 1961 an eminent psychophysiologist, Dr. Wenger, and his Indian colleagues concluded, after recording the heart rates of yogis in India, that while yogis might be able to slow their hearts nothing so dramatic as voluntarily stopping the heart was possible. Whatever slowing or stopping of hearts the yogis could induce could be seen to be due to muscle tricks such as tightening the chin on the chest. This act would cause a clamping around the major vessel of the heart and its main branches which contain receptors sensitive to pressure change and which in turn reflexly stimulate the parasympathetic nerves to slow the heart. Yet today Dr. Elmer Green of the Menninger Foundation has obtained record after record undeniably demonstrating the ability for a yogi subject of his to stop his heart for considerable periods of time, ten to thirty seconds. The hazards of conducting even physically measurable research experiments is clearly shown by such conflicting results. Perhaps the Wenger group used yogi subjects who were little interested in controlling heart rate, or perhaps they were relatively inexperienced. We don't know whether the Wenger group actually was able to obtain reliable information on these questions or perhaps they had an ideological bias that yogis, being unscientific in their pursuits, could not have anything of worth to communicate.

Dr. Elmer Green is free from such bias and in searching the world of yoga phenomena he found a yogi of long experience in manipulating his own physiologic responses, a yogi who did perform as requested and repeatedly. Submitting to the uncompromising, lie-detecting recording instruments this yogi's, Swami Rama's, quiet, mind-controlled body performed unusual feats. A simple task for his trained mind-body, he deliberately, consciously, and without moving a muscle, caused the temperature of the two sides of one hand (palm side) to change in *different directions,* achieving more than a 10° F. difference in areas less than two inches apart. Then he stopped his heart, and for twenty seconds the ventricle almost stood still, as the records appear to demonstrate.

Numerous Eastern practices emphasize a development of an inner sensitivity by the mind for its relationships to all parts of its body. The aim of this is to exert conscious voluntary control over the body by the mind. In contrast, Western practices of self-control have been dominated by science, where the dominion of matter over mind means control of the mind by physical influences. Control of heart rate came to be, in Western fashion, a function of external control—drugs, pacemakers and cardiac massage. The understanding of heart control by East and West has thus not only been antithetical, but stubbornly resistant to mutual exploration.

The difficulties of communication between East and West in this matter are not generally recognized. Language, psychology and cultural sensibilities differ enormously. The Eastern approach can communicate very little of its essence to Western laboratory-man. Eastern techniques for heart rate control are interior events, to be discussed in terms of internal experience and subjective awareness, and for this the Westerner has a severely limited vocabulary. To understand the Eastern approaches is not merely a matter of the translation of languages, it is complicated by the need to translate concepts of living, the meaning, the purpose, the existential quality of life. But the Western approach to heart rate control yields volumes of easily identified, concrete events and elements for which we have developed an extensive language.

For the Westerner with his cultural emphasis on exterior events, it is ever so much simpler to talk about mild electric shocks changing heart rates and how this can be associated with a buzzer rather than meditating on the fifth *chakra* to control the flow of blood. In the West one can talk of the intensity of shocks, their duration, the time between shocks, characteristics of the buzzer, how long it takes to make the association, what comparative changes there are, and so on ad infinitum. This difference between Eastern and Western modes of being, the great abyss that lies between exterior and interior approaches, operates to exert a profound psychologic influence on the researchers and practitioners themselves, on both what they do and how they do it. Clearly then, how we manage our own interior and exterior beings is governed by culture and a consensus of reality. It will be an exciting future if current diplomatic maneuvers and the tendency toward cross-cultural convergence can bridge the distance between Eastern and Western thought on the psychobiology of being.

And as we have seen, while the fact of voluntary control of the heart was an accepted fact of Eastern life, behavior of the body was believed in the West to be subject only to the laws of physical nature. The concept of voluntary became tied to muscles only; whatever essence of mind stuff might exist was a derivative of learning via the body's muscles. The development of learning techniques demonstrated in experimental animals and found to obey the laws of the physical world finalized the abolition of mind-body dualism; to lab-man electric shock caused the heart to speed, ergo, there was no mind stuff.

Learning: Theirs and Ours

Nearly a century of Western experimental psychology has been concentrated on theories of learning appropriate to rote, mechanical, almost automatic "learning." One of the most important learning theories to be widely adopted (and remarkably misunderstood in its implications for mind function) was the classical Pavlovian "conditioned learning." To review, the theory states that an innate body response can be conditioned, i.e., transferred from an appropriate to a nonappropriate stimulus. If an organism is repeatedly faced with two very concrete events (stimuli), one of which causes a strong, natural physiologic response (such as drinking when very thirsty), and the second event is not relevant to the selected physiology (a buzzer sounding when very thirsty), then over time the natural response tends to occur to the nonrelevant event. The classic example is (always) the hungry dog, isolated in an experimental situation and hungry due to starving, who is appeased by bits of food served only after a bell is sounded. The dog's salivary glands soon learn to become active at the sound of the bell, much as they begin to salivate when the actual food is smelled.

As applied to the heart, an electric shock to the body causes the heart to race. If the electric shock is always "paired" with (i.e., preceded by) a buzzer sounding, then after a number of pairings the heart should begin to race when the buzzer is sounded. In the next chapter we shall see that the ways of the heart obstinately challenge this simplistic notion of body behavior.

Nonetheless, the Pavlovian type of conditioned learning gave American psychologists a comfortable, convenient and inexpensive technique to explore all of the minutiae of the phenomena surrounding the transfer of natural physiologic responses from a stimulus naturally causing them to nonrelevant signals having no significance to the physiology at hand. Everything from loudness of the buzzer to type of food served to how long the animal could remember the nonrelevant event was studied.

As such learning relates to the everyday necessity to learn new bits of relevant, acceptable behavior, Pavlovian conditioned learning has little to offer. It is effective only if the organism is continuously reminded that if it doesn't perform (to the experimenter's desire), it will be punished. Either it will receive a nasty shock or it will be deprived of its "reward" of food or water.

In the 1930s Skinner's ingenuity intervened by evolving a simpler but even more challenging technique. Let the animal discover by himself the nonrelevant event in the conditioning situation. In the famous example, a hungry rat, isolated in a cage with a lever attached to a food-delivery system, explores the cage for food. By accident he hits the lever and is "rewarded" by the automatic delivery of a bit of food. Soon he "learns" to press the lever for food.

Skinnerian conditioned learning theory fostered an enormous boom in experimental learning studies. Rats were cheap, as was the equipment. It was fun to rig the experiment so that the rat was forced to adopt various schedules to obtain his reward, or such devilish tricks were tried as omitting the reward every fifth attempt by the rat to see how the rat would then alter his lever-pressing schedule. It was a great game and produced large piles of scientific papers. But the great occupation with rat learning was largely responsible for a long neglect of research into mind function.

In its bare-bones concept and when viewed from the standpoint of individual awareness and responsibility for one's own behavior, Skinnerian conditioned learning (instrumental or operant conditioning) to me has little to recommend it for everyday use,* just as Pavlovian conditioning is of little use. If an organism, rat or human, finds that he can satisfy a biologic need by accidentally brushing up against his experimenter's tricky little devices, then however much he brushes up against them and has his reward delivered, he is doing little more than perfecting his brushing-up techniques. I have

---

* This is not to say that operant conditioning isn't useful in man, but when effective, the technique is considerably modified by adding other supportive measures.

personally always felt that the rat is having a lark, chortling to himself that he can press that bloody lever faster than the experimenter can ever count, and satisfy his hunger to boot.

In retrospect it seems that the total preoccupation with the effect of external events on behavior (tone signals, lever pressing, electrical shocks) created an intellectual blindness. Researchers failed to examine with any degree of objectivity what, *exactly*, they were doing in their experiments. It took bio-feedback to do that.

To many of us in bio-feedback research it is the *information* that we give our experimental subject, man or animal, that allows him to become a successful learner. It is, to us, the kind, the amount, the fidelity, and the significance of the information which is fed back to the individual about his own interior function that leads to successful learning. The more complete the information, the greater can be the interior awareness developed by the learner. The learning is up to him.

In retrospect, too, it seems that perhaps the learning during conditioning experiments occurred because information *was always being conveyed* to the subjects unrecognized and unsuspected by the experimenters. Not only do all of the laboratory signals of lights and buzzers and electric shocks have very real meanings and messages, but if, for example, the lever-pressing rat is occasionally denied his food reward, that event itself conveys the very significant information that the lever is not always a sure bet to deliver food.

The remainder of this book attempts to develop the flow of Western concepts of how learning about one's interior being occurs. It necessarily deals with past and current prevalent research and concepts, but will, I hope, put a more meaningful, humanistic perspective on the capacity of all animal species to learn.*

---

* If you want to bone up on learning theory, see Appendix C. It may be helpful for an understanding of why we are where we are in learning to control the inner being.

SEVEN

Heartbeats: The Will of the Heart

If you stand still long enough to know an inner mind, you can feel it grow. All at once you are a scion of the world and a distant god of destiny. Why this ecstasy of soul stubbornly eludes our fumbling generations may be the tricks the outside world plays upon the world inside. It has taken a very long time to tease the soul from the heart and then to put it back again.

A Heart Learning Experiment and Its Problems

One blindness from which so many experimental psychologists seem to suffer, as we have noted before, is the almost hysterical inability to recognize the validity of common sense. Establishment theory must somehow be correct, regardless of the absurdity of the situation. The application of classical conditioning techniques to the control of heart rate is a good example. Despite the perversity of the heart's learning, despite the everyday knowledge of the integral role of heart rate to the subtlest of emotions, experimental psychologists continued to work undistractedly through stereotyped laboratory experiments to be the first to show the world that the heart could learn according to the two popular theories of the times. Through the thirties, forties, and fifties, even through the sixties, the idiosyncrasies of the heart teased the experimenters.

Bioscientific isolationism was in vogue, the era when physicists spoke only to neurophysiologists and neurophysiologists spoke only to God. Scientific specialties had proliferated like rabbits, and like rabbits each marked its territory not to be defiled by talking across borders.* Isolated from their more "scientific" peers, many a poor psychologist learned the hard way what the experimental physiologist or neurologist already knew. In a distressing way it was a comedy of errors. The young psychologist whose heart raced when he thought of the reward of returning home to his new bride, during the day divorced his academic brain from his inner feeling and settled himself in the mold of the physical sciences, administering electric shocks all day to students whose hearts he wanted to control. The scientific establishment to which he belonged argued that a change of heart rate was a mere physiological response mechanism not unlike the lab dog salivating when he heard the bell, and ergo, the heart could be conditioned à la Pavlov.†

The Heart Beats the Man

Early experiments of heart rate "control" in human beings were precise duplicates of Pavlovian techniques for dogs. There were two fundamental assumptions: first, that regarding his heart rate, man was a dog, and second, that for experimental man there were no subjective influences: no emotion, no thought, no feeling—no formation of concepts about what was going on.

A typical experiment ran as follows: E, the psychologist's depreciating abbreviation for Experimenter (possibly a subconscious technique for asserting the absence of any effect of the experimenter's presence), anyway, E attached electrodes to the arm or hand of his subject and determined just how much electric shock to the skin was just painful. He knew that such a shock elicited a change of heart rate. Next, he "paired" some external event with the electric shock in a precise manner, i.e., the experimenter consistently used a specific and unvarying short interval between dispensing the external event and giving the shock. The most convenient external events for use were either sounds or lights. E told S,

---

* Readers might be interested in researching for themselves how rabbits mark their territories (*Science*, vol. 171, p. 443, Feb. 1971). Knowing the technique adds flavor to this observation.

† I foresee the day, in some more sophisticated age, when we forswear the "objective" bonds of physics and acknowledge the reality of the subjective universe. Then perhaps we can learn what the dog was thinking when he heard the damned bell.

meaning the subject (another notation signifying the lack of any real substance to the subject other than his changing heart rate), that the electrodes on the arm were to give the shock, but the electrodes on the chest were to record the shock response. In this way E concluded (!) that S had never had an EKG recorded and so was not aware that in some way his heartbeat was being registered. At the beginning of the experiment E very carefully allowed S to "adapt" to the light or sound signal so that the event of the sudden appearance of a signal would not in itself cause a change in heart rate. Or if the light or sound did cause a change in heart rate, the change would be known.

The experiment really began by the light or sound signal appearing briefly, followed in precisely six (or five or ten) seconds by a moderately long blast of the electric shock to the arm. As the experiment wore on, S's heart began to change in a consistent manner when the light or sound signal occurred. The objective of this experiment was, of course, to train the heart to speed up when its owner saw the light or heard the sound signal. For the signal meant that if the heart didn't speed up, it would be made to do so by the shock. Yet when the results were in, the heart in fact had learned to slow down . . . in spite of the signals and in spite of the shocks.

The Pavlovian experiment (the pattern for the above experiment) of the dog learning to salivate upon hearing a bell because it had always been associated with the reward of food is cited by behavioral scientists as a gem of biological science and one of the firmest building blocks of our knowledge of the development of behavior in man. Yet in itself this Pavlovian experiment serves as the principal *dog*ma in the ruling mythology of behavioral psychology. As the noted behavioral scientist J. P. Scott observed, "The evidence which supports general theories and laws of learning rests on a remarkably narrow basis. Very few species and very few kinds of behavior have been thoroughly studied."

Someone Forgot the Physiology

Take the simple experiment outlined above as an example of a classical conditioning technique. The consensus of experimental psychologists had unequivocally stated that involuntary, automatic functions of the body were mere child's play to control by conditioning techniques. That superstition prevailed from the twenties until the last few years, despite the fact that the "teaching" was intended to speed up the heart, yet the heart "learned" to slow down. It was not until 1969 that any type of *systematic* study of the most fundamental changes of heart rate during such conditioned learning experiments was reported in the psychologic literature. There are innumerable physiologic factors that can complicate the apparently simple experiment described above.

First there is the question of what the shock itself does to heart rate. When thinking about what shock does to the heart, psychologists tend to think mainly in terms of adaptation, a psychophysiologic phenomenon where responses become less and less as stimuli are repeated, i.e., with repeated shock the actual change produced becomes less and less. And this is the case with the heart if one is evaluating the extent of the speeding or slowing caused by the stimulation. But it is not the only phenomenon; there are other important physiologic factors at work. Researchers without a "feel" and intimate knowledge for the complex inner cell and organ functioning of biological organisms tend to forget that they are not limitless, tireless sources of energy. If, for example, the shock is strong enough and repeated frequently enough, the heart muscle itself can tire. If it is forced to accelerate repeatedly and fast enough, its recovery is incomplete and there is less reserve energy for the responses to follow. Although this extreme is not likely to occur during a psychologic experiment, nonetheless there are residual effects which sap the heart's energy and can become important if there are other effects which cause fatigue.

There is another important direct consequence of repeatedly asking the heart to accelerate that has to do with the rate of recovery and state of relative excitability of the cardiac nerves which cause the acceleration. The sympathetic nerve supply to the heart is easily excited but it takes much longer to recover than even most physiologists consider. Although at first these nerves tend to remain excitable and for a time are easier to excite upon repeated stimulation, they too fatigue and begin to respond more and more sluggishly. Although psychologists do consider that the sympathetic and parasympathetic innervation of the heart may influence the heart's response quite differently in different people, they rarely identify these considerable influences mainly because it is tedious to sort out people who tend to accelerate their hearts (whose sympathetic nervous system dominates) from people who tend to slow their hearts (whose parasympathetic nervous system dominates). Yet each type of person may react differently in an experiment.

There are still other biological complications. Some individuals react more dramatically than others to shock and to the anxiety of the experiment with increased secretion of adrenaline, which heightens the speeding effect of the sympathetic nerve action on the heart. Other body activities which indirectly affect the heart rate are the effects of respiration, for example, which are direct and prompt. There are not only changes in heart rate with each inspiration and expiration, but in states of mild anxiety or alertness the breath may be held for short periods of time or big gulps of air taken quickly, and these irregular breathing patterns cause significant changes in heart rate.

The objective of the Pavlovian type of conditioned heart rate experiment (as described in the "S" and "E" experiment above) was to transfer the heart's response of accelerating when the body was shocked over to a second or neutral stimulus, in this case the tone or light signal. But just as the detailed effects of shock on heart rate were so long neglected in research studies, so the direct effects of light and tone signals were blissfully ignored although researchers had used them in their experiments for nearly forty years. One recent study, for example, showed that although the amount of speeding of the heart caused by a loud tone did indeed tend to diminish over time (adaptation), tones of lesser intensity did not have the same effect at all and speeding of the heart continued to occur. On the other hand, flashing on a light signal first caused slowing of the heart, but its effect changed to accelerating the heart when several flashes were given in quick succession. It is only recently that the researchers have decided that the responses of heart rate to the traditionally used tone and light signals are as complex as are the responses of the heart to electric shock itself. It has finally been agreed that the heart rate responds to tone and light signals first by marked acceleration, then by slowing, and finally by recovery to its normal rate.

So the earlier work, still held as gospel by many researchers and teachers, had shown, erroneously, that the heart was perverse, responding oppositely to the way it had been instructed. A great deal of work had been done in heart rate learning research only to find, finally, that nearly every element of the experiment influenced the heart's activity and in different directions and at different times, and that the heart's learning was very complex.

If, however, instead of using shock, the experimenter has compassion for his human subjects and would like to use stimuli more likely to be encountered in the everyday environment, such as unexpected, sudden noise, he is due for another surprise. Noise is apparently quite a different matter to the heart, for the heart responds to noise by slowing down rather than accelerating as it does to shock. It is interesting to observe that nowhere have the researchers used noise to try to teach the heart to slow. Apparently they had their own hearts set on teaching the heart to speed up. For one thing, it is easier for the heart to accelerate than to slow, i.e., there are more normally occurring conditions causing anxiety or alertness. So electric shock is used as the teaching device to show the heart how to accelerate, and the heart responds by learning how to slow.

In exclusively pursuing the effects of external influences, some investigators concluded that the several parts of the complex responses of heart rate to experimentally used stimuli were part of a widespread physiologic response by the organism to a suddenly occurring and novel event in the external environment. They labeled the entire response group the "orienting response."* We literally jump, for example, at a sudden, unexpected sharp sound and the whole body is involved: the heart races or momentarily stops, we gasp, heads turn, blood pressure rises, adrenaline flows. A few psychologists have believed that the widespread, vigorous muscle contractions that occur when we are violently startled (psychological experiments are notoriously vigorous) cause a change in the auto-

---

* Described in relation to skin talk, Chapter 2.

nomic nervous system and that in turn causes the heart rate to change. This would be a "passive," indirect response rather than a direct, "active" one. Orienting responses occur only when we perceive an unknown, unexpected stimulus, and diminish quickly when that stimulus is repeated, which is why we seem to get used to sonic booms or the noise of thunderstorms and to flashing neon lights. (Researchers do not tell us, however, why we do not get used to dripping faucets, squeaking shutters or buzzing mosquitoes.)

And Then They Forgot the Psychology

As sophisticated instrumentation became more available and the complex nature of heart rate changes was uncovered, the reporting of research studies also became more complex. In earlier studies the investigators simply reported the changes that seemed most obvious, that is, that people responded to the training procedures in either of the two possible ways, by speeding or slowing the heart. In recent studies, however, where more accurate equipment is used, heart rate responses are averaged for *how much* speeding or how much slowing. In the course of an experiment anywhere from fifty to several hundred responses per subject are recorded, and not only are these averaged, but the averages of all responses are put together to make a grand average. The researcher then relies on the magic of statistics to uncover the real significance of his results (i.e., he figures the probabilities; how often "on the average" people are likely to have that average kind of response).

While the averaging of results is standard scientific procedure, it is a procedure more applicable to the hard physical sciences than to psychology where individual biological differences are often striking and reflect the influence of a broad spectrum of interacting physiologic and emotional factors. These factors may profoundly influence experiments, yet be obscured and ignored by statistical analyses.

The level of anxiety or eagerness of the individual in an experiment may cause him to keep his muscles taut, accelerating the heart; or he may be uninterested or naturally calm and so run a slow heart. It is obvious that in an experiment designed to teach the heart to accelerate, the experiment is literally saturated with all of the elements that could ever excite any normal individual and cause his

heart to speed or slow or dance around. The subject walks into a
strange laboratory with strange equipment; white-coated figures of
scientific authority; worrisome instructions about what is to happen
during the experiment; warning bells and electric shocks; anxiety
that one is not performing well enough. And then the real enigma:
the researcher is trying to teach the heart to behave exactly as it
does during excitement, anxiety, and alertness. No wonder it is
puzzling that the heart learns to slow instead.

And there are other, very natural emotional and mental activities
that cloud the verities of the heart's behaving life. Heart rate is also
influenced by "anticipatory alertness," that curious suspended state
of excited expectance; and by the degree of both general and
immediate anxiety, perceptual set, how fast one adapts, and a
multitude of other subtle, seemingly remote but actually immediate
and important influences.

Many exciting clues to mind function have been lost in the
statistical averaging of the physical, physiological responses.

The Behavioristic Detour

Perhaps the confusion related to the heart's learning lies in the
researcher's head. There seems to be an unending war between the
mind of the heart and the ideas of the researcher. Take for example
the researcher's terminology of learning theory. If he wants the
subject's heart to accelerate, he reinforces acceleration by signals,
and if they work, he calls this positive reinforcement. But it is positive for the experimenter's desires, not for the heart's desire. The
heart's mind may be deciding that acceleration may be hazardous to
the health (which it is), and to the heart the reinforcement would
be quite negative. Or if the experimenter's desire is to have the heart
slow, then what was a positive reinforcement for acceleration becomes a negative reinforcement, except that since it does what the
experimenter wants, it is positive. It's all in the head of the experimenter. But the experimentee's heart has a mind, too. This is not a
mere piece of word play about semantics and differing minds, it is
an illustration of the neglect of the will of the heart. As, for example,
the willpower that successfully treated those six patients with atrial

fibrillation. The perversity of the heart in "learning" according to (classical) theory might be a clash of wills. In the experiment described above where the natural response of the heart to shock is completely reversed by pairing the shock with a tone, it may be the heart's head saying, "It is foolish and somewhat dangerous to beat faster to both the tone and then to the shock; once is enough; if I speed up for the tone, then I should slow down to the shock and keep the balance that keeps me healthy."

It became clear that the pillar of experimental learning psychology, classical conditioning, was riddled with problems when it came to training the heart. Even if these could be ironed out and ultimately support learning theory, of what practical use could such a learning method be when the heart must be constantly reminded by an electric shock or an explosive noise? In the history of learning theory, it was not too many years, as science sometimes goes, after Pavlovian concepts that Skinnerian concepts came. If the Pavlovian concepts were difficult to apply to the heart, why weren't the newer methods not tried for nearly thirty years? If Skinnerian techniques were so successful in controlling behavior, why weren't they used to teach animals and people to bring autonomic, "automatic" functions under control?

Part of the reason was that enthusiasm for American-bred operant conditioning concepts had swept the country's research laboratories. It was a dramatic new concept and so intriguingly different from Pavlovian theories. It was a joy for researchers to break from the "inferior" reflexes of Pavlov and work with the "superior" behavior possible with Skinnerian techniques. In endless studies the muscle and motor behavior of animals was re-explored by the new procedure, yet there was a thirty-year lag before it was found to be useful in bringing the body's internal functioning under control. Looking back on the long history of adamancy against exploration of possible voluntary control over internal functions in the U.S., one wonders whether some strong subconscious bias may have caused a long, relatively unproductive excursion through the expensive and minimally productive research projects of repeated conditioning experiments. The lack of enthusiasm for using a new learning technique to control the body's behavior makes an interesting window to view the behavior of the scientist.

A few casual and not very serious experiments (two) reported no success in "teaching" the autonomic nervous system by operant learning techniques. Ironically enough, one of these reports was by B. F. Skinner. He concluded, on the basis of a rather perfunctory, sketchy experiment, that the involuntary nervous system was indeed involuntary, not up to the training capacities of the "higher" nervous system functions so amenable to his operant conditioning techniques. Partly as a result, from 1938 until 1961 there was no real U.S. effort to determine whether the ANS could yield to voluntary control. The ANS was so completely inferior that it didn't qualify even to be subjected to the new mechanistic, pragmatic exploration of "superior" behavior. Then, in 1961, Gregory Razran reported Russian success in his monograph with the most delightful title, "The Observable Unconscious and the Inferable Conscious in Current Soviet Psychophysiology: Interoceptive Conditioning, Semantic Conditioning, and the Orienting Reflex." His review was widely interpreted as indicating that the Russian psychologist Lisina had successfully "taught" blood vessels to dilate by the operant conditioning techniques of Skinner. Her results jolted the American psychologists who were by now firmly entrenched in the Skinnerian tradition that the involuntary nervous system (the ANS that supplies the blood vessels with their nerves) was, by nature, completely resistant to training.

It wasn't until 1965 when a translation of Lisina's paper was published in a review by Razran that U.S. reconnaissance discovered that she herself had concluded that human subjects were able to exert voluntary control over their blood vessels by "using a number of special devices, mainly the relaxation of the skeletal musculature and changing of the depth of relaxation." In fact, Lisina suggested that her results might be explained solely as conditioned learning by skeletal muscle and respiration rather than direct learning by the ANS. In real fact Lisina had shown that such learning by small blood vessels was possible *only* if the test subjects were provided with external feedback of their activity, i.e., knowledge and feelings about whether their efforts were successful or not. But it was too late by 1965. U.S. investigators were hot on the trail of the new phenomenon: "teaching" the automatic nervous system to come under their control.

The attempt to control the heart by classical conditioning techniques was of course largely for the pleasure of theorists. Any possibility for practical application was inherently nearly impossible. Nor did Skinnerian learning theory seem to hold much promise, unconcerned as its theorists were by the influence of mental activity. But the Russians had not forgotten Pavlov's brilliant observations about the role of higher nervous activity of the higher nervous system in the evolution of higher forms of learning even though American behaviorists had. Nor had the American psychologist Neal Miller been entirely sold on the purely mechanistic, reflexologic explanations of human body behavior. Miller's work has provided a large share of the experimental underpinnings for the possibility of human voluntary control over autonomic body functions. His work, however, was conducted in animals. In the meantime it was the young psychologist Shearn who, as we shall soon see, made the break with traditional learning theory and terminology and "told it as it was."

The Heart Has a Will

While contingents of behavioral scientists busied themselves with the details of what various body functions might be responsible for the learning peculiarities of the heart, and others fussed about the failure of the experimenters to conform to the rigorous procedures espoused by experimental learning theory, the cultural revolution was sparking the resurgence of self-determination on many fronts. Youth movements, the new consciousness, and a radically changing society can be seen reflected in the new directions taken within psychophysiologic research in the mid-sixties.

In the laboratory, studies on sleep and dreams were unfolding new physiologic correlates of states of consciousness. It was becoming apparent that the complexities and shades of consciousness would have to be dealt with; the work of the mind could no longer be ignored in behavior theory studies. The influence of the mind on body behavior would have to be studied. We began to hear about "cognitive mediators" as mechanisms postulated to account for behavior rather than simple reflexology or conditioning. And what was the mind's work? It was making decisions about the information it received through all of its senses. And like the automatic control systems of spaceships, the more the mind learned about its own performance, the more improved that performance became. The mind was always being fed back information, and it learned. If the mind were fed back information about its own body's biology (i.e., bio-feedback), what now were the limits of its abilities to control its own body? Gradually the importance of bio-feedback information to the learning process has been revealed, and with it has come an unfolding of the role of cognition, of awareness, of, in fact, all of the higher mental functions. These distinguishing characteristics of human beings are finally being acknowledged.

Shearn

It is probable that Shearn's scientific paper in *Science* in 1962 was the first report of successful use of bio-feedback techniques to teach people how to control their own heart rates. Although neither he nor anyone else at that time (how primitive 1962 now seems) conjured up a *bio*-feedback concept to describe his experimental procedure, he did clearly state that he was using feedback, beginning his paper with, "While feedback would seem to characterize autonomic behavior in the biological system, little research has been directed toward the use of feedback of external origin." (The surfeit of electronic discoveries in the past decade makes the simplicity of Shearn's experiment seem like a kite-flying excursion to find electricity; nonetheless it represents both a major change in direction of psychologic research and beginning recognition of the bio-feedback process.)

Shearn used the traditional shock to the leg as a punishment to his subjects for not performing their tasks well enough. The task was to watch a timer that showed actual heart rate and to make the timer speed up by speeding up the heart. At the same time the subject could hear his heartbeat through an amplifier sound system, and that provided him with constant feedback information both visually and auditorially about his own heart rate. If he failed to increase his heart rate by the amount decreed by the experimenter and within a certain time limit, he received the shock to the leg. Every day the subjects went through hourly sessions. By the third session they were generally able to increase their heart rates enough to avoid getting a shock to the leg. Unfortunately, nowhere does Shearn tell us what he instructed his subjects to do. (In the tradition of the conditioning experiment the subjects would *not* have been told.) Regardless, it appears that the subjects learned well to keep their heart rates speeded up to prevent the shock.

More surprising were the results of the subjects who were intentionally misled about what the timer and sounds meant.* The misled subjects were told that the timer and sound signals represented their heartbeats, but in fact they did not. The experimenters deceived them by manipulating the timer and sound completely at random. The *misled* subjects, oblivious to the deception and believing that they were watching and listening to their own heart rates, *slowed* their heart rates instead of increasing heart rate as the experimental subjects did.

There are many ways to explain the results of Shearn's study. Today, after the enlightenment of bio-feedback concepts, we might ascribe a fair share of the successful results to the fact that the human mind was an important factor. It was fed back information about its interior activity. The mind may have made associations between its feelings and the visual and auditory signals, then joined these in associations with the physical sensation of increased heart rate, so that gradually the entire system became self-controlled. It adjusted like the thermostat adjusts its central control to maintain a certain heat level, that is, when the signals indicated that the heart rate was increasing, the mind-body learned to know the feeling of higher heart rate and then could generate appropriate and specialized body changes. The signals also signaled success, providing further forward impetus.†

Nineteen sixty-one was still an era of behaviorist dominance of experimental psychology, prevailed in 1961, and Shearn's study drew

---

* The fact that some subjects were misled does not imply that the other subjects were fully informed about the experiment or about what they were to do (this is psychology, not logic).

† The question of why the misled subjects slowed their hearts while receiving the same signals (but not the same information) will be considered later. A few guesses here are that they may have detected that the information claimed to be given by the signals was at odds with their inner reality. Or they may have relaxed, as their respiration indicated, and adapted to their experimental situation upon discovering that nothing was happening, pleasant or unpleasant, good or bad.

its share of criticism. First, the critics pointed out, it is well known that when one part of the autonomic system responds, most of the other parts do also, albeit at their own rates. This "fact" derived from studies on fear and intense or severe neurotic anxiety; yet Shearn's study didn't deal with obvious fear or anxiety. Nonetheless, the critics said, everyone knows the lower levels of fear and/or anxiety make respiration irregular and when that happens the heart rate accelerates or the muscles tense and the subjects become alert and that makes the heart speed up. But Shearn had used other subjects who heard and saw the same signals and they didn't speed their hearts, they slowed them. Weren't the same anxieties present in these subjects?

The use of a group of subjects who are subjected to all of the experimental elements but whose performance is deliberately misled with respect to the real purpose of the experiment, as Shearn's misled subjects were, is a common procedure in psychophysiologic research. It is called the "yoked control." It is an interesting fillip in learning research, although I believe that it serves a very limited purpose, if not, perhaps, a distinctly confusing one.*

Another way to mislead subjects is illustrated by a different type of experiment where visual and auditory signals, which actually signaled heart rate, were explained to the subjects as being signals

---

* The yoked control is a subject who is paired (yoked) with an experimental subject in that he receives the same stimuli and clues and conditions given to his experimental brother, but his performance has no effect on the outcome of the experiment. Generally the exact times of responses of the experimental subject are used for timing the stimuli, clues or other conditions being given to the yoked subject. If, for example, the experimental subject will receive a shock to the leg if he fails to accelerate his heart rate, the way his heart responds is used to govern when and at what intensity the shock is given to his "yoked" partner. Thus the "control" is continuously misinformed about his performance, and no matter what he does, he will still be punished at those times when his experimental partner is punished. In experimental psychology it was held by many that this procedure would "average out" nonspecific responses to experimental stimuli and when such changes were compared to those from a structured experiment, the fundamental, specific changes would be those "left over." In work with human beings the yoked control gained in use because it was believed to control for the effect of cognitive information on experimental results. In the heart rate game, the yoked control subject was misinformed about what the signals meant, yet he performed in a specific and discriminating manner although opposite to his yoked experimental partner. In absence of explanations offered by experimental psychologists, the influence of functional and cognitive information gained from the mechanics of the experiment and the experimental situation itself cannot be ruled out.

of their brain waves. This may be an interesting way to "control" an experiment, yet one wonders about the effect of misinformation itself. It may lead to anxiety; certainly many individuals worry about what their brain waves might reveal, and the situation could worsen considerably if they are not able to become aware of either consistent changes or make associations with themselves during the course of the experiment. In either case, whether by misleading instructions or by performance deliberately made unproductive, the subject may "work" at trying to alter what he believes he is supposed to, with the result that what he does is quite opposite to what the experimental subject is doing and would make for an unreal difference between control and experimental results.

For several years following Shearn's report, there was almost no published work on the evolving bio-feedback phenomenon. Then around 1965 a spate of new reports on the "new" feedback way of teaching people how to control heart rates began to appear in the psychologic literature. Some researchers experimented with teaching how to slow the heart, some on how to keep the heart at a regular beat, some on how to speed up the heart, while still others combined the tasks and alternated periods of having subjects slow and then accelerate the heart.

In the late sixties researchers were rejoicing because they had found that heart rate could be controlled through the simple expedient of rewarding it for performing correctly. Somehow, after thirty-odd years, the reward technique of operant conditioning was found to be effective in inducing the heart to change its rate. Except now there was a return to the terminology of reinforcement. Typically in these experiments the experimental subject was "rewarded," i.e., reinforced, for changing his heart rate. The reward was hearing or seeing a monitor of his own heart rate. Simple, unadulterated bio-feedback. Except that it was called operant conditioning, denoting that the learning and control were dependent upon the externalized signals and not upon internal intent.

Results of the many research studies were almost always positive. The heart rate of human beings could be controlled by "reinforcing" its performance. The concepts of bio-feedback had not reached the heart rate researchers and they attached little importance to the experimental trick that the reinforcement, the reward, was the feedback of a specific bit of the performer's own biology. It was enough of a reward to the researchers to have broken through the conditioning barrier that for thirty years had insisted that the autonomic nervous system and its organs could not be controlled by a system of rewards.*

Where There's a Will, There's a Way of the Heart

The idea that gradually formed in the late sixties that the body's involuntary nervous system could be brought under voluntary control represented a sharp break in the traditions of thought on the basic processes of both body and mind function. Until then all recognized authoritative biomedicine held to the concept that somewhere in the structure of the autonomic, automatic nervous system and its great diversity of end organs (heart, lungs, intestines, gall bladder, etc.) lay inherent automatic generators of primitive coping behavior, and beyond that lay nothing.

To the laboratory researcher even the whisper of the possibility of voluntary control of physiologic automatic functions was as emotionally traumatic as was the first news of heart transplants to the public. It was as if a medieval voice, long lost in the subconscious, was crying out, "Impossible; my autonomic nervous system is God-given; it is His Will not mine that gives me life. It is the work of the devil to tamper with it."† The heart is life itself; to attempt to control it by whims of the mind might be encroaching on divine powers. In whatever way the emotions of Western man may cling to magic, his intellect, anchored to the physical world, lights the path that angels fear to tread. Perhaps the rather long time between the first hints of voluntary control and the beginnings of intensive research in the United States was a period of emotional readjustment to the profound theoretical and even moral implications of the voluntary control possibility. When U.S. researchers finally got all of their information from everyone else, they really started to move.

There was now little question that the responses of the heart,

---

* For further discussion see Appendix D.

† There is an interesting equation between behavioral scientists and medieval theologians. *Beyond Freedom and Dignity* reads like the ecclesiastical mandates of the fifteenth century. To many a soul-starved scientist bio-feedback looks to be the biological equivalent of the *Summa Theologica*.

even in the most tightly controlled experiment, were governed by an internal voluntariness stemming from the mind's constant sifting and decoding of both physical and mental information. In the rigid classical conditioning studies many varieties of subjective and homeostatic (internal self-regulating) influences had confounded experiments and played havoc with interpretations. The most serious disadvantage was the gaping hole left by failure to consider the cognitive effects of experience. The experiential world is where true volition resides. What, for example, is a more obvious indicator of the heart's sensitivity to thought than the repeatedly demonstrated sudden acceleration of the heart at the mere threat of electric shock to the arm, or the mere imagining of that threat?

A great many of the investigations spawned by the puzzling possibilities of voluntary control of heart rate were not only ingenious but most revealing of the forgotten importance of the human psyche. One of the first studies (1966) which contains many more implications for human behavior than has yet been recognized was that of Brener and Hothersall. Their subjects were wired for heart rate recording; the room was comfortable and the investigators pleasant. In front of the subjects was a panel of two lights, a green one which the investigator said was a signal for a time period when high-frequency tones could be heard, and a red light when low tones could be heard. The subjects were asked to try to cause more high tones when the green light was on and to try to make more low tones when the red light was on. They were asked to do this "by mental processes only," but they weren't told that the high tones actually were their own fast heartbeats while the low tones represented their own slower heartbeats. In theory, then, all the subjects knew was that in some unknown way they had the power to produce more high or low tones and that they were to accomplish this mysterious effect exactly when signaled to do so.

Human beings are almost always quick to obey verbal commands, but to everyone's surprise even their hearts complied with the requests of the experimenters. When signaled to make more high tones, they did so by increasing their heart rates; to make low tones more often, they slowed their hearts. This happened despite the fact that their heart rates were continuing to slow during the experiment, according to the phenomenon of adaptation. The great paradox of this experiment was that *none* of the subjects guessed that the tones were controlled by their heart rates even though the electrodes on their arms and legs were strapped on exactly as they are for conventional recording of EKGs (electrocardiograms). Nearly everyone has either seen pictures of people having heart rates recorded or has actually had an EKG. Possibly some subjects were unaware that metal discs placed around wrists and ankles had a relationship to the electrical energy of the heart. More likely most were aware, but some may not have wanted to give the show away, while others perhaps weren't *quite* sure.

Then again, it seems probable that in the dead quiet of a laboratory room, darkened, and being alone, some subjects could feel their hearts beating and could relate the regular body quivers to the simultaneous occurrence of the tones. Perhaps they didn't. If they didn't, perhaps they associated their heartbeats with tones subconsciously, below the level of conscious awareness. What we *do* know is that during the experiment the subjects had information available about their heart rates that they had not had before: the tones. There was, in fact, a great deal of information—the difference between the tones, the rate of the tones and even the regularity of the tones. It is not always necessary to become consciously aware of new and different information in order to use it. It isn't necessary to conceptualize associations and relationships consciously; human beings have the capacity to formulate entire sequences of actions from subconscious mental activity.

I myself suspect that the subject fails to be aware that he is controlling his heart rate because the act of becoming aware of one's own heart rate is a new experience. When new experiences creep their way into consciousness and into memory banks of associations, they may be incomplete, distant or poorly understood, and so misinterpreted. Human beings frequently misinterpret experience. The outstanding example is the confusion that witnesses to accidents or crimes have in trying to recall the experience. The experience was new, fragmented, and poorly attended to. Law-enforcement agencies train personnel to be alertly aware during such times. It seems possible that human beings too can be trained, or train themselves, to become aware of more details of the heart rate change experience, trained to discriminate more and more finely the awareness of smaller and smaller changes. Greater attention to the fidelity and meaningfulness of the instruments and procedures may also serve to define the experience more precisely.

Another facet of Brener and Hothersall's study that has not received adequate attention is the amazing rapidity with which the heart responded to the two different signals, green and red. Each colored light signal lasted less than a minute, yet for the most part the heart promptly responded to each new request, to slow or to speed up. In general, the organs of the autonomic system are slow in responding to nervous stimulation compared to the way in which nerve stimulation can effect action in the muscular system. It is therefore surprising that the cardiac nerves can influence heart rate so quickly. Why then did the subjects respond so neatly, so cleanly, and so quickly to signals to speed or to slow? Is the efficiency of central control, the brain, so great that it can overcome the ordinariness of what happens in the rest of the body? Is there a special mechanism that governs too much speeding, too much slowing? This will become an important consideration later in this chapter.

While it is true that the difference between slowing and speeding in Brener and Hothersall's experiments scarcely exceeded twenty beats per minute, accumulated over time this could mean some fourteen thousand beats in just half a day, and this difference could be important to the organism.

Another investigator conducted an experiment to determine whether human hearts can maintain regular rates of heartbeat. Subjects were "punished" if their heart rates changed, i.e., they received a shock to the leg if they failed to keep their hearts beating in precise rhythm. The objective was to learn whether people could keep their hearts beating regularly without ever becoming aware that they were doing it. When a light signal was turned on, it meant that a shock to the leg might be upcoming. At the same time, however, the subjects were presented with a task to do that kept their attention so that they were too busy to notice the signal warning about the shock. The attention task was to detect any change in position of needles on three different meters and to note any needle change immediately. To ensure total occupation with the task, the meters were placed behind a screen which could be seen only when the subject pressed a key to light up the screen. To heighten the attention the subjects were told that if they failed to detect changes promptly, they would get the leg shock. At the beginning of the experiment the subject was exposed to what would happen if "something" about him failed to perform: he was given the shock. Naturally the heart rate increased, and it also increased when the warning light came on. The heart rate was now elevated, and the experiment was so designed that the subject was punished by the shock if he now failed to maintain the accelerated heart rate. And that is exactly what the hearts did: they maintained the accelerated heart rate as long as the warning light signal was on and they avoided the electric shock. As soon as the warning light was turned off, indicating no more shock, heart rates dropped back to normal.

But of course, all of this "heart learning" time was occurring at the same time that the mind of the subject was occupied with his task of detecting change in needle position of the meters. So his heart "learned" while he was unaware of what his own heart was doing. It learned so well that the experimenters were able to use the light signal alone, *never* followed by shock, and they could maintain the accelerated heart rate for nearly an hour. A tendency to sustain high heart rates was still evident the following day.

Control of the heart rate in these experiments was so complete that the rate could be made to "oscillate" merely by presenting and removing the warning signal at regular intervals. The authors speculated that something like this type of heart control might occur within the ordinary environment, and certainly in the absence of conscious awareness by the individual. Since there were no concurrent changes in respiration or skin resistance, the learning effect was assumed to be specific to the heart rate system.

The failure of biological scientists to participate in multidisciplinary studies is pointed up by studies such as this. A collaborating physiologist, one who knows the most intimate physiologic workings of the heart and entire cardiovascular system might have pointed out that perhaps the heart is the most sensitive responder of all autonomic organs to the least hint of emotion, such as to the warning signal. It requires merely a whiff of emotion to set the heart rate wandering. Moreover, it responds much more quickly than other organs innervated by the autonomic nervous system, and finally, it possesses a much wider range of activity through which it can re-

spond. Saliva can dry up or it can secrete, but its changes are difficult to identify in discrete stages, while the heart rate can change
100 beats per minute, and it is easy to recognize the difference between 70 and 80, for example.

One of the more interesting byproducts of the above study was
the suggestion that since the heart learned without *conscious* awareness, it was performing simply on command from the signal that
warned: perform or be shocked. If so, then perhaps subjects (or
their autonomic systems) never needed other types of learning aids
such as the light or sound signals of bio-feedback that signal *how*
the heart is performing.

While the suggestion is an interesting one, it fails to consider
subconscious processing of information. One of the most common
examples of subconscious thinking occurs when a name or bit of
information has been forgotten and seemingly can't be recalled;
then at some later time the lost item leaps to mind out of the blue.
Something had to be going on below the conscious level. So the data
presented that subjects were not consciously aware of what their
hearts were doing do not negate a subconscious reasoning process.

Subconscious Signals

A variety of curious observations about awareness has been reported
during heart rate control studies that forewarned an ensuing struggle between the psychologists' desire for physical substrates of
behavior and the emergence of man's will and mind as perhaps the
most powerful determinant of his own physical being and behavior.
Note that the experimental reports below deal exclusively with
conscious, *verbalized* descriptions of the subjective aspects of heart
rate learning. Not until later in bio-feedback history was the subconscious will probed. In several studies subjects failed to identify
their heart rate activity with the auditory or visual signals of their
own heart rates, even after days of exposure at the rate of an hour or
so every day. These reports conflict sharply with those of other
studies. Why? Was the researcher's bias in some way transferred to
the subject?

Another study insisted that only those people who *failed* to learn
any control over heart rate "guessed" they were hearing or watching

monitors of their own heart rates. The subjects who learned good control never became consciously aware that most of the information in the experimental situation concerned their hearts. Some authors suggest that such differences in performance represent two different types of people. It is well known that the sympathetic nervous system dominates in its effects over the parasympathetic system in some people and the reverse is true in the other types. With a task to slow heart rate, the people with parasympathetic dominance (ready tendency to slow) would have the edge, while the people with sympathetic dominance (tendency to speed the heart) would first have to overcome their inherent tendency before beginning to learn the task. This being true and it also being certain that the two parts of the autonomic nervous system are expressors of emotion, then any "feelings" related to the heart rate control task might be quite different in the two types of people. For example, if subjective reports in another study on heart rate slowing and speeding are examined in relationship to success of control, one notes that subjects who learned how to accelerate the heart said they concentrated on items or events or generally tensed themselves, save one who said he relaxed. But for those who successfully learned how to slow the heart, some subjects did so by relaxing while others concentrated on something other than the problem at hand. In contrast, nearly all of the nonlearners said they kept relaxed. It is difficult to extract any truly consistent subjective effort from these reports, yet the myth continues that some subjects could speed their hearts by increasing their body tension and slow them by relaxation. If the actual heart rate changes of these subjects is examined, one finds, however, *no* relationship between "learning" and their body activity.

The Heart Speaks

Although psychologists presume to deal with human behavior, experimental psychologists, struggling to model psychology after the physical sciences, by and large reject the validity of subjective reports. What a subject reports about his experiences during an experiment depends upon such a complex set of circumstances that meaningful analysis is almost impossible. The subject may or may not be attending to what the experimenter feels are the critical parts of the experiment; he may be physically tired or may be alert and responding appropriately to his physical state; he may be very intelligent or he may be poorly educated and his expressions may differ accordingly; his past experiences may make him take a dim view of the experiment or he may be curious and trying too hard to please. For such reasons experimental psychophysiologists have become defensive about subjective reports and tend to ignore their potential contribution toward understanding human behavior. Yet it is by subjective reports that we live and operate in our daily lives. Generally it takes a few encounters with a new acquaintance to establish some frame of reference with respect to his particular way of expression, to estimate the way he views his experiences, and to sift out extraneous influences until we come to a reliable mode of intercommunication. This same could be done in the laboratory.

What did experimental subjects say about their experiences in heart rate learning experiments? Try to forget that the scientist-experimenter is saturated in psychologic theory, that he has a single objective in the questions he asks, and forget that the subject might be a bit uncomfortable by the strangeness of the laboratory or annoyed by having to waste his time harnessed to apparatus. With all the resources of his academic knowledge at hand, the experimenter says, "How did you do it?" Positively brilliant. And the subject replies, "I don't know." He's not about to be trapped by making a foolish remark. Or, the experimenter may go further and ask, "How did you feel during the experiment?" And the subject replies, "Bored." Little wonder that experimenters are disenchanted with subjective reports.

While that dialogue pretty much sums up the verbal reports elicited from subjects about what they did during the experiments and how they felt about them, it should be pointed out that less than 20 percent of the investigators bothered either to question their subjects or, if they did, to report about it. As a psychiatrist-physician said, "How in the hell are we going to be able to help people to learn to control heart rates if we don't try to find out how the people who do it successfully really do it."

The laissez-faire attitude about the influence of the mind is typified in a conclusion by leading researchers and published recently in a scientific journal: "It is probably fruitless to pursue further any attempts at providing such demonstrations in humans (the pure phenomenon of instrumental conditioning) because they would require unconscious subjects to eliminate cognitive mediation and complete curarization to eliminate somatic mediation." Despite the obvious and major role of the mind and the will in learning heart rate control, voluntary effort as a specific element was never examined until 1970, after the age of bio-feedback had begun.

One of the most delightfully honest studies was that reported by Wells, in 1970, in which he constructed the heart rate control experiment to maximize results rather than to test theories. He selected the most interested and enthusiastic subjects, then he informed them fully about the experimental procedure and the meaning of the experiment. His results tell a great deal about the normal range of human ability to control heart rate and what it feels like. His subjects performed extremely well when their task was to increase heart rate, and they were more proficient than subjects in other experiments that have been reported. But none of them increased heart rate to a dangerous level. Those who achieved the greatest increase reported feelings of anxiety. This is particularly intriguing and interesting since it is so well known that during anxiety the heart rate increases. But here the subjects were increasing their heart rates voluntarily, and *then* they felt anxious. A nice chicken-or-the-egg problem. Just as surprising was the fact that they were literally unable to *decrease* heart rate voluntarily. Since other investigators had found subjects who could and did decrease their heart rates, there would seem to be something about Wells's experiment that inhibited performance of this task. Only two things were different: enthusiasm, meaning the subjects were highly motivated; and being fully informed as to the nature of the experiment.

If one were to make a guess, it might be that the enthusiasm of the subjects was primed by excitement, and excitement is primed by anticipation. But, as we have learned, the heart rate apparently slows during anticipation. Which investigators were wrong; which experiments were misguided? These are the problems of research. Wells's subjects were fully informed about the experiment and the heart rate task, suggesting the possibility that their minds had a more complete array of information to work with in making decisions about just how their hearts might respond in safety. This added increment of thinking (conscious or subconscious) would be facilitated by their eager, alert state of mind. Which just may go to show that thinking may not add a cubit to your stature, but it certainly can do something about your heartbeat.

The real jolt to the experimental conditioning learning theorists came with the 1971 study of Bergman and Johnson, who made the startling discovery that people could change their heart rates when given cognitive information only and *without* any shocks or feedback information, bells or lights of the hallowed conditioning techniques. They simply instructed their subjects: "When you hear the tone, try to increase your heart rate," or, "When you hear the tone, try to slow your heart rate." The results of this clever little study aren't much by practical standards, but with the crutch of statistics the change in heart rate *by intention only* became fairly impressive. Subjects who were asked to increase heart rate did very well, speeding the heart by some 3 beats per minute within the 6 seconds of the tone. Those asked to slow their hearts didn't, but neither did they increase the rate. As in other experiments the results point to a greater ease in speeding up the heart than in slowing it down. Although the investigators interviewed their subjects intensively, they could find no consistent technique used either to accelerate the heart nor to keep it from accelerating when asked to slow it down. But then, 6 seconds isn't much time in which to form impressions.

One can punch holes in any interesting study, especially when it is dealing with novel abilities of human beings. The Bergman and Johnson study, interesting and significant as it is, is a typical example of the obscurantism practiced by psychologic researchers. All results of the experiment were expressed in mathematical formulas. A quick calculation shows, however, that the change in heart rate never exceeded 4 percent. If the resting heart rate was 72, this amount of increase would mean the rate increased to 75 beats per minute. It would take exceptionally accurate measurements to make the results believable, for the eye makes this much error in measuring the interval between beats on a written record, and half this size of error can occur in machine-made measurements. Moreover, the heartbeat is rarely in a steady state: the normal variability of heart rate is in the neighborhood of 10 percent. Now what do we make of the study showing the remarkable effect of instructions alone on ability to increase one's own heart rate a mere 4 percent? Closer inspection of the study shows that nearly every time the subjects heard the tone, they increased heart rate. It's the consistency that counts. During other 6-second intervals without the tone, their heart rates varied scarcely at all, so by the rules of statistics it can be inferred that the change during the tone appeared specific to the time when a change in heart rate had been requested. Then again, someone else may ask, what about the expectations, the edge of anxiety about performance that might creep in? Yes, this would also increase heart rate. Psychophysiologic experiments, it would seem, are very difficult.

Two independent research studies with the same result are better than one, and Dr. Al Ax of Detroit has confirmed the fact that instructions alone, bits of cognitive knowledge, do in fact profoundly influence voluntary control of heart rate. At the 1970 BFRS meeting he reported that simply asking his subjects to increase or decrease heart rate revealed abilities to change heart rates by 20-some beats per minute. Insight into the capabilities of human beings for controlling automatic functions such as heart rate is increasing. A 1972 scientific report describes surprisingly large, 25 to 35 beats per minute, *voluntary* changes of heart rate in a bio-feedback experiment. The promptness of the changes suggested to the investigators that feedback might not be so important as other researchers had indicated. Apparently they weren't acquainted with Dr. Ax's report.

Other researchers became interested in the fact that some people can exert more control over their heart rates than can others. Two groups of researchers have investigated the difference in people classified as "externals" and "internals." In the psychology trade this refers to the way in which they control their behavior. Those with an internal locus of control are people who feel a personal responsibility for their social behavior; they feel that control lies within. The "externals" feel that their behavior is controlled by luck and fate, by what happens outside of themselves. It is an interesting notion to relate a social psychologic concept of behavior to physiologic behavior. Dr. Sophia Fotopolous has reported that people with internal control of behavior readily learned to increase their heart rates without any type of external bio-feedback, but the poor "externals," who depended upon outside events to shape their behavior, needed the external bio-feedback signal to accomplish the same thing. Also interesting is the fact that the "externals" normally have higher heart rates than do "internals." A later study not only verified these results but further showed that *with* bio-feedback external-control people were better able to learn to decrease their heart rates than were the internal-control people. Moreover, the different types of people used quite different strategies of concentration, thought, imagery and relaxation to accomplish their heart rate control.

In their 1971 study, Bergman and Johnson cite some interesting possibilities as to the mechanisms their subjects may have used to exert voluntary control. They suggest that perhaps some subjects were altering their general states of arousal by thinking about exciting or anxiety-laden things. But then, of course, others who were successful reported that they were simply relaxed and not thinking. A comparison of results in subjects who reported thinking with those who said they weren't revealed that whether or not thoughts were present had very little effect on performance. They also mention the possibility of quite other kinds of feedback information; for example, the subjects might be relating changes to success or failure and so reinforcing themselves. Some subjects, in fact, did admit to giving themselves "pep" talks during the experiments.

An ingenious piece of research was a study by Valins designed to uncover whether internal events could generate cognitive activity and so influence the subject's appraisal of the experimental situation and ability to perform. Valins showed slides of semi-nude subjects to his male subjects, and during viewing of these some of the subjects would hear a heartbeat increasing while others heard a heartbeat decreasing. The trap, however, was that those were not the subject's heartbeats. They were someone else's. Again we come up against a chicken-or-the-egg problem, for when the subjects heard a change in the false heart rate, they rated the slides they viewed then as more interesting than others. Something about their hearts remembered too, for when several weeks later they were offered some of the slides used as sort of a reward for participating in the experiment, they chose the slides they saw when they had heard the change in heart rate. This is not only a fascinating study of subconscious feedback loops in operation, but an important study showing that internal events can function as cues or stimuli and a source of cognitive information. It has become customary for us to believe psychologists who tell us that we think only when prodded by some event in the external environment. At last, science is catching up with common sense.

The opposite part of the problem was nicely demonstrated in a study by Defares and his colleagues. Using a machine which generated false heartbeats, they determined the effect of such false but physiologically potentially soothing information on subjects with different levels of anxiety. Those subjects with a high level of anxiety became calmer when they heard false *slow* heartbeats, and even more thought-provoking, *their* heart rates decreased. There are, in all, many research studies to confirm the facts that if the person is anxious his heart rate increases and/or if his heart rate increases, he becomes anxious. All one can deduce from such alternate results is that there is a powerful internal feedback loop between the brain and the heart that controls emotion, and that this feedback loop can be "entered" or acted upon at almost any point in the loop, mind or heart or in between. In some future day human beings may learn enough awareness about the infinite array of information continuously received by every part of the body, which, with their thousand mind-body feedback loops, could, for example, automatically sense the finest increment of muscle tension and instruct the heart to stay calm. A keen sensitivity to the power of the loops could herald the smallest twinge of anxiousness and seize the faint sensation to explore the cause before it dispels tranquillity. Or perhaps the reawakening of lost senses might use the faint smell of tainted air to tell the heart to beat faster and then relay the news of hazard to the mind control of flight.

Three Sex Words and the Word "Death"

One study that illustrates this perfectly is a recent report by Gary Schwartz. He has been concerned by the role of cognition in the heart control process, although at one time he was a party to a published statement that the cognitive activity could not be implicated in control of autonomic functions. Perhaps he was succumbing to the liberated, humanistic pressures of our times when he decided to investigate whether self-generated thoughts could influence heart rate. He designed a simple experiment, asking subjects to think about very specific items: precise series of numbers, letters, and specific words. They were to "think" the specific words only when they heard tones that were pacing them so that the experimenter could know when the thought item was occupying the mind. They were given a certain option as to which thoughts and at what times they would think them, e.g., of four numbers, they could "think" any of the four. Then the heart rate was measured. At the end of thinking about the number sequence, which gave the experimenter a precise starting time for what would follow, the subject then either thought of the letters A, B, C or D, or at different times thought of emotion words, these being three sex words and the word "death." The results were almost identical to the experiment where the investigator simply asked subjects to increase or decrease heart rate. The sex words caused an accelerated heart rate, the letters caused almost no change. Schwartz concludes that "different thought sequences can produce different autonomic responses." In this experiment also, the changes of heart rate were quite small, which leads one to wonder about the influences of different levels of emotional reactivity in different kinds of people. Schwartz might be interested in reviewing the work of Dixon many years ago, who tabulated differences in emotional reactivity and found that some people respond by excitement to emotionally charged words while others do exactly the opposite and their inhibition of an excitement response is shown by a depression of activity. Although Dixon used brain waves to demonstrate his results, one would suspect that, as for "internals" versus "externals," human beings may differ profoundly in the *directions* in which they respond to emotional situations.

The Role of Bio-Feedback Information

This takes us directly to the role and importance of the information provided by the experimental situation about the objective of the experiment. We will look at it in terms of bio-feedback information.

If the experimenter instructs his subject that he will receive a shock to the leg if something about him doesn't perform correctly, this in itself is information of great impact and significance. But when the experimenter does not tell the subject what he is to do, the amount of information doubles. The subject knows (a) that he is expected to do something and (b) he doesn't know what the something is. And one plus one equals two. To be sure, if the experimenter does tell the subject, the subject will exert an indefinable, unmeasurable set of influences on the experiment, but at least these are tied to the fidelity of instructions and experience. But when he *doesn't* tell the subject, a host of subconscious, emotional, mind and body influences are excited, and these too are unknown, undefinable and unmeasurable. Therefore it might be wiser to speak of Information Type A that is cognitive, consciously appreciated information, and Information Type B that is the absence of this, but contains the information of sensations and feelings that are not consciously appreciated.

In addition to the information contained in instructing subjects about their role in experiments, nearly everything in an experimental environment is information that can be perceived by the subject. Moreover, if the experimental subject is attached to apparatus, he becomes aware of his body, and that awareness is a type of bio-feedback information. In the heart rate experiments, the visual or auditory signals are, regardless of whether the subject is aware of their true significance or not, information signals concerning the subject's biology which are perceived and thus fed back to the individual. Neither awareness of body sensations nor the inferences from instructions necessarily have to be at the aware level; they can be subliminal, below the threshold for conscious recognition. Both sensations and thoughts are recognized by the organism's nervous system, are put into memory, are acted upon by his brain neurons, and have consequent effects.

Experimenters themselves are too often unaware of the fertile streams of information with which their subjects are bombarded. Sometimes the experiment is arranged so that the information available is too sparse to have even major subconscious importance; or it may be the opposite and the environment is saturated with information that confuses the mind with its diversity and novelty. Information has characteristics of time and space. Regular and irregular information are quite different kinds of information; tones and lights can be small or large, intense or soft, frequent or infrequent, regular or irregular; each change, each aspect, supplies additional information.

Understanding the role of feedback information is much more complicated than simply documenting its qualities and quantities. While the entire internal functioning of the body operates via feedback systems, some systems are more internally contained than others. Muscle systems continuously operate with an external component, the environmental clues to direction, distance, pressure, etc. But the autonomic system has been believed to react to the external environment largely by indirect association through the muscles and skin, less guided by brain-adaptive mechanisms. Certainly it is a new experience for the mind to find itself in control of automatic functions, and this alone may well color the value and importance of the bio-feedback.

Internal, self-contained feedback systems can give rise to cognitive information—thoughts—which can interact with events in the external environment to form bio-feedback loops. Take for example the phenomenon of habituation, the gradual diminution of response with repeated administrations of the stimulus. It is an enormously exciting phenomenon and has been explored to some extent by neurophysiologists. But it is coped with only by experimental psychologists. The fascinating aspect of habituation is that while a response to repeated stimulation soon disappears, say your attention to the tick of a clock, any very small, scarcely perceptible change in the stimulus re-establishes the response. In the case of the tick, should the clock stop, your attention is attracted. The best neurophysiologic explanation for this phenomenon is that neuronal systems of higher brain activity can discriminate incoming information as to its significance or meaning, and this information is fed to memory or motor circuits, depending upon whether the degree of meaning of the stimulus merits attention and action or not. The habituation process further implies a great deal of brain work to evaluate the characteristics of the stimulus to discriminate any changes in any aspect of the stimulus (or change in environment) and some decision as to whether the external event requires answering. Some experimental psychiatrists are beginning to believe that conditioned learning is actually a process of habituation.

Although there are many conflicting results, a number of researchers have found that awareness of the relationship between biofeedback signal and the heart rate is essential to successful learning. Others have demonstrated that the amount of heart rate control learned is a direct function of the amount of heart rate information fed back to the individual. As Grant discussed in relation to simple eyelid conditioning, "The conceptual relatedness of stimuli, their truth value, and their expression of commands related to the experimental contingency all affect the conditioning process in complicated ways."

Suffer the Little Rats to Come unto Me, and Forbid Them Not; for Such Is the Kingdom of Man

It has long been the tradition in American medicine and psychology that new concepts must be first proven in animals. Just exactly where the dividing line is between what can and cannot be accomplished in animals is often hard to interpret. Who would think, for example, that the concept of voluntary control over automatic, internal functions could, or would, be seriously investigated in animals, and particularly in the ordinary, lowly laboratory rat. Yet that is exactly what happened, and the story, far from being absurd, is one of the more fascinating stories of experimental psychologic research.

It should first be remembered that the great majority of experimental learning research, particularly that devoted to developing theories of learning, has been done in rats for most of this twentieth century. Although Pavlovian conditioning theories were derived from studies with dogs and other animals, production-minded American researchers found that equally good results could be obtained with rats, meaning that the less expense and greater supply of animals allowed experiments to be done on a grand scale. After Dr. Skinner broke the tie with Pavlovian tradition with the development of operant conditioning, the laboratory rat entered a new era of supremacy in the laboratory. It would be a safe guess to estimate that some 500,000 rats are used in some type of experimental learning study *per year*. Learning theorists have gotten a lot of mileage out of rats, and rats have gotten a lot of sex out of learning theorists.

There are a good many conveniences in using the laboratory rat for experimental heart rate psychologic research, one being that he is relatively easy to maintain on a respirator under paralysis by curare and it is easy to record his heart rate. The difficulty comes in selecting his reward for good performance. We have no inkling at all as to how a rat experiences his own heart rate, and certainly no thoughts about what would be a suitable reward for his performing correctly to our wishes for his heart to increase or decrease its rate. There is also, as in man, the great unknown action of the brain's cortex that associates the rat's reward with a change in heart rate.

In the early sixties Dr. Neal Miller became convinced that Pavlovian and Skinnerian conditioned learning phenomena theories were but two manifestations of the same fundamental learning process. The difficulty lay in proving it. Miller's first step was to examine the outstanding differences between the two types of learning, then to attempt to prove that the differences didn't exist. Even in the 1960s the dogma persisted that autonomic (automatic) behavior of the organism could be modified by classical, Pavlovian conditioning techniques but not by instrumental (Skinnerian) training techniques. This meant, as we have noted elsewhere, that visceral, autonomic functions, such as heart rate, could be trained to respond to some outside event only if they were frequently reinforced by a "natural" stimulus, but no learning occurred when the function was "rewarded" *after* performing.

Miller began to champion the theory that there was essentially only one type of conditioned learning and that instrumental "reward" techniques, as well as Pavlovian methods, could be used to train involuntary functions. Although there had been and were to follow many studies purporting to prove Miller's concept, they had all been subject to a strong criticism: that it really was the muscle system that learned and that changes in the involuntary functions were purely secondary to these changes in the muscle system. Since it is true that every muscle movement affects the flow of blood, the rate of the heartbeat, the flow of saliva, the emotional level of the organism, the only way to salvage the broad potential of Skinnerian conditioning was to prove that the autonomic nervous system could learn *without* any concurrent muscle activity. Proof could be obtained if an automatic organ such as the heart could be trained when all muscles of the body were paralyzed.

As the Indians of the Amazon did long before him, Miller "discovered" the drug curare, the crude tar with the magic action of paralyzing all muscles. Death by curare came because no muscles could carry out respiration, although the victim remained conscious to the end. The newer synthetically made curare substitutes provided Miller with an apparently ideal technique to separate muscle from autonomic responses. If the heart, or any automatically functioning body organ, could learn a new trick while curare was paralyzing all of the muscles, then this would be pretty convincing evidence that the autonomic nervous system wasn't so inferior after all, and that what had been thought to be different kinds of learning were really very much the same thing. Dr. Miller reports that he encountered considerable difficulty when he tried to put his unitary learning concepts into laboratory practice: the academic, scientific belief in the two principal learning theories and in the automaticity and inferiority of "involuntary" body activities was so strong that graduate students in his own department were reluctant and even refused to participate in the experiments and this caused long delays in getting the new work done. This unusual state of affairs is a profound observation on the grip that behavioristic, mechanistic views of human behavior have had on research minds at the graduate level.

One perceptive, persistent graduate student of Miller's, Jay Trowill, however, did undertake the project to demonstrate whether or not the heart could be taught to change its rate without help from the muscle system, i.e., under the effect of curare. At this point the reader should conjure up an image of a limp-as-a-rag white rat stretched out on his little pad, all of his muscles paralyzed, unable to move, unable even to breathe without the help of a respirator forcing the exchange of air in his lungs. Now, how are you going to "tell" his heart that it has performed its task of slowing or speeding up correctly? Conventionally the experimental psychologist uses rewards of food or water to appease hunger or thirst (which he has induced to make the rat "work"), or he has used a shock from which the rat must try to escape. Miller and co-workers, however, devised an ingenious experiment. They circumvented all of the sensory systems and a large part of the brain by administering the reinforcement directly into the brain.

The work of James Olds was critical here. Trowill and Miller turned to the work of Olds, the physiologist who had demonstrated the existence of "pleasure" centers in the brain. Olds had discovered that rats will work both to receive a small electric shock within the brain (pleasure areas) or to prevent a shock within the brain (pain areas). If a normal rat would work endlessly for a flick of electric shock to certain parts of his own brain, and this wouldn't require any muscle activity if his task was simply to change his heart rate, wouldn't this act also as a "reward" in a paralyzed rat? It did indeed, but then still another procedure had to be added to the experiment. First the rats had to be operated on to implant the electrodes in the right areas of their brain so that the electric shock would elicit the proper response. The proper response was to do work to get more shocks, the effect being assumed to be pleasurable, otherwise the rat wouldn't work for it. Then the amount of work the rat would do had to be measured to ensure that he would perform that same work after being paralyzed by the curare.

The experiment was designed so that when a desired change in heart rate occurred, the rat would get his "brain buzz." The researchers found that rats would indeed work to get their brain reward by changing their heart rates, either up or down, however the experimenter arranged for the buzz to be delivered. Unfortunately, after all of the early work, the amount of learning the heart showed was very small indeed, barely enough for the researchers to claim demonstration of a new phenomenon of body behavior. It is particularly interesting to discover that the reason for the rats' poor performance lay in the performance of the investigators. They had made the reward almost unattainable for the novice rats. Since in the beginning of the experiment the heart rate of the rat had to change considerably before he received his brain reward (and rats' heart rates don't normally change that much very often), the rat received his reward so infrequently that no firm association between heart rate and reward could be made. So, back to the drawing board and do another experiment making it easier for the rat to get his reward, and only gradually making it more difficult. This procedure is called "shaping." Now the rat could receive his reward with smaller changes in heart rate, and this meant that he would get them more frequently. And with shaping, the rats performed admirably, producing changes of 20 percent or more in heart rate, up or down depending upon what the experimenter wanted.

It now appeared to the learning theorists that the autonomic nervous system could learn by itself without help from muscle systems, and that in all likelihood learning behavior was accomplished by one type of central brain process, not two. There were, of course, many other questions about learning in involuntary systems, which now were not so involuntary. For example, how specific was the heart's ability? Since it was only one organ innervated by the autonomic nervous system, wouldn't all of the other visceral organs respond in their own ways at the same time that the heart was responding when it was working for a brain tickle? To answer this question Miller and another graduate student designed an experiment in which they rewarded the rats for contracting and relaxing the smooth muscles of their intestines, but also rewarded them at different times for increasing or decreasing their heart rates. Again the rats proved to be superior students. When their task was to relax the gut, they did so with no change in heart rate; when their task was to increase heart rate, they did so with no change in the motility of the gut.

Not only had a high degree of specificity of learning been demonstrated in organs receiving exactly the same kind of nerve supply (which meant the chemical reactions between nerves and organs were the same), but the researchers went on to prove that even if the system is spread out, as the blood vessels are, it is possible to learn specificity of location.

They did this by rewarding rats for learning to create a difference in the amount of blood vessel activity between the two ears. Results of this study are shown in Figure 9. Rats, paralyzed by curare, were prepared so that the vascular activity of both ears could be recorded. The task of the rat was to learn to control the blood vessel activity of *both* ears so that the amount of relaxation (vascular dilatation) of the blood vessels of one ear would be greater than in the other ear. If the rat performed correctly, he was rewarded by a mild jolt of brain electrical stimulation that had previously been found to be "pleasurable" (at least he would press a lever to get the brain stimulation).

The importance of these studies to medicine is enormous. Psychosomatic illness affects great segments of our society, yet such illnesses are among the most difficult to diagnose and often the most difficult to treat. Even more serious is the unremitting advance of destruction of function if the illness is not checked. The greatest omission of medicine, however, lies in its failures to recognize psychosomatic illness as a major area of research need. Hundreds of

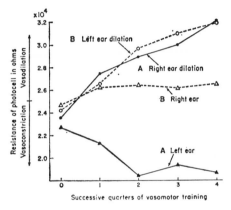

Figure 9. Learning a difference between the vasomotor responses of the two ears. Group A was rewarded for relatively more dilatation of the right ear; Group B was rewarded for relatively more dilatation of the left ear. (From L. V. Di Cara and N. E. Miller, *Science, 159,* 1485–1486, March 29, 1968, by the American Association for the Advancement of Science.)

thousands of human beings suffer from some form of emotion-induced illness or disease, yet until the problem becomes close to incapacitating, serious help is rarely found.

What the work of Miller and his colleagues really says is that something in the brain, the mind, or the will can be just as effective in relieving illnesses as it is in causing illnesses. More important, their work and that of others can even suggest that the will (or its equivalent mind-brain activity) can affect and perhaps correct disease processes of largely organic origin. On the other side of the coin, the greater the understanding of the higher, more sophisticated brain relationship to the body the more this understanding can lead to effective use of the tools of medicine and psychology.

One of the curiosities arising from Miller's work with learning in curarized animals was explored in detail by his colleague Leo DiCara. This was the astonishing fact that paralyzed rats learned very much better than nonparalyzed rats. In fact, DiCara reports that paralyzed (curarized) rats seem to learn any visceral task you ask them to do. Moreover, normally behaving rats learn much better if they have had some learning experience in the paralyzed state. There have been virtually no explanations offered for this unusual finding, yet if one thinks in terms of attention and awareness, at least one possible explanation readily comes to mind. The way in which curare and curare-like drugs act is by blocking the ability of the muscles to respond to their own nerve stimulation coming down from the spinal cord and brain. In this paralyzed state the normal feedback loop between stimulation from the outside and the normal muscle responses to that stimulation is broken. In theory some adaptation or habituation would take place so that the organism might come into some kind of equilibrium with the environment, with a consequent reduction in the amount of external stimulation or distraction requiring attention. If this were so, then attention could turn to internal events, and once an event such as the beating heart were attended to, there might come awareness. This view would hold only if the amount and diversity of normal "voluntary" activity and movement normally command the greater share of attention, at either the conscious or subconscious level.

Some of the scientist interpreters of the unusual phenomenon of enhanced learning (of visceral activity) under curare have suggested that a similar phenomenon occurs in human beings during profound relaxation. In this state there is also a marked decrease in voluntary muscle activity, and so a marked decrease in the amount of attention directed to body muscles and a concomitant increase in the awareness of internal activities, such as the gut and the heart. What this explanation doesn't reveal is whether or not a rat has "awareness"; can he comprehend sensations when he attends to them? Obviously he does when he is hungry, yet psychologic theory does not yet allow us to assume that nonverbally communicating organisms have qualities of sensations as human beings do unless we can prove it by measuring some physical change. The further exploration of just what is going on in the rat's mind when he learns to control his heart rate will undoubtedly move the science of behavior forward more than all its research to date. Yet pinpointing the neural substructure of behavior may be the imaginary pot of gold at the end of the rainbow: it may have very little to do with awareness.

The Yogi Rats

Another surprising curiosity of the learning experiments with paralyzed rats is that this particular type of learning experience dramatically changes the *behavior* of the rat. The rats that learned to decrease their heart rates came out of their experience relaxed and "cool"; the ones who had learned to increase heart rate after a month or so still appeared to be severely frightened. Behavior, however, was not the only thing changed in the rats. Nearly 20 percent of the rats who had learned to *slow* their hearts died of heart failure; many of those that didn't die developed serious cardiac problems. These extraordinary differences in behavior subsequent to the heart learning experiments apparently were discovered when the same rats were used to test whether the rats had "learned to learn." Did having learned how to control heart rate have any effect on their ability to learn a quite different task later on? Miller and DiCara tested this by an experiment in which the rats had to jump over a small barrier in order to avoid being shocked. Rats who had first learned to increase heart rate performed poorly. Rats who learned this task well were those who had first learned to *decrease* their heart rates.

Fortunately for the future of science, results like these simply open another Pandora's box. Why did learning the same task but in two different directions have such diverse effects on subsequent behavior and health? Did the learning of one direction of heart rate change affect the entire emotional structure of the animal, while learning to do the opposite thing with the very same organ, the heart, improve something in his learning structure? And why did those rats who learned the barrier-jumping task best, and had first learned to slow their hearts, fall ill or die? And the most critical question: Is psychosomatic medicine infinitely more complex than we thought?

The Public Is the Last to Know

The public is very often the last to know about new psychophysiologic concepts being explored in laboratories. Between 1965 and the present some forty scientific papers have appeared on voluntary control of heart rate. Why has it taken so long . . . from 1962 to the 1972 newspaper report that six patients learned to control their heart rates without using drugs?

We have already examined the prevailing disbelief that autonomic body functions could be brought under voluntary control. Rather a lot of money went into experiments to demonstrate that the behavior of the autonomic nervous system fit one or another of the known "learning" theories or models of body behavior used as basic building blocks in biological research.

For many decades the hallmark of basic, pure biologic research has been its unconcern for applications to the needs of society. If by chance useful techniques evolve in the course of basic research, as they often do, the first priority is to preserve the purity of the research. Many rationalizations have been developed to avoid disclosing the private laboratory affairs of bioresearchers. There is no other judge or jury; the research establishment is the sole intermediary between the products of the vast laboratory empire and an uninformed public. It feels a responsibility to protect the public against ineffective and/or harmful treatments. Since most of the research information has indicated a good possibility for the beneficial effects of heart rate bio-feedback and little chance for harm with judicious, directed use, why hasn't it moved into general use? The answer has been "It would be unfair to raise people's hopes, and if the procedure didn't help them, they might get worse just from the disappointment." Yet, how many times has the doctor said: "Now, this medication might not be the right one, but if it doesn't work, we'll try something else"? It is always a matter of percentages. The selection of what treatment is used is based *exclusively* on the principle of probabilities. A drug, for example, is explored to its final stages for clinical use on the basis that it may be effective in a certain percentage of cases of a particular illness. So the attitude that refuses to exploit a new technique which common sense and hard data say has a good chance of being helpful looks like a scientific dodge.

Why? The first reason is that our ethic states that human beings are precious and we are morally wrong if we risk the possibility of harm. Yet, here again, percentages should operate if all potential benefits for man are used on a percentage-possible basis, as they are. If there is no inkling that heart rate control training techniques can bring harm if used with caution or under good medical supervision, then the harm must lie only in the psychologic harm of potential disappointment. Surely that is a slim risk compared to the risk inherent in failing to try a treatment of reasonable promise.

If the researcher should be reasonably convinced that his new discoveries about heart rate control do have promise, how can he make them available for medical use? First he must obtain the cooperation of physicians for clinical use of treatments in his domain. The physician is also bound by a strict code of ethics: he must be as sure as possible that the new technique has a high probability for success and must be safe. He is further protected in this obligation by the Food and Drug Administration. This means that a recognized medical group or authority must re-examine the new technique in the specific context and illness in which it is purported to be effective. So there are new studies to be done. These are expensive and time-consuming.

If the new treatment is a drug, the burden of proof for effectiveness and safety is the responsibility of the drug house; moreover, the drug house pays the expense for clinical studies. Not so with new treatments arising from academic or research institution efforts. In order for such new techniques to be explored further, there must be academic scientific consensus, and here there is no coordination of effort. And there is little money. To obtain funding requires long periods of time. The scene is entirely different from developing consumer products. It is different because of procedure: there is no central authority or research funding agency that assumes responsibility for structured continuing progress on new treatment possibilities. The procedure also requires abundant evidence that the new treatment will likely succeed, and this is difficult for one individual or even one research group to secure, lacking the organization and means of the drug houses.

The researcher needs a clinician to prove the utility of his new technique, but where does one find qualified clinical researchers not already frantically busy and occupied with other demands for medical help? If the clinical man does participate, he must be compensated, and if he cannot obtain payment from his hospital or school, he must turn to funding agencies. For this he must devote considerable time to preparing convincing evidence that his projected studies will be successful. The evidence is judged by his "peers," who are almost exclusively *not* practicing physicians, but academic clinicians often more interested in theory than in potential applications.

And finally, I paraphrase the recent words of an eminent research authority speaking to a gathering of scientists: "The fact that autonomic functions, such as heart rate, can be brought under control is probably of no importance whatsoever. All that it means is that we have a new way to continue our studies."

It scarcely sounds like the philosopher's: "If you can light just one little candle, what a bright world this would be."

EIGHT

Blood Pressure: Blood Vessels and Social Tension

> While my friend Aldous Huxley and I agreed on many things, there was one idea especially we often echoed in unison: if one keeps the mind young and active, the body stays young.
>
> There is growing evidence that future health will depend upon a vigorous mind. Muscles, minds, hearts and flowing blood are the co-equals of physical life. Of these none is primary. The blood pressure we speak of is the body's pressure on the flowing blood and the body's pressure is the pressure of the mind. It may all come down to keeping the mind young.

In the current era of extraordinary ease of mass communication there is a growing awareness of the psychological and physiological effects of constant social stress. Never before in history have people become so aware of the stress in their lives. More and more people are recognizing uptight muscles, the stress headache, the nervous stomach, irregularity, drippy sinuses, chronic asthma, and above all, general physical malaise. When helpful measures are widely advertised or become fads, society avidly pursues any avenue offering possible relief from stress from a questionable panacea offered on TV ("relief is but a swallow away") to the latest diet fads in ladies' magazines. But there is still a multitude of insidious stress illnesses that are unknown to the general public. One of these may be the great unknown of essential hypertension. Its actual cause is unknown, as is a precise, permanent cure. All therapeutic measures used today are essentially preventive measures; the longer the time the unrelenting and progressive increase in blood pressure can be slowed down, the better is the chance for survival. It is *not* common knowledge that psychogenic factors may be important both in inciting hypertension and in accelerating its progress. Physicians may caution the hypertensive or hypertensively inclined patient to try to temper his emotions, but most of the advice offered is a series of negatives—don't eat, lose weight, don't eat salt, stop smoking, exercise only in moderation.

The shortage of physicians and their high cost encourages many hypertensives who have few, if any, bothersome symptoms to neglect various practices and programs which could effectively help to keep their pressures lower for longer periods of time. It is the fault of neither the physician nor the patient; the plight of the hypertensive is simply one that has not received either focused attention or broad enough perspective to provide for the kind of advertising that can make society aware of a potential danger and what it can do about it. Cancer gets a lot of focus, and the government sees to it that clinics are available for early diagnosis. But not hypertension. Which is surprising because it is probably the Number 1 Killer.

There is, however, a glimmer of hope. The initial successes of blood pressure bio-feedback in reducing arterial tension in hypertensives is showing promise. Current and planned research using bio-feedback techniques in the experimental treatment of hypertension are a new two-pronged attack designed to relieve and to prevent increased blood pressure. Some studies are directed toward the mind-body learning something about how to control blood pressure by direct feedback of its levels and fluctuations; other studies aim to use bio-feedback to produce quickly that kind of muscle relaxation which Schultz and also Jacobson found to be effective in lowering blood pressure.* The many references in this book to the therapeutic benefits of profound relaxation, as described in the scientific reports of Schultz and Luthe and of Jacobson, and the ability of muscle bio-feedback to augment the effects of relaxation and

* Their systems for muscle relaxation are described in Chapter 4.

shorten the treatment programs are particularly relevant to the problem of hypertension.

Although some authoritative medicine tends to minimize the role of psychological stress factors in the treatment of hypertension, there is abundant evidence that social stress plays an important role in accelerating the progress of hypertensive illness. If the primary reason for treatment of hypertension is to reduce symptoms and prolong life by attempting to keep the blood pressure at lower levels, then it should seem reasonable to use psychologic treatment techniques which can minimize the effect of stress on body systems. The real problem seems to be in the nature of essential hypertension itself, in that it is intimately tied to the aging process, and rarely begins until sometime after thirty. From then on its most usual course is slow, blood pressure increasing slowly, almost imperceptibly over the years. Then too, recognizable physical changes that follow rising blood pressure may be so little inconveniencing that they attract no special attention. Yet, undetected and unfelt, the walls of arteries may continue month after month to become more rigid, until finally a chance physical examination turns up elevated blood pressure or pathology of the heart, brain, eyes or kidneys. Hypertension is one of the rare illnesses whose development is not accompanied by warning signs of its inevitable deadly effect. And because there is no early-warning system for hypertension, the trick is to prepare the defenses. It has always been difficult to sell Americans on preventive medicine; free clinics are poorly attended except by the obviously ill.

At last, fortunately, the immense untapped possibilities of the communications media are beginning to attend to the mental and physical state of society. Books, newspapers, radio and television are more and more extending information for the neglected education of personal health. The public's need for personal growth and health information is being met also by the formation of lay groups to explore the mind, to ensure physical health through exercise, to try psychic healing, to meditate as a way to a more tranquil and healthful existence. Bio-feedback stands in the middle: a mind trip to inner awareness of the mind-body and a body trip to a healthy being.

Uptight Arteries?

Of all the anxieties surrounding physical ailments which human beings suffer, one of the most worrisome is learning that something is wrong with the blood pressure. American society has been indoctrinated with the potential hazards of living with high blood pressure. To a large extent it reflects the power of advertising indirectly and the type of advertising directly, for the worry is often concerned less with health than with economic security. Blood pressure readings are the staple of insurance companies, and whether or not you can get coverage often depends upon the single factor of blood pressure. For longer than I can remember newspapers and magazines have warned about the seriousness of high blood pressure, cited data to herald the need for yearly physical examination, to watch the diet, to exercise and not to exercise. For the most part the warnings have been unrealistic and without credibility, largely because medical news seems to reflect the fact that the nature of high blood pressure is obscure even in the mind of medicine. Although the causes of certain types of high blood pressure are known, there is *no known cause* for the kind of hypertension which is the most prevalent by far: essential hypertension.

For more than fifty years drug companies have spent millions of dollars searching for effective anti-high-blood-pressure drugs. Physicians have piled up data relating high blood pressure to cerebral strokes, to coronary attacks, to arteriosclerosis, to kidney failure. Yet after more than half a century of medical research, the causes and cures of essential hypertension remain nearly as obscure as when the condition was first observed.

Hypertension, the medical term for high blood pressure, has interesting connotations. The use of the word "tension" to designate the pressure that circulating blood is under in the body apparently derives from terms used in physics to indicate the pressure of fluids measured against the tension of atmospheric pressure. The blood courses through the body in a set of elastic tubes, the blood vessels, separately labeled arteries and veins, the distinction being mainly one of how much muscle tissue is in the walls and whether the vessels are coming from or going to the heart. The relative state of elasticity of the arterial system is the mechanism which sustains the pressure; the force of the heartbeat provides the major mechanism that continually renews the pressure of the blood flow. Unless there is actual heart damage, which is relatively rare, the pumping, or pressure-producing, ability of the heart is about the same in most people. The problem in hypertension is that something happens in the vast network of blood vessels to its elastic quality. When blood vessels tend to become more rigid the more the initial thrust of pressure from the heart is maintained throughout the body. There is no relaxation in the muscles of the arteries to ease the pressure. It is truly tension that keeps the blood pressure high, tension in the very real muscle cells that line the walls of the arteries and the smaller arteries, the arterioles.

Is the muscle tension of the blood vessels related to the muscle tension in the muscles surrounding our skeleton, to the muscle tension we feel in stress and anxiety? A considerable number of clinical researchers believe that this is exactly the case in many instances of hypertension, and there is the possibility as well that the same fundamental mechanisms of the increased tensions of life are implicated in all cases of hypertension. The choice of the word "hypertension" may have been more fortuitous than logical.

A Case of Medical Consensus

There is, unfortunately, a world of difference between the way physically oriented physicians and psychosomatically oriented physicians look at the causes and treatments of hypertension. Because this chapter is devoted mainly to the role of stress and tension and the potential for mind activity to effect beneficial changes in blood pressure, it is important to examine some of the differences in medical attitude about the clinical syndrome of elevated blood pressure. The views of medical opinion are widely divergent.

In a 1971 edition of a standard text of medicine the causes of hypertension are discussed exclusively from the standpoint of the pathology or disorders of various body systems and the treatment of these by drugs. The fault of this doctrine is that it deals with a profusion of medical facts not yet demonstrated to be relevant to essential hypertension. A lengthy report of a symposium on the treatment of hypertension, appearing in 1972, also confines itself to purely physical factors and stresses at some length that the recommended treatment of high blood pressure is through use of drugs along with medical advice for weight reduction, moderation in exercise, and to stop cigarette smoking. Neither of these two major medical references, representing the highest authority of medical opinion, make even passing comments on the possibility of a psychosomatic or psychologic origin of the disease. Nor do they admit to the possibility of psychologic approaches to the treatment of essential hypertension. The focus in this chapter is, however, exclusively on that same kind of hypertension of unknown cause and for which evidence of a psychosomatic origin is rapidly accumulating.

There is one powerful authority that does implicate psychologic and social factors as important in the genesis of hypertension. A third recent (1971) and more major medical authority on cardiovascular disease elaborates quite forcefully on the evidence for psychologic factors as causes of hypertension. In the light of such clear and forceful evidence (reviewed in the following section) it is ironic that it is ignored in so many authoritative texts and procedures recommended for the treatment of hypertension.

Why are these factors left to pursue their morbid course without treatment if stress, anxiety, and tension are even remotely believed to be involved in this prevalent illness known to generate distressing symptoms and shorten life?

And why does relaxation and bio-feedback lead to a lowering of blood pressure?

The answers to these questions lie in the unraveling of a complicated mixture of medical bias, the profound influence of a drug-oriented society, and the lack of an effective liaison between medicine and psychology. In biological science there has been a massive proliferation of knowledge of new details for every aspect of the biochemical, physiological, psychological, social, and drug-taking human organism. Yet a synthesis of each of these diverse influences is needed to understand that mental control of emotion may be the fundamental, pervasive regulator in the course of hypertension.

*Around and Around the Blood Pressure Goes, and Where the
Mind Is Nobody Knows*

The vascular tree of the human being is enormous and complex.
Every body cell must receive its life energy by an action of the
blood circulation. The pressure of the circulating blood determines
the effectiveness of cellular nutrition and is needed to support the
action of the kidney to clear the blood of waste materials accumulated from the body's use of its nutrition. The pressure of circulating
blood is necessary to effective mind action; too much pressure and
there is headache and potential damage, too little and thinking
becomes fuzzy or one feels giddy or may faint. Just as a normal
blood pressure is needed to ensure proper body functioning, so a
proper body functioning is needed to ensure an effective blood
pressure. It is another internal bio-feedback system, diverse, all-
pervasive and complicated. Everywhere nerves are channeled between blood vessels and the central neural core, signaling changes
and then correcting them.

The ground substance of all body operations is the elaboration
and release of biochemical substances in response to nerve stimulation. There is a wide variety of such biochemicals, but for the most
part only one or two are specific for each of the major body systems.
The release of the chemicals is reflected often in electrical changes,
such as when a nerve impulse is passing from one neuron to the
next, or at the nerve endings in functioning organs such as muscles
or stomach or heart. Generally the released biochemicals remain in
highly localized areas, but when structures of the endocrine system
are activated, they are released into the general circulation to
produce their effects in distant organs. The endocrine system is a set
of special organs such as the adrenals, the pituitary or the thyroid.

In the cardiovascular system the biochemicals released at the
nerve endings of the two divisions of the autonomic nervous system
(ANS) are the vital means by which a dynamic balance between
constriction and dilation (or relaxation) of the blood vessels is
maintained. When the sympathetic division of the ANS is stimulated, as it is in emotion and stress, epinephrine and norepinephrine
are released locally at the nerve endings and cause local constriction

of the muscles in the arteries and smaller arterioles. Because blood vessels are everywhere, the sum of all of the local vessel constrictions can have a massive effect, and if the emotional response is severe, the blood pressure can shoot up dramatically. In terms of primitive function, as for survival purposes in times of danger, this almost automatic function is part of the body's mobilization of its defense mechanisms, and once activated, the body organs return messages to the brain to indicate that preparations for defense have been made. As in spaceships, the body has backup systems to ensure adequate defense. One of these is the direct brain release of a neurohormonal substance which activates the sympathetic division and also brings into action the emergency power of the adrenal glands.

With this incalculable complexity, directly or indirectly involving the action of nearly every cell and nerve and muscle of the body, it is little wonder that hard medicine concentrates on the physical and chemical facts and ignores emotion.

It should be no surprise, either, that the cause of most hypertension is unknown. While there are specific types of hypertension which have specific causes, i.e., the result of most kidney diseases, adrenal tumors, constriction of the major artery, and a few miscellaneous, relatively rare conditions, it is estimated that in two-thirds of all cases of hypertension it is impossible to establish a cause. Medically this, the largest segment of blood pressure problems, is spoken of as "essential" or "idiopathic" hypertension, a rather neat way of obscuring the fact that the cause is unknown.

The unpredictable effectiveness of drugs in the treatment of hypertension also points a shadowy finger at the fact that psychological causes may be the triggering factors in much hypertension. Just as the causes of the disease are unknown, whether various drugs which do lower blood pressure do so by relating to the cause of hypertension is also unknown. In a sense, drug treatment is empirical. Drugs for hypertension have been chosen because they were effective in reducing blood pressure when it was *experimentally* elevated by chemically or physically manipulating body mechanisms known to influence blood pressure. The stickler is that the experimental devices have never been satisfactorily demonstrated to be of critical importance in either the cause or the treatment of high blood pressure. In a few cases drugs that lower blood pressure were found by accident, generally when the drug was being taken for quite a different purpose.

If the medical community does not know what causes most high blood pressure, why does it ignore any possible avenue of treatment such as providing relief from psychologic insults? There is, it is true, a debate about treatment of early, or mild, hypertension, but the debate is not about type of treatment, only about when drugs should be started. What follows may give some insight into why medicine has had so much difficulty in utilizing concepts of psychology and emotions to understand high blood pressure.

Those of us who favor psychologic factors in both the cause and treatment of high blood pressure have been almost, but not quite, as disadvantaged as those who favor concepts of "unknown" etiology and drug treatment. Biochemists and clinicians have, until recently, informed us that the body's chemical reactions to stress are, more likely than not, *not* significantly involved in hypertension. Certain body chemicals released during stress act to constrict blood vessels, which increases the resistance of arteries to the flow of blood, resulting in increased blood pressure. When the circulation of these "stress" substances was measured, it was found that they were generally so little involved in essential hypertension that their actions could not account for the elevated blood pressure. Thus, from conventional medical evidence, there is *apparently* no substantial evidence to implicate a general or consistent enough release of body chemicals during emotional stress accounting for sustained high blood pressure in essential hypertension. To some parochial investigators this would seem to close the book on the usefulness of psychology or study of emotion either as a tool to search for that unknown cause of hypertension or in its treatment. There are, however, large loopholes in the medical approach to hypertension that medicine itself is acutely aware of.

One obvious chink in the medical shield is the inability of experts to agree on how high is high in hypertension. This is not the fault of the physicians; it is due to the many idiosyncrasies of nature. To begin with, there is the peculiar psychology of blood pressure readings themselves. It is common knowledge that casual blood pressure readings are always suspect because they are always high. It is invariably recommended that at least several readings be taken three times in succession and at, say, weekly intervals and then under conditions affording some relaxation before a diagnosis is attempted. There is still argument; some investigators who work with round-the-clock measurements report how variable blood pressure is, while other investigators report that continuous blood pressure readings are no different than casual readings. Another study has also noted that a good bit of human error is involved in reading blood pressure. Some physicians favor certain numbers more than others and errors of 20 millimeters of mercury pressure, a highly important difference, are not uncommon.

The key question is, if the simple emotional nervousness of having a blood pressure reading taken can shoot blood pressure up to dangerous levels, then is there, despite its omission by certain medical authority, evidence that psychologic factors may actually be of primary importance in the cause of hypertension?

A second area of confusion is that surrounding the physiological (actually biochemical) effect of stress. It has long been thought that both the neurohormone that constricts blood vessels directly and its adrenal supplement should be implicated in sustaining the higher blood pressure levels of hypertension. Although hypertensive patients are notoriously hyperreactive to emotional, stressful stimuli, some biochemical medical investigations have tended to show that this excessive responsiveness is not accompanied by the usual biochemical reactions to stressor agents and their consequent deleterious effect on blood vessels as might be expected.

Stress responses are, however, typically measured in localized areas or in circulating blood or excreted urine, and measurements of such changes are both difficult and imprecise when applied to the whole organism. Although some effects of stress can be measured biochemically, in hypertension the effects have, until recently, been considered to be too small to account for a sustained high blood pressure. The fallacy here is that the amount of response to stress may be stretched over the extensive length and breadth of the vascular system. If the responses to stress of each millimeter of every blood vessel were all added together, the total effect could be enormous. No one area of stress response can provide a reliable index of the *total* amount of blood vessel tensing distributed so widely within the body. Another fallacy in the apparent failure for clinical evidence to support the contention that stressor substances (or reflexes caused by body chemicals released during stress) are important in causing hypertension is the failure to consider the role of time. When the clinical biochemist tells you that the amounts of substances released during stress are inadequate to produce the effect you are seeing, such as high blood pressure, he is rarely countered with the question: Could the effect of those small amounts build up the muscle-tensing effect day after day, even though the amount of circulating chemical remains the same? Whether or not the muscles of the vascular system could develop bad patterns of behavior in a manner analogous to skeletal muscles kept under tension has been studied only sporadically until quite recently.

We know something of the internal feedback system for skeletal muscles: that the emotion of apprehension tenses the muscles, and for short periods of time signals of the increased tension are fed back to central control and appropriate adjustments are made. And if the apprehension or worry or anxiety persists, there is a process of adaptation and over time the signals of too much tension are ignored and the muscles adapt to the new higher level of tension. But the higher tension is still there, and repeated bouts of emotion may continue to increase the tension in imperceptible increments, until suddenly the tension is so great that function is no longer normal. There is no evidence that the same progressive tensing occurs in the blood vessel musculature, but then again there is no evidence that it does not. If it does, then it would not be necessary for the body chemical responsible for increased tension to linger each time it assaults the vascular muscles. The same small amounts might build their effects upon each new increment of tension.

Sensitive Blood Vessels

Although researchers appear to differ in their experimental results regarding the detection in hypertensives of excessive concentrations of those body hormones which incite the ANS to increased activity, the difference may be traced to differences in the type of stress used to stimulate production of these biochemicals, or to the innate or

developed ability of the hypertensive to control his emotional response, or to the severity of his disease.

As noted earlier, however, it has not been possible to detect
either increased blood or urinary excretion levels of the substances
that reflect stress in hypertension with any degree of consistency. A
number of researchers feel that this does not necessarily reflect an
absence of effect from the neurohormonal substances, since, according to one theory, certain individuals may possess arterial systems
that are hypersensitive to their effects. This concept fits well with
the evidence that a genetic factor is involved in the etiology of
hypertension and with the evidence that hypertensive individuals
show hyperreactivity of their cardiovascular systems to emotional
stimulation.

Because researchers have been hard put to detect evidence of
malfunctioning body mechanisms during the long period when
blood pressure is rising but symptoms are minimal, some studies
have turned to obtaining evidence for factors that might predispose
to hypertension. In addition to the suspected influences of heredity
and of the hyperreactivity of the vascular system to stress, one of
the more interesting studies tackled one of the most sensitive body
processes involved in stress.

One of the major mechanisms of stress syndromes is detected by
the release of hormonal substances from the adrenal gland because
the release is believed to be activated through increased activity of
the hypothalamic centers of the brain and is accompanied by
increased sympathetic nervous system activity. One investigator
followed this complex process by measuring the release of cortisol
from the adrenal during mild sensory and mental annoyance of the
type that might occur in everyday life. These annoyances were a
ringing telephone bell and a flashing light which were rhythmically
interrupted. The subjects in the study were people whose personality profiles, emotional reactivity and attitudes about annoyances
had already been documented. They did *not* have hypertension.
The study revealed that when attending to the annoyances, there
was a prompt release of cortisol into the bloodstream and a concurrent rise in blood pressure and increase in heart rate. These body
reactions to stress were markedly exaggerated in those individuals
who were classed as emotionally irritable; moreover, the differences

in cardiovascular reactivity between the emotionally irritable and "normal" individuals was maintained over periods of four to five years. Since many other studies have confirmed the toxic effect of these released neurohormones over time in their stress on the heart, the evidence might suggest a more widespread cardiovascular effect and be of considerable importance in the origin of hypertension.

While there have been some medical advocates of a psycho-somatic origin of hypertension, it is only within the past five years that major clinical studies have been reported which provide solid, scientifically acceptable support for the concept. Before these efforts and before the era of specialists, there were mainly the impressions of the general practitioner whose experience fostered the conclusion that high blood pressure (the "essential" kind) was, nine times out of ten, a very ordinary process in the life history of human beings. An astounding number of studies have been made of every conceivable influence which might be related to the occurrence of high blood pressure, but more astounding is the jumble of apparently unrelated factors such as diet, genetics, race, geographical location, and occupation that appear to be important in developing hypertension. Moreover, some patients develop disturbing symptoms with only moderately elevated blood pressures while other patients tolerate high levels without any sign of distress. Although there is a heavy thread of hereditary influence, not all authorities agree that a single genetic factor is involved.

Hypertension: Where Aging Begins?

A short fifteen years ago, before drug treatment of hypertension became the acceptable way out of the hypertension dilemma, a widely held opinion was that hypertension was a straightforward result of aging. As with other tissues of the body, the elasticity of the arterial system is gradually lost, the tubes become more rigid and the blood pressure rises. And as with other manifestations of aging, some people begin the process at an earlier age than others. Although aging research holds up the prospect of increasing life-span, when the concept of aging is applied to the research of a single body system, there appears to be a natural hesitancy to acknowledge the unrelenting course of aging when it affects only one body system. Yet perhaps we can look at aging in the new perspective of bio-feedback, that we may learn to keep our blood vessels from becoming tense and constricted. And if we can do this, and protect our blood vessels from aging, then perhaps we can grow old with less pain and weariness than we do now.

People don't get old staying all to themselves—that's just withering on the vine. People age, perhaps as they always have, because of the tensions of fear and worry, insecurity and anxiety. Whether research can uncover, as it has not after some fifty years of effort, either the exact disease processes underlying hypertension or aging or both, the rationale for the treatment of hypertension will probably continue as it has in the past to be based on the observations that lowering high blood pressure prevents distressing symptoms and prolongs life.

Personal Stress and Hypertension

In sharp contrast to the biomedical studies on mechanisms of hypertension with their generally negative and disheartening results, the newer studies on the psychology and psychophysiology of the disease are replete with positive findings and are hearteningly suggestive that psychologic procedures may be as effective and infinitely safer than drugs in the treatment of hypertension. In some ways medical research in the area of hypertension is far easier than psychologic research, largely because chemical or surgical procedures can be employed experimentally both to simulate the condition of hypertension and to attempt to relieve it. The artificiality of the procedures is a necessary compromise between conducting drastic experiments in human beings and the need to elicit immediately measurable biologic changes. But when medical research edges into the psychologic domain and has the need to mimic the effects of emotion and stress, too often the artificiality of the procedures is maintained. Devices to produce experimental stress are frequently of such a severe nature as to leave the human psyche in shambles; techniques which clearly are quite different from the stream of stresses that ordinary mortals seem to endure daily. If in the psychologic approach, the human or animal experimental subject is administered a stress-producing stimulus, it is rarely one that has an analogue in real life. It is usually, in fact, a jolting flash to the eyes, a booming explosion to the ears, or that old friend, the electric shock. The justification for this specious counterpart of real-life stress is theoretically that such stress can be measured with precision, but in practice it is simply a foolish convenience.

Disturbed Emotions, Disturbed Blood Pressure

To the investigator interested in clinical realities, it is delightful to read so commonsensical a study as that reported by Heine in 1970. As a way of avoiding the use of artificial and unduly strong stress of the laboratory studies and moving directly to evaluate the effect of real-life stresses on blood pressure, he chose as his test subjects patients who unequivocally showed disturbed emotions. These were agitated depressive patients whose illnesses were sufficiently severe to warrant electroshock therapy. This category of patient, moreover, is one which generally responds well to shock treatment, and so it was possible to determine whether during recovery from the emotional illness the blood pressure would change as well. Even though there were many differences in ages and sex, the longer the illness and the more frequent the severe emotional episode, the higher the blood pressure. The patients were definitely hypertensive. After recovery from the illness, elevated blood pressures remained high for the patient group as a whole (the statistical "average") although not for individuals with differing patterns and severity of emotional problems. Detailed analysis of various factors which could have influenced the results showed that neither genetic nor medication causes were involved.

The type of psychologic state was, however, found to be an important correlate of the blood pressure level. When the patients were scored for severity of symptoms of depression, anxiety and agitation, it was found that anxiety and agitation were significantly related to elevated pressures, but depression was not. The fact that the type of emotional illness studied occurred in "bouts" or episodes allowed the investigator to estimate roughly whether successive bouts were accompanied by continuing increases in blood pressure. This relationship between emotion and blood pressure was actually found in several groups of patients, and the investigator concluded

that repeated episodes of a depressive emotional illness characterized by anxiety and agitation were also characterized by continuing
elevations of blood pressure to hypertensive levels. This is strong
evidence that whatever emotional stimuli caused the blood pressure
to increase, when sufficiently repeated, they could lead to a sustained hypertension. Another finding of considerable interest was
that those patients who had suffered relatively few bouts of severe
emotional disturbance showed a reduction of blood pressure during
and following the treatment for the emotional illness. Blood pressure levels of patients with a longer history of emotional disturbance
were relatively unaffected by the treatment. Their blood pressures
remained high. Although most of us aren't psychotic or even
severely neurotic, Heine's study should be a warning to us to pay
attention to the body as well as the emotions during our emotional
upheavals.

One of the suspicions that has haunted the biochemical-medical
research is that the tissues of the vascular system themselves might
be hypersensitive to the effects of some abnormal release of body
hormones. This would mean that blood or tissue concentrations of
the hormonal substances would not be detected under ordinary
circumstances although their effect might nonetheless be considerable.

There is some evidence from psychological studies that this
might actually be the case. In one study, for example, the experimental subjects were given a forty-minute session of the mild and
rather ordinary stress of being asked to solve some visual puzzles.
This technique, too, is a resourceful and rational method for attempting to duplicate normally encountered stress situations.
Everyday life is filled with visual puzzles to solve. These investigators, moreover, bridged the usual gulf between biochemistry and
psychology by also measuring the primary biochemical indicator of
stress used in biological studies. The rather uncomplicated and
relatively undemanding task of solving visual puzzles was found to
lead to increased blood pressure in hypertensive subjects but not in
subjects with normal blood pressures. Furthermore, there was increased urinary excretion of the stress indicator in all subjects, and
to a much greater extent in hypertensives. The researchers interpreted their results as indicating that hypertensive patients show, on

the average, a heightened response of the sympathetic division of the autonomic nervous system (ANS) to mental stress.

In another, somewhat similar study hypertensive patients with different levels of disease severity were compared to subjects with normal blood pressure. All of the subjects with high blood pressure were more emotionally responsive to stress than people with normal blood pressure and some hypertensives responded to stress by increasing blood pressure further. These results also suggested that there was dominance of the sympathetic activity of the ANS in hypertensive subjects, possibly resulting from some deficiency in regulation of the ANS. If one's blood pressure tends to be high, these two bits of research suggest that bio-feedback training might be an excellent technique to use to keep the blood pressure from rising further. The logic for this is that since it is the sympathetic ANS that constricts arterioles and keeps blood pressure up, then if one were to practice an appropriate form of bio-feedback, the sympathetic nervous system could be protected from exciting stimuli, such as nervous tension. Obviously the appropriate bio-feedback would be one leading to body tranquillity, such as muscle relaxation or brain wave control, which will be discussed in later chapters.

Another experiment demonstrating the role of emotional responsiveness in the regulation of blood pressure was simpler still and also used a familiar type of stress to elicit emotional responsiveness. The task for the subjects was merely to listen to some tones, some high- and some low-pitched, and to respond to the tones by pressing a pedal with the foot, right or left, according to what the instructions asked. Since this was an elementary task, requiring essentially only a yes-or-no decision, the length of time the subjects used to perform the task could be used as a rough estimate of the amount of information they were processing in measured time periods, and hence as an index of mental stress. Again, as in the other studies, the experimental results showed hypertensive patients to be unusually responsive to effects of the mild stress of constantly having to decide which silly lever to press. Moreover, while the blood pressure of the hypertensives rose only minimally when short work periods were used, when they spent longer times at their tasks, the blood pressure rose significantly. They also showed changes in other physiologic systems, such as heart rate, which indicated that there was perhaps, as the other studies revealed, a more general increase in responsiveness of the ANS to relatively simple mental stress in hypertensive patients. All of which says that the longer you are subjected to stress (like noise pollution), the more you may risk high blood pressure. While I would naturally recommend a relaxation bio-feedback technique to help such naturally easily stressed people to cope with the stream of silly decisions that everyday life seems to demand, an even better technique might be just to learn to ignore nonsensical situations and save the energy for really important decisions.

Talking It Over with the Boss May Save Your Blood Pressure

Social stress has also been implicated as playing a significant role in the origin and maintenance of high blood pressure. While it had been shown earlier that a group of blue-collar workers developed increased blood pressure following a permanent plant shutdown, a recent study by Kasl and Cobb followed a number of similar workers through a period of anticipated, temporary and prolonged unemployment and probationary re-employment. All of the men were in the age range between thirty-five and sixty, the age when signs of increasing blood pressure begin to appear. When they were advised of the impending plant shutdown, their blood pressures rose. In the life-stress situation this could be called anticipation of job loss. Then followed the period of unemployment. Blood pressures either remained higher or increased slightly, and the workers who were unemployed the longest showed the greatest increases in blood pressure. There were also increases when the men were re-employed but on a probationary basis. Those who were fortunate enough to find permanent re-employment also had good physiologic fortune: their blood pressures began to decrease.

An analysis of other psychologic and physiologic factors revealed that the men who tended to sustain the higher blood pressure not only were unemployed longer, but reported more subjective emotional stress and tended to have less ego resilience and self-esteem. Some of these men also had initially shown signs of insipient hypertension and rigid personalities.

The actual type of job or occupation, however, does not seem to be related to the incidence of hypertension. It seems to be more a matter of how one reacts to one's job, or whether one can handle whatever stresses it may produce. Hypertension is more frequent in people whose jobs are frustrating than in people who have demanding jobs but who can cope with them. The fact that blacks are so much more susceptible to hypertension than whites has, for example, been attributed to the fact that the social situation of blacks has continually forced them to suppress their aggressions. The incidence of hypertension is lower among rural populations, suggesting that the social stress of intensified social interactions of urban life aggravate blood pressure mechanisms as well as emotions. From information about family histories, the role of inherited factors appears to be very important in some cases, yet not in others. Perhaps the best guess one can make at the present time is that there may well be a genetic background, and when emotional assaults are superimposed, there is a strong predisposition to develop hypertension.

Coping, Personality, and Hypertension

Anytime the elements of genetic factors and patterns of emotional reactivity are combined, personality patterns emerge. So it is not surprising that many clinical researchers have found personality traits interpreted as characteristic of the hypertensive patient. Many early research studies described hypertensives as characterized by obsessive-compulsive defenses and having high standards for emotional control.

In an effort to isolate hypertensives as a distinctive psychosomatic problem from the psychologic standpoint, one study found that hypertensives were markedly field-independent, i.e., they tended to judge the environment by how they felt rather than forming their impressions from the structure of the environment. These different ways of judging sensations or perceptions are said to reveal the way in which individuals develop their own ways of interpreting the reality of the relationship between themselves and their universe. If a person relies on changes outside of himself to color his perceptions of the world, this is reflected in his personality. The field-dependent person, who clings to the structure of the external environment, is said to tend toward passivity and anxiety, to bow to the authority of others and have little esteem for himself. The field-independent individual, who apparently was found to tend toward high blood pressure, relies more on his own body sensations and feelings and tends to impose his own ideas on the structure of what he perceives. And he is more likely to be active and independent. These personality characteristics might make a hypertensive feel that he has a good bit of strength of character, but wait: not all psychologic studies of hypertensives are so kind.

One interesting but rather difficult-to-interpret study of the relationship between personality and hypertension was made by Davies in 1970. He found that blood pressure levels were *not* correlated with a history of childhood neurotic traits or even current neurotic symptoms or the neuroticism scale of a popular personality inventory test. Davies concluded that such outstanding negative relationships actually support the concept that there is a psychosomatic component in the origin of high blood pressure. This apparent paradox is seen in other types of psychosomatic illness and has prompted the theory that certain physiologic responses normally associated with emotional states can linger long after the time that the emotion is no longer outwardly apparent. In other words, the individual has learned to control his outward displays of emotion but there may still be signs of emotional turmoil within, particularly in genetically susceptible body systems. Davies further deduced that some people may be prone to develop high blood pressure when they cannot express their feelings adequately either directly or by means of neurotic symptoms. This research evidence is similar to that of the population studies indicating that the suppression of aggression in blacks is a major factor in their susceptibility to hypertension.

Two of the dominant physiologic and psychologic characteristics of hypertensive patients are, as noted, that the blood pressure of hypertensives is hyperreactive to emotional and stress stimuli, and second, that the personality of some hypertensive patients is generalized as being one of hostility in which anger cannot be expressed appropriately so that the individual may appear withdrawn and have less than satisfying social interactions. These characteristics have led some clinicians, as also noted above, to suspect the hypertensives internalize their anger to the point where the organs of the autonomic nervous system are constantly activated. A number of clinical investigators have, however, interpreted these same two characteristics as indicating a somewhat more sophisticated mechanism of the mind-body. They have theorized that perhaps the hypertensive patient actually possesses some psychologic (or biologic) awareness of his propensity to overreact physiologically and he thus develops a behavior pattern (presumably still subconsciously) designed to avoid situations which trigger his internal activating mechanisms, and in this way protects the inner body.

Some support for this contention is found in one study in which subjects were given a psychologic test with pictures of ambiguous face or body expressions that could be interpreted in many different ways. The subjects were asked to describe what story about the pictures came to mind. Hypertensive patients told drab, unemotional stories, as if pretending boredom. At the same time they showed no particular changes in blood pressure, which would have probably increased if they had brought to mind exciting stories behind the pictures. It is this kind of curious reaction that leads one to speculate that perhaps instinctively they refused to see the world except as drab and gray, erecting a physiologic wall to protect their susceptible arteries. In contrast, patients with normal blood pressure but with a variety of other illnesses told much more elaborate stories and did show blood pressure changes.

As an experiment to support this idea, a group of researchers subjected hypertensive patients, along with non-hypertensives, to viewing movies which showed in one instance a physician behaving in a friendly, relaxed, courteous manner to a patient but in a second instance the physician was annoyed, disinterested, curt, and negative.

The vascular and subjective, emotional responses of the hypertensives to the movies were exceptional. Whether the doctor in the movie was kind or rude, hypertensives showed elevation of blood pressure and increased heart rate which were of modest significance when recorded during the movie, but in an interview *following* the movie, when the subjects were asked what they thought about the movies, their blood pressures and heart rates increased to marked degrees. In contrast, their verbal expressions about the movies were almost devoid of emotion and, in fact, they generally failed to detect the obvious personalities of the physicians in the movies and sometimes even distorted or confused the roles, interpreting the good doctor as the bad doctor. Unfortunately the authors of the study tell nothing about the psychologic traits of the patients. One other interesting finding was that none of the usual biochemical reactions to stressing situations was found. While the investigators were quite cautious in their interpretations of the study, they did suggest that perhaps hypertensive patients have, or have developed, some defect in their ability to perceive their environments and this defect is used as a defense or screen against emotion-producing stimulation which would aggravate their cardiovascular hyperreactivity. This is a slightly different interpretation from that suggesting that the hypertensive develops a behavior pattern which *intentionally* protects his arteries.

All of the studies described above are of quite recent vintage, even though the greater emotional reactivity of individuals with the tendency for high blood pressure has been known for many years. The recent studies show the need to develop more reliable and specific techniques for measuring emotional responses to quite mild, ordinary stresses and slippery tricks of the mind. It is to be hoped that some researcher will begin to test for both blood pressure and the more subtle of the emotional responses in young people, following them through to middle age. In this way, along with logging in all of the emotional traumas reported by the subjects, the role of emotions in the development of hypertension could be pinpointed. Such studies might also serve well studies of aging. As a last touch, these studies would do well to include people who practice relaxation techniques and/or bio-feedback.

Frustration Is Germinal

Looking to the personality characteristics which suggested a relationship between the development of hypertension and different ways of handling mind-body responses to emotion-producing situations, one researcher explored the effects of frustration and insult on blood pressure and mood. When the experimental subjects were provoked by being told that they were failing in the experimental tests, or when they were actively insulted, their blood pressures rose. Both sexes showed the blood pressure changes, but the reported subjective emotional reactions were more intense in females. Indirectly this correlates with the higher incidence of hypertension in females in the younger age groups. Females also tended subsequently to become depressed, with less overt emotional activity. This kind of reaction fits with the evidence that suppression of emotional reactivity may be a contributing cause in hypertension. It would seem that instead of the psychophysiologist's traditional use of "representative" subject populations for his studies that more research with the susceptible females might shed even more light on how emotions influence the origin and course of hypertension. And it might be more fun, too.

If, as it appears, emotional reactions may be integral in the course of hypertensive illness, and if the seat of emotions is in the head instead of the lower body (although many researchers and theorists continue to believe the latter), then does the electrical activity of the brain reflect anything about the progress of the disease?* Apparently so, although there appears to be some minor disagreement. One study found that a mild hypertension of moderate duration in young patients was accompanied by a dominant background brain wave alpha activity, which would suggest low emotional reactivity, while another study reported that alpha activity was rare in this condition, which would suggest higher emotional reactivity. Both studies agreed, however, that with increasing severity and longer duration of the disease, more and more brain wave abnormalities occurred, and *this* would suggest that the mind does indeed have its problems in hypertension. The abnormalities were principally the occurrence of more slow waves, and even alpha activity became slower, resembling somewhat that occurring in drowsy states. Of course such abnormalities are not specific to hypertension and are a bit difficult to separate from changes occurring in some, but not all, people with advancing age. Nonetheless, this bit of information is important to remember when brain wave bio-feedback is discussed. The fact that alpha waves tend to disappear as hypertension advances could suggest that learning to control one's alpha activity might intertwine its relaxation effect in

* For a discussion of brain waves, see Chapter 9.

such a way as also to be useful in preventing or delaying the course of hypertension.*

It is well known that there is a high incidence of coronary artery disease among hypertensive patients, especially in those over age sixty. What is perhaps less well known is the overlap of both emotional and vascular reactivity in the two disorders. Quite naturally the coronary arteries are part of the arterial system, and no doubt much of what has been learned about the possible mechanisms of hypertension also apply to the development of the underlying condition that fosters coronary artery problems. The work which relates personality patterns to the predisposition to coronary problems concerns us here since our primary emphasis is on preventive medicine through learned control of body functions. In this respect, the ways in which emotional challenges are handled are of primary importance.

For the last decade or so there has been considerable controversy in the medical literature as to whether a typical personality pattern defines individuals susceptible to coronary artery disease. There has been much support for a personality pattern defined by Friedman and Roseman as being highly characteristic for individuals predisposed to this illness. They are characterized as being hard drivers, striving for achievement, competitive, restless, impatient and aggressive. In marked contrast, other clinicians have found anginal patients (those who experience cardiac pain but not coronary attacks) to be emotionally erratic and suggestible and to have less capacity for immediate interpretation and control of emotional influences, whereas post-coronary patients were found to be more controlled and inhibited and satisfied with their low level of emotional spontaneity. Another report indicated that the only outstanding characteristic of coronary patients was that they were more reflective and had more difficulty in handling aggression. While there obviously is a difference in emotional profile when chest pains are the prevailing symptoms and the sensations one has following a heart attack, there are some interesting resemblances to the personality profiles of hypertensives. In fact, the precise characteristics of

* It has been found in sleep studies, when brain waves are very slow, that blood pressure of hypertensive patients fluctuates significantly more than that of normotensive subjects.

emotional reactions may be of less importance than the fact that distorted emotional reactivity is present in patients of either or both types. The signal that should be raised by these research findings is that abnormal emotional reactions go hand in hand with disturbances of the cardiovascular system and should point directly to the need to explore more vigorously the therapeutic measures of relaxation and bio-feedback.

Can Arteries Learn Bad Habits?

It was inevitable that learning researchers would come to view the exaggerated cardiovascular activity and emotional difficulties of the hypertensive patient as a result of conditioned learning; that behavior is shaped by repeated environmental change (stimuli) into a distinctive pattern. In the laboratory the researcher continuously assaults his test organism, man or animal, with stimuli until a distinctive pattern of response emerges in the behavior. The bread-and-butter techniques are the Pavlovian bell-food-salivation system and the Skinnerian reward-reinforcement system which shapes such behaviors as lever pressing in rats. If we look at the cardiovascular system as our test organism and think of repeated episodes of excessive emotion as changes in the environment and the accompanying hyperreaction in arteries as responses of the system, then we have an exact analogue of a conditioned learning experiment. The real-life learning to be uptight, even in arteries, may be an everyday experience. The teen-age son can bang the bloody drums all day (the "natural" stimulus) rousing the automatic control of blood vessels to clamp down and make the blood pressure rise (the learning theorists' "natural" response?), until the clamping and the rising begin the very moment the son begins to hum (conditioned transfer of response?). But the mind is also responding; the tension and the thumping pressure of the swirling blood arouses sensations of anger, of frustration, of indecision or just confusion. And suddenly there it all is, irritation and upset when the son begins to hum.

Reactions such as this, whether real-life or in the laboratory, raise the possibility that psychosomatic illnesses may be "learned" in the sense that responses of the body systems are shaped by repeated exposure to events in the environment (external or internal), and whether or not mental activity intervenes. There would then be two possibilities to change this learned, misdirected behavior of the cardiovascular system. One would be to avoid the environmental change, which in the case of hypertension might be to learn to control excesses of emotional response (which one group of researchers concluded that hypertensive patients did automatically as a safety-valve defense); and the other would be to "de-condition" or unlearn bad emotional and cardiovascular habits. Because human beings are continuously responsive to change, both emotionally and with the autonomic nervous system, because they are responsive to the mildest, most ordinary stress, to recommend that a hypertensive patient try to avoid stressful situations would be impractical if not impossible.

The use of conditioned learning techniques in shaping responses of the autonomic nervous system, initiated by the Russians and by Miller and others in this country, began, as described earlier, with the heart, intestines and salivary glands. The impetus to "teach" the blood pressure was simple curiosity: Could the pressure function of the cardiovascular system, with all of its myriad nervous and hormonal influences, be brought under conditioned control?

I have viewed the insistence of American workers to use animals for studies of ANS learning with a great deal of curiosity. The great pitfall of using animal experiments for the study of human behavior is, of course, that no one knows in fact whether human behavior can be extrapolated from animal behavior. Another trap for learning theorists is that animals are almost always studied in the artificial environment of the laboratory, designed for man's convenience, and not in a natural environment that would permit natural behavior. Clearly, if one of the fundamental elements of learning is motivation, then human beings with predispositions to one or another psychosomatic illness involving misdirected or inappropriate emotional responses would be ideal subjects for such studies. If the experiments were successful, then the mechanisms could be explored. Certainly the experimental tools used in such studies are innocuous, and in the meantime success could mean relief to large populations of sufferers. So why animals? They are not suffering, and they are handicapped by their inability to communicate their emotions. It must be scientific habit. Tradition dictates that we must first determine the effectiveness and safety of new procedures in animals before exposing human beings. Certainly this applies when procedures contain uncertain and unsafe elements. But in the case of conditioned learning, the only initial unknown is the degree of success.

Those Poor Widdle Wats

One of the earliest animal studies of blood pressure learning reported was by DiCara and Miller in 1968. The procedure used was virtually identical to that of the heart rate learning experiments. The task for the rat was to either increase or decrease his blood pressure depending upon what the experimenter asked. For either task, the beginning was signaled by a tone, and if no change in blood pressure occurred within 7.5 seconds, the rat received an electric shock to the tail. If the rat "learned," i.e., if he changed his blood pressure appropriately after being alerted by the tone, then he received the reward of avoiding the shock. If he was a bit slow in understanding the task and did get shocked, he could stop the shock by changing his blood pressure. A distressingly complicated element in the experiments was that the rats had been paralyzed with a curare synthetic, mainly to answer any criticism that skeletal muscle activity was the mechanism by which the blood pressure changes occurred. Nonetheless, the rats did learn to change their blood pressures.

The researchers give us no specific information about the progress of the conditioning. For example, was blood pressure learning fast or slow compared to other kinds of learning in rats; or did the rats change their blood pressures before or after the electric shock when they began to learn? One would guess that it took the rats rather a long time to learn their tasks, being, as they were, paralyzed and in complete ignorance of what they were supposed to do. The fact that they learned at all makes one wonder whether or not rats possess a greater awareness of their internal systems than do people, but apparently this question has never been asked, probably because there is no very good way of getting an answer; their English tends to be unintelligible.*

The slow learning by animals in laboratories can be seen in this rat experiment. It took the rats somewhat better than an hour and a half, and not counting the thoughtfully provided rest periods, this amounted to somewhere around two hundred learning trials. Not bad for a rat; yet on the other hand there is always the possibility that something in the experimental procedure had an effect opposite to what was intended. The shock, for example, is a rather effective jolt to the alerting system, so in addition to performing the blood pressure task according to the experimenter's wish, perhaps the rat sometimes had to caution himself that his natural defensive elevation of blood pressure to shock wasn't a rewarding response, and so he had to lower blood pressure quickly to get the reward. I do note that it took the rats longer to learn how to lower blood pressure in this instance. Moreover, rats who were paired with the experimental rats as controls and received electric shocks at the same times as their partners regardless of what their blood pressures did showed significant rises in blood pressure. The experimental animals who were rewarded for increasing blood pressure didn't do much better than their nonrewarded partners in the first hundred or so learning trials, but after a while, they did keep on increasing. Surprisingly, although it took the rats longer to learn to decrease blood pressure, they performed this task much *better* than the task to increase blood pressure. Perhaps they became exhausted from the effort needed to reverse a natural response to shock of raising blood pressure into the correct response, a feat that lab-man would give him a passing mark for.

When the same conditioned learning method was used with rats who were not paralyzed by synthetic curare, the amount of learning in terms of amount of change in blood pressure was less than one-fifth that of the paralyzed animals. (The same thing had happened in the heart rate learning experiments.) From the research stand-

* Animals may be immeasurably closer to their internal processes and it may be that this awareness of the internal milieu helps to ensure survival. Their body functions can change quickly (have you ever seen a 'possum freeze?); they respond to internal warnings without hesitation (why does the dog seek out certain grasses with an evident urgency? when he vomits later, we know why). Perhaps animals have not confused their inner biology by words or concepts or social customs.

point this is an annoying result, although normal human beings probably consider it rather sensible. We might naturally guess that if you are totally deprived of the use of your muscles, then one-half of the body's regulatory system is missing. What is missing is that part which makes muscle adjustments to change and whispers its accomplishments to the nerve strands carrying messages back to the brain that all is well, all is adjusted for optimal living. The researcher, however, explains that the paralysis has a "de-confusing action," i.e., the rat cannot become confused having to discriminate between signals coming from body muscles (whose contractions squeeze blood vessels that indirectly change blood pressure) from signals from the blood vessels themselves (which constrict to change blood pressure directly). It is also explained that perhaps the paralysis obviates the usual attention paid to muscles so that all attention can be focused on blood pressure activity. It has even been suggested that there could be techniques for human beings to simulate the effects of muscle paralysis so that they could learn their autonomic functions better. These theorist suggestions are hardly a match for the clinical researchers who have found that merely asking people verbally to change their blood pressure is a successful technique, especially if bio-feedback is present.

Another animal study used monkeys whose task was to keep blood pressure above a certain level. Every time blood pressure fell below that level it triggered a tone in the monkey's isolation booth which could be turned off any time the monkey raised his blood pressure to the designated level for one second. If he couldn't make it, the tone finally stopped and then he got a painful shock to the feet. To get the monkeys started learning the first day of the experiment, the tone was turned off whenever the blood pressure rose slightly. Now the investigator thinks this gave the monkey or his cardiovascular system a good clue, but I still wonder whether a joyful "Atta boy!" might have urged the monkey on to victory better than an esoteric token, human-oriented bit of mechanical information. In the first place the monkeys wouldn't have had to work their way through all of the whimsy and bizarre novelty of the laboratory setting to pin down exactly what the investigator was after and worry about why the research people weren't talking to them during the agony of their chores. Then too, dog trainers know well that a

"Good boy!" is ever so much more successful than tones and shocks. Well, perhaps. When human investigators start talking to their experimental animals, at least one of the species is going to learn something.

Despite the communications lack, the monkeys proved to be most intelligent about exactly how much effort they allotted to this foreign task. Every time the investigator increased his demands by setting a new goal for the monkey's blood pressure, the monkey answered it, but if the goals were not changed, the monkey expended precisely only that amount of energy needed to answer the immediate goal. He did not increase his blood pressure any more than needed to avoid the shock. There was at least one monkey who learned to manipulate his blood pressure with great speed, and thus avoid shock, by squinching his muscles and artificially pushing up his blood pressure. Such are the hazards of research. Or of brilliant monkeys.

People Animals

But when researchers finally got around to using human beings in their blood pressure learning experiments, they continued to neglect the intellect as an influence. They also forgot a lot of physiology. Their techniques were more a caricature than serious methodology. In the most famous experiment utilizing bio-feedback of information to elicit changes in blood pressure, Harvard students were exposed to ringing bells, flashing lights, coupled with pictures of seductive nudes to cajole them into changing their blood pressures. Statistical analysis of this madness revealed astoundingly negligible changes (on the order of the normal error of reading blood pressure). Nonetheless, the authors of the study concluded that systolic blood pressure can be modified by the use of external feedback and operant reinforcement. Although I am a keen advocate of bio-feedback, I believe the conclusion is unwarranted.

Laboratory experiments such as these are the despair of many a physician and clinical researcher. They are harried enough to find safer and more effective treatments for hypertension than the ones currently available. And although the study had many methodological faults, it did try to point out new directions for therapy.

Clinicians, however, live with the everyday trauma of the patient whose hypertension is causing him real physical and real psychological problems, and they are acutely aware of the potential for hypertension to cause extensive and fatal changes in physiologic processes. The clinician is aware, as the experimental psychologist frequently seems not to be, that in the early stages of hypertension, blood pressure is "labile," that is, it can vary remarkably even within quite short periods of time. Moreover, part of this lability lies in the peculiar hyperreactivity of the hypertensive's cardiovascular system. So to the clinician, a change of a few millimeters of pressure is scarcely worth sneezing at.

The Other Blood Pressure

The clinicians have another, highly legitimate gripe. Psychologists seem to be interested in systolic blood pressure while clinicians are much more interested in diastolic pressure. When you receive a report of your blood pressure, the first of the two numbers indicates the systolic level and the second indicates the diastolic pressure. The "upper" or higher value reflects the pressure *added* to existing basal pressure coming from the pressure thrust of the ventricular contraction or beat of the heart. Since this thrust of pressure is more or less similar in everyone, except for those with actual cardiac disease, in hypertension the systolic pressure rises largely because the increasing rigidity of the major arteries results in the same amount of cardiac thrust having a greater pressure effect. The more diagnostic value is that for diastolic pressure, which reflects the actual state of rigidity or relative elasticity of the arterial system. This of course is the critical change in hypertension. Because the diastolic blood pressure, indicating relative elasticity of the arterial bed, plays the prime role in essential hypertension, it was gratifying to see the researchers turn to using bio-feedback of diastolic blood pressure in their experiments.

In the diastolic bio-feedback experiment, the experiment proper was very similar to the one described above, with one major exception. Instead of using pictures of female nudes as the reward all of the time, these fantasy rewards were used only one-third of the time, the other rewards being sometimes pictures of landscapes or sometimes pictures of how much money the subject would receive for correct performance of changing his blood pressure. (The subjects worked at a rate of $3.00 per hour plus these bonuses.) Some subjects received the flashing-light/beeping-tone feedback of successful performance when the blood pressure was a point or so higher while other subjects were similarly rewarded when the blood pressure dropped a point or two. All subjects were additionally rewarded (reinforced) after every twenty successes by the pictures. The investigators point out that their technique allowed bio-feedback with every heartbeat.

After an hour of such a procedure, which included some 55 times of inflating the blood pressure cuff, the average increase in blood pressure for the subjects who were rewarded and fed back successes for going up was around 4 mm of mercury pressure. The average decrease for those rewarded for decreasing pressure was about two points. Statistical analyses revealed (!) that these were *not* significant changes.

The real drama occurred after the study. Some of the subjects were instructed that the experiment was now over, but would they please continue to try to make correct responses although there would now be no feedback and no pictures. At this point the blood pressure of subjects rewarded for going up really bounced upward (at least in comparison to what they did during the experiment), rising on the average about eight points, while those rewarded for going down dropped about three points. Largely on the basis of this unexpected event the investigators concluded that human subjects can learn to raise or lower their diastolic blood pressure.

The study raises many interesting questions. Did, for example, the subjects unconsciously use almost imperceptible muscle activity to change blood pressure, such as the faintest tensing or the least-felt relaxation? How accurate were the researchers in reading blood pressures? For biological data there is generally assumed to be an experimental error inherent in biological variations and in equipment errors amounting to somewhere between 10 and 20 percent.

The point of greatest interest is that blood pressure changed much more when there were no longer rewards and reinforcements. Although at no time in the bio-feedback part of the experiment were they told that the bio-feedback signaled their blood pressures, it is fairly certain they had guessed it did after some fifty times of having the blood pressure cuff inflated. If they had really learned to produce the desired change of blood pressure, why didn't they go on producing the same *small* changes? And why did the subjects rewarded for going up pop up more, but those rewarded for going down change just a fraction? The researchers noted that it was easier to make the blood pressure go up than down. And it certainly is, particularly in an experiment pregnant with excitement or if your subconscious mind has learned that you get the same reward by the merest tensing of the muscles. If you are then asked to do that same trick without the rewards, you might be really motivated to demonstrate what a good learner you were. Perhaps not. But tensing is easier than relaxing, and its cardiovascular effect is magnified more than that resulting from relaxation. It is a subtle thing, but perhaps of considerable importance in experimental work. In this respect it is interesting that the researchers reported that after the experiment almost all subjects reported that they had interpreted the bio-feedback to mean an increase in arousal, attentiveness, alertness . . . and blood pressure. Often if people even think "alert" they tense, and this has been well documented in studies recording muscle activity.

Another probable reason for the surprising ability of the subjects to perform *after* the experiment has been discussed in relation to the potent effect of providing intelligent information to the subject on his ability to control heart rate.

There are other questions, too, such as was the reward effect of the landscape and money pictures any different from that of the female nudes? The investigators failed to inform us. Or, if the animal experimenters were so concerned about the effects of skeletal muscle activity on blood pressure, were muscle records made? And finally, studies using bio-feedback of diastolic blood pressure also contain many high-risk factors. Although the experiment was designed to demonstrate effectiveness of bio-feedback and operant conditioning techniques in control of blood pressure and may be well designed from the standpoint of conditioned learning theory and methodology, the tools and procedures contain an unsuspected abundance of direct physiologic and indirect psychologic factors that have been discussed in earlier pages.

Almost precisely the same conditioned learning, bio-feedback experiment was used in real hypertensive patients. There is no need to review criticisms of the method further, but one cannot help commenting on the rigidity of scientific customs. The hypertensive patients were made to suffer through exactly the same experimental procedure as had the college students except that for the really big reward they were shown slides indicating that for their 20 accumulated successes in keeping blood pressure down they would receive another nickel. They were also paid $5.00 for the sitting. Their motivation must have been enhanced by the instructions they received: that they were having their blood pressures read automatically and would they please sit still quietly for an hour while this was being done. The feedback and blood pressure cuff inflations and rewards and beeping tones and flashing lights were continued until their blood pressures refused to fall any further. Exhausted, they were released.

The data published for this study are impressive. The average decline of blood pressure for the seven patients was 16 mm of mercury pressure. Unfortunately, it was systolic, not diastolic pressure. Some rather nice averages are presented, but nowhere do the investigators discuss that notorious characteristic of hypertension: variability. All patients were on drug medication, some much more than others. Two patients suffered through some 30-odd sessions at weekly intervals, spending an hour simply sitting quietly without feedback. To the clinician this would also raise the question about placebo effect. It is well known that any treatment is always effective initially. There is also the relaxation that comes from becoming familiar with surroundings and people. Whether these influences could have produced an average of 16 mm mercury fall in blood pressure is questionable, but the question, nonetheless, should be answered.

At the time of writing this book, such was the status of bio-feedback training technology as a therapeutic tool for high blood pressure. The seeming paucity of trial runs in real patients and the stilted, theoretical laboratory approach taken by the investigators up to this point are typical examples of the incongruities that occur when one must leave the artificial simplicity of the laboratory and transfer ideas and methods to real-life difficulties. There must be a link between the experimental laboratory work and the actual therapeutic work with patients because the investigator must be assured that the ideas and concepts of the laboratory also operate with people with problems. This need tends to make new clinical studies awkward and not well tailored to the needs of the patients.

It might encourage the reader to know, however, that there are investigators who have planned new types of studies using bio-feedback in the treatment of hypertension. Since it is always hazardous to discuss other people's plans, the only planned or in-progress studies I am free to describe are my own. The reader might be interested not only in some of the details of the new studies, but also in the reasons why the particular approach is being taken.

To begin with, I reasoned that if subjects and patients had learned to change their blood pressure when they were completely *unaware* of the purpose of the experiment, then awareness about the bio-feedback procedure and its objectives should increase the ability to control one's automatic functions such as blood pressure. The obvious thing to do would be to inform the patient fully about what was happening, how it was to happen, and what was supposed to happen.

The second and perhaps more critical reason for the new study was that in the other studies the patients were being stressed at the same time they were trying to learn to control blood pressure. I reasoned that relaxation, rather than stress, might produce really significant results and be of real and perhaps permanent benefit to the patients.

There were many other reasons for making the concept of relaxation primary to the treatment procedure. First, the earlier practitioners of relaxation techniques had reported success in lowering high blood pressure. The infrequent use made of these earlier techniques was due to the long time required for therapy and many patients became dropouts, turning to less effective forms of treatment. Another reason for using bio-feedback relaxation techniques in hypertension was that nearly all psychophysiologic research has made a strong case for psychologic factors as at least part of the underlying causes of essential hypertension. If indeed those people susceptible to high blood pressure have an unusual sensitivity of their blood vessels to the effects of stress, or if normal people are found to tolerate only so much stress, then it would be logical to relieve stress-induced vascular constriction by "unstressing" the patient through relaxation. The apparent heightened emotional responsiveness of people susceptible to hypertension, along with the striking evidence that many hypertensives may repress their emotional problems and hostilities, also suggested that relaxation therapy could be important to relieving the underlying psychologic causes as well as providing measures to prevent blood pressure from continuing to rise at the rate it had been rising.

The last reason for emphasizing relaxation in the planned biofeedback treatment for hypertension was more of a theoretical nature. One of the great unknowns of biomedicine is whether the muscles of the blood vessels can relax in the same way—or by the same mechanisms—as do the large muscles covering the skeleton. Or if they do behave in a similar manner, would the willpower of bio-feedback be effective in maintaining life-prolonging blood vessel relaxation? None of the studies to date has investigated this point.

My study was designed to compare the effects on the blood pressure of hypertensive patients of a variety of techniques all related either to relaxation directly or to bio-feedback of blood pressure information. Some patients, for example, use skin temperature bio-feedback, some use muscle, and some use alpha brain wave feedback. All of these types of bio-feedback involve relaxation either directly or indirectly. The effects of these procedures on blood pressure levels are compared to the effects on blood pressure using direct feedback of diastolic blood pressure levels.

During the training procedures, the information about internal functions is presented (fed back) to the patient by means of a series of subdued light signals arranged so that each little light tells exactly how much change in blood pressure the patient is achieving as he practices to control his temperature, or muscle tension, or alpha brain waves, or his diastolic blood pressure.

Information concerning mood and feeling states is also recorded during and after all of the training sessions to document feelings of relief from tension and perhaps even an improving sense of well-being. From time to time a variety of physiologic activities are recorded to see if the body also reflects the course of improvement.

Although the study is just beginning and I don't know what the results will be, I will be happy to go on record and bet that the study will show that when hypertensive patients learn to maintain a reasonable state of relaxation through bio-feedback that they can then maintain throughout each day, not only will they show significant improvement, but their improvement will be every bit as good as that achieved by using just blood pressure feedback alone.

NINE

Alpha Brain Waves: The Importance of Being Alpha

What is so soft and tender that it cannot survive the elements but has a power so great that it can conquer the universe? Is it not a paradox that men yet negate the magic of the brain to bridge this remarkable circumstance?

A Briefing on Brain Waves

There is nothing quite so mysterious and awe-inspiring about the human body to the layman as his brain. And to biological scientists and laymen alike, the constant cryptic flow of electrical energy from the brain, called brain waves, is probably the most intriguing and at the same time the most formidable signal of the body's intricate, inner mechanisms. The astounding revelations of bio-feedback that the average human being could not only recognize his own brain waves but also learn to control them should perhaps be enough for any new discovery to disclose. But there is another startling disclosure by bio-feedback that is little appreciated even by researchers themselves. That is that during bio-feedback, the electrical activity of the brain is used as a source of electrical power.

Before the discovery of bio-feedback the electrical activity of the brain was regarded exclusively as the means by which body and mind information was communicated throughout the brain. Early in the history of neurophysiology the transmission of neural messages within the brain was compared to a telephone exchange system; after the development of electronics it was compared to a futuristic and efficient computer. The electrical aspects of brain activity were looked upon as entities which could be conveniently measured and thereby reveal the pathways and networks of message communication within the brain and between brain and body. But in bio-feedback we discovered that we were using brain electrical energy as a source of power, to do electrical work. We were taking selected brain electrical signals and using them to operate display devices, to turn on colored lights and sound-making devices.

Nearly every organ and part of the human body generates electrical current. Only a fraction of the electrical power developed in body operations is needed for optimal functioning, and for the most part the electrical power of the body spills out to be dissipated, virtually unused, into the environment. In bio-feedback both the power *and* information-transfer capabilities of electricity are used. The body's electrical signals are used to power electrical devices in the external environment and these devices transmit information about the operation of the body's vital systems that function by that same electrical energy. And behind it all is the central coordinating control center, the mind-brain.

Few people know that the brain is literally a constant storm of electrical energy. Those in the laboratories and in the clinics, who daily record the electrical energy of the brain, have somehow failed to realize that beyond its complex mental faculties, the brain is the source of considerable electrical energy. For decades technicians have been using this electrical energy to wiggle recording pens back and forth or make oscilloscope beams jump around, forgetting that this constantly flowing brain energy was also a source of power. Electrical power that could do work. And so, in one view the brain, one of the most important sources of energy, remains untapped. This is the electrical energy that our brain cells produce each millisecond of our lives. It flows constantly, day and night, never ending. Staggering amounts of this energy are dissipated almost constantly because we have not yet learned how to harness this master resource.

The concept of using brain electrical power to do work had occurred to an occasional researcher before bio-feedback: an early example was the use of brain waves to operate an anesthesia servo-mechanism in which the large brain waves signaling deep sleep activated a device to adjust the amount of anesthesia being given. The idea apparently never came to mind that brain electrical power could be used to explore the mind and be converted to provide its own therapy. But bio-feedback has now brought brain electrical power into the domain of everyday usefulness. It is a curious circumstance in biomedical history that for the same forty years since brain electrical activity has been known and studied that its potential as a source of power has been ignored. Every time a brain cell discharges its electrical message to another cell it does so by discharging electrical energy—a bit like the heat discharged when an electric light bulb is producing light. One wonders where all of the electrical energy has gone. Every being in the world is daily discharging electrical energy from its brain. Perhaps one day this excess energy of the brain will be used as a source of electrical power—or perhaps to cooperate directly with the work of other powered devices such as computers, or even be extended in its own control as a sophisticated means of nonverbal communication.*

Until the recent popular alpha bio-feedback fad, the subject of brain waves was of general intellectual interest and curiosity, but was a subject that caused considerable personal apprehension. Before bio-feedback, people were hesitant about submitting to brain wave recording, and for good reason. Brain wave recording was always associated with serious physical problems. It meant searching for brain damage, tumors and the kind of brain disorder with a poor prognosis. The only common, nondisabling disorder diagnosed in part by brain wave analysis is epilepsy, and despite the development of effective drugs to control epilepsy, the fact that it is a brain disorder has cloaked it in an undeserved mythology. Such is the power and command of the unknown.

The forebodings of the layman about the meaning of brain waves have, until recently, been wholly supported by the science of electroencephalography, the study of the electrical activity of the brain, abbreviated EEG. For most of the history of EEG work, study of abnormalities has predominated. There are real medical problems

---

* We have already noted how universally obvious these thoughts are. See Chapter 1.

where diagnosis by EEG analysis can lead to the proper selection of treatment. But for the healthy, normal human being the written record of brain waves was considered too crude, too inadequately representative of the condensed microcosm of the brain to trust for explorations of normal brain wave activity. Brain pathology is almost always marked by powerful electrical changes as compared to normal waking brain wave activity. Where there is brain disease, electrical changes in the brain can be seen to originate in specific geographic locations of the brain. In normally behaving brains, however, there is endlessly changing electrical movement everywhere.

The enormous strides made by electronic and computer engineering in the last two decades have helped a limping electroencephalography and neurophysiology to walk with renewed assurance. The tools and methods developed in the fields of electronics and computers are exactly those that studies of brain electrical activity have needed for so long. The advances in electronics and its role in implementing the operation of computers have provided the neurophysiologist with detectors of electrical activity of unbelievable sensitivity, an instantaneous analytic ability for the most complexly concealed electrical bits of the nervous system, capacious memories of computers, and multiple extensions of mind function. He can now begin to deal with the complicated, internalized substructure of the mind and behavior.

Mind-brain scientists themselves have a difficult time collecting adequate and reliable information about mind-brain function. The problem is particularly difficult when it concerns brain waves. For the most part the scientific literature on the subject of brain waves is widely scattered in the biomedical journals of numerous specialties. There are, for example, probably some ninety different kinds of scientific journals in which one might find scientific articles pertaining to brain waves. And each of these may represent a different scientific persuasion which, in addition, sponsors symposia and conferences on various aspects of brain wave function which often go unpublished for rather long periods of time. The different subspecialties are also somewhat bothersome, for each has developed its own language and concepts and criteria. These nuances of science are chronic pitfalls for the researcher who tries to span the information gap between or among specialties; the psychologist may unknowingly violate the very neurophysiology he is seeking to understand, while the neurophysiologist may unwittingly use psychologic techniques that undercut the very behavior he is trying to study. There is scientific elitism, too, and the writer for a journal of neurophysiology rarely sees fit to refer to the work of a non-neurophysiologist. The social behavior of scientists is often their own worst impediment to progress.

Information about brain waves is generally of only two types. For the most part neurophysiologists conduct complex studies designed to explore how nerve impulses (messages) are transmitted within the brain and what influences operate to channel impulses to the innumerable centers of vital brain function. Psychophysiologists, on the other hand, attempt to relate brain electrical activity to behavior, both to performing behavior and to internal body behavior, including endocrinologic activity. To whatever purpose the research is directed, the perspective has always been trying to look into the brain from the outside.

Not until bio-feedback was there a way for man to look at his mind-brain *from the inside*. Without this unique ability, knowledge of the inner universe of mind and emotional activity, personal consciousness and the subconscious could be understood only by the indirect and reflected light of probing from the outside. If one wanted to know the subjective sensation associated with a particular kind of brain wave, it was necessary either to stimulate the organism in a specific manner and *elicit* some behavioral change or to surgically remove an important brain area to observe function in the absence of one of its parts. Whichever approach was used, there was a great deal of deduction to be done from the resulting change in behavior. It is not too difficult to project major human motives and emotions into the major emotions accompanying behavior in animals when they have been overwhelmed by vigorous prodding or have suffered the loss of part of the brain. It is, however, the vital array of subtler emotions unique to man that has eluded the earthy grasp of the bioscientists. Even though the brain subserves the mental life, brain electrical activity has revealed less about the shades of emotion than skin electrical activity. Not until this decade and bio-feedback were direct communications to products of the mind made accessible.

The brain is not an easy structure to study, nor even to accumulate enough information about to appreciate its enormous complexity. Anyone who has ever attempted preparing beef brains for dinner knows the unique softness, the fragile and mushy nature of brain tissue. This delicate mass is composed of thousands of millions of brain cells, the neurons, of almost incredible fragileness, coaxed into special shape as with infinite care and with extraordinary form and structure. Groups of brain cells that assist the carrying out of body functions are clustered together and send out long ultra-fine filaments with which they communicate with other specialized clusters. Each cell is a complete universe, endowed with specialized submicroscopic elements for receiving and sending information, and is physically supplied with its own storehouse of chemicals for maintaining its health and integrity and function. Science has observed well these micro-miniature cell universes, documenting the physical attributes of their organization and isolating the intricate complexities of their chemical substance. Instruments such as the EEG machine allow orderly reports on the changes in electrical behavior of brain cells or groups of cells during their neural transactions. Yet the laborious efforts of accruing all manner of detailed information about the structure and behavior of brain cells has still not yielded the vital secret of how man thinks.

The enormity of the brain's communications network is bewildering to try to understand. One analogy is to think of the brain complex as one thinks about the planet Earth, an overcrowded Earth, for there are 20 billion brain cells packed into the skull as compared to only several billion people on Earth. Individual brain cells might represent individual people, each equipped with all of the sensing and receiving functioning aspects which make people as individual and variable and versatile as they are. Small groups of rather similar cells could represent families, and larger groups could represent communities. In the brain such cell communities may be small or large, like villages or metropolises, or modest size, as cities. The locations of groups of cells are identified partly by geography and partly by the peculiar characteristics they exhibit, much as we identify the South by its waterways and weather as contrasted to the West. There are also larger divisions, as there are Earth's major countries and continents, similar to the major brain divisions of cortex, mid-brain, cerebellum, brain stem, or thalamus. And as with Earth, the brain is a self-contained functioning unit possessing extensions outwardly to communicate with appendages, as we Earthlings communicate with those parts of us who climb mountains or dive in submarines or soar in space. As Earth has the protecting mantle of its atmosphere, brains are insulated and protected against differing environments by the massive skull structure.

The brain cell families, communities, countries and continents all communicate with each other perfectly; their social protocols are well defined. The profound paradox is that the conversation of the brain's electrical world defies translation. It has given us a multitude of modes of communication. We have developed languages that use coordinated movements of fingers, hands, bodies, mouths, and throat muscles. We discovered that what went on in our minds could be transmitted to other minds by using symbols, agreed-upon definitions of movements or voices or sense impressions. Yet we have not been able to discover how to communicate with our own brain's activity. It is like our attempts to communicate with distant elements in our own and neighboring galaxies. We know that if there is the order in the universe there appears to be, the distant elements may have an order to their structures and events that can be decoded. So it is with the brain. Its geography and its environment are known. We know that the predominant changes accompanying function of the brain are electrical and chemical in nature. But as yet we have not the faintest idea of the code the brain uses to conceive thoughts, to reason, to speculate, to envision, to symbolize, to visualize, to imagine, to form judgments, to arrive at conclusions, to understand, to be empathetic.

To Watch the Brain Perform

Neuroscience has uncovered innumerable electrical and chemical codes which operate *pari passu* with the transfer of sensory and motor, emotional and memory information within the brain. How the information is used to nourish and develop the mental life is quite a different matter. It is one thing to trace, electronically or chemically, the brain routes of, say, visual information, but quite another to define in brain activity terms just what determines why a particular bit of visual information has special meanings to any particular individual. One would have to sort out the genetic influences for that brain, explore and define its social experiences, and know why only certain bits of information are put into memory and why other certain bits are selectively recalled from memory. The end products of dynamic mental activity are far too complex for mere vocal or body expression; as we all have reflected, it would take forever to try to recount the myriad thoughts that lie behind even a simple verbal observation. Sir Francis Galton, the father of visual imagery research, tried this feat around 1870. He made shorthand notes of every thought that came to mind as he strolled down a familiar avenue. Analysis of his voluminous notes revealed new thoughts appearing at the rate of some 90 a minute. These were concrete, verbalizable thoughts, shorn of their families of subliminal and memory associations. All that we know of brain function has been derived from the outside looking in, imperfect mirrors that distort the image of the world within. The real evolution of the mind, and of mind science, awaits the growth of awareness of one's own mind from within, not the awareness that comes from the observations made by others from the outside. This is the evolutionary step that bio-feedback offers. The characteristics of our minds' activity that the neuroscientists and mind psychologists have defined for us can now be used as a ring of endless keys to explore our own withins.

The only readily available, measurable chart we have of the physical activity of the brain is that made by brain waves. It is relatively easy to tap into the endless ebb and flow of the brain's electrical energy; some electrode paste and some small metal discs to paste onto the scalp, and all that remains is to plug into an EEG recording machine. The electroencephalogram, commonly called the EEG or brain wave record, is a complex electrical record of the neuronal activity of the brain.

The 20 billion nerve cells that constitute the brain are each capable of conducting an electrical current. In a state of relative rest each brain cell has a potential electrical pressure (voltage), and when the brain cell becomes activated and is conducting a current, it does so by releasing its potential energy, which acts as an electrical pressure to push along its activity and its message. Each brain cell has one major receiver, the axon, and anywhere from one to twelve or more transmitters or outgoing contacts, called dendrites, and this allows for trillions of interconnections among brain cells. Outside, on the scalp where the electrodes are, the electrical potential, or voltage, is transferred to the electrodes and is conducted via its small wires to the amplifying system of the recorder, then to the pens.

The EEG record is generally written out by an elephantine instrument laden with buttons to poke and dials to set. The chief function of the EEG machine is to inscribe on paper a reasonably faithful representation of the electrical voice of the brain. Its main components are the powerful and selective amplifiers hidden in its cabinet and a second system which impresses the electrical changes into a magnetic field. A slender ink-writing pen is centered between the two poles of a powerful magnet, and by electromagnetic action the pen moves when the magnetic field is changed by the changes in brain electrical activity. Paper is pushed and pulled underneath the pens at a constant rate. Much like the television set, the EEG machine can be played for hours, bringing to life bustling, moving activity taking place in a distant studio. Unfortunately mechanical pens can move only so fast and all of the electrical changes of the brain waves faster than the pens can move have to be stopped before reaching the pens to prevent inaccurate recording. Thus a large part of brain electrical activity is lost before we ever see it. And as with television, the recording of EEGs can be fraught with all the difficulties of transmitting selected currents of minuscule proportion.

For some thirty-odd years study of bioelectric potentials, and especially study of the minute potentials producing brain wave patterns, was severely limited by inadequate instrumentation. Only within the last five years have truly refined, sensitive electrical detecting instruments and analyzers become available. These have stimulated renewed effort in exploring the complexities of brain waves. Older instrumentation not only amplified the small electrical signals from the brain but also amplified all of the electrical "noise" signals always present in the environment. Because of this, only the largest brain electrical signals could be displayed clearly. As technical improvements were made, many more characteristic waves of different frequencies were found in all brain wave patterns. Along with better amplifiers and specific instrumentation to discriminate unwanted (environmental) electrical signals from real brain wave activity, there are other new electronic instruments now available which permit analyses of considerably greater detail and scope. Examples are instruments which sort out the different EEG waves, count each kind, and give information about the special characteristics of each.

The small electrical signal originates from groups of brain cells and must struggle through layers of tissue and finally through the skull. As it does the electrical signals become either quite small and scattered at times, while under other circumstances the signals move together, adding to each other, producing large signals. The amplification is nearly a millionfold before we can actually see the written comings and goings of the brain's electrical activity. If one considers that there are some 20 billion brain cells, and only one small record, it can be appreciated how difficult it is to attach meanings to the written record. We can take several records, but this just makes our analyses more complex.

In its simplest terms, brain wave activity is recorded as a continuous flow of changing frequencies of electrical waves. Frequency is the term for the rate at which electrical pressure builds up and recedes. Conventionally we think of 60-cycle alternating current, which means that the direction of electron flow producing the electrical current is changing back and forth 60 times a second. Something similar happens with brain electrical waves. When brain cells discharge their electrical pressure, the push is in one direction, then during "recovery" from the discharge, the electrical pressure subsides and the electrical flow is in the opposite direction. When groups of brain cells discharge together or within microseconds of each other, recording systems can reproduce only the sum of the activity. Depending upon how quickly groups of cells fire in relationship to each other and how fast the mechanical pens can move, the resulting accumulated activity becomes manifest as brain waves of different rhythmic frequencies. Each group of frequencies from the lowest to the highest has a name, not in order of actual frequency, but named according to which seemed dominant or next dominant. The most generally prevalent brain wave frequency is called alpha—the largest, seemingly most dominant feature of brain waves. Actually alpha is *not* the most dominant, largest, or most prevalent brain wave, but it does have the distinction of being the most studied. So much is known and speculated about alpha that it is the subject of a separate section below.

I am still filled with awe and wonder when I record human brain waves in my laboratory. Watching brain waves gives me the feeling of suddenly having discovered where halos come from. I often stand entranced in front of the EEG machine, scarcely believing the beauty and indescribable complexity of the brain electrical activity being inscribed on paper and flying so swiftly past my eyes. Just to ponder the fact that living brains ceaselessly pour forth electrical activity gives one a sense of profound awe; then to be able to watch the outpouring of the infinitely varying interplay of working brain cells transcribed into familiar pen wiggles by specially engineered electronic equipment is an experience that never fails to excite.

The complexity of brain rhythms challenges the capacity of man's ability for sustained thought and perspective. It is perhaps this difficulty itself which may prove to be the ultimate barrier to understanding the functioning of the mind. The brain functions in a myriad of dimensions, not simply two or three. It is all at the same time conducting a hundred biochemical transformations in different brain areas and in different individual neurons. These are, moreover, translated into electrical impulses and changes; not the same for the various functions they perform, but almost continuously varying in number, intensity and productiveness. Brain messages are constantly undergoing diverse and complex processing, coding, distribution, verification, evaluation for significance, and so on. These activities too are not conducted in a single plane, but are multidimensional. The popular observation that it takes two to tango is overwhelmingly important in the brain, for no single nerve cell can produce a change observable on the outside. It takes many cells, often thousands, to produce an observable change. The brain is not so externalized as is muscle, where we can pool the efforts of hundreds of nerve and muscle cells to produce an observable movement. On the contrary, most brain activity by itself produces no outwardly observable effect. To add to the complexity, the actual transfer of discrete brain messages may be accomplished in a number of ways. Although traditionalists laboring under the restriction of inadequate information have told us of the "pathways" which exist for certain parts of the brain and for the handling of special types of information, newer studies which have access to highly refined instruments are showing us that although such pathways do indeed exist, they are both supplemented and modified by extra-pathway routes for exchange of information within the central nervous system. The more deeply we probe, the more mysterious and labyrinthine the world of the mind-brain becomes.

Introducing Alpha (and Perhaps Omega)

While the EEG machine scribbles out the chattering of 20 billion brain cells, laboratory-man watches with a frustration that wells within him like the tantrum of a small child. He watches the scribbling continue to send him a code of the mind, and with every new movement of the pen he searches his mind in frantic desperation for the key to the code. Every shift, every change could be significant. It is with relief that he sees the EEG record burst into a well-known pattern. The brain cells of the cortex are capable of coordinated group action. The electrical changes of each cell pull together like a tug-of-war. Their coordinated changes produce a considerable force, the voltage. Under these conditions laboratory-man can measure and correlate; he has an entity that he can recognize and can talk about. It is the ALPHA of brain electrical activity.

At the present stage in deciphering the electrical messages of the brain, laboratory-man is at the stage cryptographers were after they discovered that the great circle surrounding certain Egyptian hieroglyphs signified the name of a mighty ruler.

Alpha activity of the brain paints a truly beautiful picture. Look at the records shown in Figure 10. Notice the ebb and flow of the giant waves, giving a print of comforting familiarity in the rhythmic patterns and in the orderliness of the design. The waxing and waning is characteristic of the most easily recognized brain wave pattern as the pattern proceeds over time. This in itself is something to think about. When you look at a written record of your brain electrical activity, you *see what has been.* If the scientist wants to know your thoughts when alpha wave activity was present, you have to try to remember, and during remembering there may be little, if any, alpha activity present. It is in this netherworld of remembering, of thinking and reflecting, this meeting place between the brain and the body where alpha bio-feedback can probe the deep within, as no other known technique can, to learn whether mind substance is the same as brain substance or quite different from it.

The singular characteristic about brain waves is that they represent a continuous movement of electrical changes which coalesce from time to time to form groups or "bursts" of waves of similar time periods. The duration of the symmetrical wave and the number of similar wave forms appearing in a burst are used to express the frequency of a particular wave type. In the case of alpha waves, the total duration of its symmetrical moving shape is roughly 100 milliseconds, or one wave every 0.1 second, which, of course, is 10 waves per second.

Although alpha waves are the most easily observed of the many varieties of brain waves, they are *not,* as is generally believed, either the most frequently occurring or largest wave in the brain wave pattern. But they were discovered first, and because of the poor instrumentation of that time, they appeared to be the single most outstanding characteristic element of brain electrical activity.

Other rhythmic waves of the EEG are identified according to their frequency. In this case frequency means the incidence of occurrence per second *when* there are enough similar waves present to ensure that they are all of approximately similar wave duration. Theta activity is generally considered to have a frequency of between 4 and 7 cycles per second, and theta waves are often as large or larger than alpha waves. Faster frequencies of anything over 12 cycles per second is called beta activity. Until quite recently beta activity was not distinguished as to whether it was rhythmic or not, but there is a growing tendency to define beta as that rhythmic EEG activity occurring at 13 to 28 cycles per second. Delta waves are very slow, about 1 to 3 per second.

An abundance of alpha wave activity has classically been considered to represent states of rest (not sleep), relaxation, and relief from attention and concentration. Conversely, lack of alpha wave activity and its replacement by beta and waves of faster frequencies has been interpreted as indicating states of alertness, attention, orienting, and anxiety. Theta waves have been found to be associated with several different behavioral functions such as drowsiness, dreaming, and orienting (particularly the assimilation of new information). We are now learning that although these relationships of brain waves with emotion and behavior are true in a general way, the relationships are of infinitely greater complexity. More specific attributes of alpha, beta, and theta and their relationships to human behavior are discussed in some detail in the following sections.

Another reason why the most easily observed aspect of brain wave activity *appears* to be the alpha rhythm is that EEG recordings are generally done under conditions of relaxation. One can only imagine the amazement of Hans Berger, the pioneer of brain wave study, when in 1929 he saw this monster of the brain wave field emerge when his subject closed his eyes. It was of course most appropriate to sew the label "alpha" to this first truly recognizable cut of the mysterious cloth of brain activity. It swept on, riding like a champion over the smaller characterless waves, repeating itself in great encompassing envelopes, losing all else inside. Berger in Germany and the conservative Lord Adrian and B. H. C. Matthews in England, the dramatists of the early EEG theater, struggled to comprehend the alpha wave. Indeed, it disappeared when the eyes were opened and it returned in huge swells when the eyes were closed. Berger, Lord Adrian, and later Grey Walter were convinced that alpha waves represented that natural frequency of brain electrical activity when the pageants of the visual world were shut out. But soon they found that alpha disappeared if the subject engaged in mental activity requiring considerable attention. By 1935 alpha activity was known to be importantly related to relief from both visual activity and attention. The situation remains nearly the same today. In the thirty-odd years that have passed, alpha activity has been inspected, counted, dissected, suppressed, and distorted in a hundred ways, yet the average brain researcher is unsure whether alpha is associated with mental effort or relief from mental effort.

What exactly are alpha waves, the most obvious and dominant

energy of the brain's electrical activity? Technically, alpha waves are rhythmic changes in electrical energy, swelling up like waves of the ocean, and, like them, receding, swelling, and receding again and again. Researchers began to specify that the frequency or rate of energy rise is between 8 and 12 cycles per second. Some researchers prefer to define alpha as a rhythmic wave of between 9 and 13 c/sec; others as 8 to 13, and still others as 7 to 12, and so on. At the present time we don't know whether these differences in defining the frequency of alpha are important or not.

The electrical energy of alpha waves is measured in units just as is the energy used for the electrical supply for home appliances, but with a startling difference in magnitude. The voltage of house electricity ranges between 110 and 120 volts; that of alpha waves ranges between 20 and 150 microvolts (i.e., 20 and 150 millionths of a volt). It is truly a miracle of modern technology that we can measure not only the energy of alpha waves but also that of many other brain waves of much smaller energy, down to about two microvolts.

The Many Faces of Alpha

One of the things that startles and annoys some EEG researchers is to hear the statement that all that alpha is not alpha, that there are perhaps an almost infinite number of alphas. To many researchers alpha means any brain wave frequency between 8 and 12 cycles per second, and they let it go at that. But to the experienced alpha investigator who is concerned with the mental and emotional correlates of alpha, small alpha means quite a different set of behavioral and personality characteristics than does large alpha. So too do fast and slow alpha and all frequencies in between. People also differ quite remarkably behaviorally according to where alpha is most easily detected on the scalp and how it moves around through the brain. Not only do people differ with these different characteristics of alpha, but within the same person each differing aspect of the form or location or appearance of alpha has a multitude of different meanings with respect to his emotions or mind activity or behavior. To say alpha is to say infinite.

The Music of the Hemispheres

There are perhaps as many as six different rhythmic activities which influence alpha or denote special individual characteristics of alpha. There is the fundamental alpha rhythm obtained by averaging frequency over a specific time interval to find the most repesentative frequency. Whether alpha averages 8 or 9 or 10.6 or 11.8 cycles per second, it relates to certain basic personality traits, as do the characteristic ways that each person's alpha varies over the frequency range designated as alpha. One individual might have an average of 10.5-cycle alpha and vary little from that frequency; another might have an average of 9.8-cycle alpha and tend to vary almost continuously over the entire alpha frequency range. There are also harmonics of alpha which are both interesting and beautiful to see in EEG records. Two quite different, yet normal, EEG patterns are shown in Figures 10 and 11. These are the rhythmic brain electrical activities that are exactly one-half or twice or three times the average basic alpha frequency. Some investigators believe theta activity, at, say, 5 cycles per second, to be a subharmonic of 10-cycle alpha; or that 20-cycle beta activity is the first harmonic of alpha. No one knows why such precise multiples of the alpha frequency occur, but frequency differences are attributable to the way in which brain electrical activity in various parts acts to facilitate the development or dissolution of alpha.

Another rhythmic characteristic of alpha is the rhythms of its bursts. Notice in the illustration that while an overall reassuring pattern of orderliness is apparent, close inspection shows a vast array of new recognizable differences. The length, or duration in time, of the alpha burst is never the same. Sometimes a burst of alpha waves is short, sometimes long; rarely is it possible to find alpha bursts of exactly the same duration. Moreover, the intervals between alpha bursts vary in an independent manner, and none of these ever seems to be an exact replica of another. Another rhythm is the alternation rhythm between periods of alpha and no-alpha.

One can also see that step by step the heights of individual waves are all different, and even the spacing between waves differs from wave to wave. These wave-to-wave changes show the ever

EYES CLOSED

Figure 10. EEG pattern of a very calm individual with his eyes closed. Alpha activity occurred at each recorded scalp site. The alpha in leads 2 and 5 ranges up to about 75 μV.

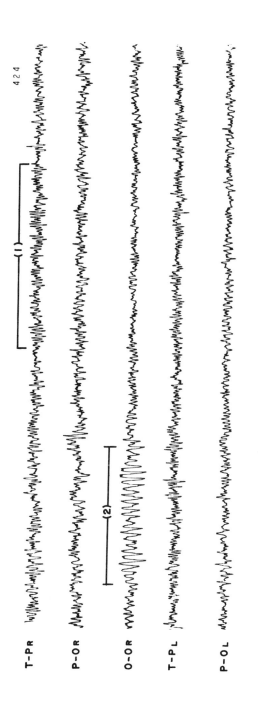

Figure 11. EEG pattern of a very alert fifty-year-old female with otherwise quite normal personality and behavioral characteristics. The eyes were closed. The EEG waves are unusually rapid and rhythmic, most of them as in (1) being classified as beta activity. The record shows one 2-second burst of alpha (2), showing how isolated alpha may be in an EEG record. This record resembles the kind of EEG pattern frequently found in people classified as "anxious." These people would be interesting candidates for alpha bio-feedback training.

T, P and O refer to locations of the scalp electrodes: temporal, parietal and occipital. R and L mean right and left hemispheres. EEG recordings are derived from pairs of electrodes.

continuing changes in the frequency of the alpha rhythm. The continuously changing characteristics of bursts of alpha activity in part reflect the normal alternation of attention and nonattention (to anything). Although the variations appear to be random and ever changing, as Mulholland has noted, they appear to be part of the eye-visual cortex auto-control system. There are other rhythms superimposed on alpha that are of such long cycles as to be generally unrecognized, but they reflect the circadian rhythms of living organisms, those daily or hourly changes that shift patterns, but in an orderly way. The best example is the differing times of appearance of alpha during sleep and wakefulness. And finally, brain rhythms may be part of a much larger continuum of the rhythmic activities of the universe, reflecting changes in atmospheric environment or social states of tension.

Not only are there a host of different kinds of alpha, but there are many influences that affect what is seen on the EEG record. Just to name a few: the type of electrodes and their placement; the type of recording device; skull thickness; electrical environmental noise; genetic factors; personality; intelligence; conditions of stress and the individual's mode of reacting to stress; endocrine factors; physiologic drives as hunger, fatigue; attention; motivation; the amount of information the individual has about his brain waves, his body and his task.

Where alpha waves arise is still an unsolved question. Alpha brain waves behave in curious ways, and to me, the alpha activity of a new subject is always strikingly different from those thousands of brain wave patterns that I've recorded. Each person appears to have highly individual patterns of brain waves.*

---

* The riddle of varying and individual alpha behavior can be better understood, to some extent, by considering the brain as a generator of one or several rhythms. The term alpha generator has quite different meanings to different investigators. It is rarely considered in the literal sense that there is actually a source of electrical current within the brain, but actually implies the functional existence of a mechanism that gathers together disparate electrical waves and emits them as smooth, continuous changes of electrical activity. To other investigators alpha generator implies a process by which excitability levels or levels of electrical conduction are matched and compared in steps, such that the result of the comparison is a constantly changing electrical value. An oversimplification of this concept suggests that there are one or several inherent frequency generators of electrical activity in the brain. In relationship to alpha these are faster or slower. But because there are so many different kinds of brain cells with so many different ways of functioning, when they are interacting with

At any particular time of an individual's ongoing brain wave activity, he may have varying proportions of slow and fast rhythms, large and slow rhythms. But for every well-marked behavioral state, such as drowsiness or visual alerting or reveries or meditation or dreaming, the mixture of brain waves is distinctively different for that individual alone. Obviously, with a finite number of basic rhythms, and a finite number of gross human behaviors, there will be many people who show quite different patterns. The unifying element appears to be the general temporal sequences in which the different patterns appear. If, for example, a person of one type possesses a relaxed type of EEG pattern as he is preparing to expend some mental effort, chances are that he will lose his alpha when he actually makes the mental effort. On the other hand, if the individual has an alerted EEG pattern when he approaches more serious mental activity, chances are good that he will actually produce alpha in his EEG (see below). Whatever assortment of EEG patterns an individual owns, he progresses through them in a fairly orderly fashion. It is a continuum of brain electrical patterns, produced by shifting patterns of activation and nonactivation of different brain cells contributing to the underlying rhythms, and it parallels quite faithfully the continuum of behavioral activities, as, for example, alerting, relaxed wakefulness, drowsiness and sleep, or smaller cycles of these within the larger cycles. But the match between the electrical and behavioral continua may start at different points in different people.

It would seem, then, that the different brain wave patterns manifest in different behavioral states are simply different manifestations, at slightly different times, of the same brain electrical continuum. This suggests that it is perhaps more the changing pattern that is important than the exact type of pattern. If this is so, then the specific characteristics of the different types of brain waves may assume important significance with respect to the nuances of

---

each other, some rhythmic activity becomes submerged in stronger rhythms, or in some cases it can add together. These different ways of interacting result on occasions when there is an apparent jumble of rhythms, which when written out on an EEG machine look like no rhythms at all; while at other times distinct rhythms like alpha emerge, but are slower or faster, larger or smaller. As noted earlier, when rhythms of distinctive frequencies exist and persist for long enough times to identify them precisely, they have been labeled by letters of the Greek alphabet.

emotion and feeling that accompany the larger states of consciousness of wakefulness and sleep. It is already clear from some bio-feedback studies that a more definitive consideration of the exact frequency of alpha, its amplitude, rate of conduction through the brain, and its appearance in various brain areas may be necessary to discriminate more precisely the various aspects of subjective states that emerge during alpha bio-feedback.

The reality and significance of the individuality of EEG patterns has not been well appreciated in research on brain wave activity. This is understandable from the standpoint of researchers who are interested in underlying mechanisms of brain electrical activity since they must study what is most commonly available. In a great deal of EEG research this means working with those kinds of people who have a fair abundance of alpha in the EEG record and who show disappearance of alpha with mental or emotional activity. Such studies cannot provide for documenting the many varieties of human brain wave patterns that exist. On the other hand, considerable confusion exists in attempting to define relationships between EEG patterns and personality or intelligence or social behavior. This is not only because of the large numbers of EEG factors that are involved, but mainly because there is an amazing variety of techniques used to evaluate brain electrical activity. Unhappily, different investigators tend to use different types of measurements, different types of subject populations, electrode placements, ways of recording, etc. Alpha activity, for example, although often measured in terms of abundance, or amount occurring per unit of time, may be measured in terms of the amplitude of the alpha signal. Rarely if ever are measurements made of the exact frequency of alpha.

With so many variations in people and scientists, it is natural that there is considerable argument in the scientific literature about the relationship between EEG patterns and characteristics of personality and intelligence. A 1948 report by Saul and co-workers contains some interesting generalizations about personality and brain waves. The report can easily be faulted scientifically for a certain lack of specifics, but by and large it summarizes the everyday subjective appraisal of people made by EEG researchers based upon just looking at the EEG records of their subjects. The generalizations of Saul et al. were based upon the constancy of the EEG pattern over a five-year period. Individuals, particularly males, having a high "alpha index" (considerable alpha in the EEG) were classified as very passive, i.e., dependent, submissive, and desiring to receive from others, particularly as these characteristics were contrasted with independence, drive, dominance, activity and masculinity.* Individuals having mixed alpha *frequencies* were characterized as showing frustration or demanding, impatient, aggressive and hostile behavior; while those with predominantly fast EEG frequencies and very little alpha were found to be the most overtly hostile, aggressive, and demanding. With respect to intelligence, however, most research supports the concept that greater intelligence also may be related to faster alpha frequencies. So to be intelligent perhaps means that you have to be a little neurotic?

Between the acute situations where the organism is aroused and becomes alerted and thus loses his alpha, and the overt behavioral disturbances of psychoneurosis where the EEG becomes distinctively abnormal lie the tangled threads of countless variations of brain wave patterns of millions of normal human beings whose behavior ranges between disturbing passivity and hypermanic states. It is in this wide range of normal activity that bio-feedback has the best opportunity to help sort out the subjective accompaniments of various brain activities, and vice versa.

Ordinary Alpha

Over the past forty years more than a thousand reports have appeared in the scientific literature mainly devoted to descriptions of the many and varied characteristics of brain wave alpha activity. Since researchers most frequently work in pairs or groups, this means that well over two thousand researchers have spent considerable time studying alpha. After all this work, it is surprising how little we can say about the meaning and function of alpha. There are still vigorous arguments about the real significance of alpha.

As Berger and Lord Adrian observed more than thirty years ago,

---

* Other studies on personality have found quite different results: e.g., that extroverts exhibit higher values of amounts of EEG alpha and also alpha amplitude. Part of the difficulty lies in provincial definitions of "abnormal" behavior as the often hazy line between normal and pathological signs of neurotic behavior.

alpha tends to appear in the brain electrical activity pattern upon closing the eyes and disappear when the eyes are opened. Both of the early investigators, along with Grey Walter, immediately deduced that the eyes' occupation with visual stimuli kept the brain active and alert during our major daily activity of looking, and when the eyes were closed there were no more stimulating visual scenes to remain alert to, allowing the brain's electrical activity to fall into a less active state marked by the appearance of alpha, as in Figure 12. The obvious relationship between alpha and *not* seeing triggered several interesting research questions. It would appear that researchers felt that the role of alpha in visual activity was tied to brain processes of attention and dealing with visual information, and for the most part they began at the beginning, exploring first various effects of attention and aroused, alert behavior on brain electrical activity. Other researchers were intrigued by the idea that alpha might help to learn something about brain activity during mental imagery, but it wasn't until the 1960s that the crucial link between alpha and eye movements was explored.

There had never really been a unified attack on deciphering the secrets of alpha until close to the time of the bio-feedback breakthrough. There are some unusual and peculiar aspects to alpha research. The great bulk of physiologic and even psychologic research is done using the dog, cat or rat; unfortunately for researchers there is no brain wave activity in these convenient laboratory animals comparable to the alpha activity of human beings. Not long ago I excitedly bought a book proclaiming to describe the physiologic basis of the alpha rhythm. There was not one single word about human alpha activity in the entire book; it was a synthesis of the most likely neurophysiologic mechanisms discovered in animals that, in theory, could be applied to human alpha. Other experimental ways of deriving information about the significance and origin of alpha have been mainly observing its changes during normal behavior and disease states during brain surgery, by watching its development in growing infants, by observing its changes during different types of mental activities, and by comparing various types of populations from different ethnic groups.

There is much more known about the significance of the disappearance of alpha from the brain wave pattern than is known about its presence. Briefly, alpha tends to disappear during mental work (see Figure 12), alerting, orienting, dreaming, hunger, visual activity and frustration. It appears when the eyes are closed, during drowsiness, relaxation, and with the rest that comes immediately after mental effort.

Almost any sensory stimulus, whether visual, auditory, or tactile, expunges alpha from brain electrical activity, particularly if the stimulus is intense or sudden. The sudden disappearance of alpha is just one of the many body changes that occur when the organism is alerted. If there is no alpha when alertness and attention are required, then one might be led to believe that alpha has no role in the assimilation or processing of new information within the brain. But even this isn't completely true because the general biological principle of adaptation appears to intervene. That is, alertness and attention occur only when there is novelty to be alert and attended to. Once the import of the newness has been assimilated, the processes adapt and they no longer mobilize themselves until another something new needs attention. Thus certain kinds of alertness and attention may be accompanied by alpha if the stimulus is not truly novel.

Researchers had become convinced that the disappearance of alpha waves from the brain wave record signaled alertness not only because they disappeared when people were startled or jerked to attention, but because this behavior of alpha also fit a very neat theory about brain electrical activity. The reticular activating theory of Morruzzi and Magoun (described briefly in Chapter 3) held, in one part, that the central core of the brain and brain stem exerted an activating effect on the cortex, and that when the organism was alerted, the synchronous or rhythmic brain electrical activity became desynchronized. Many human studies supported the notion; experiments in which alpha activity was recorded showed that it disappeared during mental tasks or when the emotions were aroused. For many years desynchrony, the absence of large, slow rhythmic waves and their replacement by small, fast waves, was believed to be synonymous with alerting, or a state of arousal.

Unlike tax loopholes, lacunae of research knowledge are ultimately filled, and within the past few years there have been sub-

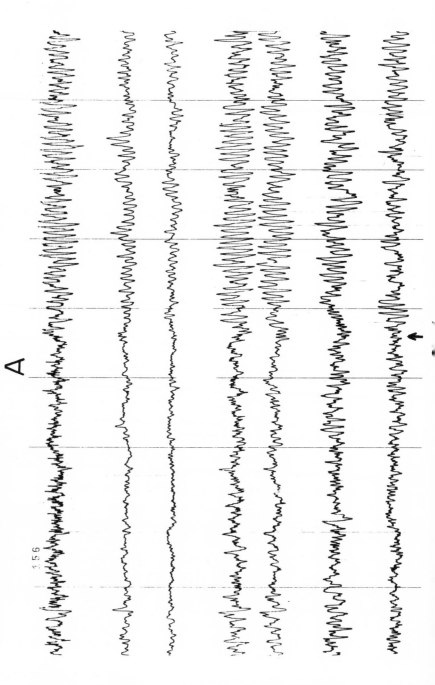

Figure 12. EEG recordings from one subject.

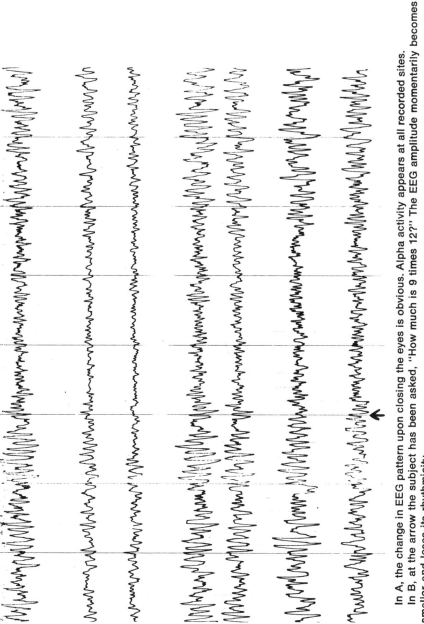

In A, the change in EEG pattern upon closing the eyes is obvious. Alpha activity appears at all recorded sites. In B, at the arrow the subject has been asked, "How much is 9 times 12?" The EEG amplitude momentarily becomes smaller and loses its rhythmicity.

stantial scientific studies demonstrating that the arousing stimuli that cause the disappearance of alpha in some people cause the appearance or increase in alpha activity in an equal number of other people. The behavior of alpha activity thus appears to be quite variable and to depend upon quite individual characteristics. The mental effort to solve a problem will make alpha disappear in some people, but in others that same type of effort will actually make alpha appear, while in still others an existing alpha activity may show specific changes in its frequency or amplitude or course of conduction through the brain. But for all people, alpha is involved whether it appears or disappears in the EEG or is changed in its fundamental characteristics.

For many years and until, in fact, around 1965, it was a firm scientific and completely erroneous conclusion that alpha activity appeared in the EEG only when the eyes were closed. Research customs are often curious, and the reason that researchers failed to find much alpha when the eyes were open was because nearly all experiments were conducted with the eyes closed!

Another point about alpha in relationship to eye activity is of critical importance in brain wave bio-feedback, particularly because of the current enthusiastic belief that alpha wave bio-feedback is a shortcut meditation technique. Westernized meditation is generally practiced with the eyes closed. Some time ago Mulholland and Dewan discovered separately, and others have adequately confirmed them, that when many people close their eyes they automatically and unconsciously turn their eyes upward. This is a common phenomenon during sleep. It so happens that in most of these people the alpha that appears in the EEG when they close their eyes is a direct function of what their eye muscles are doing. Move the eyes up and alpha appears; move them down and it disappears. The absolute reliability of this phenomenon in some people (it happens in about 30 percent) is such that Dewan was able to train them to send Morse code messages by controlling eye movements, which controlled the relative length of burst of alpha activity. The messages were written in code on the EEG machine. The utility of the technique for espionage may be limited, however, as it required about thirty seconds to develop each letter or character.

Thomas Mulholland, who ascribes to the theory that oculomotor (eye muscle) activity and alpha operate together as a control system, has provided elaborate and extensive research which demonstrates that the accommodation of the eye for visual focusing is in intimate, perhaps inseparable, relationship with the mechanisms that generate alpha activity of the brain. When an individual focuses his eyes for precise visual attention, alpha disappears, and conversely, when the eyes are de-focused, alpha reappears in the EEG. Visual focusing requires so little conscious attention that we are unaware that our eyes are almost constantly undergoing focusing and refocusing. If one intentionally, however, alternately focuses and de-focuses the eyes, it will be found that alpha activity is alternately turned on and off.

The intimacy between eyes and alpha activity may be the reason why alpha feedback faddists refer to "instant Zen" as instant. The unconscious manipulation of the smallest muscles surrounding the operation of the eye may be enough to trigger the appearance of alpha. Engulfed in the mystical meditation ritual, the learning to control one's own alpha by an unconscious twitch of the eye may not be recognized as a deception. But for the serious student of meditation the deception can be a puzzling distraction to his search for spiritual peace. Not long ago just this same experience of deception in a serious meditator was unveiled in our laboratory. A leading scientist had requested time with us for an EEG recording to check his progress with an alpha bio-feedback device he was using as a meditation aid. We first recorded the EEG of his normal activity both with the eyes open and with the eyes closed. His brain wave pattern was rather typical of a person who does a good bit of difficult thinking. As is our practice, we also recorded his eye movements. When he began his meditation practice, the recordings revealed the dismaying truth. Every brief spurt of alpha was heralded by an eye movement, and there was another to turn it off. It never failed; every time alpha appeared, there was the eye movement. He had learned to make alpha through eye movement, not to produce alpha by itself. Not surprisingly the eye movements were exaggerated far beyond normal eye movement activity. It was a disheartening experience for all of us, but it was striking evidence of the illusion and deception that can occur with improper alpha feedback training.

Blatant ignorance of alpha activity is also seen in some of the popular, nonscientific alpha feedback devices that have swamped the market in the last few years. Some of these instruct the user to place the recording electrodes in exactly the same places that are used to record eye movement in scientific studies. This makes it easy for the user to develop "control" over alpha since all he has to do is move his eyes. Moreover, fine movements of the eyebrows can trigger alpha activity. At least such devices provide the opportunity to learn to control something, even though it is only eye movements.

In the laboratory, or when using bio-feedback scientifically in therapy, it is a simple matter to rule out the effect of gross eye movements on the learning of control over alpha. It is much more difficult to rule out the effects of focusing and de-focusing. The most convenient way is to compare the amount of alpha that develops during its bio-feedback to the amount of alpha that develops when no alpha bio-feedback is given.

The placement of the electrodes for detecting brain wave activity is more crucial to the fidelity of alpha recording than their misplacement to eye movement positions would suggest. Bio-feedback researchers have tended to limit their recordings and feedback signals to the occipital scalp areas that overlie the interpretive visual cortex area, presumably because of the eye-alpha relationship. For many years researchers have concentrated on trying to define "alpha generators," brain cell areas deep within the brain, which were capable of exciting cortical cells to fire in an almost synchronous manner that we recognize as the rhythmic waves of alpha. For the most part the activity of the visual cortex was studied because it lends itself to more precise experimental manipulation (by visual stimuli) than other areas. The failure to use other cortical areas as test objects apparently gave rise to the conclusion that alpha is predominant in the visual cortex of the occiput.

Recent studies have greatly broadened the concepts of where and when alpha activity is found. Two or perhaps three more alpha generators have been postulated, and there is good experimental evidence that the alpha activity found over different locations of the brain may relate to quite different types of behavior or mental activity. Aside from the general technical difficulty and expense involved in brain wave research, only the most obvious characteristics of alpha lend themselves to easy study. But for the most part individuals vary widely in the amount and location of their alpha, in the frequency and amplitude of alpha, and the conditions under which it appears and disappears. The ability of the brain to evolve a rhythmic waxing and waning of the electrical pressure that is used to carry on its function continues to perplex researchers. Only a few scientists have had the opportunity and specialized knowledge to explore the fundamental nature of brain cell activity.

Concluding anything about alpha is perilous. The EEG machines and electrodes used to capture only the external manifestations of the operation of the brain are like the Mariner probe peeking at Mars from its thousands of miles of distance. Brain energy runs the whole mind and body; it cannot be expected that we can learn its secrets solely by examining its electrical topography. The 20 billion cellular inhabitants of the brain have nearly as many diverse ways of behavior as does the entire human body and there is as much variation in their behavioral profiles as there is in the universe of human beings.

TEN

Alpha Brain Waves: Alpha Bio-Feedback: A Tool for Medicine, Meditation . . . Or Both?

> How does the physical substance of the brain obey commands of a mind that does not consciously recognize the most abstruse, man-made symbols of itself?

In the Brown Lab with the Blue Light

By this writing hundreds of studies have confirmed the fact that when human beings can perceive their own brain wave alpha activity they can learn to control it. There have been two general research approaches, that of Mulholland and Kamiya and my approach. The former two, while having certain procedural similarities, had quite different objectives. My own approach differed in that it did not employ the conventions of experimental learning procedure, nor did it impose psychologic restraints on a neurophysiologic system. The different experimental approaches will be described and the reader can judge for himself the relative merits of each.

Probably the earliest attempts to "teach" alpha were experiments some time ago in which the objective was to condition alpha to disappear when a certain signal was sounded. Results of these early studies were equivocal but suggested that some conditioned manipulation of brain waves was possible.

My original experiments were, except for the instrumentation, of the utmost of simplicity. The subjects were seated in a comfortable chair in a modest-sized room with moderate ambient lighting and fairly good soundproofing. Pairs of electrodes were applied to the scalp to record a conventional EEG. At the same time, the brain wave activity from one pair of electrodes over the parieto-occipital area (one electrode midway on one side of the skull, the other at a midpoint on the back of the skull) was amplified and fed through an electronic filter to isolate out the range of EEG frequencies that comprise alpha activity. From there the alpha signal was treated electronically to group successive alpha waves which produced a steady electrical signal that was then used to operate a blue light. If the alpha waves had not been "grouped," each alpha wave would have triggered the blue light, resulting in an annoying flicker. As it was, this system turned the light on when alpha activity was present and turned it off when alpha disappeared. There was, however, one more feature: the intensity of the light reflected the size of the alpha.

For the experiment itself the subjects were simply asked to try to keep their eyes open and to try to find some feeling state within themselves that would keep the blue light on as much of the time as possible. It was casually explained that in some way some kind of brain activity operated the lights, but that we researchers didn't know what the feelings were, and so the subjects would have to try to discover them and then tell us. The subjects were then left alone for some 90 minutes. We experimenters worked in a separate room, running the EEG machines, adjusting the controls to ensure accurate bio-feedback of the alpha waves and listening for comments through the intercom system, noting interesting changes in brain wave patterns on the EEG record.

The bio-feedback experience was not a continuous 90 minutes. The period was broken up into alternating 3-minute rest periods and 10-minute work periods. During the rest periods the subjects were advised that the alpha feedback signal was not operating. At the end of the total practice session, the subjects were given a questionnaire and asked to write their answers to three questions: what was your subjective, "feeling" experience; what mind techniques did you use to keep the light turned on; how long did you think the experiment lasted?

Since it was alpha that activated and kept on the blue light, we measured the amount of alpha activity in the EEG in order to evaluate the ability of the subjects to generate and sustain alpha. The results were quite startling. By the end of the first practice session, the average subject had more than doubled the amount of alpha in his EEG, and he tripled the amount during the third practice session. The increase occurred with the eyes open and while the subject was trying to keep the light on. In the third practice session the abundance reached the extraordinary high of 60 percent of all EEG activity. This is as much or more than the average person shows when he has his eyes closed and is very relaxed.

At first most subjects also increased the abundance of their alpha activity during rest periods when the light signal was not operating. However, at the end of each practice session and in subsequent practice sessions, a number of subjects produced large amounts of alpha during the feedback periods, then tended to show the desynchronized or "alert" EEG patterns during the rest periods. This suggested that when they were attending to the feedback signal, they continued to increase their alpha and when attention to the task was no longer required, alpha disappeared. This was opposite to the usual sequence of changes observed for alpha: that alpha generally disappears during attention and reappears when attention is relaxed. This effect may be evidence that at least one type of selective attention does not require an alert, no-alpha EEG.

One of the most exciting consequences of the alpha bio-feedback experiment took place as the study was ending. It occurred to me that if the experimental subjects had truly learned to control their own alpha, then they should be able to perform the feat *without* the help of bio-feedback.

A month or so after their alpha experiences, we recorded the EEGs of a number of the subjects from the original study. This time there were no feedback signals. We asked them to press a button switch which would directly mark the EEG record each time they *felt* they were producing alpha, then press it twice when they felt alpha was no longer present. Over an hour's recording time, the accuracy of the subjects for knowing when alpha was present ranged between 75 and 100 percent. Even two months later, accuracy remained above 70 percent.

The written reports of the subjects describing subjective feeling states during alpha feedback were obtained in a relatively unstructured and nondirected manner, and so it was surprising to find a great similarity among the written reports of the subjects. Using the statistical rules of biological science, significant relationships were found which showed that the subjects who lost awareness of all environmental factors except the light, or who "felt dissolved into the light," were those subjects with the highest levels of alpha production. Conversely, the subjects who remained aware of the environment they were in were those who produced the smallest amounts of alpha.

Only the more significant conclusions of the alpha experiment are noted here. First, the subjects were able to produce considerably increased amounts of alpha in their EEGs some time before they were able to form a concept about how they could do it, i.e., there was a marked increase in the abundance of alpha long before the subjects were able to define their subjective feelings about the experience. Second, those subjects who formed a distinct concept about how to control the light, "learned" quite rapidly and specifically to do that task; that is, they increased alpha during the experimental trials, but during the rest periods their EEGs became "alert" and activated.

Psychologic Routes to Alpha BF

For the most part, the alpha bio-feedback research of Dr. Joe Kamiya and colleagues has followed stricter and more classical experimental psychologic procedures than mine. Kamiya and many other workers also prefer to use an auditory feedback signal. A good bit of the difference in experimental approaches lies in the type of bio-feedback information and how the information is given to the subject. Since the role of mental or cognitive activity has been minimized in psychologic research until recently, the impetus and conditions for learning lie in the hands of the programmer, who sets specific programs and rewards or signals of success for the learner.

The early alpha "conditioning" bio-feedback research, fathered by Kamiya, followed conditioned learning techniques. Such techniques emphasized the controlled presentation of both the conditioning signal and the reward. In the early experiments a tone was sounded as the conditioning signal, then when the alpha activity appeared it was rewarded, sometimes by telling the subject how much he produced or sometimes just by saying "That's good." Since the thing to be learned was alpha in the brain waves, the alpha activity had to be converted to a form which could be recognized, and this ultimately was converted into sounding a tone. The tone took the place of the conditioning signal, so that, in a sense, alpha was both its own warning signal and at the same time it was a signal requesting the production of more alpha. The essential difference here from my approach was that I did not tell the subjects what they were doing; they had to discover it by themselves, and moreover, the reward of keeping the light on was strictly a function of the inner motivation and awareness of the subject. Also, Kamiya's experiments were conducted with the subjects' eyes closed, whereas my subjects learned with the eyes opened.

It is somewhat of an operating principle in conditioned learning research that true conditioning occurs only if the thing to be learned can be manipulated both positively and negatively, or made to occur more or less frequently. In the case of brain waves this meant that true conditioned learning by brain wave alpha was accepted as such only if the same subject could be taught *both* to suppress *and* to increase his alpha. Thus, the majority of experiments followed an experimental design in which brief periods "to turn the tone (or alpha) on" (indicated by verbal instructions of the researchers to the subjects by the giving of a tone) were alternated with brief periods of "turn the tone off."

Either neurophysiologists are not very kind to psychologists or psychologists aren't very friendly toward neurophysiologists, but I have always felt that a procedure that asks individuals to carry out two quite different tasks may be all right in psychology, but in working with the body's physiology it is quite a different matter. Two different body tasks which may appear in external behavior to be opposite in direction and equal in force (such as clenching the fist and relaxing it) often involve two quite different physiologic systems and body mechanisms proceeding at different rates of activation and recovery from activation. My argument against the procedure of alternating two tasks for alpha is based upon the fact that learning such an obscure task as controlling alpha involves intricate mechanisms under any circumstances, but the particular mechanisms that underlie these two particular types of brain activity are different from each other and variable. The systems which produce alpha and the systems which make alpha disappear are neither equal nor opposite in their actions. The system which facilitates the disappearance of alpha acts rapidly and vigorously; the system that augments alpha is much less forceful and slower. Thus the physiologic effects of one system are always lagging behind the effects of the other, and it seems likely that the build-up of one effect may occur at a time when the other effect is only slowly wearing off and this would make for a confused muddle of the facts coming up to awareness. It would just take longer to learn two tasks at one time. And it did.

The Mulholland approach was the controls system approach. Many years ago Mulholland devised a feedback system in which the presence of alpha in the EEG would activate a bright light which performed the function of an alerting signal and thus caused alpha to disappear from the EEG. Then when the alerting effect was over and alpha reappeared, the light would come on again, causing alpha to disappear. The effect was much like a photocell system that opens the garage door when the path of the light beam is broken. It was an ingenious system for studying the automatic control systems relating to alpha activity. It led Mulholland into studying the role of eye mechanisms as related to alpha activity and finally into alpha bio-feedback itself.

There has been a running argument for several years about the relative merits of learning to control alpha with the eyes open or closed. As both Mulholland and I continue to point out, in our opinion, with respect to alpha the person with his eyes open is a far different person from the same person with his eyes closed. One of the arguments to support this contention is relevant to alpha bio-feedback. Upon closing the eyes about 75 percent of the people develop alpha quite quickly and rapidly reach the maximum of from 80 to 90 percent of alpha content filling the EEG. The exact amount depends upon the criteria used for measuring alpha. But with the eyes open and the individual rested and relaxed, the normal content of alpha is somewhere between 2 and 25 percent, depending upon the person. If one is trying to learn to produce *more* alpha, starting at an already high level, as when the eyes are closed, means that there the learning potential is severely limited. Any increase edges you toward the maximum, and after that there is no place to go. On the other hand, if learning occurs with the eyes open, starting from, say, a 10 percent level, there is still the maximum of 80 or 90 percent that can be achieved. That is a lot of learning room.

A more pragmatic argument for learning to control alpha with the eyes open is that it is somewhat easier, and certainly more useful, to recall the relaxing "alpha state" with the eyes open while engaged in one's daily activities.

The Feel of Alpha

Regardless of whether the learning procedure follows self-exploratory lines or laboratory conditioning techniques, the subjective sensations accompanying the increased production of alpha activity are generally quite similar. Generally the alpha bio-feedback experience has been reported to be quite pleasant, giving one the feeling of comfortable relaxation. Some people report the flow of considerable imagery, almost a day-dreaming reverie; males often reported sexual fantasies. The best alpha producers generally are those who lost awareness of their environment, tending to lose all awareness of time and reporting later that their 60- or 90-minute session seemed like only a few minutes.*

One of the problems in interpreting the subjective feeling states as being specifically related to the actual voluntary control of alpha is that the alpha learning experience in some way changes the nature of brain electrical activity. This means that there is an accompany-

* Man's knowledge of time is his experience of time—the feeling and the meaning of time. If the relationship of time to man is primarily experiential, then feelings, thoughts, and meanings that occur in time should be capable of being manipulated on an internal, subjective time base rather than on an external, physical time base, as, e.g., clock time. Experimental manipulations of subjective time have been used to promote probing of the subconscious, in meditative seeking after truth, and to facilitate learning. Perhaps this aspect of the alpha bio-feedback experience may one day be put to such uses.

ing increase in spontaneous alpha which carries over when the feedback signal is no longer present, suggesting that perhaps a rather general change occurs in the experimental subjects which persists long after the bio-feedback experience. No one yet knows whether or not this relates to an actual basic change in the subjective perspective of the subjects so that the sensation of pleasantness and relaxation is a permanent change in unconscious perspective and reaction. It is still possible that the change may be merely a quickly learned technique to de-focus the eyes and so facilitate the development of alpha.

The enduring change in human subjects both of more pleasant feelings and the accompanying increase of alpha strongly recommends alpha bio-feedback for the treatment of anxiety and tension. The possibility of permanent change in level of alpha activity caused me considerable worry in the early bio-feedback days. Some subjects increased their alpha activity several hundred percent. If the subjective sensations were also changed in a beneficial direction, this would be useful to the individual. But the changes are so subtle that there is no ready way to evaluate whether the changes are good or bad. There are, however, several clinical research studies under way using alpha bio-feedback to treat neuroses that have a high anxiety component, and rather encouraging results are being obtained.

There has been some criticism by learning theorists that the subjective feeling states experienced during various bio-feedback procedures pertain solely to the two contrasting and gross physiologic states of tension (alert behavior) and relaxation and have little or nothing to do with finer, more personal distinctions among sensations.

It seems to be a bit early in the development of bio-feedback to criticize the relative inability of individuals to describe in fine detail their subjective sensations. Bio-feedback is a new experience. As with all new experiences, there is first a global, general reaction of either pleasantness or unpleasantness. It is only with further experience that the finer shades of feeling can be identified. Critics have cited the failure, for example, of experimental subjects to discriminate their sensations when they learned to increase or decrease their heart rates. Reports of the feeling states accompanying the learning to increase heart rate are said to be the same as those reported for decreasing heart rate, although it should be pointed out that the subjects were changing their heart rates only slightly and probably not beyond the usual variation encountered in mental tasks. The criticism fails to note the well-discriminated feeling states described in the chapters about heart rate. Moreover, the criticism cannot apply to brain wave control, since most individuals discriminate feeling states occurring during alpha from those occurring in the absence of alpha, albeit they do so in rather general terms. Biofeedback allows the person to experience his interior for the first time. If we don't know how a particular physiologic function *feels,* either consciously or subconsciously, it is doubtful that we can be very discriminating in describing the initial feelings of becoming aware of a new sensation. There is no prior information to tell whether the physiologic activity being learned is increasing or decreasing. A starting point must be found, a reference. In the beginning of learning to control a biologic function, the reference may be an increase or a decrease in activity, but only after such a reference is discovered can other feeling states be compared. Even then, it seems likely that the first changes would have to be of considerable magnitude in order to accumulate enough "feeling" information to allow subconscious processes to carry the information through to consciousness where it can be verbalized and communicated.

Because the mind-body is continuously reacting to both external and internal changes, it is difficult to identify subjective feeling states with any accuracy unless an opportunity is provided to remain in a relatively steady state where there is time for awareness to develop. Experimental evaluations usually hurry the experiment along, as, for example, in the alternating of requests to produce more alpha and then to suppress it. And there are countless other influences which may affect the development of awareness, such as the experimental environment, the attitude of the researchers, the attitudes and feelings of the subjects, and their capabilities for reacting and expressing. And there is also the failure of language, and the differences in the ways people use language and the ingrained cultural differences of emotional reactions.

Most psychologic work with subjective states is concerned with the influence of elements in the external environment, and this complicates the discovery of the internal self by requiring expression of subjective feelings in terms of the external world. But in bio-feedback mental and emotional activities of the within are the primary influences. The very human factors of attention, motivation, imagination, conceptual association, free recall, reasoning, expectancy, and attitude are all modulated by the individual's inherited, acquired and experiential characteristics. Where he is with respect to all of these constantly varying factors determines where he will go when he is generating his own changes of internal environment during the bio-feedback experience. The scientific requirement to describe and measure these changes and influences can be made only in terms of the physiologic indicator with which the individual is working: his EEG or heart rate or skin electrical activity. Even then we are not sure that there is any type of precise relationship between the higher mental functions and the underlying physiology. But the ability of an individual to "tag" aspects of his own subjective activity by means of bio-feedback displays implies that he has perceived, isolated and identified aspects of the inner self and has learned the rudiments necessary to control it. The internal processes used to activate the external monitors of the internal physiologic activity would appear to include, at least, processes of internal orienting and searching, internal attention, internal recognition and recall.

One of the more revealing neurophysiologic surprises to come from bio-feedback is that the attention which alerts the organism and desynchronizes his brain wave pattern has little relationship to the physiology claimed to underlie externally directed attention. Intense, concentrated attention can prevail while the EEG pattern is in a state identified with behavioral relaxation and inattention. An individual who learns to control his EEG alpha or theta activity and is able to produce these specific brain waves at will must be expending considerable energy to the process of paying attention, yet his EEG shows no sign of the usual pattern associated with alerted attention to the external environment. It would appear that the kind of attention paid to the internal environment during bio-feedback may be quite different from the kind of attention used in concentrating on the external environment. Or possibly that conscious and subconscious focusing of attention are reflected quite differently in the EEG.

The Alpha Mantra

Alpha bio-feedback has had its greatest popular attraction as an aid to meditation or even as a technologic technique to facilitate the goals of meditation. Early in the development of alpha feedback, the resemblance of certain subjective phenomena as well as of the accompanying brain wave patterns to those reported for certain Zen and yoga states was recognized. A number of research reports revealed that practicing students of Zen and yoga developed large quantities of EEG alpha activity of considerable amplitude almost immediately upon beginning their meditative practice. Then, as meditation continued, the frequency of alpha began to decrease, melding into the slower theta waves. The subjective reports too were similar, the Zen and yoga practitioners reporting that the mind and consciousness were turned inward, with the identity of the external universe lost although awareness of it could remain at certain stages. On the surface meditation and alpha bio-feedback appear to be extremely similar. Even the sensation of separation from the material universe can occur in both; a depersonalization, loss of individual identity, and a feeling of becoming aware of the unifying thread of life.

The popularization of alpha bio-feedback as a meditative technique has raised many questions. Many advocates, including some researchers, believe that alpha is instant Zen, instant satori; that the filling of the head with alpha waves with its accompanying sensation of divorcement from material reality is the exact equivalent of the Zen no-mind state. They tend to believe that the no-mind is the absence of thoughts of material attachments to the self, a dissolution of the ego. The experience is described as the ecstatic, mystical state of unity with the universe.

Just how much of the subjective experience is illusory and self-deceptive is difficult to say. There may indeed be no dividing line between the nothingness of mind and the nothingness of sleep except remembered awareness. At one time Arthur Koestler equated the supreme universal consciousness with the unconsciousness of sleep and death. No one except perhaps the sages knows whether nonordinary states of consciousness are illusion or whether the universal mind is an unconsciousness of nothingness. The use of alpha feedback in meditation is not likely to be resolved by discussion. It is the new perspective gained by becoming aware that there are other states of consciousness than those we are familiar with, and each change in perspective is valuable.

While I question the value of alpha feedback for the advanced meditator, I see nothing wrong in its use as an educational aid in learning to become aware of the vast stores of mental resources available to human beings to be used as they desire, for meditation, for understanding, or for learning. There are scientists, however, already at work to strengthen the dichotomy between science and spiritual development. One recent report presumably designed to denigrate the reality of the alpha experience seems to illustrate nicely the importance and the influence of the experimenter's objectives and attitudes. One must first remember that some twenty or more studies of alpha bio-feedback have reported increased production of alpha results in pleasant and interesting experiences. The new report describes how volunteers were subjected to procedures to learn how to increase and decrease alpha. Some of the experimental sessions lasted as long as twelve consecutive hours. Reports of subjective feelings apparently indicated that the subjects were bored by the whole experience, and the researchers concluded that the beneficial effects claimed for alpha feedback machines now on the market were probably not due to increasing alpha activity but were self-deceptive, subjective, wish-fulfilling dreams excited by "the placebo effect resulting from the application of electrodes to the scalp."

While twelve continuous hours of any precisely restricted activity does tend to become quite boring, the investigators do not reveal whether they gave any instructions of significance to their subjects, or what their own attitudes were. If it were, perhaps, a rather stiff, scientific environment, populated by uninteresting people, and with the overhanging threat of having to be successful in a scientific experiment and with no other information available, then it is little wonder that boredom intervened.

The elements of subconscious, social and situational pressures are important influences on any mental and emotional activity. We are so accustomed to behaving in a socially acceptable way that we are frequently deceived about our own motives. Social pressures usually supersede private emotional pressures. We daily deceive ourselves in a large part of our activities. We buy products that are attractively advertised by seeing what we, and the advertisers, want to see, not what is really there. This may be true of some of the effects of bio-feedback, particularly of alpha bio-feedback because there has not been time enough yet to sort out the real from the imagined. Nor may this be an important endeavor, for the gains in awareness may discover that much of reality is only agreed upon and not real. It may expand the consensual reality.

There has long been a taboo against adventuring in one's own mind. Regardless of the future of alpha feedback, at least it has actively driven a wedge to split the superstitions of mind taboos. Not only does alpha, and other brain waves as well, bring the interior of self back into the realm of acceptable study, but it brings with it a renewal of attention to other mind-affecting techniques. There is, for example, a curious relationship between alpha feedback effects and hypnosis.

Coincident with the development of alpha bio-feedback was the study of brain electrical activity as related to susceptibility to hypnosis. People with a fair amount of alpha in the EEG were found to be those who were most susceptible to hypnosis. Then, with the advent of alpha BFT, new studies were made which discovered that successful learning to control alpha was accompanied by an increased susceptibility to hypnosis. This phenomenon gives rise to a family of interesting speculations. Is the increased susceptibility due to that particular state of consciousness accompanying large amounts of alpha that allows one's self to be peculiarly open to suggestions, or is it that the "alpha state" gives one the narrowing of consciousness that is needed to focus all mental, psychologic and physiologic attention on a discrete, specific command, whether self- or other-generated? Or, is the efficiency of mental activity used for logic, reason and judgments turned off by the innocent no-mind alpha state, allowing personal behavior to be guided effortlessly but indiscriminately into just any channel that happens to command attention? Whoever generates the command, the self or another, the commands are likely to originate from social pressure rather than from awareness of the self.

If the increased susceptibility for hypnosis by alpha feedback training means increased and indiscriminate susceptibility to suggestion, then the alpha faddists may offer a large potential market for retailers of consumer products. But if the increased susceptibility implies the mobilization of psychologic and physiologic energy toward a specific purpose, then alpha bio-feedback may indeed be a new step in the individuation of man.

Alpha BFT also seems to foster imagery, a mental process which may contribute to the apparent importance of alpha in both susceptibility to hypnosis and in meditation. It is probably natural that mental and visual images would develop with those types of alpha feedback that recommend practice with closed eyes, in view of the relaxing effect of sitting still in a quiet place, with nothing more than the feedback signal of one's own alpha to disturb the silence. Whether or not visual imagery occurs in the presence of alpha waves has long been disputed. The delayed resolution to this question only serves to point out the serious lack of information about mental activities and how they relate to brain wave patterns. It was long believed that people capable of visual imagery had virtually no alpha activity, but over the years it was discovered that their chief characteristic was the rapid disappearance of alpha during mental tasks that involved imagery, such as visualization itself or tasks such as mental arithmetic.

My own work has contributed the fact that a curious relationship exists between imagery and the EEG. People capable of vivid visual imagery do actually have large quantities of alpha, but it is promptly lost during imagery tasks. In sharp contrast, people who have no capacity to conjure up visual images have very little alpha normally, and when they do, they do not lose their alpha during such mental tasks; on the contrary they frequently make more alpha. Thus, when visualizers learn to control alpha, they are also learning something else. They are learning to sustain alpha all the while they are having the visual images which ordinarily cause alpha to disappear. There is a great deal of such scattered bits of neurophysiologic evidence to indicate that during "alpha states" there is a shift in level of consciousness along with the brain electrical changes which say that the brain is quite capable of handling its business in a variety of ways, while at the same time being under voluntary control. In classical neurophysiology there has been a tendency to assume that different types of brain electrical activity of the major states of consciousness, i.e., alert, awake, drowsy, etc., are reflected in quite different EEG patterns. Yet during each state there are many mental activities that go on; this speaks to the concept that either the different manifestations of brain electrical activity have very little specific relationship to various mental activities or that the methods for analyzing brain waves are still unsophisticated.

Hazards of Alpha BFT

Assuming proper and intelligent supervision for alpha BFT, the dangers of it lie mainly in problems of the instrumentation. Many skilled neurophysiologists watch in horror the neurophysiology done by less sophisticated colleagues. The electrical and neural complexity of neurophysiology, particularly in brain electrical work, is enormous and requires extensive background knowledge to be interpreted properly and safely. I too watch the pop alpha artists with their feedback machines with a feeling of some horror. There are as many traps and hidden dangers in this microcosm of the brain electrical universe as were real booby traps in Vietnam. For example, with the exception of a few specially engineered devices, most scientific systems used to detect and isolate brain wave activity are highly susceptible to the electrical "noise" of the environment. Brain electrical currents are smaller than most environmental electrical noise, and only with special designs can such interference be effectively eliminated as contaminants of the brain wave record. Although the alpha waves are generally larger, they also undergo some distortion by the very electronic circuits used to eliminate the interference. So the alpha waves that one sees are not always as real as one would like.

Then there are miscellaneous, non-brain-wave electrical changes that use the same circuitry as alpha to activate instruments to read that alpha was present when it wasn't. Such artifacts can result from sweating in the area of the electrodes, imperceptible hair movements, scalp twitches, unnoticed twitches of the eyebrows, eye movements, eye blinks, and gulping. Other artifactual changes can also profoundly influence the EEG record, such as changes due to respiration, or heartbeat, or ocular tremors which so frequently occur normally, or unnoticed body muscle activity and simple tension. More serious are the danger signals of real disease, such as the many variants of EEG activity that are found in epilepsy. Many of these abnormal EEG elements can pour through the electronic equipment as easily as can alpha and could result in the inadvertent training of people to aggravate or even incite actual illness.

There is another area of potential danger in the use of alpha training. This is the characteristic change in brain electrical activity that occurs with certain social behavior problems. The alpha activity of adolescents with behavior problems has been documented to be of a slightly slower frequency than "normal" alpha, and it is also distinguished by less variation in frequency. A similar change occurs in certain types of depression as well as following treatment by certain drugs. Many habitual drug users, particularly of marijuana and heroin, may have predominantly slow EEG patterns with slow, steady alpha activity. The hazard of alpha bio-feedback might be that such states could be strengthened by alpha BFT since one objective of alpha BFT is to produce a brain wave pattern similar to those which may accompany certain behavioral problems or drug use. While it has never been satisfactorily established that there is a correspondence between patterns of brain electrical activity and different subjective or affective states, nonetheless, the EEG characteristics of people with behavior problems or who use dangerous drugs suggest that alpha BFT should be used with caution in such people.

Theta and Beta

Learning to exert voluntary control over other brain waves still lies in the future. No scientific reports are yet available on the learned control of either theta or beta. Several interesting studies are, however, currently being conducted. And while the scientists are reluctant to discuss the studies before their results are completed, there is enough scientific gossip around to indicate that the experiments in progress will yield some exciting results. New insights into both brain electrical mechanisms and their accompanying subjective states are to be expected on the basis of what is already known about the behavioral correlates of other brain electrical activities.

Brain wave theta activity is that rhythmic activity having a frequency of between about 4 and 7 cycles per second. In some individuals it appears as exactly half the frequency of alpha. Mainly, though, theta wanders variously around the frequency range. It may be large or small, and it can be found almost anywhere, although older neurophysiology claimed it to be generally absent from occipital areas of the visual cortex. Once really looked for, it has been found everywhere. The main problem with theta is its relative scarcity. Under normal waking conditions it pops into the EEG record randomly and then only briefly. It has been found to relate to a wide variety of human and animal behaviors, such as drowsiness, orienting, dreaming, during recall and recognition.

As with alpha activity, theta comes in many different forms. The question for the future is, What form relates to what behavior? It may be found, for example, that very slow theta is more specific to drowsiness, while a slightly faster theta might accompany the effort of recalling memories. Or that the theta of dreaming has quite specific characteristics for each individual or for different types of dreams, as the imagery of daydreaming. Obviously, the use of theta bio-feedback to isolate and learn to control these different behaviors which give insight into the more abstruse mental activities should provide an exciting time in the future of bio-feedback. An example of the possibilities as done in my laboratory is illustrated in Figure 13.

Dr. Elmer Green of the Menninger Foundation has recently offered some verbal comments on the type of theta wave training that he and his wife Alyce are conducting. Dr. Green, one of bio-feedback's more ingenious and creative researchers, is zeroing in on the type of reverie and visual imagery that occurs in the hypnotic state just before drifting off to sleep. By some electronic wizardry he is able to capture the change from alpha to theta and use this for feedback purposes. One can only imagine what tours through inner space this technique will allow. If one could extend the time of that delightful presleep imagery, then the content and flow of imagery could be salvaged and remembered and examined. Dr. Green is particularly interested in the processes of creativity. How often we have heard of discoveries being made by the imagery or flow of thoughts in sleep and presleep, and now here is a technique that might make the process of creativity more readily available to everyone.*

The most abundant and least known component of brain electrical activity has attracted the least attention of bio-feedback researchers. This is the family of small, fast waves lumped together under the label of beta activity, regardless of whether the waves are rhythmic, such as alpha, or whether the large variety of fast frequencies are mixed together. The general observation is that it occurs when the organism is aroused or alerted. This is not saying much, since for most researchers, the frequency range of beta is considered to be anything faster than alpha. There are, however, many exciting exact frequencies of rhythmic activities in the beta range such as 14- or 18- or 22- or 24-cycle-per-second rhythmic waves. Virtually nothing is known about the subjective or behavioral correlates of these frequencies except the 14-cycle rhythm that occurs mainly in sleep, and higher frequencies that may appear in individuals with high intelligence combined with very high energy levels. I have studied several such cases of the latter, and in all instances the EEG patterns were highly rhythmic although ranging through at least from 14- to 30-cycle activity of high amplitude, occurring in all areas of electrode placement. And in each instance the individuals were of quite remarkable intelligence but at the same time were, although under some reasonable emotional control, always casting about for something new to think about, to discuss profound philosophies, or solve problems.

One of the reasons that little information has been accumulated about beta activity is that it is extremely difficult to record by conventional recording techniques. The EEG patterns are of lower amplitude than is necessary for recording alpha, and the many problems of EEG recording of "clean" records increases the diffi-

* For experiential demonstrations of imagery and creativity as a connected process, see *Mind Games* by Robert Masters and Jean Houston (New York: Viking Press, 1972).

Figure 13. EEG record of a subject learning voluntary control over theta brain waves.

A

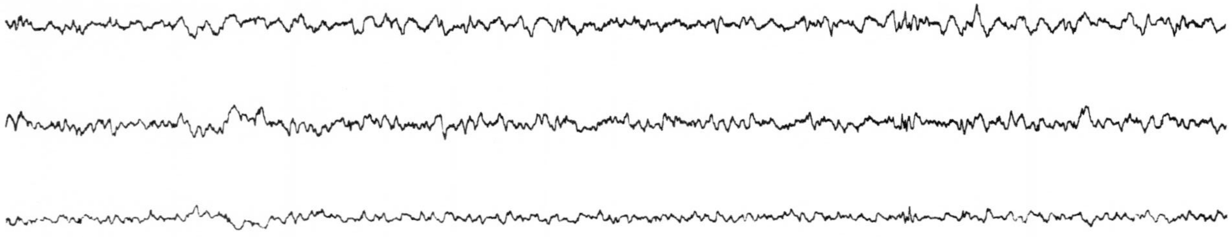

In A, about five minutes after beginning, there are sporadic episodes of poorly defined theta waves in the temporo-parietal area (first line). The subject understands what theta waves look like on an EEG record and he is concentrating on producing them by mental effort alone.

B

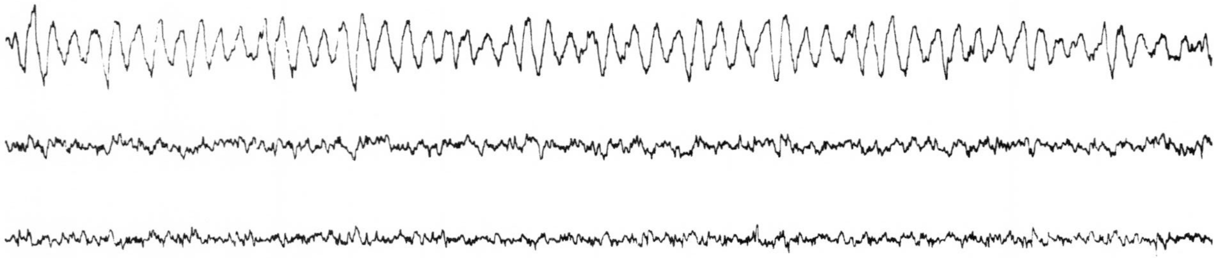

Record B is twelve minutes later. The subject has formed exceptionally clear theta waves in Lead 1. They are much more regular and abundant than is generally seen spontaneously.

C

In Record C the subject has decided to produce theta waves in Leads 2 and 3. They are not as large as those in Lead 1 but are fairly regular. At this point the subject felt that he was in a "hyper-trance" state—that he was totally concentrated but very alert.

D

D. Five minutes later the subject has produced large and quite regular theta waves in all leads.

E

E. In trying to "think" his theta brain waves larger, those in Leads 2 and 3 become quite large, but those in Lead 1 are now yielding to an alpha rhythm.

F

F. Five minutes later. The subject can no longer sustain theta waves. They have disappeared from Leads 2 and 3 and are being replaced by alpha in Lead 1.

culties. Individuals with considerable beta also have an overabundance of muscle artifacts which make EEG recording difficult because muscle artifacts obscure the original tracing. Typically EEG researchers refuse to record from such people, noting in their scientific papers that more than 50 percent of the subjects originally intended to be used in their studies showed low-voltage records and insufficient alpha, and so were discarded from the study. It seems likely that many subjects have not been employed in experimental EEG work because of these difficulties.

In addition to the normal occurrence of beta during alert behavior, beta activity may also dominate the EEG pattern in certain neuroses and after taking certain barbiturates or tranquilizers. The first phase of the sedative action of drugs is the production of high-voltage fast activity in the 13-to-28-cycle-per-second range, the slowing of the EEG typical of sleep coming only with larger doses or at a later time.

Although large quantities of beta activity in the EEG are generally considered to relate to high levels of arousal, there are research reports that indicate many frequencies of beta are normally occurring components of brain waves, particularly during the early phases of sleep. Some investigators have found beta to be an accompaniment of the mental processing of visual information, while others have found beta activity to be predominant when individuals are processing new information. There is also a genetic factor in rhythmic beta, several investigators finding that quite specific beta frequencies are inherited.

What the future of beta bio-feedback may be cannot be projected with any degree of clarity at the moment because so little is known about its behavioral significance. At present we don't know whether a beta frequency of 15 cycles per second is much different from 20 cycles per second when it comes to manifest behavior. This is an area of brain exploration in which bio-feedback can contribute more to new discoveries about the meanings of brain activity than can most techniques. With the feedback of specific frequencies within the beta range, experimental subjects can describe to investigators their subjective states and feelings until some consensus about the significance of various beta frequencies can be derived.

It is, of course, tempting to speculate that if beta activity of 13 to 28 cycles per second is a characteristic of the action of sedatives, then bio-feedback training with these frequencies might replace the need to take sedatives or tranquilizers.

On the other hand, if it is really true that particular beta frequencies reflect certain mental processes involved in the understanding of either new or visual information, perhaps beta BFT might lead to techniques for dramatically speeding up learning processes. The neglected world of beta may soon produce some remarkable new applications for mental growth.

ELEVEN

Identifying One's Own Brain Waves:
A Trial Run to the Subconscious

In Western civilization the comfort of the self has been troubled for many centuries by a bewildering polarity cultivated by those who claim wisdom and the ability to offer us advice. We have been torn between the gurus of science and the gurus of the soul. Both have persuaded us to believe their wisdom separately. In the experiential life the division between physical and mental being is not clearly defined. We may now be on the threshold of experiencing an inner wisdom that may heal the breach between science and the spirit.

Recognition of Different Waves in One's Own EEG

Not all work with brain wave bio-feedback need be exclusively learning how to control different brain components. With bio-feedback also came the opportunity to explore whether sensations and feelings and thoughts actually did have some relationship to the mysterious brain waves. The only information we biological scientists had about the correspondence between brain waves and mental activity had been learned most indirectly. Before bio-feedback no scientist pulled out certain brain waves, held them up for view, and asked, "Here's alpha, how do you feel now?," or "Here's beta, what sensations do you have, what mood?"

I took advantage of my early entry into bio-feedback, and of the laboratory of special instruments built for me, to see whether it

353

might be possible for human beings to identify various brain waves of their own directly, and in terms of their feeling states or thoughts. It seemed to be a straightforward task: let people watch their brain waves and let them describe their sensations or thoughts that seemed to go along with each different kind of wave. Now that part actually is easy; what complicates the problem is making sure that any correlation between subjective activity and EEG components is so accurate and reliable that other scientists will believe you. Scientific procedure is very rigid and that complicated my project enormously.

Nonetheless, the experiment was fairly simple, although the instrumentation was considerably more complex than in the alpha work. The same EEG activity was used: that recorded from the parieto-occipital area (from midway on one side of the skull to a midpoint on the back of the skull). This time the EEG activity was fed into three filters simultaneously, so that alpha, theta, and beta frequencies were simultaneously being filtered throughout the experiment. The beta activity in this case was specifically a frequency between 13 and 28 cycles per second; the theta was 4 to 7 cycles per second.

These three EEG frequencies were used to operate lights of three different colors. Again, electronic circuitry was used so that recognizable trains of waves of adequate amplitude were required to be present in the EEG in order to activate the lights, and once on, the lights remained on for the duration of the rhythmic burst. As in the alpha experiments, the intensity of the lights was proportional to the amplitude of each of the signals.

The experimental situation was similar to that of the previous one with a few exceptions. The only instructions to the subjects were to keep their eyes open but this time they were asked to try to identify feeling states which they felt were related to any particular color of light. Red, green, and blue lights were used and were paired, in random fashion, to one of the three EEG frequencies, alpha, beta, or theta. The subjects, all completely naïve about brain waves, were told that the lights were being operated by their own brain waves, and that it was believed that these mirrored feeling states in some way.

In this first experiment using three colored lights to feed back information about the three most commonly occurring brain wave frequencies, the subjects were simply allowed to watch these light indicators of their own brain wave activity for about an hour. Nothing else. Afterward they were asked to write a description about what feelings or moods or thought states they related to the different light colors.

The experimental subjects of course knew that the different colored lights represented different brain waves, but they didn't know *which* colors represented *which* waves. Moreover, for some subjects theta waves were displayed via a green light, others were displayed by a red light, etc. Because the brain waves of different people were being fed back by different colored lights, in order to prove that particular subjective feelings related to specific brain waves, all of the different people would have to discriminate and describe similar feelings or thoughts for each brain wave regardless of the color of light used to display those waves. This was a large request to make of a bunch of normal human beings who didn't know an alpha wave from a hole in the wall and cared little about brain waves anyway.

After the entire study had been completed, my assistants and I had before us a stack of written experiences about the bio-feedback experience. As we analyzed the descriptions, we had to decode the color the subjects were talking about as to whether the color had represented alpha, beta, or theta brain wave activity. We were surprised to find that regardless of the color of light used to indicate any particular brain wave, the descriptions of subjective feelings and thoughts tended to be quite similar for any particular brain wave.

In describing alpha waves, regardless of light color used, the experimental subjects tended to use quite similar phrases. Fourteen of twenty-six said that the light gave them feelings of "pleasantness," or "well-being," or "pleasure," "tranquillity," or "relaxation"; and there were seven subjects who described alpha as giving them "an increased awareness of thoughts and feelings." Two reported that during alpha they were reviewing personal experiences and only three had nothing to say about alpha. On the other hand, in describing their feelings about beta activity (again regardless of light color used), there was general agreement among subjects, nine

reporting "worry," "anger," "fear," or "frustration" while five reported "tension, alertness, excitement." One said it gave a feeling of
hunger and surprise, while eight subjects had no particular sensations. There were, interestingly, three people who said that the beta
lights gave them feelings of contentment, warmth, and love.

The feelings and thoughts described for theta activity were quite
different and strongly reflected the influence of more thought than
feeling activity. These descriptions were chiefly "memory of problems," "uncertainty," "problem solving," "future planning," "switch-
ing thoughts," "solving mechanical or financial problems," and "day-
dreaming." There were ten such reports, but there were also
thirteen subjects who could recall no specific feelings or thoughts
that related to the colored light that had represented theta.

One can easily see a conceptual unity among the descriptions
noted above for each different brain wave. For alpha, for example,
most descriptions implied an awareness of body feeling, while other
descriptions implied less attention to body and somewhat more
attention to an experience of consciousness. By contrast, the descriptions of feelings produced by the lights representing beta, i.e.,
fast brain wave activity, appear to be directed toward unpleasant
feelings and thoughts. Those few indicating a pleasant experience
cannot be explained at this time.

When theta activity was observed, the agreement between brain
wave and a subjective state was less clear-cut. Nearly one-third of
the subjects related theta waves to feelings and thoughts suggesting
the thinking process, while the majority were not able to identify
any relationship between the theta light and subjective experience.
Even though success in identifying theta was just 30 percent, we
had expected much less success than this because very little theta
activity is normally present in brain waves during quiet, awake
states. We know, moreover, that two almost diametrically opposed
feeling states can relate to theta: drowsiness and serious thinking.
With so little theta present in the EEG, trying to identify a feeling
or thought state for theta might be quite a confusing task.

This first experiment with the three-light system demonstrated
the obvious ability of human beings to identify specific components
of their own brain waves. If indeed brain cell activity does reflect

our mental functioning, then the result is not surprising. It simply hadn't been done before.

Toward Identifying the Subconscious

A second experiment using the three-light system was much trickier. The objective was to attempt to identify any subconscious influences or elements that might be used in the ultimate process of learning to control different specific brain wave components. This presented a difficult task since, after all, we have not yet been able to identify any physical monitors of mental activity let alone subconscious activity. It seemed to me that the experiment might be valuable since a great deal of our thinking and feeling activity takes place when we are not consciously aware of it. Although the mission seemed impossible, my own subconscious momentum to experiment took over and I didn't argue with it.

I was using colors to feed back the three dominant brain wave activities, and this meant that a person's feeling about a particular color might influence or dominate over the feeling he could develop about a certain brain wave. This problem was solved in part by the procedure used in the first experiment—that is, changing the pairing between color and brain wave component in a scientific, random fashion such that one subject might see his alpha activity as a red light, beta as a blue light, etc., while another subject might see *his* alpha as a green light, his theta as a red light and so on. This arrangement meant that the consensus of a large group of subjects about the feelings and thoughts they related to a specific brain wave component would not be influenced by the feelings they had about the specific colors.

But this, of course, raised another problem. In some circumstances the feelings and thoughts relating to a specific color might be exactly the same as those feelings and thoughts related to a specific brain wave. Now this is the sort of thing which complicates science and the reason that biological scientists are so often hung up on the concept of control. How could I control for this contingency—that the feelings and subjective response to colors might be the same as that to certain brain waves?

The answer is surprisingly simple. First, let me restate the problem. If we want to know what feelings relate to a specific brain wave, and the brain wave is represented by a color and yet the feelings that relate to brain waves are unknown, then what items in this formula do we already know? Simple: We know how we feel about colors. If we feel that calmness is a blue word and if we should find that calmness is also an alpha brain wave word, then shouldn't we get some indication of this if we represent alpha waves by some color *other* than blue?

So the first procedure was to survey average people about their feelings about colors. First I prepared a list of words which are descriptive of feelings, thoughts, moods, and emotional responses, such as happy, distracted, tired, excited, etc.—150 of them—and printed these on cards. Then I prepared four colored boxes: red, blue, green, and white. Nearly a hundred people were surveyed for how they related feelings and colors. They were asked to sort all of the cards with descriptor words into the colored boxes as fast as they could. The faster the sort the more possible might be the representation of subconscious influence. The white box was for descriptor words for which they had no color-feeling relationship. After the survey I had quite specific data about how most people felt about colors and was in a position to go ahead with the experiments.

Relationships between feelings and color are very strong. In general most people feel that angry is a red word, frustrated is a red word, or that peace is a blue word. Naturally people differ in some respects, but the majority agree about many relationships between feelings and color.

The bio-feedback experiments were exactly as they had been for the people who wrote descriptions about how they felt watching three colors of lights signaling their brain wave activity. The subjects sat watching the colors displaying their different brain wave components for an hour. Immediately after the bio-feedback experience they were asked to sort the descriptor cards to the same red, blue, green and white boxes, just as the people had done for the control data who didn't have the bio-feedback experience.

The results were quite astonishing. An analysis of the card sorts to color by the subjects who had just had an hour of watching their brain waves represented by colored lights revealed totally different relationships between feelings and colors from people who hadn't had the experience. No longer did all of the subjects feel that angry was a red word. If their *beta* brain wave activity had been displayed by a green or blue light, they now tended to relate the concept of angry either to green or to blue. Or, for example, they related the words peace or calm to red or green instead of to blue—provided their alpha activity had been represented by a red or a green light.

What this meant was that the hour's experience of watching their own brain waves had not only reorganized their usual feelings about color, but had given them an awareness of those feelings that were specifically related to certain brain waves. The way in which different brain wave patterns, containing different amounts of alpha, beta, and theta, relate to subjective feeling states is illustrated in Figure 14. There is an interesting point that I will discuss later concerning the question of whether feelings about color modify brain waves or whether brain waves are first affected by colors and then feelings developed later.

In any event, we had now found that as human beings we could identify different elements of our own brain wave activity if we were given a suitable indicator of that activity. But the exciting aspect was that this identification appeared to take place largely on a sub- or pre-conscious level before becoming consciously aware of the association between brain wave and feeling or thought. The reason for deducing this was that the associations between feelings and brain waves overrode normal, deeply entrenched associations between feelings and color. There was other evidence for the con-clusion because the cards describing feeling and thought had been sorted as quickly as possible (150 into four colored boxes) and virtually no contradictory synonyms of varieties of mental activity were found when the card sorts were analyzed. Moreover, the feeling states that the card sort data indicated as being perceived were *not* found to relate to any change in the *amount* of the brain waves with which they were associated, as has been found for conscious feeling states induced by experimental procedures. There were some marginally significant changes in the *amplitudes* of alpha, beta, and theta in subjects who agreed about related subjec-tive feelings but they pertained more to rather general mood and feeling states. All in all, the two experiments indicated that we had

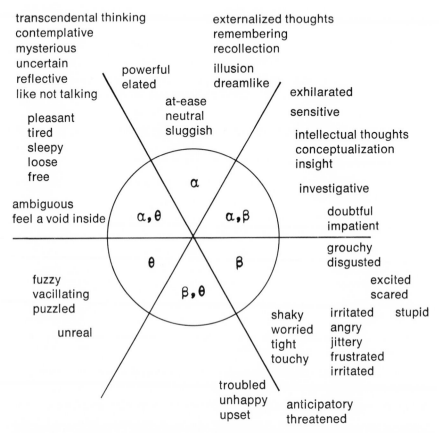

Figure 14. A graphic representation of the relationship between subjective feeling states and the relative amounts of alpha, theta and beta found in the EEG as obtained in the experiment described. The descriptors of subjective feeling shown for each point around the circle are those selected by a statistically significant number of people with similar quantities of the three major EEG frequencies. The midpoint of each segment of the circle indicates that the EEG contained relatively large amounts of the frequencies noted, while at either side of the midpoints the respective frequencies occurred in smaller quantities.

It should be noted that although the results represented here have been replicated in other studies, they are by no means intended as conclusive.

the prospect of having actual physical and/or physiological indicators of aspects of pre-conscious activity.

A Concept of How It Happened

The unique characteristics of the experimental situation were that they allowed the subjects to interact with aspects of their own physiologic functioning in the *absence* of either directed or pre-formed concepts. (In psychologic experiments, particularly conditioning experiments, the experimenter or the experimental situation directs the behavior and programs the number and type of behavioral responses allowed.)

The colored light monitors of the individual's own EEG activity (i.e., of the three major frequency components of the EEG) provided continuing perceptual information about the electrical activity of the brain's functioning. We all know how difficult it is to sustain a single thought, or even to sustain a single feeling state. Conscious awareness, particularly conscious awareness of directed thought and feeling activity, is continuously varying both in degree and direction and in content and range of perspective. Brain electrical activity is also a continuously varying activity and is a reflection of the continuously varying dimensions of mental or subjective states. If a relationship between subjective and brain electrical states is even approximately true, then the *temporal* characteristics of both elements of the relationship constitute the most important aspects requisite for establishing associations between these two variables. That is, the feeling state should coincide with the presence of the particular brain wave in the EEG. The more frequently this occurs the more opportunity there is to identify a particular feeling or thought to a particular brain wave.

If the information from the alpha learning experiment and from the experiment demonstrating ability to identify subjective relationships to specific brain wave components are combined, one can conjecture on the role of mental activity in the bio-feedback control system. Because the subject is allowed to interact with aspects of his own physiologic functioning without either direction or conceptual information, the experiment cannot proceed unless the subject generates the specific physiologic activity (such as alpha or beta) which will activate the machine. Activation of the bio-feedback display occurs only when a specific brain wave is present in the total brain wave pattern. It thus monitors precisely the selection of the appropriate brain wave, and this selection evolves from mental effort by the individual. During the first minutes of such a bio-feedback experience, the feedback monitor (the light signal) operates strictly according to the probability for occurrence of the desired brain wave in any individual. When the desired brain wave occurs, the monitor faithfully signals its presence. At this point in time the subject has no prior knowledge of how that particular brain wave relates to his subjective feelings. He does, however, have a store of memory information by which he can relate the subjective feeling state present to previous similar subjective feelings when the light signal is on.

Thus, during the bio-feedback training, the subject is receiving two different sets of information about himself. He is receiving perceptual data via the light monitor which tells him many characteristics about the brain wave in question: its rate of occurrence, how long it is present at any one time, how fast it appears and disappears, etc. At the same time the subject is undergoing the experience of interacting with specific aspects of his own physiologic substrates of emotion and with past experience. He has been instructed to try to identify his feelings and thoughts at those specific moments when the monitor light signals the presence of a certain type of brain wave. The second set of information available during the feedback experience is thus experiential data which, either because of the instructions to the subject or because of the nature of the feedback system, generate subjective exploratory activity. The individual searches his memories of experiences first in order to identify his present state and then to verify whether the subjective state is similar each time the monitor signals the selected brain wave.

During the bio-feedback learning experience the subject thus has two streams of information available for subsequent integration: the perceptual data and the experiential data. As the training continues, the repeated availability of these data provides the opportunity to verify the characteristics of their relationship over time. The individual continues to perceive the experience of interacting with specific aspects of his own internal experience and is able to verify the relationships of the experience such that subsequently he is able to form a concept about it.

The verification of perception of the experience implies that some organization of data has occurred. In this case we are talking about the association, organization, or structuring between two sets of internally originating information, one set of which has been

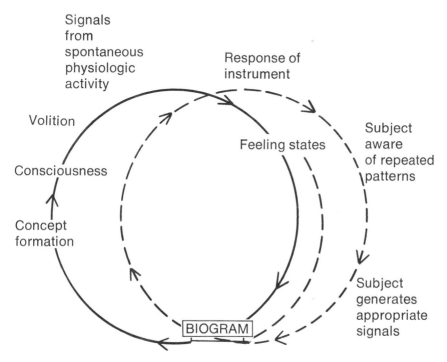

Figure 15. Diagram of possible events occurring during bio-feedback learning.

externalized and has been perceived as part of the external environment.

My conception of the phenomenon is represented by the diagram in Figure 15. First, unelicited random brain wave activity produces a response of the instrument. Now, because of instructions to the subject, two quite different processes begin: the subject becomes aware of certain patterns, or repetitions of patterns, of the lights coming on and staying on, which is, or represents, the perceptual data; and at the same time he is undergoing the normal ranging of subjective thought and feeling, which provides internal orienting and memory experiential data. At some point he begins to generate appropriate signals, i.e., signals that are appropriate to the instrument's ability to respond. It is at this time that the gap between the two streams of information has narrowed sufficiently for some type of associational structuring to occur between the two types of information.

In order to refer conveniently to this point, I have proposed the term biogram. Although the term has been used elsewhere to describe a relationship between an individual and his biologic environment, it is a useful temporary term in bio-feedback because it relates semantically to the word engram, denoting a memory trace. Some kind of memory record has to have been made of the association between the perceptual and experiential data, and this memory record is the result of internal biologically originating experience. It is essentially now a subconscious representation of an experience, hence the name biogram.

Since the two previously unrelated sets of information have at this point now been brought into a relationship with each other and have some type of structure, verification of the experience becomes possible. During verification the mind becomes aware of the organized perceptual and memory data, and continued verification of the biogram leads to conscious recognition and finally conscious voluntary control of the now internalized relationship between mind and body activities. With this information in consciousness, the subject can voluntarily retrieve components of the biogram and can adjust both his behavior and awareness of his behavior. In the latter stage no external signals are necessary to sustain the relationships between feeling states and EEG activity. Since the physiologic changes, such as alpha, appear to occur before the individual can conceptualize the experience, the process may operate entirely on a subconscious level.

When the process becomes completely internalized, voluntary control can be exerted exclusively with respect to the subjective activity. The physiologic changes now become a consequence of the phenomenon of voluntary control over internal states rather than a necessary component in the elaboration of the response. Note that voluntary control does not necessarily imply conscious control.

The concept of the biogram as a pre-conscious entity provides an interesting base for studying relationships between experiential and perceptual data. Variations in the degree of organization of the biogram may account for differences in ability to conceptualize the relationships between mind and body activities.

Color, Brain Waves, and Feeling States

In addition to the information which related feeling states to brain waves obtained during the three-light, three-brain-wave experiment, substantial information was accumulated on the relationships between color and brain waves.

These fascinating interrelationships are easily illustrated using Venn logic diagrams as in Figure 16. There are three primary variables of color, feeling state, and brain wave represented by the circles. Each variable relates to each other in varying, unknown degrees. If we say, as we have found, that some colors relate to some brain waves and that the *same* colors relate to some feeling states, then we can conclude that some feeling states relate to some brain waves, and this is exactly what the experiments revealed.

The overlap between the associations between color and feeling states and the associations between color and brain waves, shown by the overlapping circles, suggests the possibility that subjective activity relating to colors may originate from the same underlying neuronal processes as do the brain waves. We will probably never know exactly which came first, the relationship between brain waves and feeling states or the relationship between brain waves and color, but we can make a number of conjectures about it. I tend to favor the concept that the brain cell, neuronal, response to color came first, since in my studies and those of others the brain electrical response to red is one of alerting or arousal, whereas the brain electrical response to blue is one of relaxation. This happens in animals as well as man.

As discussed in Chapter 2, if we think about the color of the environment of animals, we immediately recognize that the color

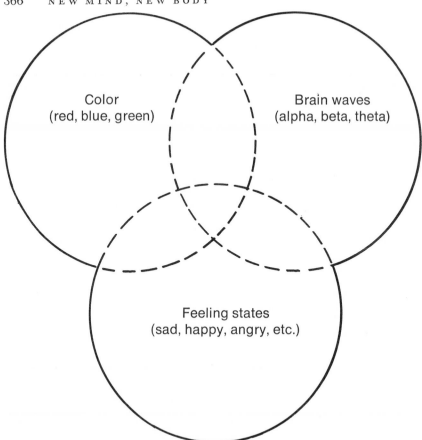

Figure 16. Venn diagrams to illustrate the syllogism that if some colors relate to some brain waves and the same colors relate to some feeling states, then some feeling states relate to some brain waves.

red is predominantly associated with blood that is spilled out into the environment during a kill and which is a sign of danger. When blood is present in the environment, animals are probably alerted. On the other hand, the presence of a perfect blue sky in the environment might well signal a time of peace and tranquillity, the absence of potential harm from the elements. The color green might be associated with foliage for hiding or grass for eating and stalking, and hence be intermediate between rest and alerted states.

One role of color in man's life might be that of an early warning system, an instinctive response to be modulated by specific circumstances. Such subjective associations with color may provide a bridge between pre-conscious associations among perceptual and experiential data and the synthesis of conscious awareness.

Bio-Feedback Is a Different Way of Learning

There are many unusual aspects that suggest bio-feedback learning may be quite a different process from other known modes of learning. In general, learning theories must rely on evidence for internal, thinking processes by the ways in which they can be modified and measured by elements in the external environment. Because of these restrictions and the hesitancy to accept various ways of reporting subjective feelings and awareness as reliable, there is little known about the details of higher levels of mental activity that provide man with his extraordinary ability for learning much more than stereotyped behaviors. Man and many animals are capable of symbolic thinking and behavior; they have the facility to integrate, spontaneously, wide varieties of learning and information in their reasoning processes to evolve solutions and insights.

The unique characteristics of the bio-feedback learning process classify it as an awareness or cognitive process. It is, ultimately, awareness of the relationship between subjective activity and the feedback signals operated by physiologic activity which is the behavior that is learned. The majority of bio-feedback experiments, whether learning to control heart rate or single muscle units or skin electrical resistance or brain waves, all indicate that complex learning takes place on a pre- or subconscious level, and that this learning is orderly, symbolic, specific and highly discriminating.

The information that the brain uses during bio-feedback is an abstraction, a man-made symbol to represent continuously varying body activity. The abstraction contains the synthesis of physiologic, psychologic, conceptual and mechanical information. Moreover, the control to be learned is in itself a complex process of abstraction of the relevant information from both the feedback symbol and elements of past experience as integrated with the information content of the surrounding environment, including attending human attitudes.

In learning to control a selected item of mind-body behavior, the item must first be identified. But the feedback signal is *not* the item to be learned; it serves only to label the item, or response, once it has occurred. It remains neutral and meaningless until some intelligence of the central nervous system identifies it as an abstract label for a complex, dynamic event having certain *temporally* reproducible characteristics. The feedback signal initially becomes activated only accidentally according to the probability for the behavioral event to occur, and only later is its activation intentional. It accrues significance only as a result of continued activity and as the identification of its meaning becomes successful. To add to the complexity, confirmation of the identification of the feedback symbol appears not to be complete until the signal is discontinued by termination of the behavioral event that activates it. In this sense, the behavioral event to be learned is its own detector and its own selector.

The learning in bio-feedback evolves from an internal circular process. The behavior to be learned can be learned only by self-analysis of the symbols of its occurrence. In other modes of learning, behavior is either directed or judged by events external to the system, i.e., both the behavior to be learned and the criteria for learning it are indicated and judged externally. In bio-feedback, successful learning depends completely upon internal effort by the learner. He must generate both his behavior to be learned and his rewards for learning it. He must even select the qualities of his own rewards. He must select the significant values of his own behavior in order to generate a signal that is his own reward for successful learning, and it must be appropriate or learning does not occur. The circuits of the feedback system are either closed and operating or they are not closed and not operating.

In the feedback system the entire learning process is internally directed. The subjective attributes and influences of motivation, reward, error, anticipation, preparation, expectancy and drive all stem from verification and awareness of an internal event. In bio-feedback, learning is entirely dependent upon the consequences of the behavior while it is being learned. The consequences are organized into a flexible scheme that systematically uses the information provided by itself to learn about itself.

One of the major deficiencies of all learning concepts is the failure to define the ways in which information during learning is handled. It is customary to evaluate learning in terms of the information provided, but rarely, if ever, is learning evaluated according to the ways in which the information to be learned is used. This largely accounts for the failure of conventionally used intelligence and performance tests to reveal the rather remarkable efficiency of many minority groups for using the limited amount of information that has been provided to them. Further analysis of bio-feedback learning offers a new approach to evaluating differences in *ways* of using information rather than *how much* information is used in learning.

TWELVE

Within the Near Future: Seeds
of Conjecture

No era of history has failed to record its wisdom that man
could control his own destiny. In no era of history has man
listened. He may not be listening today.

Awareness and a Long, Healthy Life

In the bustle and stress of modern life, the average man has little
time to reflect upon what he is or what he could be. His behavior,
his thoughts, and even his dreams are regulated, and often controlled, by forces outside himself—his boss, his job, his spouse, his
television set, his newspaper, his new car, his son. The overwhelming material luxury of today's living leaves little room for intangibles. Suddenly, today the intangibles of life no longer seem so
alien and remote—they are taking on form and substance. Millions
of people attest to the power of positive thinking; millions more are
exploring new avenues for the communication of emotions. And
with the impetus supplied by two young women who reported on
Russian efforts in psychic phenomena, there are new movements
abroad to induce the best of science to explore the paranormal. The
explosion of interest in the magic of the mind is not an emotional
reaction of a perplexed society; it appears to be the result of objective confirmation that the mind, the psyche, the soul, the attitude,

the emotion of man possess powerful abilities and energies that can shape his own evolution of mind and body.

And for this moment in time bio-feedback appears to be one of the most potent and practical tools for explorations of the power and the energy of the mind. The principle that the mind and body can use information about themselves to teach themselves a new awareness and greater vitality *is* the essential principle underlying bio-feedback. This fact triggers fascination and compels conjecture. The number of immediate uses of bio-feedback far exceeds the present capacities of medicine, psychology, and biology to explore them. There are countless physical and emotional problems where bio-feedback can be used to relieve causes and symptoms as well as being a convenient, effective practice to prevent illness. Its basic nature and the global reach of its effects will take many years to document. Because the processes that underlie the bio-feedback phenomenon encompass the entire spectrum of an individual's physical, mental and emotional being, future uses of the bio-feedback principle can cover just as broad a spectrum. It can play a major role in a new era of mental and physical health, and the dimensional perspective it gives on mental life will impress its change on social life as well. It is difficult to sketch future benefits separately; improved physical health leads to improved emotional mental health, and the converse is also true. Together these lead to improved social and cultural well-being.

As we learn more about the phenomenon it seems that bio-feedback has almost unlimited potential in terms of social and human needs, and as a personal survival health kit for every man, woman, and child. Because we have not yet learned to become aware of the "feel" of our interior body functionings, consciousness becomes cognizant of their being and existence only when some body disturbance upsets the normal mode and range of functioning. Sometimes our subconscious rumbles vague warnings about internal problems, but generally by the time a suffering interior awakens consciousness to the internal need, the internal problems are already in need of medical or psychological attention. There is, in bio-feedback, the very real possibility to be both the protector of health and its physician.

Probably the most immediate potential benefit of bio-feedback lies in its ability to reveal the well-beingness of inner man. Never before has man had the opportunity to inspect his interior physical being *before* it becomes disordered. If man wishes, he can use bio-feedback techniques to make regular inspections of the internal physical self, learning to become aware of failings of normal function which, if left unchecked, can lead to real illness. What a different society it would be if people learned what it feels like to be in a state of good health, not only for the whole organism but for all different parts of the organism, a learning to know what is normal—or even *better*—what better-than-well-being is really like. In a state of health we ignore our bodies; it is only in a state of illness that we become aware of our bodies or pieces of them. And when we are sick we forget the feeling of wellness (we only yearn for it) and the loss of the memory of wellness renders us incapable of using our mind-body systems to correct the problems of illness. We have forgotten because we really never knew the *feeling of being healthy*. We have learned the "feel" of illness, and we can, with some effort and attention, learn the "feel" of wellness.

The close tie between physical and emotional well-being also increases the probabilities for early detection of emotional illness. There are special techniques such as brain wave or skin electrical bio-feedback that can be used as sensitive detectors of emotional well-being. There is, with bio-feedback, the opportunity to explore the self to establish the most effective operating ranges of both physical and mental or emotional function.

The education of the awareness of internal body functions is a bit like learning physiology, not as in a college course, but from the inside out. Once learned, it is like having a highly skilled doctor inside of us always watching for errant body behavior. The awareness learner can come to discriminate normal, satisfactory, and satisfying body function from not-quite-normal function. Learning to become aware of comfortable mind-body function is the education necessary to detect the early warning signs of potential problems. When ranges of normal activity are exceeded too much or for too long a time, the aware being can seek therapeutic help at the earliest moment. Then practice with bio-feedback techniques can be used therapeutically to either reverse or delay damage to body systems and to the mind.

Even when actual physical problems are developing, the awareness gained by bio-feedback practice yields more benefits than simply acting as an early-warning system for detection of a developing illness. The heightened awareness also vastly improves communication with the physician. The new understanding of the physical interior makes it easier to describe with accuracy the place and intensity of gnawing distress.

In the future it seems likely that bio-feedback techniques will be highly specific, and with their practice, illnesses can be detected by practiced awareness and the course of many illnesses can be shortened. Even now, whether for specific or for general purposes, learned muscle relaxation serves to reduce both the intensity and the length of illness that are the ever-present impediments to the success of any treatment.

The ability to detect the state of well-beingness of the body, along with the ability to practice procedures to ensure well-being, have impelling implications for increasing life-span. There will be little or none of the actual tensions that keep body systems pulled out of shape, and less energy will be expended in misdirected use of the body's energy; thus bio-feedback offers an extraordinary means for preventive medicine and for extending one's life-span.

Out of the Tension Trap

Future uses of bio-feedback stem from learning greater awareness of normal biologic activity. One could, for example, become so aware of the mind-body changes during the onset of sleep that control over sleep itself could be learned, even the exact depth of sleep desired. Or we could, perhaps, increase the efficiency of such sleep substitutes as rest, cat-napping, and momentary relaxation. Perhaps the most remarkable example of probing and understanding and directing dream life has been practiced by the Senoi tribe of the Malay peninsula. This "primitive" tribe has attained an extraordinary degree of control over the dream life. Recognizing, as does Western psychiatry, that dreams contain reproductions of the difficulties and frustrations of social life (as well as its pleasures), the analysis of dreams is a daily family function as well as a group social function. Through such education and psychotherapy of the significance of the social and emotional impact of dreams, the Senoi developed a society which rarely suffered from the socio-psychologic distresses of our own society—emotional distress, conflict, violence, crime, and psychosomatic disease. They also apparently have enjoyed unusually good physical health.

There are other examples in less materially advanced cultures of the use of the feedback principle to achieve emotional and physical well-being. For example, it has been said that the people of the famous Hunza valley, up in the tri-corner where Afghanistan, Tibet, and Russia meet, are famous for their exceptional longevity and vigor because of their diet of apricots and whole grains, living actively for perhaps 130 or so years. But they have another secret. From early childhood the Hunzas practice profound relaxation several times a day. It is not an unusual sight to see children and adults alike stop any place, sit, and sink into deep relaxation for 10 or 15 minutes, arising restored and renewed. While no one has proved that this is their own special form of bio-feedback, it doesn't take much imagination to conclude that to achieve deep relaxation requires becoming aware of the muscles and their tensions. This is not to say that the Hunzas have the type of muscle tension associated with the social climate of Westerners, but then perhaps the awareness of the total state of being that flows from an altered state of consciousness in profound relaxation may in itself be an active deterrent to social tension.

Perhaps many of the new mind-awareness movements in the United States are fostering types of deviceless bio-feedback as practiced by the Senoi and by the Hunzas. The popularity of various schools of meditation and contemplation may be occurring not only because of the spiritual insights they may afford, but in large part because of an apparent increase in life energy that follows practice. That such energy changes do occur has been clearly confirmed in experimental studies. Although other forms of Oriental meditation practice have not been similarly documented in the laboratory, adherents claim that meditation exercises do increase energy and improve health. Many meditation exercises concentrate on developing an awareness of body processes, much as bio-feedback does, except that the body information needed to develop the awareness is less readily available than in bio-feedback form.

But the emotional self has its own existence and its own problems. The relief from and prevention of emotional problems is another important benefit that bio-feedback lends to the human being under stress. Bio-feedback techniques and practice can provide insights about body reactions and lead to a steadier emotional state; they may also provide a dramatic new means of communicating with the subconscious. As noted in the discussions of skin electrical responses, heart rate, the behavior of muscle cell groups and brain waves, there are a variety of bio-feedback techniques which can furnish new and precise avenues to interior emotional life. As in the use of bio-feedback to keep a satisfying control of physiologic functions, it can also be used both to guard a state of emotional well-being and to be sensitive to developing emotional problems. Apart from these aids, it is a useful communications medium in working with therapists to explore conflicts or emotional disquiet more deeply.

If, through bio-feedback, people can learn awareness of physical and emotional states of well-being and detect the earliest signs of changes signaling trouble, what then of hospitals and doctors? The most immediate effect would be a more efficient use of medical facilities. If the average person could sustain physical and emotional health for longer periods by himself, scarce medical facilities would not be diverted to unraveling psychosomatic from organic pathology. There is every likelihood that there would be a drastic reduction in the incidence of psychosomatic illness.

Medical research could also develop numerical profiles for each individual that would indicate his optimal level of biologic function and emotional behavior. These profiles might indicate anything from normal blood cell count to blood cholesterol to relaxation levels of muscles to attitudes about sex or scholars. Such profiles might be on computer cards, available to each individual for exact reference should he detect undesirable changes occurring in his body. He might also update his profiles yearly on the basis of increased knowledge about his body and mind, and the changes of emotion and age. If troubles arose, he might work with a health profile specialist to direct his bio-feedback practice and other mind-body therapies to help lead him rapidly back to physical or emotional well-being.

Even if It Weren't Real

No doubt to many completely physically oriented physicians the effects and potential of bio-feedback will be denigrated, for some time at least, as being just another placebo. The role of the placebo in medical research is generally viewed as an annoying intrusion of the patient's self-deception about the merits of the treatment he is receiving. In medicine and medical research the placebo is a drug or treatment which is both innocuous and without the possibility of exerting an influence on the course of the illness. Yet regularly the placebo *does* produce beneficial effects; sometimes as many as 35 percent of an experimental patient group will show substantial improvement by use of a placebo alone. The effect is generally interpreted as a psychologic result of changing medication, or increased attention to the patient, or the patient's ability to sense a change in the treatment routine.

Acknowledging the reality of the placebo effect is important to the future of bio-feedback. They are both drugless and their benefits originate in the activity of the mind. The only difference is that the placebo action stems from nebulous subconscious desire; bio-feedback effects are accomplished by awareness and learning.

The curious part of the placebo problem is that it has rarely been recommended as a treatment procedure by itself, except by an occasional insightful practicing physician. Now, with the apparently universal principle of an internal control system for individuals that is revealing an ability for ordinary human minds to influence the processes of illness, it would seem that the role of the placebo should be inspected from a different perspective.*

Will There Be a Future for Drugs?

There are numerous defense systems in the body capable of preventing the assaults of illness and disease. We are all familiar with our occasional immunity to colds or the flu, or our rapid recovery from surgery. What we have *not* done in medicine and psychology is to explore ways to strengthen these defenses naturally (although food

* For a bit more on placebos, see Appendix E.

faddists certainly try). The awareness learning in bio-feedback training should provide a proper tool to arouse our natural defenses and keep them effective and on the alert.

All that many drugs do in the body is try to mobilize the natural defenses. As far as infections are concerned, it is believed by many that the most effective therapy is a future chemical isolated from natural body defense mechanisms that prevents the spread of invading organisms. Nearly every drug is capable of producing deleterious effects in the body if not used with care; often the undesirable side effects of drugs cause more problems than they cure.

The ability of bio-feedback to produce intentional and profound changes in one's own physiologic functioning should prove to be of considerable value in the therapeutic use of drugs (and to the drug industry). It is a very real possibility that everyone who now uses drugs to alleviate the symptoms and causes of disease, every physician who prescribes drugs, every addict or potential addict who uses drugs as an escape or defense, will all be influenced by the availability of bio-feedback to aid in the control of mind and body. There are many roles that bio-feedback can play in conjunction with or by replacing drugs. If the illness can be managed by bio-feedback alone, as many doubtless can, then fine; but if a drug is required to facilitate recovery, then bio-feedback can be used to augment the drug effect.

In many instances the therapeutic action of bio-feedback may be so effective that when drugs must be added to the treatment, smaller doses can produce their effects more readily and more completely. The combined therapeutic effectiveness with a drug may increase the specificity of the drug effect and also reduce the incidence of undesirable side effects. Because the drug and bio-feedback are both directing their actions toward the same beneficial end, they enhance the effects of each other.

The capability of BFT to reveal to the patient more precisely the nature of the internal difficulty also means that it can be used to assist in distinguishing between organic illness and the subjective emotional overlay that aggravates the symptoms, and this would allow for greater accuracy in diagnosis. If, for example, bio-feedback procedure can relieve the physical problem only to a certain degree, then the remainder of the problems not so controlled provides a rough estimate of the actual amount of pathologic involvement.

One of the more troublesome problems in medicine is to distinguish between the real effects of a drug and the psychologic responses which occur simply because the illness is being treated. Bio-feedback can assist in making this distinction because it allows the patient to document the physiologic changes along with the accompanying subjective changes, both with and without the addition of drugs to the treatment. Working with the doctor in this way offers the physician more insight into the various realities of the illness and allows him to select his treatments for greater and more specific effectiveness. And this shortens the duration of the illness.

And for Drug Abuse

The use of bio-feedback techniques to rehabilitate drug abusers may become one of its more outstanding uses. The prevalence of drug abuse and its attending disasters are so well known that they need no comment. There are many guesses about the reasons for drug addiction and drug abuse which cover a variety of biologic, psychologic and sociologic factors. The current consensus is, however, that therapeutic attacks on the drug abuse problem based on such guesses and hypotheses have been disappointing at best.

Prominent among the hypothesized psychologic causes for drug use and misuse are anxiety, alienation, peer pressure, the need for relaxation, and neurotic compulsion. No single factor has, however, been productive of a treatment directed specifically against it. Joel Fort has stressed that it is not any one single factor, it is the *interrelatedness* of the causative factors.

It is frequently observed that indulgence in certain drugs, particularly marijuana and alcohol and possibly heroin itself, occurs in part because of the urge to find a rapid and effective way for relaxing. While this might be considered as relatively insignificant in relation to the severity of the drug abuse problem, the reasons for the need to relax, i.e., tension and anxiety, are problems of even greater magnitude in present-day society. It follows also that perhaps a large share of the population is vulnerable to the effects of tension and anxiety and seek their relief in the very few avenues available for relaxation. The sale of tranquilizers and alcohol confirms the magnitude of the problem. It is an unusual circumstance of modern life that there are only two major avenues to relaxation available to the American public: entertainment and drugs. Although education may discuss problems of tension and anxiety, virtually no education in techniques for relaxation of the body (and the extension of the capacities of the mind and body) is offered.

Few, if any, professionals dealing with mental health problems and drug misuse have ever experienced the effects of hallucinogens, nor have they lived in a drug society. The conceptual and operational gap between the drug abusers and the well-meaning professionals who attempt to deter and to treat drug abuse may stem largely from the inability to convey the experience induced by the drugs. Many drug users have noted the similarities to mystical and peak experiences, and the descriptions for such experiences of non-ordinary reality, such as ineffable or cosmic union, all express the difficulty in communicating the experience. Much of the almost incomprehensible new street language reflects the need for non-ordinary expression as an attempt to communicate not only drug experience, but to communicate the experience of a new consciousness. The old reality is not the present reality; earth is no longer the center of the universe; drug experience is not a drug but a social experience; the boundaries of self have flexed and opened, and these revolutions in apparent reality demand new modes of communication.

If reports of subjective experience are compared between certain drug states and those occurring in certain bio-feedback training exercises, it is surprising to find many similarities, such as sensations of floating, a feeling of dissolving into the feedback signal, the loss of time perception, detachment, and other non-ordinary states and feelings.

Experimental studies in bio-feedback have also brought out the resemblance between both the psychologic and physiologic aspects which develop to those occurring during certain yogic or Zen meditation exercises. Both the Eastern and Western techniques appear to have common elements involving increased awareness of self and of internal events, and it is common consensus that the types of individuals who seek mystical experience, psychic experience and even bio-feedback experience are similar in many respects to those who seek drug experience. Such individuals prefer the world of profound experience, of mystical insights, of deep probings for identity of the individual, and eschew the traditional, commercial, the purely physical and empirical ends. In this new philosophy the bio-feedback "machine" appears to represent an impersonal tool for self-realization, uncontaminated by manipulations of a distrusted establishment, and is particularly attractive to just those people who are seeking new experiences, individuation and identity.

The actual nature of experience has been rather consistently ignored in the culture of psychologic academia, except as it ultimately becomes manifest as behavior, because academic scientific tradition demands tidy measurements, reproducibility, expressibility, and an observable parameter or variable. The effect of nonordinary experience on personality, behavior, motivation, and other ingredients which determine human behavior is virtually unknown in a meaningful, predictive way. In the history of cannabis and heroin, for example, there are countless ecstatic reports of pleasurable experiences when the drugs were used casually; the same is true of the newer hallucinogens. In a less puritan day these reports were considered with interest and conjecture; today the reality of the nonordinary experience of drugs is clouded by an outmoded puritan ethic which fails to recognize the drug experience for what it really is—an action to unveil the new consciousness and a reaction against the old consciousness. Drug use is only a symptom of societal frustration and the desire to fulfill the long unrealized mind potential of evolving man. Forward-looking researchers are only now beginning to incorporate concepts of a changing reality into studies of human emotion.

Experienced investigators in the field of drug abuse generally do tend to agree (particularly since no known psychologic or sociologic technique has successfully influenced drug abusers) that drug abusers are seeking new experiences to relieve anxieties and frustrations, and to make them feel more capable and to enhance self-esteem. If this is true, then an effective treatment for actual and potential drug abuse would be greatly enhanced *by providing the user with an experience which is more meaningful, useful, and inner-directing than that of the drug experience.* One interesting illustration of this conclusion is found in the work of Dr. Herbert Benson of Harvard and the Massachusetts General Hospital. In a recent interview he reported nearly 90 percent success in weaning some 1,800 young drug abusers away from drugs by teaching them Transcendental Meditation.

Certain experiences obtained with bio-feedback training not only share aspects of drug and mystical experience but may add an important dimension to such experiences. The new dimension is the consequence of focusing attention on the relationship between internal physiologic events and internal mental, emotional, and conceptual events. If, as experiments suggest, this occurs, the drug user may find at least partial answers to his questions of identity and social acceptance, answers to why he has anxiety and tension. It should be possible to enhance the process by appropriate supportive therapy or counseling.

The sustained interest of subjects in bio-feedback experiences is an expression of the interesting and pleasurable nature of the subjective states they induce. The sensations of increased awareness of internal events serve as a continuing motivation for pursuing new discoveries of the inner self. Several forms of bio-feedback—most notably muscle and brain wave—can lead to altered states of consciousness. Even during mildly altered states of consciousness attention shifts from anxiety-producing elements of the environment toward elements of internal functioning not previously available for perception and the new focus reduces anxiety proportionally.

The distressing side effects of drug abuse are apathy, purposelessness, loss of will. Individuals tend to become more autonomous and alienated. Any modality of treatment must deal with substantially reducing such side effects. There are also inherent, self-perpetuating motivation and self-regulatory mechanisms which occur with bio-feedback training, which can enhance awareness and develop a concept of internal control and individuation. Such evidence lends support to the thesis that highly significant experiences can be obtained with bio-feedback techniques and that these may rank equally well with the drug abuser's concept of the drug experience. Preliminary explorations using complex pattern feedback of both EKG and EEG along with autonomic and EMG feedback have disclosed that the actual experiences of altered awareness may be quite dramatic and profound. These new experiences would not only be infinitely safer but have the potential to supply incentive for continuing the "inner search" for meaningful insights about one's own inner self.

Many of us who use brain wave bio-feedback in our research studies have discovered many a drug "abuser" among our experimental subjects. While we must exclude them from further study for scientific reasons, from time to time we had our own feedback about their subsequent behavior. Some of these troubled subjects have reported to us that the alpha feedback experience provided such a powerful insight into their internal world of experience that in some way it rearranged their values and they became no longer interested in the drug experience. In laboratories where the subjective experience of feedback only is studied and more young people are involved, a significant number of subjects have been found who stopped drug-taking after intensive involvement with alpha bio-feedback. Moreover, such subjects often charged headlong into acceptable, meaningful, productive pursuits. It will be some time before completely verifiable, scientifically acceptable studies can be put together to confirm these sporadic observations, but the fact that they are reported from widely scattered laboratories lends credence to the observations.

Returning to Health

Most illnesses require extensive rehabilitation attention, that is, a bridge between optimal therapeutic effects for recovery and the individual's ability to function fairly independently of medical or psychologic support. The gist of psychotherapeutic thinking is that awareness of self, self-confidence, and a realistic picture of social (interpersonal) interactions are the desired end points of treatment for emotional disturbances. In all medical problems there is also an inherent concern for well-being and ability to function. These range from the normal concerns of the medical patient to the abnormal concerns of the psychoneurotic patient. Any unwarranted concern, whether it be anxiety, depression, or lack of confidence, is an obstacle to the adequate and necessary functioning of the individual. Social disturbances are often even more serious than emotional or medical problems and frequently require long periods of rehabilitation. Any dependency or resistive reaction of individuals (usually groups of individuals) to their society results in sequestered or socially deviant behavior. The focal point of treatment of these disturbances is also in awareness of self, self-confidence, and a realistic understanding of interpersonal relationships.

For these various psychophysical pathologies there exists a large gray area between adequate recovery produced by currently used therapeutic measures and the goal of returning the patient to a useful, satisfying and productive existence. Since the underlying mechanism of the feedback system evokes awareness of self and of one's ability to produce a useful, enjoyable, and confident frame of mind, it is reasonable to deduce that a significant number of individuals will benefit from the new technique. Bio-feedback therapy can provide confidence that appropriate behavior can be both learned by the patient *teaching himself* and recalled at will for those moments of stress which normally perpetuate the disturbance.

Such "self-therapy," which may be assisted by professional attendants, could effectively reduce the number of hours now required for counseling and guidance, reduce the number of visits to a therapist, prevent a certain percentage of patients from returning to the hospital or medical care units, reduce loss of time away from the job (or school), and reduce the number of services required for the patient. Aside from the benefits to mental and physical health, the savings in medical time and money alone should interest the government in exploring bio-feedback techniques for rehabilitation.

The procedure for many types of rehabilitation could be quite general. One might be as follows: The subject is told that various colored lights are actually operated by his own brain waves or muscle activity (or by his own feelings, whichever is more appropriate), and that these are controlled by his own feelings and thoughts and moods. The subject is told that he, himself, can control the lights by the way he feels and thinks. He would be asked to identify as many moods, thoughts, and feelings as he could to specific colors, positions, patterns, or sequences of the lights, then asked to concentrate on those feelings and thoughts which he feels will be of the greatest help to him. He is told that after some practice he can prove to the therapist that he can control the light displays at will.

The subject is informed that the therapist will *not* know his inner feelings and thoughts—only that he, the subject, can control them at will. If muscle activity were used as the bio-feedback signal, emphasis of the instructions also include instructions for relaxation. Treatment sessions could last 60 minutes or so each, and the number of sessions required to achieve effects would depend upon the individual's responses and the evaluations made by the observers.

While the treatment sessions are under way, the subject would be allowed to confirm impressions of his progress and to alter aspects of the light arrangement to those which he felt would be most effective for him. In this way the subject could come to learn that indeed the therapist can't read his mind, but that he, the subject, actually can manipulate the order, color, intensity, and arrangement of the lights by the way he feels and thinks.

Imagine that a patient with asthmatic tendencies has a possible 12-light display, say 4 different colors each with 3 hues, in front of him. He notes that more and brighter or darker red lights are lighted when he feels "tight" and has a feeling of respiratory distress, but discovers that the more relaxed he becomes and has easier respiration, more and brighter blue lamps light up. He begins to try to keep on the blue lights first by actively keeping himself relaxed, and later, by reproducing only the mental feeling of relaxation. He "passively" teaches himself to keep the blue lights lit; i.e., he allows it to happen rather than actively trying to make it happen. Later, he finds that he has no need for the lights to be able to recall the feeling state that accompanies easier respiration. He can then recall the feeling at times of impending stress and block the incipient asthma attack before it can develop.

Each subject for treatment would be informed that he has the potential to operate the visual displays by his own particular feelings and thoughts, and moreover, that he alone knows how he accomplishes the task. It seems logical to assume that when individuals learn how to manipulate bio-feedback displays by their own subjective activities, and realize that this is the accomplishment of the individual only, then some degree of confidence will emerge. The fundamental experience of becoming aware of one's "inner self" is the mechanism by which the displays operate. Thus two factors of great importance for achieving identity and motivation have been uncovered by the subject himself, and they provide a base of information about and control of self which is henceforth available to the individual.

As we are seeing, there are an astounding number of physical, psychologic, and social disabilities to which the simple bio-feedback training procedure can be applied with a reasonable confidence that it will be of benefit in the rehabilitation of the patient. Aside from neurologic, muscular, cardiovascular, and psychosomatic problems that have been discussed in preceding chapters, there are large areas of psychoneurotic and social disability where bio-feedback can provide important help during rehabilitation.

There are numerous examples of patients, such as those with severe psychoneurotic problems, who have been treated in the hospital and face further emotional difficulties when they are released and returned to society. This is a time when confidence is weak and the support of continuous medical attention and counseling have been withdrawn. Here a procedure as described can provide the support of the confidence needed that one can control one's own being.

Using appropriate bio-feedback techniques, the patient can train himself before leaving the hospital to regulate his heart, his breathing, his level of tension, or whatever affords him the fastest recovery. Such a precaution may help to remedy a curious paradox of illness: that one recovers from one illness only to return to the hospital with another. In illness serious enough for hospitalization it is rare that full recovery occurs in the hospital; rather the distresses of physiology linger and the weakened system is not just one system, the entire body is weakened. If the body drain is not also attended to, other systems become susceptible to illness and the cycle of illness begins again.

And Returning to Social Health

There are today more than ever before the socially handicapped, those who suffer the socio-psychologic disturbances of behavior which isolate them from "normal" social activity. They are the addicts to one or more of the "dangerous drug" group or to alcohol, to overeating, to milder forms of sexual neuroses, or they are the school dropouts and the chronically unemployed.

The core problems of the socially handicapped are primarily a lack of self-awareness and identity, lack of confidence in the self which impedes activation of inherent survival activity that provides the ground substance of motivation. Feedback therapy is particularly appropriate to these groups of socially handicapped persons.

As one of the socially handicapped groups, for example, the hard-core unemployed consists partly of people who have the mental and physical ability to hold jobs. What these individuals lack are the attitudes necessary to gain and maintain employment. Such problems of attitude could be helped through bio-feedback by providing a counseling-assisted situation in which these individuals could identify their established attitudinal sets with the aid of the feedback mechanism. These sets of attitudes could then be re-evaluated within the subject's own experiential frame of reference for their positive or negative value in relation to employment.

For example, visual feedback could be presented in the form of a matrix of light cells of varying colors and intensities. The various changes of brain wave patterns or body activity would activate various changes in the light patterns depending upon the changes occurring within each individual subject. If different mental attitudes produce different light matrix patterns for the individual, then the individual can learn to identify the different emotional attitudes. Because particular attitudes are now immediately available for re-evaluation, the subject can weigh their desirable or undesirable characteristics. When attitudes conducive to gaining and maintaining employment are recognized and become manifested as motivational drives, a major obstacle to unemployment would be removed.

Since each individual operates within his own attitudinal frame of reference and corresponding brain wave or muscle pattern, only the individual subject will be able to identify and manipulate the light matrix pattern. Control and awareness of one's own attitudes and attitude changes enhance confidence within the individual and in the case of BFT would allow transfer into the real-life situation after mastery of the light matrix is accomplished in the treatment situation. Any beneficial effects would rely solely upon whether a significant difference in rate of job acquisition and length of job tenure occurred.

The observation that one of the major negative characteristics of the hard-core unemployed is anxiety about both the acquisition of the job and performance suggests another use of the feedback technique to provide a self-teaching desensitization treatment of job-related anxiety. A series of pictures of typical interview and on-the-job situations might be projected onto a diffusion screen in front of the subject. A series of small colored lights placed along the edge of the plastic of the diffusion screen allows for developing a series of colors and hues to illuminate the diffusion screen. The colored lights are operated by brain wave activity or by muscle activities. Pictures of interview or job situations related to anxiety projected on the screen would be seen in the colors and hues developed by the brain wave or muscle activity that occurs in anxiety situations, and the color of lighting for the picture would change as the emotional set related to the situation pictured changed to a more relaxed attitude. The brain wave or muscle patterns are universal, and the underlying concept is that the subject can both become aware of the specific situations that cause him anxiety and learn how to change his response.

In Learning

One of the most constructive future uses of bio-feedback may be in education. It seems quite feasible that bio-feedback can be used in conjunction with teaching machines to alert the student to his optimal mind-body state for any given learning situation. Children generally learn to control their physiologic processes more quickly than they do their mental processes. By learning to control the phenomena of their selves, they could acquire certain mental and physical disciplines more quickly than they normally would. They might, for example, learn the physiologic patterns accompanying concentration, thereby setting the groundwork to learn to concentrate all the more effectively.

A simple but very meaningful use of a bio-feedback technique could be in conjunction with teaching machines. It is well known that the attention span of children is short. An accurate indicator of the length of each span of attention would be useful in maximizing the use of the teaching machine. The display screen of the teaching machine might, for example, be capable of changing color: greenish for periods when the child's attention level is high—a go-ahead signal; and reddish for periods when attention begins to wander—a stop signal. The color of the screen would be controlled by the two basic brain wave patterns, the "alert" EEG associated with high attention levels, and the "nonalert" EEG pattern associated with nonattention. Similarly, physical and mental attitudes more suitable for learning could be learned more readily as well as improvement of their attention span by their own volition. Feedback could initiate in Western education something that it has lacked since the time of Plato—a holistic education, an education of mind and body together so that finally the student might truly be educated in terms of that ancient but futuristic motto: *mens sana in corpore sano*.

THIRTEEN

Or the Distant Future? Flowers of Fantasy

It is strange that the impact of the seemingly simple operation of bio-feedback is so easily intuited but is so ill understood by the intellect. Despite the constant changes in daily life, we seem not to be prepared to acknowledge that its many electrical activities are sources of significant electrical power, nor that the mind needs only symbols to affect the behavior of its body.

To the Subatomic Self

To most of us the future of man means flights in space to the edges of our galaxy and beyond. For ourselves we think of the future in terms of a long life, free from physical and mental discomfort. We think of how to survive if our life's pace and the population continue to increase, if the environment is sacrificed or atomic energy goes astray. Can bio-feedback be of use in these critical concerns? There is solid scientific evidence emerging to justify the belief that it can. But beyond the very real help that bio-feedback can provide to improve mental and physical life as we know it now, there still lie far-distant spheres of consciousness and understanding to which bio-feedback may guide the mind in a journey through inner space.

Flight into outer space depends now more on the endurance of man than of his machines. Endurance implies the ability to withstand assaults to the being while maintaining an effective integrity of the whole. The billions of space dollars have coped admirably with the hazards of the external environment of the spaceman; current technology assures the space traveler relative body safety and relative comfort when space flights are limited to a few weeks. But the new problems that might limit future space travel are temporary physiologic changes in the astronauts that could lead to permanent damage or perhaps death if return to Earth's atmosphere is not in time to allow recovery.

Suppose, for example, that one physiologic problem might be leakage across cell membranes of one of the body's vital mineral elements. Could it ever be possible that human thought alone might control this dangerous seepage of a mineral from a cell where it is essential to sustain life? Sounds impossible? Not a bit; remember what hypnosis can do. One of the tests used in some hypnosis courses is to suggest to the subject that a nickel placed in the hand is getting hotter and hotter. You pass Hypnosis One if your subject thinks "hot" so intensely that a blister is raised. Or there is the old trick of sticking pins into someone to see how deeply he is hypnotized. Both tricks are tricks of consciousness that involve the passage of minerals and fluids across cell membranes. In the case of the blister, fluids along with the minerals they contain seep out of places where they are normally restrained by the cell membranes of the small blood vessels and the subcutaneous tissues. On the other hand people usually bleed when pricked hard by a pin, but under hypnosis the cell membranes tighten up and no fluid escapes, even though there is all the power of the blood pressure exerting its force to push the blood through the pinhole.

Medical hypnosis has become an accepted tool of modern anesthesiology, yet surprisingly, there have been few if any research explorations into the physiologic efficiency of hypnosis, nor have there been any serious studies of the effectiveness of autosuggestion in the control of physiologic processes. No one knows how far the control can go. Psychologists have long been arguing the theory and rightful use of hypnosis, and many use it empirically and on a limited basis, confining its use to replace anesthesia during surgery. It is as if medicine fears the potential power of the mind; certainly it has kept the mind under its own control. Yet if hypnosis can control bleeding as well as pain, it is a major oversight that hypnosis has not been explored scientifically and systematically for its effect on other body functions.

Both hypnosis and bio-feedback are capable of controlling body functioning without drugs and without surgery. Now there are two fingers pointing toward the dominion of mind over matter, and a third, acupuncture, has just emerged from its Eastern medicine chest.*

The demonstration by Basmajian and others that human beings can voluntarily control the electrical activity of a single motoneuron cell in the spinal cord would seem to be the ultimate in voluntary control over the body. Speculation suggests that the ultimate lies further beyond this. The microsystems that are necessary both to conduct and not to conduct a nerve impulse are biochemical in nature. If an individual activates one cell at will, then he is also affecting the internal chemistry of the cell at the same time. More remarkably, he is simultaneously turning off the electrochemistry of tens or hundreds of other cells which must be suppressed in the process of isolating a single cell for activation.† If the human mind can select one of a million unknown, unseen cells in the spinal cord and learn to control it so quickly, then one must admit that the possibility exists of selecting out any other cell, spinal cord or else-where. The new key is bio-feedback, i.e., the technique for supply-ing the human mind with information about the unfelt within. The fact that many and diverse cellular processes are involved in bio-feedback hint another future for its ability to control complex patterns of body activities effectively, one that may one day be used to control one's own endocrine or metabolic life. Perhaps never to grow old or infirm.

Bio-Feedback to Sleep

A cursory examination of sleep and bio-feedback research suggests that many of the physiologic changes occurring during sleep induc-tion and in the maintenance of sleep can be employed as feedback signals to train subjects to control or facilitate sleep induction. Since

* The way in which acupuncture produces its effects is not known in Western terms. One Chinese tradition indicates the existence of energy pathways that the West may or may not discover. The network of "meridians" which trace the connections between inner organs and the areas on the skin for which they have a particular affinity may be electromagnetic fields or body nerves or a mode of channeling energy as yet unknown.

† If this ability were fully realized, it might mean that the control of genetic engineering could occur by human consensus rather than by computer.

many of the currently used feedback procedures involve training for relaxation effects, the effect of practicing selective control over body indicators of sleep would undoubtedly develop useful techniques for control of the induction, quality and amount of sleep.

The sequence of brain wave and other body activities during sleep induction is generally similar for all individuals. Incipient drowsiness (presleep but awake state), for example, is characterized by large amounts of alpha activity of increasing amplitude. As sleep intervenes, alpha waves give way to slow, irregular waves of lower voltage where theta waves may become prominent. As sleep deepens, these waves continue to decrease in frequency. Training subjects to decrease the frequency of their alpha waves down to the theta range and then lower in frequency may provide an efficient way of inducing sleep. Voluntary control of alpha itself theoretically should predispose one to less anxiety and distraction by the simple expedient of providing a point of habitual focus of attention away from the anxiety-producing stimulus.

A large area of research important to the useful applications of sleep research has been largely neglected. This is the determination of what type of physiologic activities might qualify as effective substitutes for sleep. It is well known in anecdotal literature that certain forms of rest, relaxation, or diversion can act as restoratives in instances of sleep loss. It is not known to what degree this is a function of the individual.

In situations of high anxiety, for example, effects of sleep loss appear to be very pronounced. It has not been established whether the complaints of sleep loss are due to loss of sleep or whether the complaints might not be actually due to a continuing inability to utilize effective sleep substitutes, such as voluntary control over anxiety, voluntary control over muscle tension, or control of attention. For the most part mild sedatives or tranquilizers do not in themselves induce sleep but act by raising the thresholds of various physiologic systems so that they are more difficult to activate, excite, or arouse. It is these effects that facilitate both the rate of onset of sleep and the depth of sleep which determines their effectiveness.

Sleep substitutes, such as short periods of deep relaxation, have rarely been assessed for effectiveness in maintaining the well-being of the body and mind. In the recent review of the methods and medical applications of autogenic training, Luthe noted that subjects who have continued training for some time exhibit brain wave changes which are suggestive of pre-sleep, and that one of the benefits of autogenic training is relief from sleep problems. Since brain wave and muscle feedback training appears to produce similar states more quickly and more effectively, similar effects on sleep induction might well be achieved.

If body indices of sleep or substitute-sleep can be brought under voluntary control, the effects of such control would be of considerable value for all biomedical disciplines. Recovery from many illnesses is facilitated by sleep or forced rest, and they are used as supportive treatment in a wide variety of medical and psychologic problems. If sleep or sleep substitutes can be brought under voluntary control they would be helpful in everyday living, in addition to their therapeutic help.

An Awareness of Awareness

One of the most fascinating mental activities of man is his production of sudden "insights." Sometimes without conscious thought or sometimes after years of intensive mental effort, the real significance of many seemingly unrelated items suddenly snaps into place. Some insights are called the "aha!" reaction—that sudden awareness of meaning that occurs, for example, when you study the meaningless colors and shapes of a jigsaw puzzle and suddenly see how the pieces fit. The same thing happens in learning something new. You might be trying to learn how computers work. Even if all the pieces of information you need are given in an array of precise logic, step by step, there comes a moment when the missing link slips into place and in an instant all of the information flows together to make a whole and becomes meaningful. At this moment the human mind recognizes that understanding has occurred. It has become aware of becoming aware.

The biological groundwork and the technical aids by which awareness can be amplified and magnified already exist. There is already considerable research evidence to demonstrate that the assimilation of new information is accompanied by a specific set or sets of brain electrical events. A part of this physiologic pattern also includes signs of alertness, anticipation and preparation for brain activity that will follow. The entire group of brain electrical events can be used as bio-feedback signals. For a particular individual or for a particular circumstance (or anything from jigsaws to piecing gossip together or to learning math), the brain electrical events *might* be x amounts of alpha, x frequencies of alpha and theta, y amounts of beta, and z of some other neuronal event. Whatever the pattern is, it is the *pattern* that can be conveyed via feedback to the individual who generated it. Since human subjects appreciate and learn rather complex bio-feedback patterns rapidly, there is a reasonable likelihood that they can learn the significance of their own biologic signals that are indicating the actual act of assimilating new information. This new knowledge can also provide a basis for consolidating feelings and sensations or impressions about the learning "set" and come to be consciously recognized. The training should sharpen the awareness and focus of the optimal learning set and so be available for recall on a voluntary basis.

There is certainly adequate evidence that attitudinal "sets" or mental-emotional postures for effective learning can be acquired. They involve conscious awareness and control of motivation, attention, reasonable emotional and physical tranquillity, relevance and other faculties of the human mind. Once these factors are adjusted for the learning experience, the individual begins searching for and assimilating information. It is in this aspect that bio-feedback may offer new clues for accelerated and expanded learning since the moment of "closure" or insight about the meaning of new information appears to be accompanied by its own set of brain electrical events. An example is illustrated in Figure 17. Phenomena which seem to attend creative states—imagistic thinking, automatisms, time distortions, symbolic process, high-energy states—may also have special clusters of brain electrical events. These could be used in bio-feedback training, not only to study the curious phenomenon of insight, but to practice accelerating the process of arriving at new insights, or to sustain fleeting moments of understanding, and open up the still inaccessible area of complex mental activities and processes.

Possibly the most futuristic use of bio-feedback in expanding awareness and consciousness depends upon laboratory experiments that have not yet been done. Since the moment of insight is signaled by a specific set of brain wave events, it is logical to deduce that the occurrence of such events had to be preceded by other electrical events which signaled their coming. One can conjecture then that there are specific brain electrical activities that exist which predict the times and conditions when perceptual and conceptual systems become "set" for the optimal utilization of new information. (This *might* be the peculiar appearance or type of several different brain wave components occurring in specific relationships to each other: obviously if brain waves reflect mental activity, then they must do so in some orderly fashion that the appropriate electronic dissection can isolate and identify, much as complex body biochemicals are isolated and identified.) When such antecedent brain electrical events are isolated and characterized, they can be converted into externalized bio-feedback displays and used in training to reinforce them and bring them under voluntary control. Such control would mean expanded and accelerated awareness, acceleration of the process of recognition of information, and perhaps of the rate and extent of thought processes themselves.

Becoming aware and *becoming aware of becoming aware* are two of the superior mind abilities that bio-feedback might well be used to expand and hasten in their evolution. Training to expand awareness means increasing the awareness, both in amount and intensity, of things perceived of both inner and outer worlds. With the appreciation of more information, there is a firmer, more diverse field of knowledge from which concepts or symbols of the products of reflective thought can be derived to make the mind more capacious and expand its perspectives on the several realities. Obviously, the new horizons of mind revealed to an expanded awareness will be known only when awareness takes us there. The one thing that we can anticipate is a new state of consciousness.*

---

* Even at the furthest limits of today's expanded consciousness we resort to the models of mysticism of an earlier age to describe our moments of altered states of consciousness. We use words like supraconsciousness, hallucinatory, metaphysical, intangible, or other-world, borrowed from a consciousness that changed in different times. The capturing of different subjective states enjoyed by different minds at different times may in fact have no relationship to the changes in consciousness which appear to be evolving now through new techniques and a new technology designed to explore the more distant realms of consciousness. Our expansions of awareness might lead to an entirely new conceptual reality.

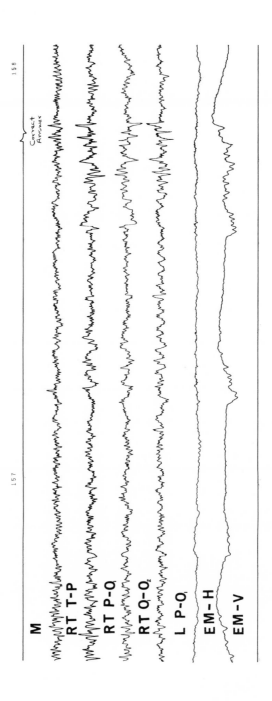

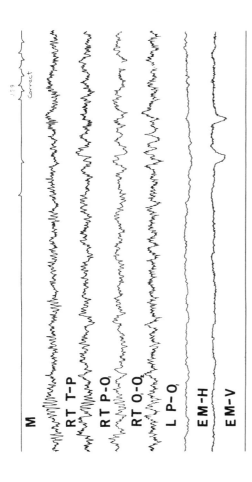

Figure 17. EEG records from experiments in which subjects were asked to unscramble letters to make real words (e.g., CEEAP unscrambled is PEACE).

The marker indications on the top line toward the right note when the subjects made correct answers. Just prior to giving the correct answer the subject shows EEG theta activity in the right occipital area, RT O–O. The appearance of theta may be specifically related to "closure"—the *aha!* response, as when suddenly aware of solving a problem, or it may merely be related to up-and-down eye movements, as indicated by the line marked EH–V, which is a record of horizontal eye movements. This is a problem for future research.

The Voluntary Control of Death

The extraordinary power of the human will over the most vital of the body's functions is illustrated by an experience of a friend of mine. As the Chief of Surgery of a state hospital, he was called upon to perform a complicated, serious operation on a prisoner. The prisoner-patient made an astounding and rapid recovery, indicating his physical vigor and resiliency. Some two years later the prisoner was appearing before a parole board, which recommended immediate release from prison. A moment after release was ordered a court deputy read a summons from another state ordering the prisoner to be transferred to another prison to serve an additional ten years. As the order was read, the prisoner collapsed, dying. My friend, in the next building, arrived within minutes. Resuscitation procedures were instituted immediately, but it took all the resources of experienced medical treatment to recover the patient. There was no heart attack, no asthma attack, no cerebral stroke; there was, in fact, no physical reason that could be detected in thorough examination to account for the imminent death. The prisoner admitted that he could not face further imprisonment and had simply decided to die.

There is of course the natural end to life when it can no longer defend against the elements and time, yet before that comes there is sometimes a circumstance that begs for consideration of early termination. The voluntary control of death is not as unlikely an ability as it often seems. Our Western culture values life so highly that we are disturbed and bewildered by suicide. This value system does not exist in many countries where the ethic teaches that death is a rewarding step toward unity with God.

The Western ethic is, however, becoming ambivalent. There is growing criticism of God-playing physicians who prolong life in terminal, irreversible, agonizing illnesses against overwhelming humanitarian impulses and logic. It is a singular contrast to the behavior of certain Eskimo tribes where the elderly, when the end of their usefulness and life and happiness is obvious, walk off to die alone. Voluntarily. Death comes quickly in the subfreezing cold of the Arctic, an anesthetic numbing away of life that is no doubt a more acceptable mode of voluntarily ending life than the violence of

shooting or hanging oneself. With extended control over body processes, in some future morality, it may someday be possible to make
as smooth a voluntary transition from life to death as we do from
wakefulness to sleep.

Who knows best when life is ended than the mind-body itself?
Growing old means that we have grown in the wisdom that comes
from experience, we can compare the old self with the young self,
count up the problems, judge how much we can live with them,
compare realities, compromise between the here and the not-here,
understand and even desire the continuity of life that means both
beginning and ending. If and when the time comes that death is
desired more than life, the voluntary control of the mind and body
might solicit death for release from unbearable suffering.

Beyond the Mind: the Pattern of Its Music

Today in neurophysiology and psychophysiology there is a growing
emphasis on the meanings of body processes as they occur *in
patterns*. In the past most scientific work was confined to study of a
single isolated bit of body chemistry or behavior. A number of bio-
feedback researchers have occasionally used the feedback of biologic patterns of brain electrical or body signals in experiments and
have been deeply impressed by the dramatic ability of naïve subjects to identify and reproduce rather complex patterns of their own
biologic functioning. In my own laboratory, for example, we provided our subjects with a crossword-puzzle type of visual display in
which each square represented a different bit of brain wave activity
(in color) and were startled to find that within as little as 15
minutes subjects were able to light up certain groups of squares
selectively and with no apparent effort. The astounding fact was
that the bits of brain wave activity used to light up the squares were
not, according to good neurologic theory, ones believed to be so
intimately related that they could occur together. In a way this
unexpected ability resembled the results of Basmajian and a number
of others who have demonstrated that human beings are extremely
efficient in developing control over temporal sequences and patterns
of muscle or brain neuron firing but do poorly with individual
components. A good bit of current bio-feedback research suggests

that the information an individual derives from the external part of the bio-feedback loop is identified chiefly as part of a large pattern of information which involves how the information is patterned both in space and time (e.g., the *where* and *when* of alpha and other waves) rather than information being appreciated as technologically isolated bits of information (as *here* is an alpha wave).

Moreover, a profound subjective experience can be obtained when a representation of a whole physiologic function is fed back to the individual as it is functioning through distance and time. This might have been expected because isolated components of a physiologic activity cannot begin to characterize the dynamic nature of the way in which the components needed to effect a meaningful body activity interact with each other. So it might be reasonable to assume that the bio-feedback of isolated parts of biology may be less efficient for learning voluntary control than feedback of patterns which can give more inclusive information about the total function of the system. It might also be argued that the operational mode of an individual's functioning is one of balanced interaction, and that the sensations arising from the awareness of one's own physiology are in the nature of a cluster. If one would like to control a new movement, for example as in relearning how to use an injured arm, it is more meaningful and efficient to do so with a picture of the complete, 3-D movement in mind rather than being aware of only what each muscle does individually. Knowledge of the complete pattern of function is not only necessary but often the pattern is the only information needed to learn to control the function. Certainly we have never learned to control each muscle separately or even serially in learning to walk. So it may be with brain waves or blood pressure: knowledge of the whole may be more important than knowledge of the sum of its parts.

Certainly an awareness of the totality of functioning is different from the awareness of an isolated part. Gardner Murphy and others have postulated that the maintenance of a particular state of mind is heavily dependent upon a particular configuration of the physiologic variables of the body and the internal and external sensations reaching the brain. It would then follow that changes in the patterns of spatial-temporal configuration of information to the mind can lead to altered states of consciousness.

Many neurophysiologists believe that the brain electrical activity of human beings is best definable in terms of individual patterns, both of the continuously fluctuating spontaneous activity and the brain wave patterns that develop during different types of mental and emotional activity. The principle of using patterns to represent the dynamics of brain activity may be infinitely more complex and subtle than the types of extended life activities that one can absorb, for example, by watching colonies of ants or bees who work for the well-being of the colony and not for the individual. In the last decade other models have been suggested to explain the ability of small groups of brain cells or perhaps even single brain cells to participate in an amazing variety of brain functions. The hologram (spatial) and holophone (temporal) models of information input, storage and retrieval emphasize the directions of newer thinking, i.e., that the representation of all details of a multidimensional pattern or picture also occur in each component part, however small, of the entire pattern—even in bits of time. The use of both temporal and spatial patterning of bio-feedback information may provide a powerful tool in the study of brain function as well as defining the more elusive states of consciousness, and perhaps develop new techniques for learning.

Mind-Body Music

One such currently widely discussed but futuristic use of the feedback of patterns of body function lies in translating them into patterns of music and art, which also have dimensions in space and time. The conversion of arrays of body signals into forms that can be perceived by the senses as meaningful patterns may at first glance seem to be only an idea for a science fiction story. Yet the appetite of the human organism for meaningful *patterned* symbols, such as the work of artists, musicians and writers, or simply harmony in the environment, that offer new insights into being is a substantial rationale for making an effort to realize the patterned bio-feedback concept. This is a rather difficult technologic and physiologic task, but not at all impossible. Some laboratories, including my own, have already developed primitive forms of bio-music. The concept of transforming biological signals into aesthetically acceptable music or art forms theoretically appears to offer exciting new forms of therapy and therapeutic approaches. Music itself has been amply demonstrated to be of invaluable therapeutic assistance, particularly in relieving emotional distress of both emotional problems and the anxieties of real body illnesses.

There is a good bit of evidence to indicate that music is an inherent *physiologic* expression of man. One such characteristic that may be of critical importance to the success of bio-music is that man is capable of remembering long sequences of musically or vocally related items, but his memory for sequences of nonmusically or nonvocally related items (such as noise) is quite short. This characteristic suggests that the degree of voluntary control over physiologic function could be markedly extended by providing bio-feedback information in the form of music. Moreover, brain wave or body music productions would have considerable meaning attached to them, facilitating memory and learning to duplicate large and extended patterns of brain or body action.

In music (or art) the compositions developed by brain wave activity, including muscle and autonomic nervous system activity when desired, during different moods or feeling states, or types of mental activity or states of consciousness, can be of value for therapeutic and research purposes. The subject might listen to his bio-music productions over short intervals and try to classify them according to his subjective mood and sensations. Or paint colored pictures with his body's energy. And he could attempt to duplicate those compositions which express a feeling of well-being, or conversely learn to suppress those he associates with undesirable states. At the same time the researcher can analyze the patterns of physiologic activity which comprise the compositions for content of various types of body activities. Another interesting use of bio-music might lie in determining the significance of dreaming. Individuals could be recorded for their brain wave music during dreaming, then listen to it after waking.

Music and/or art produced by the functions of the mind and body and faithfully translated do not merely represent the person's being, they literally *are* the person's being. The activities of the totality of being can be translated into a dynamic, moving physical form where it can be perceived as part of the external world in a perceptually ordered set of events. The individual can identify with the perceived form because it represents an undivided, one-to-one full representation of himself. Because brain wave patterns and body physiology vary with mood, feelings, mental activity, stress and the total state of being, it barely strains the imagination to believe that the individual can distinguish among the various states of his being, the degree of health or illness, the essence of any mood, the awareness of thought, of reasoning, of feeling. Millions of human beings have caught the moods of Beethoven, the feelings of the Beatles, the passions of Baez. Once the relationships between man's external form as music and his internal state or activity are recognized, the individual may be inherently directed to sustain those external indicators that aid in his survival physically, socially, and psychologically.

The therapeutic community is geared to deal with medical, psychologic, and social problems only when such problems are serious enough to affect the environment. There are, however, millions of human beings who are either not yet seriously ill but who will be unless help is given, or who are no longer seriously ill but who will be again if they do not receive help. Whether the illness is not yet or has just receded, mind-body music or art forms can serve as guides to a safe, operating state of health.

When a person is not well he knows it; *he* is not functioning properly, he doesn't feel well, he is not "in tune" with himself. But he can rarely receive help because the feeling of wrongness, the feelings of discomfort, the feelings of *not* well-being are the most difficult of all feelings to communicate. We understand what it means simply not to feel well, whether in spirit or body, but we can do little to detect a specific reason, to isolate one specific cause.

Mind-body music or art compositions could provide the means to recognize the special circumstances surrounding those "wrong" feelings. When the individual producing his own mind-body music feels good, or less ill, he produces a mind-body composition that he "feels" is right. Those compositions produced when not well are identified as not-quite-well compositions because *he* produced them. Since most of us are motivated to seek and capture those things which are most helpful to our well-being, we can teach ourselves to eliminate the wrong directions of our minds and bodies because the mind-body compositions provide direction.

The well person too has many problems to contend with. He must solve problems of everyday living, of his own behavior, his relationships with others, his concepts of life and eternity. Until now he has been dependent upon either the conclusions arrived at by others or upon the labored questioning of his own reflective self-education. Now, with his own mind-body music, his own compositions, he can inspect his interior self for the rightness of his mind and emotion responses as they relate to the functioning of his being *as a whole*. He can, in large part, be his own guide and teacher chiefly because he will now possess strong and accurate indicators of the degree of harmony between himself and life.

If the individual's illness or neurotic tendencies cause him difficulty in recognizing such relationships, he can enlist the assistance of a therapist-doctor, psychiatrist or psychologist. It should not take long before therapists learn of the similarities between particular forms of mind-body music and their medical or psychological origins.

Mind-body music or art also offers a means of replacing the computer in the diagnosis of illness since such compositions are *patterns* produced by the totality of the person's functioning, i.e., his entire nervous system, body and mind, as they are interacting, rather than the isolated, discrete bits of indirect clues about the interior of man which we now work with in medicine and psychiatry. The music or art has the potential to represent man faithfully as he is inside and a composite picture of his state of being. He recognizes patterns much more easily than he does conglomerates of isolated bits of information. Mind-body music or art patterns may succeed over the computer (whether a real computer or a man organizing bits of information) because they can convey the essence of the being.

Bio-music may also provide a new means of communication. Who can deny the force of human communication through music? From the tribal beat of the African drums to the harmony of Bach to the sophisticated complexities of harmonic structure created by Ives, Stravinsky and Copland, the feelings and thoughts of men and women have been universally communicated through music. One has but to look at the social force produced by rock and roll, the Beatles, acid rock, and the frantic forms of the new music.

The impact of mind-body music is potentially great. Man establishes rapport with other men because he identifies his feelings in other men. He has variously expressed these by means of poetry, music, art, and friendship, but now he has the possibility of communicating directly a unified representation of his being and his feelings without words. The devices he will use are merely extensions of himself; they are not merely representations but describe a totality of man himself.

Man understands patterns. He understands his own whole pattern even though he does not understand its parts. His mind and body function as a unit; when one part is affected, many parts are affected. When one part is made well, other parts are made well. An integrated person rarely has illness; he is a whole pattern in which all parts function in harmony. Now man may be able to communicate directly his harmony or disharmony. It may not take long before man recognizes either in his fellow man. He may be able to communicate his patterns not only to his fellow man, but also to his doctor, his teacher, his neighbor. Inadequate verbal descriptions can be replaced by meaningful, completely truthful messages from the inner self. Even at a fraction of its estimated effectiveness, mind-body music or art could produce a positive influence in solving problems related to the welfare of our society.

Psi and Meta-Psi

The characteristic feature and most exasperating aspect of psychic phenomena, or parapsychology, is its unpredictability. This feature alone, which intrudes upon the orderliness of the rest of the universe, may incite the skepticism prevalent in so many scientists. Yet science itself knows relatively little about normal mind function, and much less than is needed to determine where our minds are and what they are doing. If we know so little about what is normal, how can we know whether paranormal is paranormal or normal. Yet the probabilities are high that psi is not so much unpredictable as it is our inability or failure to ferret out some aspect of psychic phenomena upon which some type of predictability can be based. Most people who are psychics have specialties, such as precognition, psychometry, or clairvoyance, and in this sense, what *kind* of event might happen in the future may be predicted, but it is apparently impossible to predict *when* a psychic event will occur.

There is some hope that bio-feedback can be used to bring at least some psychic ability under voluntary control. If this becomes a reality, it will likely be the most explosive, far-reaching discovery that bio-feedback can make. Psychical researchers and the general public alike have, for years, yearned to find a tangible handle to psychic phenomena. Only today are smatterings of biological research activity beginning to reveal faint clues that there is indeed a brain substrate for supranormal behavior. The research of Honorton and Schmeidler and Lewis with alpha bio-feedback hints at the involvement of brain mechanisms, as does the work of Ullman with psychic dreams and bits of corresponding brain wave changes.

If we accept the premise that our mental and emotional activity does truly originate from or involves our brain cells (and for this there is considerable proof), then it is logical to assume that the psi phenomenon also invokes these same brain cells whatever other means it may use. We assume this because psychic activity involves a change in both mental and emotional activity; otherwise, it could not be integrated, stored, recalled and communicated by human means. If, for example, a sensitive "receives" telepathic information, then somehow that information had to have entry into the universe of the brain cells where the concept or "picture" of the pattern of the information developed in order to be communicated through the usual avenues available to human beings. Even if the psychic information gets into the brain supranaturally, in order to get *out* of the brain to be communicated, it must go through the ordinary channels of brain processing. This means that there is a brain physiologic impression of the psychic experience, and if that impression is there in the brain, then we should be able to find it.

I have suggested the following approach to parapsychologic researchers.* Record as much of the physiologic, particularly brain electrical, activity of proven sensitives for as long as possible. It

---

* Banquet address, "Auto-control of Consciousness," Parapsychological Association Annual Convention, New York City, September 10, 1970.

might take days, weeks, or months, although proven psychics have fairly frequent experiences. Then, whenever a psychic experience has occurred, that physiologic information would be analyzed extensively to isolate special events that are not found when psychic experiences did not occur. It may, of course, also be necessary to measure as many environmental factors as feasible such as weather, nearby electromagnetic fields, body electrical fields, as well as the psychologic and sociologic characteristics of the psychic and their interaction with the researchers. But if the brain truly does contribute to thought and communication and emotion, the chances of finding a characteristic, accurate, and reliable predictor of psychic activity would seem to be fairly good.

Suppose that one biologic indicator is found, then where are we? On the brink of a new adventure for bio-feedback and prepared for the most exciting excursion for mankind. For the indicator would be much more than just an indicator of psychic activity, it would be a superb candidate for bio-feedback. It would be coaxed into electronic circuits and returned to the sensitive to give him information about what his mind-body is doing during psychic experience. And as with any bio-feedback, the information can be used to learn to control the experience. No doubt there might be a scarcity of information because of the relative infrequency of the experiences; however, once a reliable indicator of the experience is found, it can be simulated. The researcher has a model; he can supplement the spontaneous biologic accompaniments of psychic activity by simulated bio-feedback. Or, it seems quite possible that the indicators or biologic changes accompanying psychic experiences actually do occur in attenuated form even when a psychic experience is not recognized and fails to come to consciousness for communication; the indicators may be sufficiently present in other bio-information that they can be extracted and used.

Another fascinating conjectural use of bio-feedback may lie in the exploration and voluntary control of the remarkable energy conversions that may occur in some types of psychic phenomena. Science may have prematurely judged such phenomena. Evidence from the Iron Curtain countries seems to indicate that there may be ways to utilize bioelectric body energy or mental energy to interact empirically with events or elements that can also be empirically observed, as in telekinesis. It appears that mental or psychologic energy is in some way transformed into physical energy. In these instances, too, documentation of the accompanying biological changes may offer the way to uncover key effects, and these in turn could be used as bio-feedback signals both to identify the energy conversion process more specifically and to learn to make the conversion efficient by voluntary control.

The excitement that bio-feedback has generated is deserved. It is a powerful and effective tool for the future of the mind. Its potential may be unlimited, or it may be merely a step toward a new reality. Beyond this we cannot predict. What new resources man will find within the depths of his mind cannot be foretold. One can but guess that new forces of mental energy will be unleashed, for we are all familiar with the repressive constraints exerted upon our minds during the entire age of materialism and technology. Now technology has come full circle and is allowing us to begin the exploration of the recesses of our inner space.

Appendixes

A. *Six of One, Half a Dozen of the Other*

At the present rate of research interest and progress, along with public interest, the near future should see the availability of convenient, sophisticated instruments to assist in learning the self-control of certainly most of the major body functions, and perhaps as well an assortment of instruments specialized for the more obscure or rare body functions that only occasionally become troublesome.* At the same time current clinical studies are bringing to light more and more efficient ways to ensure the success of bio-feedback procedures.

How medicine or psychology or biological science will make instruments and treatment regimens available to the public is already a subject of controversy. Bio-feedback has posed quite new problems for medical authority; it seems to be neither fish nor fowl. It is not a drug, a chemical foreign to the body that needs years of extensive study to prove its safety and efficiency, nor is it a purely psychologic technique which can be used by thousands of psychotherapists and counselors after only a short course of instruction. Some research experts, sequestered in highly specialized areas and unaware of the broad scope of bio-feedback and its already countless accomplishments, are inclined to relegate the effectiveness of bio-feedback solely to the research domain for use as an experimental tool. They defend their failure to advocate or even attempt clinical use of bio-feedback by citing a lack of overpowering evidence for the efficiency of bio-feedback as a therapeutic measure. It is of some importance to recognize that this apparent lack is a function of the researchers themselves. There is, for example, a paradoxical tendency among researchers

---

* Unless the techniques of bio-feedback are improperly applied, or instruments are inadequate for accurate feedback, or the set and setting of the experience act at cross-purpose. Many such faults have occurred in early bio-feedback work and will probably continue until the processes of bio-feedback are designed specifically for individual body needs and objectives.

409

to use procedures in clinical studies that were designed to test theories in laboratories and are, more often than not, inappropriate to the clinical condition under study as well as impractical and imprecise.

Possibly the largest obstacle that some researchers have had in acknowledging the validity and efficiency of bio-feedback is its inseparability from the naturally endowed, normal operating ability of ordinary human beings. Daily the average human being receives bio-feedback signals from his gut to notify central control that commands to ingest food should be issued. Or central control receives signals that the exercising body should dissipate its heat by perspiration. All that bio-feedback does is insert a technical device between body substance and central control.

It is the Gestalt of bio-feedback that confirms its validity. Several hundred scientific studies have demonstrated the fact of voluntary control over all types of body functions. Bio-feedback's broad spectrum of effectiveness demonstrates its fundamental and universal nature. The scientific bickering and criticism that do exist can invariably be found to be insular to a particular theoretical point. When negative results and conclusions have been cited, they can generally be found to indicate more about the experimental conditions than about the effectiveness of the bio-feedback procedure itself. A powerful testimonial to the reality of bio-feedback is found in observations that have been made for each physiologic function in which the amount and type and quality of both bio-feedback and other intelligent information given to the subjects or patients was optimized. These studies clearly demonstrated that for many body functions and under many different conditions nourishment of the mental being is the basic element in the learning of voluntary control.

The new dimension that bio-feedback brings to the evolving mind is the mind's ability to use information to control the material substance of man's being. More directly, bio-feedback may have provided the instrument to excise the cataracts of scientific vision that so long have prevented participation of the mind of man in the survival and evolution of his own consciousness and psyche.

The dangers of bio-feedback can lie in no other place but the mind of man himself. The instruments and devices used in bio-feedback, provided they transfer high-fidelity information, do nothing more than externalize intellectualized symbols of parts of the body's interior activity. Body systems and organs do not function by means of feedback lights or tones or oscilloscope beams of changing electrical currents; they function by the dynamic interplay of all that is both elemental and complex in the worlds of chemistry and physics. And the unknown of the mind. Bio-feedback signals are artificially isolated abstract symbols, poor substitutes to represent the perpetual, diffusive transmutations of the world within. Yet, perhaps because the abstractions are products of the mind, the mind has little trouble identifying the reality that the symbols represent.

The question of the safety of bio-feedback is thus primarily a question of whether the mind can, by its conscious or subconscious intellect, cope with information about itself and its body without bringing itself to harm. In this respect it is unlike all other medical and psychologic procedures. It appears to be strictly a function of information. If the user of bio-feedback, or the patient, is not properly instructed or is poorly informed about the process, the phenomenon, and the biology involved, he may bring harm to himself by misinterpreting and end by practicing to deceive himself. Such may be the hazards of evolution.

B. *Further Notes on the Basics of Skin Talk*

By isolating all of the particular parts of the waves, it was possible to begin relating skin electrical events to the matter of sweating. As it turned out, the coincidence between skin talking and sweating was not at all what it had seemed at first. Measuring the skin voltage, it was found that the first, small negative deflection heralded the pre-secretory activity of sweat glands, as if the emotional signals from the brain were fast-talking the sweat glands to get ready for an emotional surge. This caused some small shift in the chemical relationships between the sweat glands and the skin where the recording electrodes were, and this warning of coming events was signaled through the recording system to the pens. The opposite positive and large wave which followed was discovered not to be related to sweating, but to some hydration-dehydration change going on in the skin caused by the sweating, and having to do with the movement of ions. Each chemical change was a reflection of a different type of brain information and caused by impulses coming down from the brain to skin cells. As more parts of the story were uncovered, the more extensive and complex it became. As with the unidirectional waves of resistance and conductance, the bidirectional waves of the skin's own voltage were different in how quickly waves occurred, how large they were, how frequently they occurred, how long they lasted. Even the way the wave returned to its resting position was found to contain quite different kinds of information. If the wave, or pen deflection, returned quickly, it was associated with the positive deflection and the period when sweat was being resorbed, which has been interpreted as reflecting a mobilization for goal-directed behavior (to be discussed later). A slow descent of the pen, indicating recovery of the skin responding, was found to be associated with the negative deflection and with sweating. There were other differences. Many of the skin electrical waves which occurred spontaneously did not resemble the waves which were intentionally elicited by stimuli, either physical or emotional. And there is a component of the skin response that still stumps the researchers, so that one aspect of the response remains unknown as far as its underlying body biochemistry and nervous supply is concerned.

Drugs, particularly those chemicals affecting or involved in processes of the transmission of nerve messages, were used to uncover what parts of the nervous system were involved in skin responses. A rather curious circumstance was found; the nerves that transmitted the messages were those of the sympathetic division of the ANS, but the chemical transmitter was that of the parasympathetic division of the ANS. Since some of the same nerves supplied the blood vessels in the skin, and the changes in the vascular beds are easily brought about by emotional activity, having the same groups of nerves involved in these two separate but related body functions tended to complicate the decoding of skin language. Nonetheless, the two different body activities were finally separated and found to be largely independent of each other, although the vascular change did change fluid content and that changed the basic electrical properties of the skin. The use of chemicals in the study of skin activity also revealed that the sweating brought on by arousal or anxiety states served a further purpose, that of protecting the skin against mechanical injury, and moreover assisted in modulating the sensitivity of the skin to pain quite independently of sweating but complexly related to the electrical activity of the skin. The contribution of the changes in the vascular bed to the well-being of the skin were also integral to its ability to assist in the regulation of body temperature, and this was another physiologic factor that had to be dissected out of the skin talk vocabulary.

C. *Boning Up on Learning Theory*

In the Western world the dominion of the Scientific Method over explorations into human behavior crystallized with the physiologist Pavlov's well-known experiments with a salivating, hungry dog, food, and bell (originally, actually a metronome). This was the first and became the classical example of "teaching" the involuntary, life-supporting systems of man to respond on cue. It would not be long until disciples of Pavlov undertook to "teach" the electrical system of the skin, the heart rate, blood vessels, and other "automatic" body activity by similar methods of rewards, shocks, buzzers, and bells. Work with these more internal organs only awaited development of adequately sensitive instruments to monitor their special types of changes. In the twenties a few perceptive American and British emissaries returned from training experiences with Pavlov with the technical knowledge and facility for the first time to attack the inner mechanisms of externally expressed behavior in a systematic way. They returned with an exciting new model of behavior, and like kids with new electric trains or erector sets, they set about to vary the model in every way the basic parts allowed.

The scientific events in the United States leading to the discovery that autonomic body functions could come under voluntary control grew out of an interesting dispute which arose some thirty years after Pavlov's work when Skinner developed a second model of conditioned behavior which was equally as amenable as Pavlov's to ready experimental manipulation. Although a great deal of learning derives from instinct, imitation, modeling, habit chaining, cognition, etc., these modes of learning are much more difficult to study under controlled laboratory conditions. Throughout this century American experimental psychologists have occupied themselves chiefly with the two learning models, Pavlovian and Skinnerian.

A reasonable definition of learning is that learning is a process by which the performance of an organism (or part of an organism) is changed by its experience. A large amount of learning, particularly that which becomes a habitual way of behaving, can be reduced to some simple and quite general formulations, provided they are based upon laboratory observations in which conditions are controlled by the researcher. In a nutshell, these simple formulations (for the simplest kind of learning models) say that according to the Pavlovian model, a response can be transferred from one stimulus to another, i.e., from one environmental change or event to another, while according to the Skinnerian model any experimenter-selected behavioral activity emitted by an organism can be made to recur by the proper reinforcement. The process for both forms of learning is known as conditioning, a word and process now so well known that it is a part of everyday vocabulary. To learning theorists and practitioners of experimental psychology conditioning comes in these two primary forms: classical (Pavlovian) and operant (Skinnerian).

Classical conditioning generally refers to simple or primitive reflexes. The adherents of classical conditioning work exclusively with an external stimulus to elicit or *provoke* naturally occurring responses of the animal. Learning is demonstrated experimentally by using two stimuli, one of which causes some innate response of the organism, such as salivation, tearing, coughing, the knee jerk—or any natural body reaction—and a second stimulus which does not cause such a response and which under ordinary circumstances has no significance to the organism. If the second signal is given in some close time relationship with the primary stimulus, the response caused by the primary stimulus gradually becomes associated with the secondary signal. The objective of course is to transfer the natural response so that it occurs when the secondary signal is given.

The following classical conditioning experiment describes the procedure used in thousands of learning theory experiments and, as we shall see, the exact procedure used to try to condition skin electrical activity, the heart and other body activities in human experiments. (As you scan the description, note the amount of bio-feedback information contained in the experimental situation, the emphasis on physical manipulations, and the lack of emphasis on the behavioral state or mind-state of the animal.) The experimenter arranges a shock to be given to the skin of the leg and regulates the intensity of the current, the length of time the shock is applied, and the time intervals between shocks. He does this to find a schedule and intensity which ensure a leg jerk every time. Then he introduces a second stimulus which has no significance or relationship to the reflex being studied and usually is a tone or light signal, sometimes a touch. This second, or neutral, stimulus is "paired" with the stimulus causing the innate response of the organism. It can precede, follow, or overlap time-wise the physiologic stimulus. After a number of pairings, sometimes as few as one or two or sometimes as many as several hundred, the leg will jerk in response to the second signal, the tone or light, in a way which resembles the leg jerking in response to the electric shock. When this happens it is said that the leg jerk reflex has been conditioned, it has been "learned."

What it has learned is a moot question and whatever it is it doesn't last long. In order for the second signal to continue to be effective, the first or shock signal must be continued frequently, otherwise the response to the neutral signal falters and disappears. In fact, the prime criterion for effectiveness of transfer of response from primary to secondary stimulus is the number of responses produced by the secondary stimulus after the primary one has been discontinued.

A great deal of ambiguity has arisen over the years in interpretation of the classical conditioning model of learning. It could be demonstrated in a single-celled organism where it strains the imagination to implicate "higher mental activity" in the learning process. Yet when a Pavlovian disciple rings a bell just before giving food to a dog and finds the dog associating the two events and salivating in anticipation of food merely at the sound of the bell, then the "simpleness" of the learning is confounded by the obvious but currently unde-fined participation of complex brain mechanisms. For several decades psy-chologists themselves have tended to ignore the intervening effects of the higher nervous system on elicited behaviors, viewing the internal mechanisms of the organism as relatively simple mechanical events. It has only been recently that "cognitive" intervention and mediation have been identified as indis-pensable elements in most learning, even of simple reflexes or autonomic body behavior. It is doubtful that Pavlov ever intended to leave his simplified but experimentally productive model of animal behavior at a primitive level. It is not generally remembered that he elaborated many novel and testable con-cepts about the role of higher nervous activity in behavior. Yet many be-havioral scientists seem to have taken him at his experimental word.

The late Gregory Razran, one of only two experimental psychologists with long dual experience in both Russian and American behavioral research, put it very bluntly: the 1927–1928 translations of Pavlov's work, "showed American neobehaviorists, irrespective of brand, what might be done with learning con-fined to the study of an organism by one simple method: (1) the vast amount of interrelated (parametric) information that could be obtained, (2) the vast opportunity to systematize—or extrapolate—this information. As is known, no American neo-behaviorist has verified the work of Pavlov with the method and organism that he had used, but all were quick to parallel him. B. F. Skinner (1938) did the paralleling by replacing salivation with lever-pressing." He concluded, "The main establishment of present-day American psychology is sharply severed into two antagonist, yet in one sense allied, camps: unevolu-tionary conditioners, for whom the minds of worms and men are the minds of rats, and unevolutionary cognitionists, to whom the minds of worms and rats are the minds of men."

Razran's words are difficult but his prejudice is obvious. It is based upon the fact that the most logical, parsimonious sequence of increasing complexity of behavior is an evolutionary one. In 1935 Razran wrote, "It would really be a curious freak of organismic evolution, the outstanding feature of which is the evolution of the brain and that special modifiability called learning capacity, if the laws of the modifiability remained fixed and did not evolve." The way I translate this is, "The outstanding feature of living creatures is the evolution of the brain and that special ability of the brain for learning. It would, therefore, be a curious freak in the evolution of living beings if the laws of learning remained fixed and did not also evolve."

Although it was the experimental psychologist Edward Lee Thorndike who began laying the groundwork for the second model of conditioned behavior around the turn of the century, it was not until the late 1930s that Skinner demonstrated concretely and convincingly that a "reversal" of the classical conditioning procedure could also lead to control of behavior. The new technique created a new storm of research activity. The new twist, the reversal of procedure (what Razran called paralleling Pavlov), was essentially to let the animal *select* the reward he wanted from an assortment provided by the experimenter. The reward was that item in the environment which reinforced the particular behavior employed to obtain the reward. In other words, for any behavior which the experimenter desired to be duplicated, and so analyzed by the experimenter, the animal probed its environment until, by trial and error, he discovered the reward for performing that specific behavior. If the animal was suitably motivated, then it continued to repeat that behavior to obtain the reward. In most cases motivation has been ensured by altering the animal's physical state or environment. The now well-known example of operant conditioning is that of the rat who is hungry and is placed in a small cage with a lever. If and when he presses the lever, food is delivered to him. It is, for practical purposes, a *sine qua non* that the rat must be starved. Obviously, if he is starved, he is most likely in a state of almost constant hunger and searching for food, and as he searches, he very likely will hit the lever and presto, there comes the food. When food arrives each time he presses the lever and there is no other way to obtain food, then the animal soon "learns" to press the lever to get his reward of food.

From a mechanistic point of view, much human behavior can indeed be called operant in type, particularly if we use a bare-bones definition which applies only to fundamental body processes and ignores mental influence or defines mental influence as simply a more complex but basically similar physiologic process. That is, if we receive a reward for doing something, we are more likely than not to repeat that behavior. In the learning theories we are discussing, nearly every stimulus (or external event which causes a change in behavior) is fitted into a simple hierarchy of rewards depending upon how it gives pleasure or satisfies the organism. The external events may be either rewards or the taking away of rewards, and may be primary or secondary. The events that deny rewards are generally termed aversive, since most organisms attempt to escape encounters with unpleasant events. Another terminology describes the behavioral reinforcement properties of the external events: if the event brings out a desired behavior, it is called positive reinforcement; if the event suppresses a specifically designated behavior, it is called negative reinforcement. Then there are secondary reinforcers of behavior. Pavlov initially encountered a host of these, as do conditioning experimenters to this day. If, for example, the experiment is instrumented to deliver a food reward, the noise of the mechanism delivering the food can also serve as a signal that food is on the way. Secondary reinforcers are of such common occurrence that they are often overlooked. Dogs and cats, for example, often "know" what you are going to do some time before you actually do it. It takes only one bad experience at the vet's, and on the way for the next visit, anywhere from leaving the house to waiting in the office, the animal may begin to shake or balk. Some change in the animal's environment (including perhaps your own behavior) was associated backward in time and served as a secondary reinforcement, the primary one being either the vet himself or his office.

In actual laboratory experiments, however, operant conditioning procedures are rather severely restrained, largely to allow the investigator to isolate a particular aspect of behavior for study. In real life a wide variety of events can serve as rewards, which makes this model useful in deriving applications modifying human behavior.

The practical difference between the two conditioning concepts of learning lies in the relationship between the reinforcement and the behavior that is reinforced. Reinforcement is an operational definition. Most experimental psychologists employ reinforcements for their value as rewards (either their presence or absence), but there are other theorists who hold out for other interpretations about the function of rewards, particularly those relating to the information-containing role of rewards, as in bio-feedback.

In classical conditioning the reinforcement is that stimulus or event which automatically triggers some inborn behavioral response. The trigger is forced upon the organism so often that almost any other selected secondary stimulus given in association will come to produce that same innate response. But once the reinforcing trigger is taken away, the effectiveness of the secondary event quickly fails.

In operant conditioning almost anything can function as a reinforcement, but items in the environment *do* function or qualify as reinforcements only if they become effective in eliciting the desired response. Operant conditioning is almost exclusively a reward model of behavior. If an animal is destined to receive a shock should he fail to perform some desired activity, his reward is the escape or avoidance of the shock when he performs correctly. In operant conditioning, too, forgetting is rapid when performance is no longer rewarded.

In classical conditioning some association has to take place between the two types of stimuli so that in a sense the animal must "learn," i.e., come to change his behavior. If he performs when he perceives the warning signal (the conditioning signal), he is then successful in obtaining the reward of something he accepts for certain reasons (water when thirsty) or of avoiding something unpleasant (the shock). The essential question is *when* (i.e., when he should respond) he learns.

In operant conditioning also the animal must make an association between two events which relate what particular behavioral activity is successful in obtaining a reward. The essential question here, however, is *what* (i.e., which behavior of his repertoire) he learns.

The essential difference between classical and operant conditioning is thus often claimed to be a matter of *when* versus *what*, i.e., when a behavior occurs versus what behavior occurs. In classical conditioning the experimenter determines *when* the behavioral reinforcement is to be given (i.e., when a food reward is given following the warning or alerting signal), whereas in operant conditioning the reinforcement occurs when the animal performs correctly (i.e., the experimenter determines what behavioral act can obtain the reward). Theorists generally fail to point out that in operant conditioning, although the experimenter does not determine *when* the reward is given, he allows the rat so few options for correct performance that once the rat discovers the means to the reward, the timing of the delivery of the reward is dependent in part upon the physiologic needs of the animal and the timing of these needs as well as the animal making an association between *when* to do *what*.

The most useful difference between the two types of conditioning is the way in which the reinforcement of desired behaviors can be used. In classical conditioning the reinforcement is by the stimulus causing the innate response, and that is all that it can reinforce. In operant conditioning, the reinforcement or reward can strengthen any immediately preceding response, and the same reward can, moreover, be used to strengthen many quite different responses.

What operant conditioning procedures have allowed is a way to measure performance once it has occurred. Some theorists point out that if an animal finds that pressing a certain lever will produce food, then no matter how many times he presses the lever he is not learning anything new.

When operant conditioning came into vogue, difficulties immediately arose in using it for anything considered automatic and involuntary. Somehow the conclusion had become accepted that classical conditioning held for simple reflexes and the "inferior" involuntary, automatic body functions that didn't require complex action of the nervous system, and that operant conditioning applied only to higher, more complex functions requiring integration by higher neural function. The concept apparently arose largely because operant conditioning techniques allowed the reward or reinforcement to select the behavior desired for control from the repertoire of the behaving organism as a whole.

Throughout this century, until the concept that mental processes may influence even the most primal of body function began to be supported by laboratory evidence, it has been that simplest kind of learning, conditioning, which was used almost exclusively in research dealing with "learning" by physiologic processes. It has been recognized by some psychological theorists that psychologic laws established by watching animal behavior do not necessarily apply to human behavior; however, the main thrust of experimental learning endeavors, particularly by physiologic processes, has been according to the principles of conditioning as determined in animals.

The application of conditioning techniques to human behavior, however, generally entails change, often considerable change, in the procedures to produce successful results. Such changes raise questions about the relevance to the understanding of behavior of behavioral research that is constrained by requirements to quantify behavior in terms of purely external, purely physical events. Why, for example, does the association between the nonsignificant event (the conditioning stimulus) and the innate response, or the association between performance and reward, fail to be stored in memory the way nonlaboratory, infrequently reinforced associations are so readily stored and easily recalled in both animals and human beings? Is it that some unlooked for, internal intelligence is continuously making evaluations and judgments? Perhaps a rat also may evaluate the significance of his situation in terms of *his* heredity, his environment, and his experience (not those of the experimenter), and perhaps judges the experiments to be a waste of energy and decides to forget the experience as irrelevant to reasonable behavior.

It is the interpretation and extrapolation of animal conditioning studies that are scientifically violated when applied to human learning that causes real problems. What we have discussed here has derived from studies of relatively simple animal or physiologic behavior functions under highly controlled conditions. Animals have been considered to be limited in the number or type of events which they consider to be rewarding or useful. But again, we are not animal mind-readers, and perhaps it is our inability to communicate with the animal that complicates our study of behavior rather than a lack of thought-type process in the animal. On the one side, study of behavior in human beings is complicated by the errors of subjective, feeling colorations, while on the other side, the animal side, we have little means to discover, or we choose to ignore, any subjective phenomena at all in animals. Although unwarranted extrapolations from animal studies have been applied in the psychology and education of human beings, the procedures and concepts have been applied straightforwardly in "teaching" the body's physiologic processes. It is whether the latter application is warranted that is the subject of this book.

D. *Voluntary Heart Rate Control or Muscle Reflex?*

Many problems arose, however; an energetic and conservative school of researchers insisted that it was not the ANS that was being directly controlled; the ANS was responding as a secondary effect to a conditioned learning by muscles or respiration (also muscle). These researchers conducted many experiments to prove their point. It is true that one of the truly confounding factors present in all of the experiments on heart rate control is the influence of undetected muscle activity on the part of the subject.

Paul Obrist and co-workers have provided some powerful research to support this concept. First they pointed out that there are always "anticipatory" changes in heart rate which are coincident with somato-motor activity. Later they found a metabolic link betwen cardiac and body muscle systems that related to the behavior of both systems, suggesting a common (neural, biochemical) mediator within the central nervous system. Then, by observing numerous indices of muscle activity, they have generally found an absence of heart rate learning provided the various somatic influences were eliminated and learning only when muscle activity became conditioned simultaneously with heart rate. They did discover, however, an influence which modified heart rate that was independent of both somatic activity and the effect of the reward or reinforcement which elicited the conditioned responses.

It is argued by many of the conditioning schools of experimental psychologists that the autonomic nervous system responds continuously and somewhat passively to muscle activity. The mildest muscle tension or the slightest irregularity of respiration can "induce" changes in the ANS, one being a change in heart rate. Unless the experimenter has electrodes on all of the body's muscles recording muscle tension, he can only infer muscle tension from subjective reports. Muscle tension is always dynamically shifting. It is an *ad absurdum* argument. The influence of respiration is also troublesome. If the breath is held for a few seconds, the heart speeds up; if breathing is fast, the heart slows, and these changes also occur on smaller scale for every respiratory effort made. These types of concurrent changes, physiologically intrinsic to the organism, are difficult to weed out from the rest of the influences. Nonetheless, some experimenters were able to show that, on the whole, respiration had little to do with voluntary control of heart rate. When the subject's task was to sustain periods of increased heart rate and then sustain periods of decreased rate, breathing patterns remained relatively unaltered. Other investigators asked their subjects to either over-breathe or under-breathe, and they still obtained desired changes in heart rate.

The problems with heart rate control experiments continued to multiply. It soon became apparent that most of the investigators were comparing the degree of heart rate change to a level which was induced by the experiment itself, not to the *normal* level of the subject's heart. And taking that into consideration changed the look of heart rate control quite a bit. When Mary Headrick and others compared so-called learned changes to normal heart rates, they found significant changes when the task was to increase the heart rate but virtually no change when the subjects were to slow the heart. The general finding that speeding up the heart is easier to learn is logically related to the natural response of the heart to situations containing elements of fear or anxiety. Anytime a subject is exposed to the unknowns of an experiment, and it deals with *his* body, he is anxious and somewhat fearful. Furthermore, the majority of human beings have sympathetic dominance, the tendency to speed their hearts under such circumstances.

Moreover, the Headrick study is the single study to date in which the sensation of a marked voluntary increased heart rate was elicited from the subject, rather than simply asking the subject: "How did you do it?" This one report indicated that the subject experienced tension, uneasiness, and something akin to anxiety.

E. *Faith Is a Safe "Drug"*

Not long ago I heard a radio medical reporter recounting a story about the origin of the placebo. It was such a delightful story and so illustrative of the controversies surrounding the placebo effect that I did not check its authenticity for fear of destroying the importance of the message. It seems, the story went, that in the early years of this century when patent medicines were in vogue and a booming business venture, certain legislators and medical experts decided to prove that most patent medicines were worthless because they were either completely ineffective as drugs, or if they were effective, it was because of the alcohol content. Congressional hearings on the matter were arranged under the leadership of Senator Placebo. The Senator insisted that the hearings be closed to the public, but reporters' interviews with the witnesses called soon revealed that all expert testimony concluded that the patent medicines were indeed worthless. There began to be a hue and cry for a hearings report. The agitation for the report grew; the safety of the public was at stake; the Senate should recommend vigorous legislative action to ban their sale. Finally Senator Placebo made his report.

There will be no report, he said, I have destroyed all records of the hearings. No medical evidence was given to prove the medicines were in any way harmful to human beings. They are safe, so why should I deny their effect? Belief is as powerful as drugs. And ever after, drugs with no effects were called placebos.

Today, some fifty years later, there is a revival of the same effort. The FDA is actively attacking the sale of over-the-counter remedies that cannot be proved in rigorous laboratory and clinical studies to have a discernible effect on the physical ailment they claim to affect. Medical expertise concludes that such drugs fail to produce the specific physical effects used to judge the efficiency of powerful chemical agents. Powerful chemicals are sold by prescription only because they also produce undesirable effects when used without expert direction. Such one-sided emphasis and insistence on permitting for sale only chemicals with measurable effects by currently known testing procedures acknowledges only the absolutes of physical or physiologic change and fails to consider the interaction between physical nature and the psychologic and social milieu of the suffering patient. It also fails to consider that many illnesses are psychosomatic, caused almost exclusively by emotional distress, and that faith and belief can relieve and ameliorate the distress as well as, if not perhaps better than, chemicals.

It is as if the FDA and medical zealots are waging war on belief. Ignored is the subtle effect accompanying drug use of paying attention to and trying to become aware of body effects that in itself may, through subconscious action, prove beneficial. Mind-body is not divided. Many sufferers suffer because of emotional deceptions, and if so, they can recover the same way. On the other hand, there is no evidence to indicate that despite the ineffectiveness of the drugs, the attention and awareness of the physical problem that surround the concept of self-treatment do not in fact perform an important recovery function by virtue of the same kind of willpower that appears to be so large a part of the bio-feedback process. If the drug is nothing more than a catalyst for willpower and a vehicle for belief, why must authority deprive a public of the rightful exercise of its own mind abilities?

Bibliography

CHAPTERS 2 AND 3: Skin Talk

Andreassi, J. L. Effects of regular and irregular signal patterns upon skin conductance and reaction time. *Percept Motor Skills,* 1966, *23:*975–978.

Archer, J., Jr.; Fiester, T.; Kagan, N.; Rate, L.; Spierling, T.; and Van Noord, R. New method for education, treatment, and research in human interaction. *J Counseling Psychol,* 1972, *19:*275–281.

Averill, J. R. Autonomic response patterns during sadness and mirth. *Psychophysiology,* 1969, *5:*399.

Ax, A. F. and Bamford, J. L. Validation of a psychophysiological test of aptitude for learning social motives. *Psychophysiology,* 1968, *5:*316.

Badia, P. and Defran, R. H. Orienting responses and GSR conditioning: A dilemma. *Psychol Rev,* 1970, *77:*171–181.

Barland, G. H. and Raskin, D. C. An experimental study of field techniques in "lie detection." *Psychophysiology,* 1972, *9:*275.

Beloff, J.; Cowles, M.; and Bate, D. Autonomic reactions to emotive stimuli under sensory and extrasensory conditions of presentation. *J Amer Soc Psychical Res,* 1970, *64:*313–319.

Berlyne, D. E. and Borsa, D. M. Uncertainty and the orientation reaction. *Percept Psychophysica,* 1968, *3:*77–79.

Bernal, M. E. and Miller, W. H. Electrodermal and cardiac responses of schizophrenic children to sensory stimuli. *Psychophysiology,* 1970, *7:*155.

Bernstein, A. S. Phasic electrodermal orienting response in chronic schizophrenics: II. Response to auditory signals of varying intensity. *J Abnorm Psychol,* 1970, *75:*146–156.

Brotsky, S. Classical conditioning of the galvanic skin response to verbal concepts. *J Exp Psychol,* 1968, *70:*244–253.

Broughton, R. J.; Poire, R.; and Tassinari, C. A. The electrodermogram (Tarchanoff Effect) during sleep. *Electroenceph Clin Neurophysiol,* 1965, *18:*691–708.

Burdick, J. A. Autonomic lability and neuroticism. *J Psychosom Res*, 1966, 9:339–342.

Burstein, K. R.; Fenz, W. D.; Bergeron, J.; and Epstein, S. A comparison of skin potential and skin resistance responses as measures of emotional responsivity. *Psychophysiology*, 1965, 2:14.

Campos, J. J. and Johnson, H. J. The effects of verbalization instructions and visual attention on heart rate and skin conductance. *Psychophysiology*, 1966, 2:305.

Carey, C. A.; Schell, A. M.; and Grings, W. W. Effect of ISI and reversal manipulations on cognitive control of the conditioned GSR. *Psychophysiology*, 1972, 9:266.

Christie, M. J. and Venables, P. H. Effects on "basal" skin potential level of varying the concentration of an external electrolyte. *J Psychosom Res*, 1971, 15:343–348.

Cole, G. H. M.; Spurgeon, N.; and Sipprelle, C. N. Extinction of a classically conditioned GSR as a function of awareness. *Behav Res Ther*, 1967, 5: 331–337.

Cole, G. H. M.; Gale, A.; and Kline, P. Personality and habituation of the orienting reaction: tonic and response measures of electrodermal activity. *Psychophysiology*, 1971, 8:54.

Cole, G. H. M. and Gale, A. Physiological reactivity as a predictor of performance in a vigilance task. *Psychophysiology*, 1971, 8:594.

Cook, S. and Harris, R. E. The verbal conditioning of the galvanic skin reflex. *J Exp Psychol*, 1937, 21:202–210.

Corah, N. L. and Tomkiewicz, R. L. Classical conditioning of the electrodermal response with novel stimuli. *Psychophysiology*, 1971, 8:143–148.

Corteen, R. S. Skin conductance changes and word recall. *Brit J Psychol*, 1969, 60:81–84.

Coules, J. and Avery, D. L. Human performance and basal skin conductance in a vigilance-type task with and without knowledge of results. *Percept Motor Skills*, 1966, 23:1295–1302.

Craig, K. D. and Wood, K. Physiological differentiation of direct and vicarious affective arousal. *Canad J Behav Sci*, 1970, 1:98–105.

Crider, A.; Shapiro, D.; and Tursky, B. Reinforcement of spontaneous electrodermal activity. *J Comp Physiol Psychol*, 1966, 61:20–27.

Darrow, C. W. Problems in the use of the galvanic skin response (GSR) as an index of cerebral function: implications of the latent period. *Psychophysiology*, 1967, 3:389–396.

Darrow, C. W. Differences in the physiological reactions to sensory and ideational stimuli. *Psychol Bull*, 1929, 26:185–201.

Darrow, C. W. and Gullickson, G. R. The peripheral mechanism of the galvanic skin response. *Psychophysiology*, 1970, 6:597–600.

Defran, R. H.; Badia, P.; and Lewis, P. Stimulus control over operant galvanic skin responses. *Psychophysiology*, 1969, 6:101–106.

Dengerink, H. A. and Taylor, S. P. Multiple responses with differential properties in delayed galvanic skin response conditioning: A review. *Psychophysiology,* 1971, 8:348.

Dickson, H. and McGinnies, E. Affectivity in the arousal of attitudes as measured by galvanic skin response. *Amer J Psychol,* 1966, 79:584–589.

Docter, R. F. and Friedman, L. F. Thirty-day stability of spontaneous galvanic skin responses in man. *Psychophysiology,* 1966, 2:311–315.

Dureman, I. and Palshammer, A. Differences in tracking skill and psychophysiological activation dynamics in children high or low in persistence in schoolwork. *Psychophysiology,* 1970, 7:95.

Edelberg, R. Electrical properties of the skin. In *Methods in Psychophysiology,* Clinton C. Brown, ed. Baltimore: Williams & Wilkins, 1967.

Edelberg, R. The information content of the recovery limb of the electrodermal response. *Psychophysiology,* 1970, 6:527.

Edleman, R. I. Effects of differential afferent feedback on instrumental GSR conditioning. *J Psychol,* 1970, 74:3–14.

Edwards, D. C. and Alsip, J. E. Intake-rejection, verbalization, and affect: effects on heart rate and skin conductance. *Psychophysiology,* 1969, 6:6.

Elias, M. F. Heart rate, skin potential response, and latency of overt response, as indicators of problem recognition and solution. *Psychonom Sci,* 1970, 18:337–339.

Epstein, S. Heart rate, skin conductance, and intensity ratings during experimentally induced anxiety: habituation within and among days. *Psychophysiology,* 1971, 8:319.

Fisher, L. E.; Kotses, H.; and Christie, D. J. Negro-white differences in GSR response components and experimenter race effects. *Psychophysiology,* 1972, 9:279.

Fletcher, J. E. The orienting response as an index of mass communication effect. *Psychophysiology,* 1971, 8:699.

Forbes, T. W. Problems in measurement of electrodermal phenomena—choice of method and phenomena—potential, impedance, resistance. *Psychophysiology,* 1964, 1:26–30.

Fowler, R. L. and Kimmel, H. D. Operant conditioning of the GSR. *J Exp Psychol,* 1962, 63:563–567.

Fowles, D. C. and Venables, P. H. The reduction of palmar skin potential by epidermal hydration. *Psychophysiology,* 1970, 7:254.

Freeman, G. L. The galvanic phenomenon and conditioned responses. *J Gen Psychol,* 1930, 3:529–539.

Fried, R.; Friedman, M.; and Welch, L. High and low anxiety and GSR adaptation. *Psychonom Sci,* 1967, 9:635–636.

Fuhrer, M. J. and Baer, P. E. Cognitive processes in differential GSR conditioning: effects of a masking task. *Amer J Psychol,* 1969, 82:168–180.

Furedy, J. J. Novelty and the measurement of the GSR. *J Exp Psychol,* 1968, 74:501–503.

Furedy, J. J. Electrodermal recovery time as a supra sensitive autonomic index of anticipated intensity of threatened shock. *Psychophysiology*, 1972, 9: 281–282.

Gale, A.; Bull, R.; and Haslum, M. Cumulative expectancy, subjective report of alertness and electrodermal activity. *Psychophysiology*, 1972, 9: 383–392.

Gavalas, R. J. Operant reinforcement of an automatic response: two studies. *J Exp Anal Behav*, 1967, 10:119–130.

Germana, J. and Chernault, G. Patterns of galvanic skin responses to signal and non-signal stimuli. *Psychophysiology*, 1968, 5:284.

Goldstein, M. J.; Rodnick, E. H.; Jackson, N. P.; Evans, J. R.; and Bates, J. E. The stability and sensitivity of measures of thought, perception and emotional arousal. *Psychopharmacologia*, 1972, 24:107–120.

Greene, W. A. and Nielsen, T. C. Operant GSR conditioning of high and low autonomic perceivers. *Psychonom Sci*, 1966, 6:359–360.

Grings, W. W. and Carlin, S. Instrumental modification of autonomic behavior. *Psychol Rec*, 1966, 16:153–159.

Grings, W. W. Anticipatory and preparatory electrodermal behavior in paired stimulation situations. *Psychophysiology*, 1969, 5:597.

Gruber, R. P.; Reed, D. R.; and Block, J. E. Transfer of the conditional GSR from drug to non-drug state without awareness. *J Psychol*, 1968, 70: 149–155.

Gustafson, L. A. and Orne, M. T. The effects of verbal responses on the laboratory detection of deception. *Psychophysiology*, 1965, 2:10.

Hare, R.; Wood, K.; Britain, S.; and Shadman, J. Autonomic responses to affective visual stimulation. *Psychophysiology*, 1970, 7:408–417.

Helmer, J. E. and Furedy, J. J. Operant conditioning of GSR amplitude. *J Exp Psychol*, 1968, 78:463–467.

Hirschman, R. and Katkin, E. S. Relationships among attention, GSR activity, and perceived similarity of self and others. *J Personality*, 1971, 39: 277–288.

Holloway, F. A. and Parsons, O. A. Unilateral brain damage and bilateral skin conductance levels in humans. *Psychophysiology*, 1969, 6:138.

Hughes, W. G. and Shean, G. D. Personality and ability to control the galvanic skin response. *Psychophysiology*, 1971, 8:247.

Johnson, H. J. and Campos, J. J. The effect of cognitive tasks and verbalization instructions on heart rate and skin conductance. *Psychophysiology*, 1967, 4:143.

Johnson, H. J. and Schwartz, G. E. Suppression of GSR activity through operant reinforcement. *J Exp Psychol*, 1967, 75:307–312.

Johnson, L. C. and Lubin, A. Spontaneous electrodermal activity. *Psychophysiology*, 1966, 3:8.

Jones, B. E. and Ayres, J. J. B. Significance and reliability of shock-induced changes in basal skin conductance. *Psychophysiology*, 1966, 2:322.

Juniper, K. and Dykman, R. A. Skin resistance, sweat-gland counts, salivary flow, and gastric secretion: Age, race, and sex differences, and intercorrelations. *Psychophysiology*, 1967, 4:216.

Kaplan, B. E.: Psychophysiological and cognitive development in children. *Psychophysiology*, 1970, 7:18.

Kaplan, S.; Kaplan, R.; and Sampson, J. R. Encoding and arousal factors in free recall of verbal and visual material. *Psychonom Sci*, 1968, 12:73–74.

Katsube, A. and Tadaki, E. Studies on the psychogalvanic phenomenon in physical movements. V. The psychogalvanic phenomenon in response to kendo play and kyudo play in mind image pictures and viewed in motion pictures. *Res Phys Educ, Kyushu Univ*, 1964, 8:7–13.

Kelly, D.; Brown, C. C.; and Shaffer, J. W. A comparison of physiological and psychological measurements on anxious patients and normal controls. *Psychophysiology*, 1970, 4:429.

Kilpatrick, D. G. Differential responsiveness of two electrodermal indices to psychological stress and performance of a complex cognitive task. *Psychophysiology*, 1972, 9:218–226.

Kimmel, H. D. and Hill, F. A. Operant conditioning of the GSR. *Psychol Rep*, 1960, 7:555–562.

Kimmel, H. D. Instrumental conditioning of autonomically mediated behavior. *Psychol Bull*, 1967, 67:337–345.

Kleinman, K. M. and Stern, J. A. Task complexity, electrodermal activity and reaction time. *Psychophysiology*, 1968, 5:51.

Klinge, V. Effects of exteroceptive feedback and instructions on control of spontaneous galvanic skin responses. *Psychophysiology*, 1972, 9:305–317.

Kodman, F., Jr. Validity of GSR conditioning. *Psychol Rep*, 1967, 21:813–818.

Kopacs, F. M. and Smith, B. D. Sex differences in skin conductance measures as a function of shock treatment. *Psychophysiology*, 1971, 8:293.

Korn, J. H. and Moyer, K. E. Effects of set and sex on the electrodermal orienting response. *Psychophysiology*, 1968, 4:453.

Koumans, A. J. R.; Tursky, B.; and Solomon, P. Electrodermal levels and fluctuations during normal sleep. *Psychophysiology*, 1968, 5:300.

Krupski, A.; Raskin, D. C.; and Bakan, P. Physiological and personality correlates of commission errors in an auditory vigilance task. *Psychophysiology*, 1971, 8:304.

Kugelmass, S. and Lieblich, I. Effects of realistic stress and procedural interference in experimental lie detection. *J Appl Psychol*, 1966, 50:211–216.

Kugelmass, S. and Lieblich, I. Relation between ethnic origin and GSR reactivity in psychophysiological detection. *J Appl Psychol*, 1968, 52:158–162.

Lader, M. H. Palmar skin conductance measures in anxiety and phobic states. *J Psychosom Res*, 1967, 11:271–281.

Lader, M. and Mathews, A. Physiological changes during spontaneous panic attacks. *J Psychosom Res*, 1970, 14:377–382.

Lader, M. and Mathews, A. Comparison of methods of relaxation using physiological measures. *Behav Res Ther*, 1970, 8:331–337.

Levine, H. I.; Engel, B. T.; and Schulkin, F. R.   Patterns of autonomic responsivity in identical schizophrenic twins. *Psychophysiology*, 1967, 3:363.

Lovibond, S. H. Positive and negative conditioning of the GSR. *Acta Psychol (Amst)*, 1963, 21:100–107.

Luborsky, L. and Blinder, B. Eye fixation and recall of pictures as a function of GSR responsivity. *Percept Motor Skills*, 1963, 16:469–483.

Lykken, D. T. Direct measurement of skin conductance: a proposal for standardization. *Psychophysiology*, 1971, 8:656–672.

Lykken, D. T.; Miller, R. D.; and Strahan, R. F. Some properties of skin conductance and potential. *Psychophysiology*, 1968, 5:253.

McNair, D. M.; Droppleman, L. F.; and Kussman, M. Finger sweat print tape bands. *Psychophysiology*, 1967, 4:75.

Mandler, G.; Mandler, J.; and Uviller, E. Autonomic feedback: the perception of autonomic activity. *J Abnorm Soc Psychol*, 1958, 56:376–383.

Mandler, G.; Preven, D. W.; and Kuhlman, C. K. Effects of operant reinforcement on the GSR. *J Exp Anal Behav*, 1962, 5:317–321.

Martin, I. and Venables, P. H. Mechanisms of palmar skin resistance and skin potential. *Psychol Bull*, 1966, 65:347–357.

Martin, R. B.; Dean, S. J.; and Shean, G. Selective attention and instrumental modification of the GSR. *Psychophysiology*, 1968, 4:460–467.

Martin, R. B. and Dean, S. J. Instrumental modification of the GSR. *Psychophysiology*, 1970, 7:178.

Mefferd, R. B., Jr. and Wieland, B. A. Modification in autonomically mediated physiological responses to cold pressor by word associations. *Psychophysiology*, 1965, 2:1.

Mordkoff, A. M.; Edelberg, R.; and Ustick, M. The differential conditionability of two components of the skin conductance response. *Psychophysiology*, 1967, 4:40–47.

Neumann, E. and Blanton, R. The early history of electrodermal research. *Psychophysiology*, 1970, 6:453.

Nourse, J. C. and Welch, R. B. Emotional attributes of color: A comparison of violet and green. *Percept Motor Skills*, 1971, 32:403–406.

Obrist, P. A.; Webb, R. A.; and Sutterer, J. R. Heart rate and somatic changes during aversive conditioning and a simple reaction time task. *Psychophysiology*, 1969, 5:696.

O'Gorman, J. G. Latency and habituation of the electro-dermal response. *Psychophysiology*, 1971, 8:280.

Ohman, A. Differentiation of conditioned and orienting response components in electrodermal conditioning. *Psychophysiology*, 1971, 8:7.

Orne, M. T. and Thackray, R. I. Group GSR technique in the detection of deception. *Percept Motor Skills*, 1967, 25:809–816.

Patton, G. W. R. Combined autonomic effects of concurrently-applied stressors. *Psychophysiology*, 1970, 6:707.

Pillard, R. C.; Carpenter, J.; Atkinson, K. W.; and Fisher, S. Palmar sweat prints and self-ratings as measures of film induced anxiety. *Percept Motor Skills*, 1966, 23:771–777.

Pishkin, V. and Shurley, J. T. Electrodermal and electromyographic parameters in concept identification. *Psychophysiology*, 1968, 5:112–118.

Prescott, J. W.: Neural timing mechanisms, conditioning, and the CS-UCS interval. *Psychophysiology*, 1966, 2:125–131.

Purohit, A. P. Personality variables, sex-difference, GSR responsiveness and GSR conditioning. *J Exp Res Personality*, 1966, 1:166–173.

Rappaport, H. and Katkin, E. S. Relationships among manifest anxiety, response to stress, and the perception of autonomic activity. *J Consult Clin Psychol*, 1972, 38:219–224.

Roessler, R. and Collins, F. Personality correlates of physiological responses to motion pictures. *Psychophysiology*, 1970, 6:732.

Sadler, T. G.; Mefferd, R. B.; Wieland, B. A.; Benton, R. G.; and McDaniel, D. C. Physiological effects of combinations of painful and cognitive stimuli. *Psychophysiology*, 1969, 5:370.

Satterfield, J. H. and Dawson, M. E. Electrodermal correlates of hyperactivity in children. *Psychophysiology*, 1971, 8:191–197.

Schwartz, G. E. and Johnson, H. J. Affective visual stimuli as operant reinforcers of the GSR. *J Exp Psychol*, 1969, 80:28–32.

Senter, R. J. and Hummel, W. F., Jr. Suppression of an autonomic response through operant conditioning. *Psychol Rec*, 1965, 15:1–5.

Shapiro, D.; Crider, A. B.; and Tursky, B. Differentiation of an autonomic response through operant reinforcement. *Psychonom Sci*, 1964, 1:147–148.

Shapiro, D. and Watanabe, T. Reinforcement of spontaneous electrodermal activity: A cross-cultural study in Japan. *Psychophysiology*, 1972, 9: 340–344.

Shaver, B. A., Jr.; Brusilow, S. W.; and Cooke, R. E. Origin of the galvanic skin response. *Proc Soc Exp Biol Med*, 110:559–564.

Shean, G. D. The relationship between ability to verbalize stimulus contingencies and GSR conditioning. *J Psychosom Res*, 1968, 12:245–249.

Shean, G. D. Vasomotor conditioning and awareness. *Psychophysiology*, 1968, 5:22–30.

Shean, G. D. Instrumental modification of the galvanic skin response: conditioning or control? *J Psychosom Res*, 1970, 14:155–160.

Shmavonian, B. M.; Miller, L. H.; and Cohen, S. I. Differences among age and sex groups in electro-dermal conditioning. *Psychophysiology*, 1968, 5: 119–131.

Shnidman, S. R. and Shapiro, D. Instrumental modification of elicited autonomic responses. *Psychophysiology*, 1970, 7:395.

Snider, I. J. and Bregman, A. S. The effect of GSR confirmed perception of bisensory input on immediate verbal memory. *Psychophysiology*, 1970, 7:169.

Solley, C. M. and Thetford, P. E. Skin potential responses and the span of attention. *Psychophysiology*, 1967, 3:397.

Stern, J. A.; Surphlis, W.; and Koff, E. Electrodermal responsiveness as related to psychiatric diagnosis and prognosis. *Psychophysiology*, 1965, 2:51.

Stern, R. M. and Kaplan, B. E. Galvanic skin response: voluntary control and externalization. *J Psychosom Res*, 1967, 10:349–353.

Stern, R. M. and Lewis, N. L. Ability of actors to control their GSRs and express emotions. *Psychophysiology*, 1968, 4:294–299.

Stern, R. M.; Gaupp, L.; and Leonard, W. A comparison of GSR and subjective adaptation to stressful stimuli. *Psychophysiology*, 1970, 7:3.

Sternbach, R. A. and Tursky, B. Ethnic differences among housewives in psychophysical and skin potential responses to electric shock. *Psychophysiology*, 1965, 1:241–246.

Streiner, D. L. and Dean, S. J. Expectancy, anxiety, and the GSR. *Psychonom Sci*, 1968, 10:293–294.

Surwillo, W. W. Statistical distribution of volar skin potential level in attention and the effects of age. *Psychophysiology*, 1969, 6:13.

Swenson, R. P. and Hill, F. A. Effects of instruction and interstimulus interval in human GSR conditioning. *Psychonom Sci*, 1970, 21:369–370.

Tart, C. T. Patterns of basal skin resistance during sleep. *Psychophysiology*, 1967, 4:35.

Thackray, R. I. and Orne, M. T. A comparison of physiological indices in detection of deception. *Psychophysiology*, 1968, 4:329.

Thayer, R. Activation states as assessed by verbal report and four psychophysiological variables. *Psychophysiology*, 1970, 7:86.

Tizard, B. Evoked changes in EEG and electrodermal activity during the waking and sleeping states. *Electroenceph Clin Neurophysiol*, 1966, 20:122–128.

Ton, W. H. and Boulger, J. R. Voluntary inhibition of galvanic skin response. *Psychol Rep*, 1971, 29:603–606.

Tursky, B. and O'Connell, D. N. Survey of practice in electrodermal measurement. *Psychophysiology*, 1966, 2:237.

Tursky, B. and Sternbach, R. A. Further physiological correlates of ethnic differences in responses to shock. *Psychophysiology*, 1967, 4:67.

Tursky, B.; Greenblatt, D.; and O'Connell, D. Electrocutaneous threshold changes produced by electric shock. *Psychophysiology*, 1970, 7:490.

Uno, T. The effects of awareness and successive inhibition on interoceptive and exteroceptive conditioning of the galvanic skin response. *Psychophysiology*, 1970, 7:27–43.

Verschoor, A. M. and Van Wieringen, P. C. Vigilance performance and skin conductance. *Acta Psychol (Amst)*, 1970, *33*:394–401.

Wallace, R. M. and Fehr, F. S. Heart rate, skin resistance, and reaction time of mongoloid and normal children under baseline and distraction conditions. *Psychophysiology*, 1970, *6*:722.

Wieland, B. A. and Mefford, R. B., Jr. Identification of periodic components in physiologic measurements. *Psychophysiology*, 1969, *6*:160.

Wilcott, R. C. Adaptive value of arousal sweating and the epidermal mechanism related to skin potential and skin resistance. *Psychophysiology*, 1966, *3*:249.

Wilson, A. and Wilson, A. Psychophysiological and learning correlates of anxiety and induced muscle relaxation. *Psychophysiology*, 1970, *6*:740.

Wilson, G. D. An electrodermal technique for the study of phobias. *New Zeal Med J*, 1966, *65*:696–698.

Wilson, G. D. Arousal properties of red versus green. *Percept Motor Skills*, 1966, *23*:947–949.

Wilson, G. D. Reversal of differential GSR conditioning by instructions. *J Exp Psychol*, 1968, *76*:491–493.

Wilson, G. D. Personality, GSR conditioning and response to instructional set. *Psychol Rep*, 1968, *22*:618.

Wineman, E. W. Autonomic balance changes during the human menstrual cycle. *Psychophysiology*, 1971, *8*:1–6.

Wishner, J. Studies in efficiency: GSR conditioning as a function of degree of task centering. *J Abnorm Soc Psychol*, 1962, *65*:170–177.

Wolfensberger, W. and O'Connor, N. Relative effectiveness of galvanic skin response latency, amplitude and duration scores as measures of arousal and habituation in normal and retarded adults. *Psychophysiology*, 1967, *3*:345.

Worrall, N. Differential GSR conditioning of true and false decisions. *J Exp Psychol*, 1970, *86*:13–19.

Wyatt, R. and Tursky, B. Skin potential levels in right and left handed males. *Psychophysiology*, 1969, *6*:133.

Woy, J. R. and Efran, J. S. Systematic desensitization and expectancy in the treatment of speaking anxiety. *Behav Res Ther*, 1972, *10*:43–49.

Zeiner, A. R. and Schell, A. M. Individual differences in orienting, conditionability, and skin resistance responsivity. *Psychophysiology*, 1971, *8*:612.

CHAPTERS 4 AND 5: Muscles

Agras, W. S.; Leitenberg, H.; Barlow, D. H.; Curtis, N.; Edwards, J.; and Wright, D. Relaxation is systematic desensitization. *Arch Gen Psychiat (Chicago)*, 1971, *25*:511–514.

Antonelli, D. J. and Waring, W. Circuit for a one degree of freedom myoelectric control. *Med Res Engin*, 1967, 4th quarter, 35–38.

Baginsky, R. G. Voluntary control of motor unit activity by visual and aural feedback. *Electroenceph Clin Neurophysiol*, 1969, 27:724.

Bair, J. H. Development of voluntary control. *Psychol Rev*, 1901, 8:474–510.

Bartoshuk, A. K. Electromyographic gradients as indicants of motivation. *Canad J Psychol*, 1955, 9:215–230.

Basmajian, J. V. Control and training of individual motor units. *Science*, 1963, 141:440–441.

Basmajian, J. V. and Simard, T. G. Effects of distracting movements on the control of trained motor units. *Amer J Phys Med*, 1967, 46:480–486.

Basmajian, J. V. Control of individual motor units. *Amer J Phys Med*, 1967, 46:1427–1440.

Basmajian, J. V. Electromyography comes of age. The conscious control of individual motor units in man may be used to improve his physical performance. *Science*, 1972, 176:603–609.

Bizzi, E. and Evarts, E. V. Central control of movement: translational mechanisms between input and output. *Neurosci Res Program Bull*, 1971, 9:31–59.

Block, J. D. Operant conditioning with augmented feedback: New perspectives in motor rehabilitation of the brain damaged. Invited address to the N.Y. Soc. Phys. Med. & Rehabilitation at the N.Y. Academy of Medicine, June 4, 1969.

Boman, K. Effect of emotional stress of spasticity and rigidity. *J Psychosom Res*, 1971, 15:107–112.

Booker, H. E.; Rubow, R. T.; and Coleman, P. J. Simplified feedback in neuromuscular retraining: An automated approach using electromyographic signals. *Arch Phys Med*, 1969, 50:621–625.

Budzynski, T.; Stoyva, J.; and Adler, C.: Feedback-induced muscle relaxation: application to tension headache. *J Behav Ther Exper Psychiat*, 1970, 1:205–211.

Butler, K. N. The effect of physical conditioning and exertion of the performance of a simple mental task. *J Sports Med*, 1969, 9:236–240.

Deecke, L.; Scheid, P.; and Kornhuber, H. H. Distribution of readiness potential, pre-motion positivity, and motor potential of the human cerebral cortex preceding voluntary finger movements. *Exp Brain Res*, 1969, 7:158–168.

DeLong, M. Central control of movement: Central patterning of movement. *Neurosci Res Program Bull*, 1971, 9:10–30.

Evarts, E. F. Central control of movement: Feedback and corollary discharge: A merging of the concepts. *Neurosci Res Program Bull*, 1971, 9:86–112.

Fetz, E. E. and Finocchio, D. V. Operant conditioning of specific patterns of neural and muscular activity. *Science*, 1971, 174:431–435.

Fruhling, M.; Basmajian, J. V.; and Simard, T. G. A note on the conscious controls of motor units by children under six. *J Motor Behav*, 1969, 1:65–68.

Gray, E. R. Conscious control of motor units in a tonic muscle. The effect of motor unit training. *Amer J Phys Med*, 1971, *50*:34–40.

Green, E. E.; Walters, E. D.; Green, A. M.; and Murphy, G. Feedback technique for deep relaxation. *Psychophysiology*, 1969, *6*:371–377.

Green, E. E.; Green, A. M.; and Walters, E. D. Voluntary control of internal states: Psychological and physiological. *J Transpersonal Psychol*, 1970, *2*:1–26.

Grim, P. F.: Psychotherapy by somatic alteration. *Ment Hyg*, 1969, *53*:451–458.

Hardyck, C. D.; Petrinovich, L. F.; and Ellsworth, D. W. Feedback of speech muscle activity during silent reading: rapid extinction. *Science*, 1966, *154*:1467–1468.

Harrison, V. F. and Mortensen, O. A. Identification and voluntary control of single motor unit activity in the tibialis anterior muscle. *Anat Rec*, 1962, *144*:109–116.

Hefferline, R. F. The role of proprioception in the control of behavior. *Trans NY Acad Sci*, 1958, *20*:739–764.

Hefferline, R. F.; Keenan, B.; and Harford, R. A. Escape and avoidance conditioning in human subjects without their observation of the response. *Science*, 1959, *130*:1338–1339.

Hefferline, R. F. and Perera, T. B. Proprioceptive discrimination of a covert operant without its observation by the subject. *Science*, 1963, *139*:834–835.

Hutton, R. S. Kinesthetic after effect, a measure of kinesthetic awareness. *Percept Motor Skills*, 1966, *23*:1165–1166.

Jacobs, A. and Felton, G. S. Visual feedback of myoelectric output to facilitate muscle relaxation in normal persons and patients with neck injuries. *Arch Phys Med*, 1969, *50*:34–39.

Jacobson, E. Neuromuscular controls in man: methods of self direction in health and disease. *Amer J Psychol*, 1955, *68*:549–561.

Jacobson, E. *Progressive Relaxation*. Chicago: University of Chicago Press, 1958.

Jacobson, E., ed. *Tension in Medicine*. Springfield, Ill.: Charles C Thomas, 1967.

Kahn, M.; Baker, B. L.; and Weiss, J. M. Treatment of insomnia by relaxation training. *J Abnorm Psychol*, 1968, *73*:556–558.

Krauklis, A. A. Role of muscle tension in self regulation of the functional state of the brain. *Acad Sci (Latvia)*, 1970, *8*:277.

Lader, M. H. and Mathews, A. M. A physiological model of phobic anxiety and desensitization. *Behav Res Ther*, 1968, *6*:411–421.

Lieblich, I. Note on Thysell's "reaction time of single motor units." *Percept Motor Skills*, 1970, *30*:152.

Luthe, W. Autogenic training: method, research and application in medicine. *Amer J Psychother*, 1963, *17*:174–195.

Marsden, C. D.; Merton, P. A.; and Morton, H. B. Servo action in human voluntary movements. *Nature (London)* 1972, *238*:140–143.

Mathews, A. M. and Gelder, M. G. Psychophysiologic investigations of brief relaxation training. *J Psychosom Res*, 1969, *13*:1–12.

Noble, P. J. and Lader, M. H. An electromyographic study of depressed patients. *J Psychosom Res*, 1971, *15*:233–239.

Okaichi, H. The effects of induced muscular tension and original muscular tension in verbal learning. *Jap J Psychol*, 1970, *41*:20–29.

Pallas, J. R. L. Mental and motor efficiency as a function of induced muscle tension, relaxation and level of manifest anxiety. *Diss Abstr*, 1971, *31*: 4343–4344.

Paul, G. L. Extraversion, emotionality, and physiological response to relaxation training and hypnotic suggestion. *Int J Clin Exp Hypn*, 1969, *17*:89–98.

Paul, G. L.: Physiological effects of relaxation training and hypnotic suggestion. *J Abnorm Psychol*, 1969, *74*:425–437.

Paul, G. L. Inhibition of physiological response to stressful imagery by relaxation training and hypnotically suggested relaxation. *Behav Res Ther*, 1969, *7*:249–256.

Peacock, S. M. Some considerations of motor and electrical activity in states of diminished awareness. *Exp Med Surg*, 1969, *27*:169–176.

Petajan, J. H. and Phillip, B. A. Frequency control of motor unit action potentials. *Electroenceph Clin Neurophysiol*, 1969, *27*:66–72.

Petajan, J. H. Motor unit frequency control in facial neuropathy. *Electroenceph Clin Neurophysiol*, 1969, *27*:718.

Phillips, R. E.; Johnson, G. D.; and Geyer, A. Self-administered systematic desensitization. *Behav Res Ther*, 1972, *10*:93–96.

Prentke, E. M. and Beard, J. E. A surface electrode design for myoelectric control. *Orthot Prosth*, 1969, *23*:63–67.

Ranji, J. and Kato, M. Volitionally controlled single motor unit discharges and cortical motor potentials in human subjects. *Brain Res*, 1971, *29*:343–346.

Rubow, R. T. and Smith, K. U. Feedback parameters of electromyographic learning. *Amer J Phys Med*, 1971, *50*:115–131.

Sargent, J. D.; Green, E. E.; and Walters, E. D. Preliminary report on the use of autogenic feedback training in the treatment of migraine and tension headaches. *Headache*, 1972, *12*:120.

Scully, H. E. and Basmajian, J. V. Motor-unit training and influence of manual skill. *Psychophysiology*, 1969, *5*:625–632.

Simard, T. G. and Basmajian, J. V. Methods in training the conscious control of motor units. *Arch Phys Med*, 1967, *48*:12–19.

Simard, T. G. and Ladd, H. Conscious control of motor units by thalidomide children: An electromyographic study. *Develop Med Child Neurol*, 1969, *11*:743–748.

Simard, T. G. Fine sensorimotor control in healthy children. An electromyographic study. *Pediatrics*, 1969, *43*:1035–1041.

Simard, T. G. and Ladd, H. W. Pre-orthotic training. An electromyographic study in normal adults. *Amer J Phys Med,* 1969, *48:*301–312.

Smith, K. U.; Gould, J.; and Wargo, L. Sensory feedback analysis in medical research. II. Spatial organization of neurobehavioral systems. *Amer J Phys Med,* 1964, *43:*49–83.

Smith, K. U. and Henry J. P. Cybernetic foundations for rehabilitation. *Amer J Phys Med,* 1967, *46:*379–467.

Teuber, H. L. Perception. *Handbook of Physiology.* 1960, 3:1595–1668. John Field, ed. American Physiological Society, Washington, D.C.

Trombly, C. A.: Myoelectric control of orthotic devices: for the severely paralyzed. *Amer J Occup Ther,* 1968, *22:*385–389.

Wagman, I. H.; Pierce, D. S.; and Burger, R. E. Proprioceptive influence in volitional control of individual motor units. *Nature (London)* 1965, *207:*957–958.

Whatmore, G. B. and Kohli, D. R. Dysponesis: a neurophysiologic factor in functional disorders. *Behav Sci,* 1968, *13:*102–124.

Wickramasekera, I. Effects of EMG feedback training on susceptibility to hypnosis: preliminary observations. *Proc Ann Conv Amer Psychol Ass,* 1971, 6:783–784.

Williams, R. B. and Eichelman, B. Social setting: Influence on the physiological response to electric shock in the rat. *Science,* 1971, *174:*613–614.

Wilson, A. and Wilson, A. S. Psychophysiological and learning correlates of anxiety and induced muscle relaxation. *Psychophysiology,* 1970, *6:* 740–748.

Wyke, B. The neurology of stammering. *J Psychosom Res,* 1971, *15:*423–432.

CHAPTERS 6 AND 7: Heartbeats

Bergman, J. S. and Johnson, H. J. The effects of instructional set and autonomic perception on cardiac control. *Psychophysiology,* 1971, 8:180–190.

Bergman, J. S. and Johnson, H. J. Sources of information which affect training and raising of heart rate. *Psychophysiology,* 1972, 9:30–39.

Blanchard, E. B.; Young, L. D.; and McLeod, P. Awareness of heart activity and self-control of heart rate. *Psychophysiology,* 1972, 9:63–68.

Brener, J. and Hothersall, D. Heart rate control under conditions of augmented sensory feedback. *Psychophysiology,* 1966, 3:23–28.

Bull, K. and Lang, P. J. Intensity judgments and physiological response amplitude. *Psychophysiology,* 1972, 9:428–436.

Chatterjee, B. B. and Eriksen, C. W. Cognitive factors in heart rate conditioning. *J Exp Psychol,* 1962, 64:272–279.

Collen, A. and Libby, W. L. Effects of hunger upon the cardiac deceleratory response to food pictures. *Psychophysiology,* 1972, 9:280.

Costello, C. G. and Hall, M. Heart rates during performance of a mental task under noise conditions. *Psychonom Sci,* 1967, 8:405–406.

Craig, K. D. and Lowery, J. J. Heart-rate components of conditioned vicarious autonomic responses. *J Personality Soc Psychol*, 1969, *11*:381–387.

Crow, L. T.; Godfrey, C. C.; and Parent, R. J. Repeated heart rate acceleration with a pre-verbalization stimulus complex. *Psychophysiology*, 1972, *9*:277.

Deane, G. E. Cardiac activity during experimentally induced anxiety. *Psychophysiology*, 1969, *6*:17–30.

Defares, P. B.; van Enkevort, G. M.; van Gelderen, M. H.; and Schendelaar, J. K. Pseudo-heartbeatfeedback and the reduction of anxiety. *Nederl T Psychol*, 1969, *24*:117–135.

DiCara, L. V. and Miller, N. E. Long term retention of instrumentally learned heart-rate changes in the curarized rat. *Comm Behav Biol*, 1968, *2*:19–23.

DiCara, L. V. and Miller, N. E. Changes in heart rate instrumentally learned by curarized rats as avoidance responses. *J Comp Physiol Psychol*, 1968, *65*:8–12.

DiCara, L. V. and Miller, N. E. Heart-rate learning in the noncurarized state, transfer to the curarized state, and subsequent retraining in the noncurarized state. *Psychol Behav*, 1969, *4*:621–624.

DiCara, L. V. and Weiss, J. M. Effect of heart rate learning under curare on subsequent noncurarized avoidance learning. *J Comp Physiol Psychol*, 1969, *69*:368–374.

Donelson, F. E. Discrimination and control of human heart rate. *Diss Abstr*, 1967, *27*:457.

Dronsejko, K. Effects of CS duration and instructional set on cardiac anticipatory responses to stress in field dependent and independent subjects. *Psychophysiology*, 1972, *9*:1–13.

Dykman, R. A. and Gantt, H. Cardiovascular conditioning in dogs and in humans. In W. H. Gantt, ed., *Physiological Bases of Psychiatry*. Springfield, Ill.: Charles C Thomas, 1958, pp. 171–195.

Elliott, R. and Graf, V. Visual sensitivity as a function of phase of cardiac cycle. *Psychophysiology*, 1972, *9*:357–361.

Engel, B. T. and Hansen, S. P. Operant conditioning of heart rate slowing. *Psychophysiology*, 1966, *3*:176–187.

Engel, B. T. and Chism, R. A. Operant conditioning of heart rate speeding. *Psychophysiology*, 1967, *3*:418–426.

Engel, B. T. and Gottlieb, S. H. Differential operant conditioning of heart rate in the restrained monkey. *J Comp Physiol Psychol*, 1970, *73*:217–225.

Engel, B. T. Operant conditioning of cardiac function: A status report. *Psychophysiology*, 1972, *9*:161–177.

Fenz, W. D. and Dronsejko, K. Effects of real and imagined threat of shock on GSR and heart rate as a function of trait anxiety. *J Exp Res Personality*, 1969, *3*:187–196.

Frazier, T. W. Avoidance conditioning of heart rate in humans. *Psychophysiology*, 1966, *3*:188–202.

Fuhrer, M. J. Differential verbal conditioning of heart rate with minimization of changes in respiratory rate. *J Comp Physiol Psychol*, 1964, 58:283–289.

Fuhrer, M. J. and Baer, P. E. Differential classical conditioning: Verbalization of stimulus contingencies. *Science*, 1965, 150:1479–1481.

Graham, F. K. and Clifton, R. K. Heart-rate change as a component of the orienting response. *Psychol Bull*, 1966, 65:305–320.

Granger, L. Variations of cardiac rate in different types of situations of visual attention. *Canad J Psychol*, 1970, 24:370–379.

Hare, R. D. Response requirements and directional fractionation of autonomic responses. *Psychophysiology*, 1972, 9:419–427.

Harwood, C. W. Operant heart rate conditioning. *Psychol Rec*, 1962, 12: 279–284.

Headrick, M. W.; Feather, B. W.; and Wells, D. T. Voluntary changes from baseline heart rate with augmented sensory feedback. *Psychophysiology*, 1970, 6:636.

Headrick, M. W.; Feather, B. W.; and Wells, D. T. Unidirectional and large magnitude heart rate changes with augmented sensory feedback. *Psychophysiology*, 1971, 8:132–142.

Hein, P. L.; Cohen, S. I.; and Shmavonian, B. M. Perceptual mode and cardiac conditioning. *Psychophysiology*, 1966, 3:101–107.

Higgins, J. D. Set and uncertainty as factors influencing anticipatory cardiovascular responding in humans. *J Comp Physiol Psychol*, 1971, 74: 272–283.

Hnatiow, M. and Lang, P. J. Learned stabilization of cardiac rate. *Psychophysiology*, 1965, 1:330–336.

Hnatiow, M. Learned control of heart rate and blood pressure. *Percept Motor Skills*, 1971, 33:219–226.

Jenks, R. S. and Deane, G. E. Human heart rate responses during experimentally induced anxiety: A follow up. *J Exp Psychol*, 1963, 65:109–112.

Jennings, J. R. Cardiac reactions and different developmental levels of cognitive functioning. *Psychophysiology*, 1971, 8:433–450.

Jones, G. B. and Fenz, W. D. Relationships between cardiac condition-ability in the laboratory and autonomic control in real life stress. *Psychophysiology*, 1972, 9:267.

Kahneman, D.; Tursky, B.; Shapiro, D.; and Crider, A. Pupillary, heart rate, and skin resistance changes during a mental task. *J Exp Psychol*, 1969, 79:164–167.

Kaplan, B. E.; Corby, J. C.; and Liederman, P. H. Attention and verbalization: Differential responsivity of cardiovascular and electrodermal systems. *J Psychosom Res*, 1971, 15:323–328.

Katkin, E. S. and Murray, E. N. Instrumental conditioning of autonomically mediated behavior: Theoretical and methodological issues. *Psychol Bull*, 1968, 70:52–68.

Lang, P. J.; Sroufe, L. A.; and Hastings, J. E. Effects of feedback and instructional set on the control of cardiac-rate variability. *J Exp Psychol*, 1967, 75:425–431.

Levene, H. E.; Engel, B. T.; and Pearson, J. A. Differential operant conditioning of heart rate. *Psychosom Med*, 1968, 30:837–845.

Libby, W. L. Awareness of own cardiac and pupillary response to pictures. *Psychophysiology*, 1972, 9:273.

Malmstrom, E. J. Heart rate synchronization to rhythmic auditory stimuli. *Psychophysiology*, 1970, 6:626–627.

Miller, N. E. and DiCara, L. Instrumental learning of heart rate changes in curarized rats. *J Comp Physiol Psychol*, 1967, 63:12–19.

Miller, N. E. and Banuazizi, A. Instrumental learning by curarized rats of a specific visceral response, intestinal or cardiac. *J Comp Physiol Psychol*, 1968, 65:1–7.

Miller, W. H. Extinction of learned heart rate deceleration as a function of awareness. *Diss Abstr*, 1969, 29:4851.

Morgenson, D. F. and Martin, I. The orienting response as a predictor of autonomic conditioning. *J Exp Res Personality*, 1968, 3:89–98.

Morgenson, D. F. and Martin, I. Personality, awareness and autonomic conditioning. *Psychophysiology*, 1969, 5:536–547.

Murray, E. N. and Katkin, E. S. Comment on two recent reports of operant heart rate conditioning. *Psychophysiology*, 1968, 5:192–195.

Obrist, P. A. Heart rate and somatic-motor coupling during classical aversive conditioning in humans. *J Exp Psychol*, 1968, 77:180–193.

Obrist, P. A.; LeGuyader, D. D.; Howard, J. L.; Lawler, J. E.; and Galosy, R. A. Operant conditioning of heart rate: somatic correlates. *Psychophysiology*, 1972, 9:270.

Ray, W. J. and Strupp, H. Locus of control and the voluntary control of heart rate. *Psychophysiology*, 1972, 9:270.

Razran, G. The observable unconscious and the inferable conscious in current Soviet psychophysiology: Interoceptive conditioning, semantic conditioning, and the orienting reflex. *Psychol Rev*, 1961, 68:81–147.

Rushmer, R. F. and Smith, O. A., Jr. Cardiac control. *Psychol Rev*, 1959, 39:41–68.

Saxon, S. A. and Dahle, A. J. Auditory threshold variations during periods of induced high and low heart rates. *Psychophysiology*, 1971, 8:23–29.

Saxon, S. A. Detection of near threshold signals during four phases of cardiac cycle. *Alabama J Med Sci*, 1970, 7:427–430.

Schulman, C.; Kreiter, R.; and Murray, J. The relationship between heart rate change threshold and audiometric threshold in hearing impaired children. *Psychophysiology*, 1972, 9:274.

Schwartz, G. E. and Higgins, J. D. Cardiac activity preparatory to overt and covert behavior. *Science*, 1971, 173:1144–1146.

Schwartz, G. E. and Higgins, J. D. Response imperativeness and the cardiac wave-form during the preparation of a motor and "mental" reaction response. *Psychophysiology,* 1971, 8:244.

Schwartz, G. E. Cardiac responses to self-induced thoughts. *Psychophysiology,* 1971, 8:462–467.

Shearn, D. Does the heart learn? *Psychol Bull,* 1961, 58:452–458.

Shearn, D. W. Operant conditioning of heart rate. *Science,* 1962, 137:530–531.

Snyder, F.; Hobson, J. A.; Morrison, D. F.; and Goldfrank, F. Changes in respiration, heart rate, and systolic blood pressure in human sleep. *J Appl Physiol,* 1964, 19:417–422.

Spence, D. P.; Lugo, M.; and Youdin, R. Cardiac change as a function of attention to and awareness of continuous verbal text. *Science,* 1972, 176: 1344–1346.

Stephens, J. H.; Harris, A. H.; and Brady, J. V. Large magnitude heart rate changes in subjects instructed to change their heart rates and given interoceptive feedback. *Psychophysiology,* 1972, 9:283–285.

Stern, R. M.; Bott, R. W.; and Herrick, C. D. Behavioral and physiological effects of false heart rate feedback: A replication and extension. *Psychophysiology,* 1972, 9:21–29.

Surwillo, W. W. Human reaction time and endogenous heart rate changes in normal subjects. *Psychophysiology,* 1971, 8:680–682.

Sutter, J. M. and Gerard, R. Psychic factors in cardiac arrhythmias. *Un Med Canada,* 1968, 97:1055–1068.

Tursky, B.; Schwartz, G. E.; and Crider, A. Differential patterns of heart rate and skin resistance during a digit-transformation task. *J Exp Psychol,* 1970, 83:451–457.

Valins, S. Cognitive effects of false heart-rate feedback. *J Personality Soc Psychol,* 1966, 4:400–408.

Valins, S. Emotionality and autonomic reactivity. *J Exp Res Personality,* 1967, 2:41–48.

Varni, J. G.; Clark, E.; and Giddon, D. B. Analysis of cyclic heart rate variability. *Psychophysiology,* 1971, 8:406–413.

Weiss, T. and Engel, B. T. Operant conditioning of heart rate in patients with premature ventricular contractions. *Psychosom Med,* 1971, 33:301–321.

Wells, D. T. Large magnitude voluntary heart rate changes under conditions of high motivation and extended practice. *Psychophysiology,* 1970, 6:636.

Wood, D. M. and Obrist, P. A. Effects of controlled and uncontrolled respiration on the conditioned heart rate response in humans. *J Exp Psychol,* 1964, 68:221–229.

CHAPTER 8: Blood Pressure: Blood Vessels and Social Tension

Benson, H.; Herd, J. A.; et al. Behavioral induction of arterial hypertension and its reversal. *Amer J Physiol,* 1969, 217:30–34.

Benson, H.; Shapiro, D.; Tursky, B.; and Schwartz, G. E. Decreased systolic blood pressure through operant conditioning techniques in patients with essential hypertension. *Science,* 1971, *173:*740–741.

Bohm, M.; Trlica, J.; and Veljacikova, N. The Czechoslovak EEG commission: The EEG in different phases of essential vascular hypertension. *Electroenceph Clin Neurophysiol,* 1967, *22:*286–287.

Conn, Hadley L., ed. Systematic arterial hypertension. *Cardiac and Vascular Diseases,* 1971, *2:*882–972.

Davies, M. Blood pressure and personality. *J Psychosom Res,* 1970, *14:*89–104.

DiCara, L. V. Learning in the autonomic nervous system. *Sci Amer,* Jan 1970, 30–39.

DiCara, L. V. and Miller, N. E. Instrumental learning of systolic blood pressure responses by curarized rats: Dissociation of cardiac and vascular changes. *Psychosom Med,* 1968, *30:*489–494.

Eastwood, M. R. and Trevelyan, H. Stress and coronary heart disease. *J Psychosom Res,* 1971, *15:*289–292.

Ettema, J. H. Blood pressure changes during mental load experiments in man. *Psychother Psychosom,* 1969, *17:*191–195.

Frankenhaeuser, M. Behavior and circulating catecholamines. *Brain Res,* 1971, *31:*241–262.

Gentry, W. D. Sex differences in the effects of frustration and attack on emotion and vascular processes. *Psychol Rep,* 1970, *27:*383–390.

Hein, B. Psychogenesis of hypertension. *Proc Roy Soc Med,* 1970, *63:*1267–1270.

Henry, J. P. and Cassel, J. C. Psychosocial factors in essential hypertension. Recent epidemiologic and animal experimental evidence. *Amer J Epidem,* 1969, *90:*171–200.

Jenkins, C. D.; Zyzanski, S. J.; and Rosenman, R. H. Progress toward validation of a computer-scored test for the type A coronary-prone behavior pattern. *Psychosom Med,* 1971, *33:*193–202. ·

Kakolewski, J. W. and Takeo, Y. Relationships between EEG patterns and arterial pressure changes. *Electroenceph Clin Neurophysiol,* 1967, *22:*239–244.

Kasl, S. V. and Cobb, S. Blood pressure changes in men undergoing job loss: a preliminary report. *Psychosom Med,* 1970, *32:*19–38.

Korner, P. I. Central nervous control of autonomic function. Possible implications in the pathogenesis of hypertension. *Circ Res,* 1970, *27:*159–168.

Lee, S. G.; Carstairs, G. M.; and Pickersgill, M. J. Essential hypertension and the recall of motives. *J Psychosom Res,* 1971, *15:*95–105.

Liljefors, I. and Rahe, R. H. An identical twin study of psychosocial factors in coronary heart disease in Sweden. *Psychosom Med,* 1970, *32:*523–542.

Mai, F. M. M. Personality and stress in coronary disease. *J Psychosom Res,* 1968, *12:*275–287.

Miller, N. E. Learning of visceral and glandular responses. *Science,* 1969, *163:*434–445.

Miller, N. E. Psychosomatic effects of specific types of training. *Ann NY Acad Sci*, 1969, *159*:1025–1040.

Miller, N. E.; DiCara, L. V.; Solomon, H.; Weiss, J. M.; and Dworkin, B. Psychological aspects of hypertension. Learned modifications of autonomic functions: A review and some new data. *Circ Res*, Suppl I, July 1970.

Mitschke, H. EEG in arterial hypertension. *Electroenceph Clin Neurophysiol*, 1969, *27*:660.

Nestel, P. J. Blood pressure and catecholamine excretion after mental stress in labile hypertension. *Lancet*, 1969, *1*:692–694.

O'Leary, J. P.; Columbaro, R. L.; Schwab, J. J.; and McGinnis, N. H. Anxiety in cardiac patients. *Dis Nerv Syst*, 1968, *29*:443–448.

Peart, W. S. Arterial hypertension. In *Textbook of Medicine*, 13th ed. Cecil-Loeb, 1971, 1050–1062.

Plumlee, L. A. Operant conditioning of increases in blood pressure. *Psychophysiology*, 1969, *6*:283–290.

Raab, W. Correlated cardiovascular adrenergic and adrenocortical responses to sensory and mental annoyances in man. A potential accessory cardiac risk factor. *Psychosom Med*, 1968, *30*:809–818.

Richter, H. E. and Sprung, H. Psychophysiological studies in the initial stage of essential hypertension. *Z Ges Inn Med*, 1969, *24*:17–21.

Rossen, R.; Jeub, R.; and Eiken, J. EEG patterns in coronary heart disease. *Electroenceph Clin Neurophysiol*, 1971, *31*:635.

Rubin, R. T. and Bodie, M. W. Blood pressure measurement in the study of manic depressive diseases. *Dis Nerv Syst*, 1969, *30*:392–395.

Sapira, J. D.; Scheib, E. T.; Moriarity, R.; and Shapiro, A. P. Differences in perception between hypertensive and normotensive populations. *Psychosom Med*, 1971, *33*:239–250.

Schwartz, G. E.; Shapiro, D.; and Tursky, B. Self control of patterns of human diastolic blood pressure and heart rate through feedback and reward. *Psychophysiology*, 1972, *9*:270.

Shapiro, D.; Tursky, B.; Gershon, E.; and Stern, M. Effects of feedback and reinforcement on the control of human systolic blood pressure. *Science*, 1969, *163*:588–589.

Shapiro, D.; Tursky, B.; and Schwartz, G. E. Control of blood pressure in man by operant conditioning. *Circ Res*, Suppl. I, 1970, *26–27*:27–41.

Shapiro, D.; Schwartz, G. E.; and Tursky, B. Control of diastolic blood pressure in man by feedback and reinforcement. *Psychophysiology*, 1972, *9*:296–304.

Shatlov, N. N. and Murov, M. A. The influence of intense noise and neuropsychic tension on the level of the arterial pressure and the incidence of hypertensive vascular disease. (Russian) *Klin Med (Moskva)*, 1970, *48*:70–73.

Silverstone, S. and Kissin, B. Field dependence in essential hypertension and peptic ulcer. *J Psychosom Res*, 1968, *12*:157–161.

Torgerson, S. and Kringlen, E. Blood pressure and personality. A study of the relationship between intrapair differences in systolic blood pressure and personality in monozygotic twins. *J Psychosom Res*, 1971, *15:* 183–191.

Wenger, M. A.; Bagchi, B. K.; and Anand, B. K. Experiments in India on "voluntary" control of the heart and pulse. *Circulation*, 1961, *24:*1319– 1327.

Williams, D. H. and Cartwright, R. D. Blood pressure changes during EEG monitored sleep. A comparative study of hypertensive and normotensive Negro women. *Arch Gen Psychiat (Chicago)*, 1969, *20:*307–314.

Williams, R. B. and Eichelman, B. Social setting: Influence on the physiological response to electric shock in the rat. *Science*, 1971, *174:*613–614.

CHAPTERS 9, 10, AND 11: Brain Waves

Adrian, E. D. and Matthews, B. H. C. The Berger rhythm: Potential changes from the occipital lobes in man. *Brain*, 1934, *57:*355–385.

Albino, R. and Burnand, G. Conditioning of the alpha rhythm in man. *J Exp Psychol*, 1964, *67:*539–544.

Anand, B. K.; Chhina, G. S.; and Singh, B. Some aspects of electroencephalographic studies in yogis. *Electroenceph Clin Neurophysiol*, 1961, *13:* 452–456.

Bagchi, B. K. and Wenger, M. A. Electrophysiological correlates of some Yogi exercises. *Electroenceph Clin Neurophysiol*, 1957, Suppl. 7:132–149.

Barlow, J. S. Rhythmic activity induced by photic stimulation in relation to intrinsic alpha activity of the brain in man. *Electroenceph Clin Neurophysiol*, 1960, *12:*735.

Barratt, P. E. Use of the EEG in the study of imagery. *Brit J Psychol*, 1956, *47:*101.

Becker-Carus, C. Relationships between EEG, personality and vigilance. *Electroenceph Clin Neurophysiol*, 1971, *30:*519–526.

Berger, H. *Nervenkr*, 1929, 87:527.

Berger, H. *Psyche*, 1940. Jena: Gustav Fischer.

Berger, R. J.; Olley, P.; and Oswald, I. The EEG, eye movements and dreams of the blind. *Quart J Exp Psychol*, 1962, *14:*183.

Berkhout, J.; Walter, D. O.; and Adey, W. R. Alterations of the human electroencephalogram induced by stressful verbal activity. *Electroenceph Clin Neurophysiol*, 1969, 27:457–469.

Berlyne, D. E. and McDonnell, P. Effects of stimulus complexity and incongruity on duration of EEG desynchronization. *Electroenceph Clin Neurophysiol*, 1965, *18:*156–161.

Brown, B. B. Specificity of EEG photic flicker responses to color as related to visual imagery ability. *Psychophysiology*, 1966, 2:197–207.

Brown, B. B. Subjective and EEG responses to LSD in visualizer and non-visualizer subjects. *Electroenceph Clin Neurophysiol,* 1968, 25:372–379.

Brown, B. B. Recognition of aspects of consciousness through association with EEG alpha activity represented by a light signal. *Psychophysiology,* 1970, 6:442–452.

Brown, B. B. Awareness of EEG-subjective activity relationships detected within a closed feedback system. *Psychophysiology,* 1970, 7:451–464.

Brown, B. B. Some observations on eye movement and EEG activity during different sensory modalities of perception and recall. In *The Oculomotor System and Brain Functions,* ed., V. Zikmund. Slovak Acad of Sci, 1973.

Brown, B. B. Additional characteristic EEG differences between smokers and nonsmokers. In *Smoking Behavior: Motives and Incentives,* ed. W. L. Dunn, Jr. Washington, D.C.: Winston & Sons, 1973.

Bundzen, P. V. Autoregulation of functional state of the brain: an investigation using photostimulation with feedback. *Fed Proc,* Trans Suppl, 1966, 25: 551–554.

Carmona, A. B. Trial and error learning of the voltage of the cortical EEG activity. *Diss Abstr,* 1967, 28(3-B):1157–1158.

Chapman, R. M.; Shelburne, S. A.; and Bragdon, H. R. EEG alpha activity influenced by visual input and not by eye position. *Electroenceph Clin Neurophysiol,* 1970, 28:183–189.

Clusin, W. EEG and the measurement of visual performance. *Electroenceph Clin Neurophysiol,* 1969, 27:707.

Cohn, R. The influence of emotion on the human electroencephalogram. *J Nerv Ment Dis,* 1946, 104:351–367.

Costa, L. D.; Cox, M.; and Katzman, R. Relationship between MMPI variables and percentage and amplitude of EEG activity. *J Consult Clin Psychol,* 1965, 29:90.

Daniel, R. S. Alpha and theta EEG in vigilance. *Percept Motor Skills,* 1967, 25:697–703.

Daniel, R. S. Electroencephalographic pattern quantification and the arousal continuum. *Psychophysiology,* 1965, 2:146–160.

Danilova, N. N. Electroencephalographic responses to flickering light in the alpha rhythm frequency range. *Pavlov J Higher Nerv Activity,* 1961, 2:8.

Deliyannakis, E.; Panagopoulos, C.; and Huott, A. D. The influence of hashish on human EEG. *Clin Electroenceph,* 1970, 1:128–140.

DeLucchi, M. R.; Garoutte, B.; and Aird, R. B. The scalp as an electroencephalographic averager. *Electroenceph Clin Neurophysiol,* 1962, 14: 191–196.

Dewan, E. M. Communication by voluntary control of the electroencephalogram. *Proc Symp Biomed Eng,* 1966, 1:349–351.

Dixon, N. F. Feedback and the visual threshold. *J Commun,* 1962, 12:97–105.

Dixon, N. F. and Lear, T. E. Electroencephalograph correlates of threshold regulation. *Nature (London),* 1963, 198:870–872.

Dixon, N. F. Incidence of theta rhythm prior to awareness of a visual stimulus. *Nature (London)*, 1964, 197:167.

Drever, J. Some observations on the occipital alpha rhythm. *Quart J Exp Psychol*, 1955, 7:91.

Drever, J. Further observations on the relation between EEG and visual imagery. *Amer J Psychol*, 1958, 71:270.

Eberlin, P. and Yager, D. Alpha blocking during visual after-images. *Electro-enceph Clin Neurophysiol*, 1968, 25:23–28.

Emrich, H. and Heinemann, L. G. EEG and perception. *Psychol Forsch*, 1966, 29:285–296.

Engstrom, D.; London, P.; and Hart, J. Hypnotic susceptibility increased by EEG alpha training. *Nature (London)*, 1970, 225:1261–1262.

Fetz, E. and Finocchio, D. V. Operant conditioning of specific patterns of neural and muscular activity. *Science*, 1971, 174:431–435.

Gaarder, K. Control of states of consciousness. I. Attainment through control of psychophysiological variables. *Arch Gen Psychiat*, 1971, 25:429–435.

Gaarder, K. Control of states of consciousness. II. Attainment through external feedback augmenting control of psychophysiological variables. *Arch Gen Psychiat*, 1971, 25:436–441.

Gale, A.; Coles, M.; and Blaydon, J. Extraversion-introversion and the EEG. *Brit J Psychol*, 1969, 60:209–223.

Galin, D. and Ornstein, R. Lateral specialization of cognitive mode: An EEG study. *Psychophysiology*, 1972, 9:412–418.

Gastaut, H.; Dongier, S.; and Dongier, M. Electroencephalography and neuroses: Study of 250 cases. *Electroenceph Clin Neurophysiol*, 1960, 12:233–234.

Giannitrapani, D. EEG average frequency and intelligence. *Electroenceph Clin Neurophysiol*, 1969, 27:480–486.

Giannitrapani, D. WAIS I.Q. as related to EEG frequency scores. *Electro-enceph Clin Neurophysiol*, 1970, 28:102.

Giannitrapani, D. Scanning mechanisms and the EEG. *Electroenceph Clin Neurophysiol*, 1971, 30:139–146.

Glass, A. Mental arithmetic and blocking of the occipital alpha rhythm. *Electroenceph Clin Neurophysiol*, 1964, 16:595–603.

Glass, A. Intensity of attenuation of alpha activity by mental arithmetic in females and males. *Physiol Behav*, 1968, 3:217–220.

Goldstein, L.; Sugerman, A. A.; Stolberg, H.; Murphree, H. B.; and Pfeiffer, C. C. Electrocerebral activity in schizophrenics and non-psychotic subjects: quantitative EEG amplitude analysis. *Electroenceph Clin Neurophysiol*, 1965, 19:350–361.

Golla, F.; Hutton, E. L.; and Walter, W. G. The objective study of mental imagery. I. Physiological concomitants. *J Ment Sci*, 1943, 89:216.

Green, E. E.; Green, A. M.; and Walters, E. D. Self-regulation of internal states. *Proc Inter Cong Cybernetics*, London, Sept. 1969.

Green, E. E.; Green, A. M.; and Walters, E. D. Voluntary control of internal states: psychological and physiological. *J Transpersonal Psychol*, 1970, 2:1–25.

Grunewald, G.; Simonova, O.; and Creutzfeldt, O. D. Differential EEG-alterations during visuomotor and cognitive tasks. *Arch Psychiat Nervenkr*, 1968, 212:46–69.

Harding, G.; Jeavons, P. M.; Jenner, F. A.; Drummond, P.; Sheridan, M.; and Howells, G. W. The electroencephalogram in three cases of periodic psychosis. *Electroenceph Clin Neurophysiol*, 1966, 21:59–66.

Hart, J. T. Autocontrol of EEG alpha. *Psychophysiology*, 1968, 5:506.

Hirai, T. Electroencephalographic study on the Zen meditation (Zazen)—EEG changes during the concentrated relaxation. *Psychiat Neurol Jap*, 1960, 62:76–105.

Honorton, C. and Carbone, M. A preliminary study of feedback-augmented EEG alpha activity and ESP card-guessing performance. *J Amer Soc Psychical Res*, 1971, 65:66–74.

Honorton, C.; Davidson, R.; and Bindler, P. Shifts in subjective state associated with feed-back–augmented EEG alpha. *Psychophysiology*, 1972, 9:269.

Hoovey, Z. B.; Heinemann, U.; and Creutzfeldt, O. D. Inter-hemispheric "synchrony" of alpha waves. *Electroenceph Clin Neurophysiol*, 1972, 32: 337–347.

Hord, D.; Naitoh, P.; and Johnson, L. C. EEG spectral features of self-regulated high alpha states. *Psychophysiology*, 1972, 9:278.

Hord, D.; Naitoh, P.; and Johnson, L. Intensity and coherence contours during self-regulated high alpha activity. *Electroenceph Clin Neurophysiol*, 1972, 32:429–433.

Hubel, D. H.; Henson, C. O.; Rupert, A.; and Glambos, R. "Attention" units in the auditory cortex. *Science*, 1959, 129:1279.

Jacobs, L.; Feldman, M.; and Bender, M. B. Are the eye movements of dreaming sleep related to the visual images of the dreams? *Psychophysiology*, 1972, 9:393–401.

Jasper, H. and Shagass, C. Conditioning the occipital alpha rhythm in man. *J Exp Psychol*, 1941, 28:373–387.

Jasper, H. and Shagass, C. Conscious time judgments related to conditioned time intervals and voluntary control of the alpha rhythm. *J Exp Psychol*, 1941, 28:503.

Jung, R.; Creutzfeldt, O.; and Grusser, O. J. The microphysiology of cortical neurones. *German Med Monthly*, 1958, 3:269.

Kamiya, J. Conditioned discrimination of the EEG alpha rhythm in humans. Paper presented Western Psychol Assoc, 1962.

Kamiya, J. Conscious control of brain waves. *Psychology Today*, 1968, 1:56–60.

Kamiya, J. Operant control of the EEG alpha rhythm and some of its reported effects on consciousness. In C. Tart, ed., *Altered States of Consciousness*, 1969, 507–556.

Kasamatsu, A.; Okuma, T.; Takenaka, S.; Koga, E.; Ikeda, K.; Sugiyama, H. The EEG of "Zen" and "Yoga" practitioners. *Electroenceph Clin Neurophysiol*, 1957, Suppl 9:51–52.

Kasamatsu, A.; Hirai, H.; and Ando, N. EEG responses to click stimulation in Zen meditation. *Proc Jap EEG Soc*, 1962, 77–78.

Keesey, U. T. and Nichols, D. J. Fluctuations in target visibility as related to the occurrence of the alpha component of the electroencephalogram. *Vision Res*, 7:859–877.

Korein, J.; Maccario, M.; Carmona, A.; Randt, C. T.; and Miller, N. Operant conditioning techniques in normal and abnormal EEG states. *Neurology (Minneap)*, 1971, 21:395.

Kreitman, N. and Shaw, J. C. Experimental enhancement of alpha activity. *Electroenceph Clin Neurophysiol*, 1965, 18:147–155.

Kuprianovich, L. The process of instruction during sleep can be regulated. *Technika-Molodezhi (Moscow)*, 1965, 11:26–28.

Leader, H. S.; Cohn, R.; Weihrer, A. L.; and Caceres, C. A. Pattern reading of the clinical electroencephalogram. *Electroenceph Clin Neurophysiol*, 1967, 23:566–570.

Lehmann, D. Topography of spontaneous alpha EEG fields in humans. *Electroenceph Clin Neurophysiol*, 1971, 30:161.

Lille, F.; Provaznik, K.; and Pottier, M. Effects of auditory and visual stimuli on electroencephalograms during psycho-sensory tasks. *Travail Humain*, 1970, 33:77–86.

Lindsley, D. B. Foci of activity of the alpha rhythm in the human EEG. *J Exp Psychol*, 1938, 23:159–171.

London, P.; Hart, J. T.; and Leibovitz, M. P. EEG alpha rhythms and susceptibility to hypnosis. *Nature (London)*, 1968, 219:71–72.

Lorens, S., Jr. and Darrow, C. W. Eye movements, EEG, GSR and EKG during mental multiplication. *Electroenceph Clin Neurophysiol*, 1962, 14:739–746.

Lubin, A.; Johnson, L. C.; and Austin, M. T. Discrimination among states of consciousness using EEG spectra. *Psychophysiology*, 1969, 6:122.

Lynch, J. J. and Paskewitz, D. A. On the mechanisms of the feedback control of human brain wave activity. *J Nerv Ment Dis*, 1971, 153:205.

Marjerrison, G.; Krause, A. E.; and Keogh, R. P. Variability of the EEG in schizophrenia: Quantitative analysis with a modulus voltage integrator. *Electroenceph Clin Neurophysiol*, 1968, 24:35–41.

Matousek, M.; Volavka, J.; and Roubicek, J. Electroencephalogram in normal population. II. Influence of physiologic changes on EEG. *Psychiatry*, 1967, 63:73–78.

Morrell, L. K. Some characteristics of stimulus-provoked alpha activity. *Electroenceph Clin Neurophysiol*, 1966, 21:552–561.

Mulholland, T. and Runnals, S. Evaluation of attention and alertness with a stimulus-brain feedback loop. *Electroenceph Clin Neurophysiol,* 1962, *14*:847–852.

Mulholland, T. and Evans, C. R. Oculomotor function and the alpha activation cycle. *Nature* (London), 1966, *211*:1278–1279.

Mulholland, T. B. Feedback electroencephalography. *Activ Nerv Sup (Praha),* 1968, *10*:410.

Mulholland, T. The concept of attention and the electroencephalographic alpha rhythm. *Attention in Neurophysiology.* London: Butterworth, 1969.

Mulholland, T. Feedback electroencephalography II. *Activ Nerv Sup (Praha),* 1971, *13*:266–277.

Mulholland, T. B. and Peper, E. Occipital alpha and accommodative vergence, pursuit tracking and fast eye movements. *Psychophysiology,* 1971, *8:* 556–575.

Mundy-Castle, A. C. The electroencephalogram and mental activity. *Electroenceph Clin Neurophysiol,* 1957, *9*:643.

Nencini, R. and Pasquali, E. Variation in the amplitude of the alpha rhythm during controlled presentation of images. *Arch Psychol Neurol Psychiat,* 1969, *30*:337–350.

Nowlis, D. P. and Rhead, J. C. Relation of eyes-closed resting EEG alpha activity to hypnotic susceptibility. *Percept Motor Skills,* 1968, *27*:1047–1050.

Nowlis, D. P. and Kamiya, J. The control of electroencephalographic alpha rhythms through auditory feedback and the associated mental activity. *Psychophysiology,* 1970, *6*:476–484.

O'Malley, J. E. and Conners, C. K. The effect of unilateral alpha training on visual evoked response in a dyslexic adolescent. *Psychophysiology,* 1972, *9*:467–470.

Oswald, I. The EEG, visual imagery and attention. *Quart J Exp Psychol,* 1957, *9*:113.

Oswald, I. The human alpha rhythm and visual alertness. *Electroenceph Clin Neurophysiol,* 1959, *11*:601.

Paskewitz, D. A. and Orne, M. T. Visual effects during alpha feedback training. *Psychophysiology,* 1972, *9*:269.

Peper, E. Feedback regulation of the alpha electroencephalogram activity through control of the internal and external parameters. *Kybernetik,* 1970, *6*:107–112.

Peper, E. and Mulholland, T. Methodological and theoretical problems in the voluntary control of electroencephalographic occipital alpha by the subject. *Kybernetik,* 1970, *7*:10.

Pillsbury, J. A.; Meyerowitz, S.; Salzman, L.; and Satran, R. Electroencephalographic correlates of perceptual style: Field orientation. *Psychosom Med,* 1967, *29*:441–449.

Puskina, V. G. and Talavrinov, V. A. Spatial synchronization of alpha-activity in the cerebral cortex in the paranoid form of schizophrenia. *Zh Nevropat Psikhiat Korsakov*, 1967, 67:76–83.

Regestein, Q. R. Alpha waves produce boredom. *Science News*, 1972, *101*:331.

Remond, A. and Leseve, N. EEG and emotion. *Electroenceph Clin Neurophysiol*, 1957, Suppl 6:253.

Rodin, E. A.; Domino, E. F.; and Porzak, J. P. The marihuana-induced "social-high." Neurological and electroencephalographic concomitants. *JAMA*, 1970, *213*:1300–1302.

Rosenfeld, J. P.; Rudell, A. P.; and Fox, S. S. Operant control of neural events in humans. *Science*, 1969, *165*:821–823.

Roubicek, J.; Zaks, A.; and Freedman, A. M. EEG changes produced by heroin and methadone. *Electroenceph Clin Neurophysiol*, 1969, 27:667.

Rynearson, R. R.; Wilson, M. R.; and Bickford, R. G. Psilocybin-induced changes in psychologic function, electroencephalogram, and light-evoked potentials in human subjects. *Mayo Clin Proc*, 1968, *43*:191–204.

Sacks, B.; Fenwick, P. B. C.; Marks, I.; Fenton, G. W.; and Hebden, A. An investigation of the phenomenon of autocontrol of the alpha rhythm and possible associated feeling states using visual feedback. *Electroenceph Clin Neurophysiol*, 1972, *32*:461–463.

Saul, J. J.; David, H.; and Davis, P. A. Psychologic correlations with the electroencephalogram. *Psychosom Med*, 1949, *11*:361.

Saunders, D. R. Further implications of Mundy-Castle's correlations between EEG and Wechsler-Bellevue variables. *J Nat Inst Personnel Res*, 1960, 8:91.

Scheich, H. and Simonova, O. Parameters of alpha activity during the performance of motor tasks. *Electroenceph Clin Neurophysiol*, 1971, *31*:357–363.

Schmeidler, G. and Lewis, L. Mood changes after alpha feedback training. *Percept Motor Skills*, 1971, *32*:709–710.

Schwartz, G. E.; Shaw, G.; and Shapiro, D. Specificity of alpha and heart rate control through feedback. *Psychophysiology*, 1972, 9:269.

Shagass, C. Conditioning the human occipital alpha rhythm to a voluntary stimulus. A quantitative study. *J Exp Psychol*, 1942, *31*:367–379.

Shaw, J. C. and McLachlan, K. R. The association between alpha rhythm propagation time and level of arousal. *Psychophysiology*, 1968, *4*:307–310.

Shipton, J. and Walter, Grey. Alpha and intelligence, personality cultural differences and social activity. *Electroenceph Clin Neurophysiol*, 1957, Suppl 6:185–202.

Silverman, S. Operant conditioning of the amplitude component of the EEG. *Psychophysiology*, 1972, 9:269.

Slatter, K. H. Alpha rhythms and mental imagery. *Electroenceph Clin Neurophysiol*, 1960, *12*:851.

Stanford, R. G. and Lovin, C. EEG alpha activity and ESP performance. *J Amer Soc Psychical Res*, 1970, *64*:375–384.

Sterman, M. B. and Friar, L. Suppression of seizures in an epileptic following sensorimotor EEG feedback training. *Electroenceph Clin Neurophysiol,* 1972, *33:*89–95.

Stern, J. A.; Das, K. C.; Anderson, J. M.; Biddy, R. L.; and Surphlis, W. "Conditioned" alpha desynchronization. *Science,* 1961, *134:*388–389.

Stevens, J. R. Endogenous conditioning to abnormal cerebral electrical transients in man. *Science,* 1962, *137:*974–976.

Sugarman, L. Alpha rhythm, perception and intelligence. *J Nat Inst Personnel Res,* 1961, 8:170.

Torsten, S. F. Electroencephalographic alpha frequency and mental disease. *Acta Psychiat Scand,* 1970, *70:*67–75.

Travis, T. A.; Kondo, C. Y.; and Knott, J. R. A controlled study of alpha enhancement. *Psychophysiology,* 1972, 9:268.

Ulett, G. A.; Gleser, G. C.; Winokier, G.; and Lawler, A. The EEG and reaction to photic stimulation as an index of anxiety proneness. *J Neurophysiol,* 1953, 5:23.

Vogel, F. The genetic basis of the normal human electroencephalogram. *Humangenetik,* 1970, *10:*91–114.

Vogel, W.; Broverman, D. M.; and Klaiber, E. L. EEG and mental abilities. *Electroenceph Clin Neurophysiol,* 1968, *24:*166.

Volavka, J.; Grof, P.; and Mrklas, L. EEG frequency analysis in periodic endogenous depressions. *Psychiat Neurol (Basel),* 1967, *153:*384–390.

Volavka, J.; Matousek, M.; and Roubicek, J. Mental arithmetic and eye opening. An EEG frequency analysis and GSR study. *Electroenceph Clin Neurophysiol,* 1967, *22:*174–176.

Volavka, J.; Zaks, A.; Roubicek, J.; and Fink, M. Electrographic effects of diactyl-morphine (heroin) and naloxone in man. *Neuropharmacology,* 1970, 9:587–593.

Wallace, R. K. Physiological effects of transcendental meditation. *Science,* 1970, *167:*1751–1754.

Walter, R. D. and Yeager, C. L. Visual imagery and EEG change. *Electroenceph Clin Neurophysiol,* 1956, 8:193–199.

Walter, W. G. and Shipton, J. Alpha characteristics. *Electroenceph Clin Neurophysiol,* 1957, Suppl 6:253.

Walters, C. Clinical and experimental relationships of EEG to psychomotor and personality measures. *J Clin Psychol,* 1964, *20:*81–91.

Wenger, M. A. and Bagchi, B. K. Studies of autonomic functions in practitioners of yoga in India. *Behav Sci,* 1961, 6:312–323.

Zappoli, R. The possibility of conditioning in man. Some types of discharges and epileptic attacks of reflex nature. *Riv Neurol,* 1969, 1:31–35.

MISCELLANEOUS

Bakers, J. H. C. M. and Tenney, S. M. The perception of some sensations associated with breathing. *Resp Physiol,* 1970, *10:*85–92.

Ballard, P.; Doerr, H.; and Varni, J. Arrest of disabling eye disorder using bio-feedback. *Psychophysiology,* 1972, 9:271.

Bloch, S. and Davies, B. Forearm blood flow in anxious and non anxious patients. *Aus New Zeal J Psychiat,* 1969, 3:86–88.

Block, J. D.; Logerson, J.; Zohman, L.; and Kelly, G. A feedback device for teaching diaphragmatic breathing. *Amer Rev Resp Dis,* 1969, 100:577–578.

Borge, G. F.; Buchsbaum, M.; Goodwin, F.; Murphy, D.; and Silverman, J. Neuropsychological correlates of affective disorder. *Arch Gen Psychiat,* 1971, 24:501–504.

Brady, J. V.: Emotion revisited. *J Psychiat Res,* 1971, 8:363–384.

Bull, K. and Lang, P. J. Intensity judgments and physiological response amplitude. *Psychophysiology,* 1972, 9:428–436.

Cannon, W. Vodoo death. *Amer Anthropologist,* 1942, 44:169–181.

Carrera, F., III. and Adams, P. L. An ethical perspective on operant conditioning. *J Amer Acad Child Psychiat,* 1970, 9:607–623.

Cleghorn, J. M. Psychosocial influences on a metabolic process: The psychophysiology of lipid mobilization. *Canad Psychiat Ass J,* 1970, 15:539–547.

DiCara, L. V. and Miller, N. E. Instrumental learning of vasomotor responses by rats: Learning to respond differentially in the two ears. *Science,* 1968, 159:1485–1486.

Dickens, G. and Sharpe, M. Music therapy in the setting of a psychotherapeutic centre. *Brit J Med Psychol,* 1970, 43:83–94.

Dixon, N. F. Feedback and the visual threshold. *J Commun,* 1962, 12:97–105.

Dongier, M. The psychosomatic approach in cardiology: art, science or pseudoscience? *Un Med Canada,* 1968, 97:1097–1103.

Dorsey, J. M. Etiology and treatment of emotional factors in allergic diseases. *Ann Alerg,* 1972, 30:223.

Dykman, R. A. and Gantt, W. H. Cardiovascular conditioning in dogs and in humans. In *Physiological Bases of Psychiatry,* W. H. Gantt, ed. Springfield, Ill.: Charles C Thomas, 1958, pp. 171–195.

Dykman, R. A. On the nature of classical conditioning. In *Methods in Psychophysiology,* Clinton C. Brown, ed. Baltimore: Williams & Wilkins, 1967, pp. 234–290.

Efron, R. The minimum duration of a perception. *Neuropsychologia,* 1970, 8:57–63.

Fischer, H. K. and Dlin, B. M. Man's determination of his time of illness or death. *Geriatrics,* 1971, 26:89–94.

Forrest, M. and Kroth, J. A. Psychometric and physiological indices of anxiety. *J Clin Psychol,* 1971, 27:40–42.

Fox, S. S. and Rudell, A. P. Operant controlled neural event: Formal and systematic approach to electrical coding of behavior in brain. *Science,* 1968, 162:1299–1302.

Frank, J. D. The influence of patients' and therapists' expectations on the outcome of psychotherapy. *Brit J Med Psychol*, 1968, *41*:349–356.

French, J. R. P., Jr. and Caplan, R. D. Psychosocial factors in coronary heart disease. *Industr Med*, 1970, *39*:383–401.

Friedman, M.; Byers, S. O.; Rosenman, R. H.; and Neuman, R. Coronary-prone individuals (type A behavior pattern) growth hormone responses. *JAMA*, 1971, *217*:929–932.

Gelder, M. G. and Mathews, A. M. Forearm blood flow and phobic anxiety. *Brit J Psychiat*, 1968, *114*:1371–1376.

Gellhorn, E. and Kiely, W. F. Mystical states of consciousness: Neurophysiological and clinical aspects. *J Nerv Ment Dis*, 1972, *154*:399–405.

Gilman, L. and Paperte, F. Music as a psychotherapeutic agent. In *Music and Your Emotions*, ed. Emil A. Gutheil, M.D., Liveright, N.Y., 1952.

Goldie, L. and Green, J. M. Changes in mode of respiration as an indication of level of awareness. *Nature (London)*, 1961, *189*:581–582.

Hackett, T. P.; Cassem, N. H.; and Wishnie, H. Detection and treatment of anxiety in the coronary care unit. *Amer Heart J*, 1969, *78*:727–730.

Hare, R. D. Response requirements and directional fractionation of autonomic responses. *Psychophysiology*, 1972, *9*:419–427.

Hilf, F. D.; Winner, W. K.; and Kopell, B. S. Feedback utilization styles of paranoid patients. *J Nerv Ment Dis*, 1969, *149*:491–495.

Jenkins, C. D.; Hames, C. G.; Zyzanski, S. J.; Rosenman, R. H.; and Friedman, M. Psychological traits and serum lipids. I. Findings from the California Psychological Inventory. *Psychosom Med*, 1969, *31*:115–127.

Kerr, T. A.; Schapira, K.; and Roth, M. Relationship between premature death and affective disorders. *Brit J Psychiat*, 1969, *115*:1277–1282.

Krantz, D. L. The separate worlds of operant and non-operant psychology. *J Appl Behav Anal*, 1971, *4*:61–70.

Lader, M. H. Psychophysiology of clinical anxiety. *Brit J Hosp Med*, 1969, *2*:1448–1451.

Lesse, S. *Anxiety. Its components, development, and treatment.* New York: Grune & Stratton, 1970.

Lowinger, P. and Dobie, S. What makes the placebo work? A study of placebo response rates. *Arch Gen Psychiat*, 1969, *20*:84–88.

Luparello, T.; Lyons, H. A.; Bleecker, E. R.; and McFadden, E. R., Jr. Influences of suggestion on airway reactivity in asthmatic subjects. *Psychosom Med*, 1968, *30*:819–825.

Lynch, J. L. The stimulus—the ghost—the response. The carousel of conditioning. *Cond Reflex*, 1970, *5*:133–139.

Machac, M. Vasomotor response to intentional autoregulative operations of the relaxation activation method. *Activ Nerv Sup (Praha)*, 1969, *11*:42–45.

Maher-Loughnan, G. P. Hypnosis and autohypnosis for the treatment of asthma. *Int J Clin Exp Hypn*, 1970, *18*:1–14.

Maher-Loughnan, G. P. Emotional aspects of chest diseases. *Geriatrics,* 1971, *26:*120–139.

Margolin, S. G. Consciousness: An interface between brain and mind. *J Nerv Ment Dis,* 1972, *154:*395–398.

Marks, I. The origins of phobic states. *Amer J Psychother,* 1970, *24:*652–676.

Maslach, C.; Marshall, G.; and Zimbardo, P. Hypnotic control of complex skin temperature. *Proc Ann Conv Amer Psychol Ass,* 1971, *6* (Pt. 2):777–778.

Masserman, J. H. Is uncertainty a key to neurotogenesis? *Psychosomatics,* 1970, *11:*391–402.

Masuda, M.; Perko, K. P.; and Johnston, R. G. Physiological activity and illness history. *J Psychosom Res,* 1972, *16:*129–136.

McAdam, D. W., et al. Conative control of the contingent negative variation. *Electroenceph Clin Neurophysiol,* 1966, *21:*194.

McCollum, M.; Burch, N. R.; and Roessler, R. Personality and respiratory responses to sound and light. *Psychophysiology,* 1969, *6:*291–300.

Menzies, R. Conditioned vasomotor responses in human subjects. *J Psychol,* 1937, *4:*75–120.

Morgenson, D. F. and Martin, I. Personality, awareness and autonomic conditioning. *Psychophysiology,* 1969, *5:*536–547.

Moritz, A. R. and Zamcheck, N. Sudden and unexpected deaths of young soldiers. Diseases responsible for such deaths during World War II. *Arch Path (Chicago),* 1946, *42:*459–494.

Murphy, G. Experiments in overcoming self-deception. *Psychophysiology,* 1970, *6:*790–799.

Onomitsu, I.; Nagata, M.; and Tsuji, T. Control of chronic noninfectious diseases, especially cardiovascular diseases. I. Study on patients with cardiovascular disorder as viewed from emotional life (Japanese). *Kitakanto Med J,* 1969, *19:*50–59.

Plutchick, R. Psychophysiology of individual differences with special reference to emotions. *Ann NY Acad Sci,* 1966, *134:*776–781.

Razran, G. The observable unconscious and the inferable conscious in current Soviet psychophysiology: Interoceptive conditioning, semantic conditioning, and the orienting reflex. *Psychol Rev,* 1961, *68:*81–147.

Razran, G. In *Mind in Evolution,* Boston: Houghton Mifflin, 1971.

Reckless, J. B. A behavioral treatment of bronchial asthma in modified group therapy. *Psychosomatics,* 1971, *12:*168–173.

Rees W. D. and Latkins, S. G. Mortality of bereavement. *Brit Med J,* 1967, *4:*13–16.

Richter, C. P. The phenomenon of unexplained sudden death in animals and man. In W. H. Gantt, ed., *Physiological Bases of Psychiatry,* Springfield, Ill.: Charles C Thomas, 1958.

Russell, H. L. Fingertip temperature changes during relaxation and psychotherapy. *Psychophysiology,* 1972, *9:*279.

Sandars, N. K. *The Epic of Gilgamesh.* New York: Penguin Books, 1971.

Sargent, J. D.; Green, E. E.; and Walters, E. D. The use of autogenic feedback training in a pilot study of migraine and tension headaches. *Headache,* 1972, *12:*120.

Scott, J. P. *Animal Behavior.* Garden City, N.Y.: Doubleday Anchor, 1963.

Shean, G. D. Vasomotor conditioning and awareness. *Psychophysiology,* 1968, 5:22–30.

Shmavonian, B. M. Methodological study of vasomotor conditioning in human subjects. *J Comp Physiol Psychol,* 1959, 52:315–321.

Smith, K. Conditioning as an artifact. *Psychol Rev,* 1954, *61:*217–225.

Smith, K. U. and Henry, J. P. Cybernetic foundations for rehabilitation. *Amer J Phys Med,* 1967, *46:*379–467.

Snyder, C. and Noble, M. Operant conditioning of vasoconstriction. *J Exp Psychol,* 1968, 77:263–268.

Spilken, A. Z. and Jacobs, M. A. Prediction of illness behavior from measures of life crisis, manifest distress and maladaptive coping. *Psychosom Med,* 1971, *33:*251–264.

Stephenson, S. E.; Young, W.; Montgomery, L. H.; and Batson, R. Physiologic autocontrol of mechanical respirators. *Dis Chest,* 1961, *39:*363–371.

Taub, E. and Berman, A. J. Movement and learning in the absence of sensory feedback. In S. J. Freedman, ed., *The Neuropsychology of Spatially Oriented Behavior.* Homewood, Ill.: Dorsey Press, 1968.

Teichner, W. H. Interaction of behavioral and physiological stress reactions. *Psychol Rev,* 1968, 75:271–291.

Ullman, M. An experimental approach to dreams and telepathy. Methodology and preliminary findings. *Arch Gen Psychiat,* 1966, *14:*605–613.

Van Praag, H. M. Complimentary aspect in the relation between biologic and psychodynamic psychiatry. *Psychiat Clin (Basel),* 1969, 2:307–318.

Volow, M. R. and Hein, P. L. Bidirectional operant conditioning of peripheral vasomotor responses with augmented feedback and prolonged training. *Psychophysiology,* 1972, 9:271.

Waggoner, R. W. and Waggoner, R. W., Jr. Somatic concomitants of depression. *Southern Med J,* 1969, *62:*285–289.

Weber, S. J. and Cook, T. D. Subject effects in laboratory research: An examination of subject roles, demand characteristics, and valid inference. *Psychol Bull,* 1972, 77:273–295.

Weiner, H. Current status and future prospects for research in psychosomatic medicine. *J Psychiat Res,* 1971, 8:479–498.

Weiss, J. H.; Martin, C.; and Riley, J. Effects of suggestion on respiration in asthmatic children. *Psychosom Med,* 1970, *32:*409–415.

Williams, R. B. and Eichelman, B. Social setting: Influence on the physiological response to electric shock in the rat. *Science,* 1971, *174:*613–614.

Wineman, E. W. Autonomic balance changes during the human menstrual cycle. *Psychophysiology,* 1971, 8:1–6.

Young, J. P. R.; Fenton, G. W.; and Lader, M. H. The inheritance of neurotic traits: a twin study of the Middlesex Hospital Questionnaire. *Brit J Psychiat*, 1971, *119*:393–398.

Zuckerman, M.; Persky, H.; and Curtis, G. C. Relationships among anxiety, depression, hostility and autonomic variables. *J Nerv Ment Dis*, 1968, *146*: 481–487.

Index

74 75 76 77 10 9 8 7 6 5 4 3 2 1